Fiscal Federalism and Equalisation Transfers

Studies in Territorial and Cultural Diversity Governance

Series Editors

Francesco Palermo
Joseph Marko

VOLUME 21

The titles published in this series are listed at *brill.com/tcdg*

Fiscal Federalism and Equalisation Transfers

Balancing Regional Autonomy and Solidarity

Edited by

Mikel Erkoreka

BRILL | NIJHOFF

LEIDEN | BOSTON

The International Association of Centers for Federal Studies (IACFS) funded this book project.

This book has undergone a peer review process as a prerequisite for its publication.

Library of Congress Cataloging-in-Publication Data

Names: Erkoreka, Mikel, editor.
Title: Fiscal federalism and equalisation transfers : balancing regional autonomy and solidarity / edited by Mikel Erkoreka.
Other titles: Fiscal federalism and equalization transfers
Description: Leiden ; Boston : Brill/Nijhoff, 2025. | Series: Studies in territorial & cultural diversity governance, 2213-2570 ; vol. 21 | Includes index.
Identifiers: LCCN 2024050837 (print) | LCCN 2024050838 (ebook) | ISBN 9789004524507 (hardback) | ISBN 9789004524514 (ebook)
Subjects: LCSH: Intergovernmental fiscal relations. | Central–local government relations. | Local finance – Law and legislation. | Revenue sharing – Law and legislation. | Transfer payments--Law and legislation. | Decentralization in government – Law and legislation. | Cultural pluralism – Political aspects. | Autonomy. | Global Financial Crisis, 2008–2009. | COVID-19 Pandemic, 2020.
Classification: LCC K4655 .F57 2025 (print) | LCC K4655 (ebook) | DDC 336.3–dc23/eng/20241026
LC record available at https://lccn.loc.gov/2024050837
LC ebook record available at https://lccn.loc.gov/2024050838

Typeface for the Latin, Greek, and Cyrillic scripts: "Brill". See and download: brill.com/brill-typeface.

ISSN 2213-2570
ISBN 978-90-04-52450-7 (hardback)
ISBN 978-90-04-52451-4 (e-book)
DOI 10.1163/9789004524514

This book is printed on acid- free paper and produced in a sustainable manner.

Contents

Figures and Tables

Figures

Tables

Notes on Contributors

Miguel Angel Asensio
was Professor and Director of the Public Administration Doctoral Program in Littoral University, teaching Public Finance, Economic History and Thinking (UNL, UCSF and UNER). He was Fulbright Scholar at the University of Pittsburgh, visiting professor at Canadian Universities and consultant for World Bank and OAS. He holds a PhD in Economics and a PhD in History (UA & UTDT). He served as Minister of Public Finance in the Province of Santa Fe, in the Federal Commission for Taxes and National Senate's Adviser (Argentina). His research fields are economic history and public and federal finances.

Daniel Béland
is Director of the McGill Institute for the Study of Canada and James McGill Professor in the Department of Political Science at McGill University (Montreal, Canada). A student of fiscal federalism and comparative social policy, he has published more than 20 scholarly books and 200 articles in peer-reviewed journals.

Eva Maria Belser
holds a Chair in Constitutional and Administrative Law at the University of Fribourg (since 2008) and a UNESCO Chair in Human Rights and Democracy (since 2014). She teaches and researches in the fields of Swiss and comparative constitutional law, federalism, decentralisation and globalisation, human and minority rights, democracy as well as development cooperation, constitution-making, and conflict resolution. She is co-director of the Institute for Federalism, heads its international centre and regularly accepts mandates as a Swiss expert in international cooperation and consulting projects. She was honoured with the 2019 Federalism Prize for her achievements in the field of comparative federalism. She is currently President of the International Association of Centres for Federal Studies (IACFS), Vice Dean of the Faculty of Law Fribourg and on the Advisory Board of International IDEA.

Govind Bhattacharjee
is a retired bureaucrat who has served in various capacities in India and abroad during his civil service career which included a tenure of four years as Tax Advisor to a foreign government and a number of assignments with the United Nations. Apart from being a Visiting Senior Fellow at the Centre for Multilevel Federalism, New Delhi, he is also a Professor of Practice at the Arun Jaitley National Institute of Financial Management where he teaches

Public Finance and Public Policy and a Visting Professor at the Indian institute of Management, Calcutta. Dr Bhattacharjee is a prolific writer and a regular columnist with versatile interests in diverse areas. He has so far published 10 books and authored more than 300 research papers and articles in academic journals and national newspapers.

Tinashe Carlton Chigwata
is an Associate Professor and Head of Multilevel Government at the Dullah Omar Institute (DOI) based at the University of the Western Cape (UWC), South Africa. He undertakes research, teaching, and consultancy on local and regional governments, multi-level government (devolution, federalism etc), democracy and good governance. He teaches in the Postgraduate Programmes in Multi-level Government and Local Government offered by the Dullah Omar Institute. He has authored and edited several academic publications, including four books on local government and multilevel government in South Africa, Zimbabwe and Zambia. He is the Chief Editor of the Local Government Bulletin, which publishes regular and accessible articles, policy briefs, reports on judgment and summaries of new bills on local government and multi-level government in South Africa and the region.

Mikel Erkoreka
is Director of the Ituna Center for Basque Economic Agreement and Fiscal Federalism Studies and Senior Lecturer of Public Policy and Economic History at the University of the Basque Country (UPV/EHU). His main research fields are public finances, economic history, fiscal federalism, comparative federalism and European Union fiscal and economic integration process.

Pamela Jesica Fadul
is National Public Accountant graduated from the Faculty of Economic Sciences of the National University of the Litoral, Argentina and Candidate for the Master in Public Administration. During 2018 to 2022 she worked administratively in the specialization and management of public organizations of the aforementioned University participating as professional researcher in the specific program for strengthening research in Economic Sciences (PROMCE). Since December 2023 has been appointed as high local public official in Rojas (Buenos Aires, Argentina).

Gisela Färber
is Senior Fellow at the German Research Institute for Public Administration Speyer (Germany). She is Professor Emeritus at the Chair of Public Finance, German University of Administrative Sciences; since 2020 is she Adjunct

Professor at the Curtin University in Perth (WA Australia). She was and still is member of a broad variety of advisory commissions of German Federal and State Governments and Parliaments and has worked as advisor for the European Commission and other foreign governments. Her main research fields are fiscal federalism, local finance, demographic change, civil servants' salaries and pensions, reforms of public administration; reduction of regulatory burdens; China's economy and administrative system.

Tracy Beck Fenwick
is Associate Professor in Comparative Politics and Director of the Australian Centre for Federalism in the School of Politics and International Relations at the Australian National University. She is an Honorary Fellow of the Institute of Intergovernmental Relations at Queen's University, Canada. Her books include Avoiding Governors: Federalism, Democracy, and Poverty Alleviation in Brazil and Argentina (2016, University of Notre Dame Press) and Beyond Autonomy: Practical and Theoretical Challenges to 21st Century Federalism (Brill Press, 2021). She completed her doctorate specializing in Comparative Politics at the University of Oxford, U.K. in 2009 (St. Anthony's College). She holds a M.A. in Comparative Politics and a B.A. in Latin American Studies and Economics from McGill University, Canada.

Ana Herrero-Alcalde
is a Public Economics Professor at the UNED and a member of the *Centro de Investigación sobre Gobierno Multinivel y Políticas Territoriales*. She has been an external researcher at the Spanish Institute of Fiscal Studies and a visiting researcher at the Andrew Young of Policy Studies (Georgia State University) and at the Institute for Comparative Federalism (Eurac). Her fields of expertise are fiscal decentralization, intergovernmental transfers, and the devolution of the Welfare State.

Olivier Jacques
is Assistant Professor in the Department of Health Policy Management and Evaluation at the School of Public Health of the Université de Montréal. He received his PhD from the Department of Political Science at McGill University and has been a postdoctoral fellow at Queen's University. His research concern the political economy of public finance, health policy, fiscal federalism and public opinion on fiscal policy. His research have been published in Social Science & Medicine, Journal of European Public Policy, Party Politics, European Political Science Review, Journal of European Social Policy, Social Policy & Administration, Regional Studies, Territory, Politics and Governance,

Canadian Journal of Political Science, Canadian Journal of Public Health, Canadian Public Administration and Canadian Public Policy, among others.

Mario Kölling

is a lecturer in the Department of Political Science at the UNED and senior researcher at the Manuel Giménez Abad Foundation. He is involved in the LEGITIMULT project, funded by the Horizon Europe programme, and principal investigator together with César Colino in the project: Institutional Reforms in Multilevel Systems: Paradigms, Constraints, Processes and Outcomes. He is also country expert for Spain in the Sustainable Governance Indicators (SGI) project of the Bertelsmann Stiftung. His research covers issues of territorial decentralisation and multilevel governance. Furthermore, he focuses on the EU budget and comparative federalism.

André Lecours

is Professor in the School of Political Studies at the University of Ottawa, Past President of the Canadian Political Science Association, and Fellow of the Royal Society of Canada. His main research interests are nationalism and federalism. He is the co-author (with Daniel Béland) of Nationalism and Social Policy. The Politics of Territorial Solidarity (Oxford University Press, 2008); the co-author (with Daniel Béland, Gregory Marchildon, Haizhen Mou and Rose Olfert) of Fiscal Federalism and Equalization Policy in Canada. Political and Economic Dimensions (University of Toronto Press, 2017); and the author of Nationalism, Secessionism, and Autonomy (Oxford University Press, 2021).

Florencia Martino

holds a degree in Economics from the National University of the Littoral, carrying out the PhD in Economics of the Pontifical Catholic University Argentina (UCA) with a doctoral scholarship granted by CONICET. She has made presentations in the Montevideo Group, in the Fiscal Federalism Seminar at the University of Mendoza and in the National Congress of Political Science, having published in co-authorship in the Review of the Giménez Abad Foundation (2023), and other papers in the Reviews of the UNL (Económicas) and National University of Entre Ríos (Axes).

Andoni Montes-Nebreda

is Lecturer in Public Economics at the University of the Basque Country (UPV/EHU), and associate researcher at Ituna Center for Basque Economic Agreement and Fiscal Federalism Studies and Complutense Institute of International Studies (ICEI-UCM). His research is focused on Fiscal and Tax

Policy, Federalism, and Welfare State. He collaborates with international institutions, such as the OECD, and think tanks, such as Fundación Alternativas.

Francisco Javier Romero Caro
(PhD) is Senior Researcher at the Institute for Comparative Federalism of Eurac Research in Bolzano/Bozen. He won the XVII 'Manuel Giménez Abad' Award for his book on the Canadian federal system and the integration of Quebec, and the European Commission awarded him with the Seal of Excellence in the Horizon 2020 Marie Skłodowska-Curie call to develop a project on fiscal federalism and diversity accommodation. He has been a visiting researcher at the CEPC, the Max Planck Institute for Comparative Public Law, the University of Ottawa and the University of Edinburgh. His research interests encompass fiscal federalism, the territorial distribution of powers in multilevel systems (with a special focus on federal states) and the territorial integration of national minorities in secessionist contexts. He has authored several articles and book chapters on these topics.

Miranda Stewart
is Professor specialising in taxation law and policy at the Melbourne Law School, University of Melbourne, an Honorary Professor at the Crawford School of Public Policy, Australian National University and an International Research Fellow of the Centre for Business Taxation, Said Business School, The University of Oxford. Miranda is vice-chair of the Permanent Scientific Committee of the International Fiscal Association and was recently a visiting fellow at the Australian Treasury. Her books include Tax, Social Policy and Gender (2017, ANU Press) and Tax and Government in the 21st Century (2022, Cambridge University Press).

Nico Steytler
is a professor emeritus in the Faculty of Law, the University of the Western Cape, and continues as a team member of the Multilevel Government Project of the Dullah Omar Institute of Constitutional Law, Governance and Human Rights. Previously, he held the South African Research Chair in Multilevel Government, Law and Development (2013 to 2022). His research focus is constitutional law, multilevel government and local government in South Africa, elsewhere in Africa and further afield. In addition to his publications in these fields, he has served as a consultant on multilevel government in a number of countries across the world.

Alice Valdesalici

(PhD) is Research Group Leader and Senior Researcher at the Institute for Comparative Federalism of Eurac Research. She has been visiting scholar at the Instituts d'Estudis Autonòmics in Barcelona and at the Deutsche Forschungsinstitut für öffentliche Verwaltung Speyer. She got her PhD in Italian and European Constitutional Law at the Graduate School of Law of the University of Verona in May 2016. For her research she has been awarded the 'Ronald Watts Young Researcher Award 2016', by the International Association of Centres for Federal Studies (IACFS), and the 'Award for Federal and Regional Studies 2016', by the Austrian Landtagspräsidentenkonferenz and the Institute for Federalism in Innsbruck'. Her main research interests are Comparative Fiscal Federalism, Federal and Regional Studies, Italian and European Constitutional Law, and Institutional Innovation. She authored several papers on these topics in academic journals as well as edited books. She has provided consultancies to the Council of Europe and to regional and local governments in Italy.

Jaap de Visser

is National Research Chair in Multilevel Government, Law and Development in the Dullah Omar Institute at the University of the Western Cape's Faculty of Law. His research, teaching and consulting focuses on multilevel government, local government, good governance and federalism in Africa, and he has published widely on these topics. He is co-author of Local Government Law of South Africa, and has overseen and conducted postgraduate and contract research on multilevel government in a South Africa, Mozambique, Uganda, Zimbabwe, Ethiopia, Lesotho, Zambia and Kenya. He is co-convener of the annual African School for Decentralisation and Vice-President of the International Association of Centres for Federal Studies.

Bizuneh Yimenu

is a Lecturer in Comparative Politics at Queen's University Belfast. Previously, he was a Teaching Fellow at the School of Government, University of Birmingham. He holds a PhD in Comparative Politics from the University of Kent. His research focuses on decentralisation, federalism, political economy, authoritarianism, and ethnic politics. Bizuneh has published in journals, including Publius, Public Administration and Development, and Regional and Federal Studies. Bizuneh is a Fellow of the Higher Education Academy. He is also a steering committee member of the ECPR Regionalism and Federalism standing group and an editorial board member of Regional and Federal Studies and Ethnopolitics. He regularly provides expert comments on major international media outlets like BBC and Al-Jazeera.

INTRODUCTION

State Intervention and the Development of Fiscal Equalisation Systems in Federal Countries: An Historical Introduction

Mikel Erkoreka

Ituna Center for Basque Economic Agreement and Fiscal Federalism Studies (UPV/EHU - University of the Basque Country)

The liberal revolution and the new ideologies that spread through large parts of the world during the 19th century, established a new form of understanding and structuring of relations between the citizen and the state. In this new framework of political, economic and social relations, the frontier between individual freedom and the collective interest has been the object of constant discussion and revision since the origins of the "modern" state: what should be the extent of state intervention and what functions should this assume?

Determining the limits of this intervention depends on the ideology, the objectives, the system of priorities and the economic and legal framework that regulate the state's activities. The classical liberal ideology predominant in the governments of the first generation of liberal states defended a state model involving little intervention, principally focused on promoting capitalist and industrial development within a market economy, protecting private property and guaranteeing public order and external security. Questions of a social nature, such as the fight against economic inequality or the development of social protection mechanisms, were not a priority or did not directly form part of the political agenda. These questions were circumscribed to the private sphere of the citizens. In this way, industrialisation provided enormous wealth to the beneficiary countries, but also opened up a great divergence between countries, and internally, between territories (industrialised vs. non-industrialised) and individuals.

Supported by the power of industrialisation and the strength of their armies, the European countries spread the principles of classical liberalism all over the world through the networks of the global capitalism, the revolution in transport and communication, the creation and diffusion of new currents of thinking and philosophy, as well via the imperialist military path. In the period leading up to the First World War few countries of the world escaped – with

DOI:10.1163/9789004524514_002

greater or lesser intensity- the influence of this "modernising wave", whether through conviction or imposition.

In response to the growing social tension and workers' mobilisation, the liberal state took timid steps to gradually increase its intervention in social questions during the last decades of the 19th century and the first third of the 20th century. However, the milestone that marked the turning point in the interventionist evolution of the state was the international economic crisis of 1929.

The first decades of the 20th century saw the emergence and consolidation of alternatives to the liberal system, both from the left (especially communism) and from the right (especially fascism). In contrast to classical liberalism, both systems were committed to strengthening state intervention in order to implant a new model of political, economic and social relations and organisation under the direction and control of the government. The fight against the inequality gap (especially in the case of communism) and against the power monopoly exercised by the capitalist elites won these alternatives the support of broad social masses that felt unprotected under the liberal model of limited state intervention.

The great crash of 1929 exposed the limitations and lacks of the classical liberal model: its inability to respond to the dire economic and social crisis fractured the societies in a large part of the industrialised powers, jeopardising the survival of the liberal system. Facing this threat, liberal ideology changed, evolving towards a new more interventionist state model, with a greater sensitivity to the social question.

Following the Second World War, the geopolitical and ideological map of the world was reshaped. On one side, Europe definitively lost its "position of dominion", which initiated a complex process of decolonisation and independence of the former colonies. On the other, the new world order was divided into two opposing ideological blocs in the Cold War. Within this framework of ideological confrontation and its consequences, the objective of fighting against inequality to guarantee a social and economic balance and cohesion was accepted by the majority of societies in the liberal-capitalist bloc (with a different focus and intensity depending on the particular characteristics of each country). Thus, the "new" liberalism was committed to increasing the level of state interventionism in both the economic and the social spheres, with the inclusion on the political and government agenda of the fight against inequality as a function and priority of the state. In some countries this led to the configuration of the welfare state.

In the new stage that opened after the Second World War, the state increasingly took on a greater role in the fight against economic inequalities, both interpersonal and inter-territorial. For example, regional policies and convergence programmes were developed to reduce territorial inequalities. Similarly, in federal and fiscally decentralised countries (whose number has been increasing in recent decades), the implantation of formal equalisation systems became widespread, with the aim of reducing regional disparities in fiscal capacity and/or expenditure needs among constituent units through horizontal and vertical fiscal redistribution mechanisms. From their origins up to the present, fiscal equalisation systems have faced the difficult challenge of seeking a balance between the objectives of equity and efficiency, while safeguarding the effective autonomy of the constituent units. The OECD defines the pillars, scope and objective of fiscal equalisation policies as follows:[1]

> Fiscal equalisation is a transfer of fiscal resources across jurisdictions with the aim of offsetting differences in revenue raising capacity or public service cost. Its principal objective is to allow sub-central governments to provide their citizens with similar sets of public services at a similar tax burden. Fiscal equalisation can be seen as the natural companion to fiscal decentralisation as it aims at correcting potential imbalances resulting from sub-central autonomy. If sub-central governments had no fiscal power, no fiscal equalisation would be needed. Distinct fiscal equalisation arrangements first emerged during the 1940s and 1950s in a number of federal countries, and today most OECD Member countries have introduced some explicit or implicit fiscal arrangement that reduces fiscal disparities across jurisdictions.

But equalisation policy is not a purely fiscal and financial issue. It has political and legal implications, which affect the essence and principles of federal systems. The equalisation systems have an important political component as an element of internal accommodation and cohesion, generating ties of solidarity and belonging (however, fiscal equalisation can also have a negative aspect if it becomes a source of grievances and resentment between territories). Therefore, fiscal equalisation policy has an impact on the political and institutional dynamics and intergovernmental relations of federations. Amongst others, it has a direct impact on the sensitive balance between autonomy/sovereignty vs. centralisation. Its adoption implies entrusting a powerful tool with a horizontal scope to the federal government, with a great potential for actively intervening in shaping the framework of intergovernmental relations.

---

1 Blöchliger, H., Merk, O., Charbit C. & Mizell, L. (2007). "Fiscal equalisation in OECD countries". *OECD Working Paper*, 4/2007, p. 5.

In any case, the implications of fiscal equalisation systems are not the same in federations of long historical standing and those created more recently. For example, for diverse reasons, the United States stands out as one of the federal exceptions that has not so far established a stand-alone equalisation system. Conversely, in the countries that have developed processes of federalisation or decentralisation following the Second World War, the implantation of systems of fiscal equalisation have, in general, been accepted and formalised in a "more pacific" and natural way. The model of fiscal federalism of each country has also been influential when it comes to facilitating or hindering the fit of the equalisation systems: implanting an equalisation mechanism in systems where sub-central governments exercise broad fiscal autonomy and operate in a framework of fiscal competence is not the same as implanting such a mechanism in systems that are more fiscally centralised and more dependent on federal transfers. Other elements and factors have also conditioned the design, scope and working of fiscal equalisation systems in federal or decentralised countries, such as for example: the a/symmetrical character of the system of federalism or fiscal federalism; the degree of territorial inequalities; the multi/mononational composition of the state; the presence/absence of challenges to the state's territorial integrity; the rigidity/flexibility of the institutional model and the legislative process; or the capacity of intervention of the Federal Court, amongst others.

In spite of the difficulties that accompany the inception and subsequent implantation of systems of fiscal equalisation, in light of the flexibility that characterises federalism, at present the majority of federal or decentralised countries have a system of equalisation adapted to the particularities, idiosyncrasies and political and institutional dynamics specific to each system, in order to alleviate problems arising from territorial fiscal inequalities and facilitate internal cohesion. That is why, as chapters of this book make clear, the working, configuration, scope and objectives of the systems of equalisation vary substantially between countries.

Since the 1990s the debate on inequality has re-emerged strongly at the international political, institutional and academic levels. The neoliberal turn that spread through the capitalist countries in response to the 1973–1979 oil crisis, the dissolution of the Soviet Union, the economic and industrial development of China, India and other players, the battle to dominate the new international order and the international crisis of 2008, amongst many other factors, have altered the map of inequality (both at the international level and internally within each country). Although since the 1990s there has been a reduction in total global income inequality between countries, in many cases internal territorial fiscal disparities have increased appreciably (both in terms of fiscal capacity and expenditure needs). The social, financial and political implications of this increase in territorial disparities have become a source of concern and tension for many federal and decentralised countries. The crisis of COVID-19 has aggravated this situation, reviving the debate on the role that the state should play in confronting interpersonal and inter-territorial inequalities.

The periods of crisis provide an ultimate testing ground for evaluating the resistance of the systems of governance and historically have played an important role in transforming the functioning and intergovernmental dynamics of federal countries. Both the 2008 financial crisis and the COVID-19 health crisis have strained federal systems – with greater or lesser intensity, depending on the case –, forcing the intergovernmental financial transfer model to be revised and adapted in most countries. This review and adaptation process has also affected equalisation transfers. In some countries it has led to profound reforms in the fiscal equalisation system. The main aim of this book is to study the state of the question of territorial inequalities, intergovernmental transfers and fiscal equalisation systems in federal or decentralised countries after the two deep crises of 2008 and 2020. This book places the spotlight on the effects, challenges and risks provoked by territorial fiscal inequalities in federal systems, and on the diversity of mechanisms and instruments created by the different federations in confronting or mitigating its adverse consequences. How did both crises affect within the framework of intergovernmental financial transfers and in the equalisation systems of the federal/decentralised countries? What is the current situation and the challenges for the future? What debates and tensions has the issue of territorial inequality provoked? In this respect, the book aims to serve as a reference on the present and future of fiscal equalisation systems in federal countries.

To this end, we have counted with the participation of leading authors and research institutions on federalism from all over the world, thanks to the network of the International Association of Centers for Federal Studies (IACFS). The IACFS is an association of institutions with interests in independent research and publication about political, constitutional, legal, administrative, fiscal, economic, social, cultural, historical and philosophical issues relevant to political systems which have federal features. One of the strengths of this book is its multidisciplinary approach to the subject. As reflected in this introduction, the question of fiscal equalisation has a multidimensional character: fiscal, financial, political, legal and institutional, amongst others. The union of experts from different disciplines (especially economists, lawyers and political scientists), offers a certainly novel approach to this book, and allows us to understand the complexity of the topic from a broad and transversal approach. In this sense, some chapters approach the issue from a more legal perspective, others, more political, and others, more financial. In this way, the full reading of the book provides us with a comprehensive view on the debates generated by fiscal territorial inequalities and equalisation policies both in the different federal or decentralised systems analysed, as well as in the different fields of research on federalism.

Besides this introduction, the first part of the book contains two chapters with a theoretical and comparative character that characterise and delimit the current framework of the systems of fiscal equalisation in federal or decentralised countries: the first from an economic and financial perspective; the second, from a legal and constitutional perspective.

The second part of the book studies the equalisation policies and systems adopted to confront territorial fiscal inequalities in nine federal or decentralised countries. The book has achieved a geographical balance, encompassing federal or decentralised countries throughout the five continents: Argentina, Australia, Canada, Ethiopia, Germany, India, South Africa, Spain and Switzerland. The book thus makes it possible to analyse, compare and contrast the different formulas implanted in these countries, focusing especially in the evolution during the first quarter of the XXI century. In this way, the book aims to facilitate research on trends within the framework of comparative fiscal federalism and makes it possible to compare and contrast the evolution, working, accommodation, particularities and the current problems and future challenges of fiscal equalisation systems and intergovernmental transfers between different federations.

Some of the chapters that form part of this book were presented at the Conference of the International Association of Centers for Federal Studies (IACFS) held in Bilbao on 27 and 28 October 2022. The IACFS conference was organised by the Ituna Center for Basque Economic Agreement and Fiscal Federalism Studies (UPV/EHU – University of the Basque Country). On behalf of the Ituna Center, I would like to take this opportunity to thank the speakers and participants at the IACFS Conference, as well as the Basque institutions for their support during the organisation (especially, the government of Bizkaia and the Basque government).

I hope that the resulting book will prove interesting and contribute to furthering research in the field of fiscal federalism and intergovernmental relations in federal systems.

PART 1

Theoretical Framework of Fiscal Equalisation

CHAPTER 1

The Economics of Fiscal Equalisation

Andoni Montes-Nebreda

Ituna Center for Basque Economic Agreement and Fiscal Federalism Studies (UPV/EHU – University of the Basque Country) & Complutense Institute for International Studies (ICEI-UCM)

1 Introduction

Whether they are considered federations or not, fiscal equalisation is among the most characteristic elements of fiscally decentralised countries' institutional machinery. Despite the existence of diverse intergovernmental fiscal transfer programmes, fiscal equalisation stands out for three main reasons: it is a solidarity tool that supports minimum provision of local public services, it is formula-based, and it is usually the largest transfer scheme. With few exceptions, such as the United States, all fiscally decentralised countries apply a fiscal equalisation mechanism.

Indeed, according to OECD data, fiscal equalisation programmes represent a very relevant part of general public expenditure. This is particularly true in Australia, Japan, Germany and Korea, where more than 8% of the public sector's budget is devoted to finance it. In contrast, in Belgium and Italy, the weight of fiscal equalisation does not even reach 1% of public spending. In between, it is possible to find fiscal decentralisation models traditionally analysed in comparative federalism studies, such as Spain (4%), Canada (2%), or Switzerland (2%).

The theoretical discussion on fiscal equalisation schemes has been extensively developed by literature at Boadway and Flatters (1982), Boadway and Wildasin (1984), Usher (1995), Mieszkowski and Musgrave (1999), Boadway (2004), or Martinez-Vazquez and Searle (2007). For a more policy-oriented practitioner's guide on equalisation see Shah (1994), Boadway and Hobson (1998), and Boadway and Shah (2007, 2009).

There are as many types of equalisation programmes as federal, quasi-federal or decentralised countries. In this chapter we will provide common guidelines to classify them. We will look into what is equalised, whether it is fiscal capacity or expenditure needs (or both). Partial equalisation will be discussed in contrast to full equalisation. Risks of fiscal equalisation, the tax-back problem

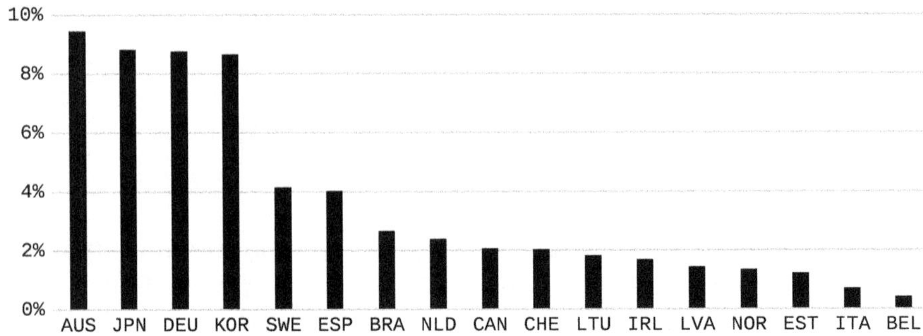

FIGURE 1.1 Size of fiscal equalisation programmes across OECD countries (2017 or latest available) (% public expenditure)
Note: AUS: Australia; AUT: Austria; BEL: Belgium; BRA: Brazil; CAN: Canada; CHE: Switzerland; CHL: Chile; CRI: Costa Rica; CZE: Czech Republic; DNK: Denmark; DEU: Germany, ESP: Spain; EST: Estonia; FIN: Finland; FRA: France; GBR: United Kingdom; GRC: Greece; HUN: Hungary; IRL: Ireland; ISL: Iceland; ISR: Israel; ITA: Italia; JPN: Japan; KOR: Korea; LTU: Lithuania; LUX: Luxembourg; LVA: Latvia; MEX: Mexico; NLD: Netherlands; NZL: New Zealand; NOR: Norway; POL: Poland; PRT: Portugal; SVK: Slovakia; SVN: Slovenia; SWE: Sweden; USA: United States
SOURCE: (OECD, 2021, P. 53)

and the flypaper effect will be explored too. But we will first try to understand why fiscal equalisation is so widespread, its causes and consequences.

2 Justification, Debates and Advantages of Fiscal Equalisation

Despite debate and criticism raised in some countries around how much should fiscal equalisation redistribute (e.g. Canada, Belgium, or Spain), the existence of some kind of fiscal equalisation is generally pacific as it is justified on both equity and efficiency arguments. This section will elaborate on the causes that make fiscal equalisation so widespread across federations. Depending on the regulation and design of the fiscal equalisation mechanism, sometimes the advantages listed below will be among their explicit objectives, or they will be spontaneous positive consequences of the dynamics of the scheme.

2.1 *Vertical Imbalances*

The first reason why the need for fiscal equalisation can be justified is the existence of vertical fiscal imbalances. These imbalances are a mechanical consequence of the application of the subsidiarity principle. This principle suggests that policy responsibilities should be attributed to the lowest level of government possible, as long as side-effects are not large enough to recommend the next higher level of government should get in charge.

Musgrave's (1983) prescriptions for revenue-side decentralisation are stricter than Oates' (1972) for expenditure decentralisation. Consequently, and without exception, fiscal decentralisation is always asymmetric. Following guidelines of the theory of Fiscal Federalism, revenue-side responsibilities are less often decentralised, or at least to a lesser extent, than expenditure-side responsibilities (Boadway and Keen, 1996). Therefore, central governments have more revenue available than that needed to run public services under their competence. On the contrary, subnational governments (SNG) lack enough resources to support public services they are responsible for. Vertical transfers are the response provided by federalism to address these imbalances.

Figure 1.2 illustrates the size of vertical imbalances across OECD countries as reported by the OECD Fiscal Decentralisation Database. The difference between the two columns, subnational expenditure and revenue, results in the scale of vertical imbalances. Large imbalances are observed for heavily decentralised countries such as Denmark, Belgium, Spain, and Austria. However, vertical imbalances are also high for centralised countries such as Ireland, Greece, Slovakia, and Lithuania.

Vertical imbalances are present in every OECD country but New Zealand, Chile, and Costa Rica, which are also examples of heavily centralised institutional models. In addition, vertical imbalances are also relatively small in highly decentralised federations that follow a more equilibrated approach, such as Germany, Switzerland, Australia, and to a lesser extent, Canada and the United States.

The horizontal or vertical nature of fiscal equalisation is not pacific and has been long discussed by literature. On the one hand, Castells (1988), López-Laborda (1991), or Boadway and Tremblay (2006) consider that equalisation can be both vertical and horizontal, depending on whether a vertical or horizontal imbalances are to be filled. On the other hand, Dahlby (2014), and Onrubia and Ruiz-Huerta Carbonell (2019) consider that the term fiscal equalisation should be reserved for transfers that aim to correct horizontal imbalances. As it can be interpreted from this debate, it is clear that fiscal equalisation is required to address horizontal imbalances. However, there are more doubts regarding the link between fiscal equalisation and vertical imbalances.

Our view is that vertical imbalances do not necessarily need to be addressed by fiscal equalisation, as any other kind of vertical transfer scheme, such as block grants, could do the job (Dahlby, 2014). However, this is the most typical case, since treating vertical imbalances without providing fiscal equalisation would require distributing funds on a purely per capita basis. Yet, allocating

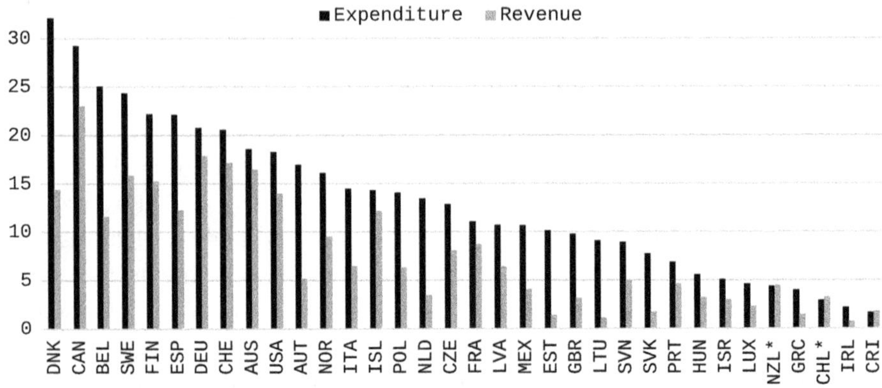

FIGURE 1.2 Subnational expenditure and revenue in 2021 (% GDP)
Note: data for countries marked with * corresponds to 2020
SOURCE: OECD FISCAL DECENTRALISATION DATABASE

the same amount of transfers to all jurisdictions is not perceived as an equitable response, and therefore central governments' transfer allocations usually consider fiscal capacity or/and expenditure needs.

2.2 *Equity*

Equity is the most easily observable justification for fiscal equalisation. In contrast with the unitary public service provision, decentralised provision alone cannot result in an equitable result due to differences in fiscal capacity and needs across jurisdictions. Without fiscal equalisation, those differences would translate into uneven access and quality of healthcare or education across territories, which represents a horizontal equity issue. Two citizens in the same position would receive a different treatment by the public sector depending on their residence. To a certain extent, this is innate to federalism and can be considered desirable as it suggests there exists a diverse policy menu offer to choose from (Tiebout, 1956). However, when very large, these differences could turn both into a political problem and into an efficiency problem, due to induced suboptimal mobility.

Precisely, the main objective of fiscal equalisation is related to equity (Bird and Vaillancourt, 2007). It aims to ensure that all jurisdictions, despite their differences in terms of fiscal capacity or needs, can provide a common minimum level of local public services when charging similar taxes. In other words, it aims to ensure that citizens can enjoy similar access to public services of even quality disregards where do they live.

Although fiscal equalisation often gets mixed up with regional policy (Pérez et al., 2020), it is important to explain that following Tinbergen's rule, they are separate tools for separate problems (López-Laborda et al., 2024). Oppositely to what it has been explained for fiscal equalisation, regional policy pursues to close regional divergences in income levels, in development stages. Regional policy programmes are devoted to public investment, in contrast to current spending, which is the focus of fiscal equalisation. Therefore, regional policy is often instrumented through earmarked grants, opposite to unconditional grants that define fiscal equalisation (Boadway and Shah, 2007).

Indeed, in most federations, fiscal equalisation is the largest cross-territorial redistribution tool, even larger than regional policy. National public pension schemes or income tax can also work as implicit interregional equity instruments. However, they are based and thus designed along the lines of interpersonal equity. It can be argued that fiscal equalisation is to a large extent behind the in-kind income redistribution in federations since it supports healthcare and education, which are the main in-kind redistributive programmes managed at the subnational level (OECD, 2021).

However, authors such as Oakland (1994) question the equity-favourable nature of fiscal equalisation. First, from the interregional equity point of view, he argues that financial flows in fiscal equalisation take place between jurisdictions with higher fiscal capacity and lower expenditure needs towards those with lower fiscal capacity and higher expenditure needs. This does not necessarily need to be from high-income towards low-income territories, and therefore fiscal equalisation could work in the opposite direction to that expected and be regressive. And second, from the interpersonal equity perspective, Oakland (1994), Usher (1995), and Wilson (2007), argue that even if fiscal equalisation would redistribute income from "rich" to "poor" jurisdictions, equalisation could still transfer resources from a low-income household at a rich region to contribute paying for better quality local public services used by a high-income household living in a poor region.

2.3 *Efficiency*

Finally, after the budgetary and equity rationales for fiscal equalisation, we will briefly discuss its efficiency grounds. Most efficiency gains in this field are explained by the use of fiscal equalisation as an internalisation mechanism for externalities emerged from the interaction between jurisdictions, from horizontal spillovers. Boadway and Keen (1996) suggest that the efficiency-related justification of fiscal equalisation is so powerful that even in an ideal model without fiscal imbalances, it would be needed to address vertical and horizontal fiscal externalities.

2.3.1 Restoring the Fiscal Equivalence

Olson's (1969) fiscal equivalence theorem states that optimality in the local provision of public goods requires full identification between recipients and contributors. This would be the guarantee of efficiency as users' demand would be limited by the cost signal represented by local taxation used to finance it. However, we are aware that there are several reasons why, in most cases, users do not face the full cost of public services. On the one hand, progressive taxation distorts that relationship, since high-income taxpayers might not be the heaviest users of local public services. User fees, mostly used at the local level (e.g. sports facilities …) address this issue to a certain extent, as still they usually set a price under production cost.

On the other hand, residents in other jurisdictions may use local public services of the neighbouring jurisdiction, where they do not pay their taxes. This is the most evident case of the existence of horizontal spillovers and is related to the nature of public goods, whose consumption is not excludable. For example, this phenomenon takes place when a patient attends a doctor in a neighbouring region. However, it also takes place in less tangible situations, such as good air quality breathed by residents of the neighbouring town thanks to the creation of a low emissions zone. This kind of horizontal externalities, which partially shift the cost of local public policies from their beneficiaries, can be addressed through horizontal transfers, which could be fiscal equalisation (Smart, 1998). It is also not uncommon for federations to create *ad hoc* federal funds to help internalise these spillovers.

2.3.2 Disincentive to Tax Competition

Tax autonomy has several advantages, among them, opening space for tax competition (Olson, 1969; Musgrave 1983). Tax competition works as a fiscal discipline device, limiting the excessive growth of the public sector size (Brennan and Buchanan, 1980). In addition, since it allows for a differentiated revenue-side policy menu, it can foster policy innovation; and, as citizens can compare the tax menu offered by each jurisdiction, also accountability can improve. However, if tax requirements set by subnational governments start decreasing following a domino-effect dynamic at which this behaviour is copied by the rest of jurisdictions, then taxes could become suboptimally low (Zodrow and Mieszkowski, 1986). This phenomenon is known as "race to the bottom" and is particularly likely to take place in contexts of competitive fiscal federalism, and to affect capital taxation, as this is the most mobile tax base (Sinn, 2003).

Fiscal equalisation is particularly useful to cope with harmful tax competition. Indeed, fiscal equalisation can set powerful disincentives against these dynamics when its formula considers not actual revenue but fiscal capacity instead. In those cases, transfers are allocated according to potential tax revenue, this is the tax base and not revenue raised. This way, a decrease in revenue caused by lower taxation is not compensated by fiscal equalisation. Oppositely, jurisdictions can retain revenue increases generated by higher taxation or more effective tax administration, setting an interesting incentive to improve efficiency but against harmful tax competition (Bucovetsky and Smart, 2006; Kotsogiannis, 2010).

2.3.3 Slowing Down Inefficient Mobility: Congestion Costs and Economies of Scale

One of the consequences generated by fiscal equalisation affects both efficiency and equity. By limiting the differences in local public service provision across jurisdictions, fiscal equalisation reduces the variance in fiscal residuals too. Fiscal residual is defined as the net gain from local public goods and services obtained by a resident in a specific jurisdiction, after paying taxes (Buchanan, 1950). While living in a high fiscal capacity and low needs region should offer a large fiscal residual, the opposite should be true for low capacity and high needs territories.

Without fiscal equalisation (and if wages would not differ across jurisdictions), the incentive to "vote with one's feet" would be very powerful, both for the high-income looking to pay lower taxes, and for the low-income looking for more redistributive or generous local public spending (Tiebout, 1956). This is considered inefficient migration as it would be solely driven by fiscal policy, and not by wage differentials, which should be the signal driving optimal mobility (Buchanan, 1950). Change in residency would concentrate tax bases in to-have jurisdictions leaving in-need jurisdictions empty.

The increase in geographic imbalances would generate inefficiencies in both places. On the one hand, the attractive jurisdiction could suffer from increased congestion costs derived from an excessive concentration of population within its regional boundaries (Buchanan and Wagner, 1970; Baldwin and Krugman, 2004). On the other hand, the emptied jurisdiction could become in danger of not reaching the minimum scale to provide local public services involving large fixed costs.

The case of congestion and economies of scale is a good example of how a well-designed fiscal equalisation system could improve both equity and efficiency, breaking the traditional trade-off discussed in the field of Public Economics. Indeed, fiscal equalisation serves as a tool to reduce differentials in the fiscal residual across jurisdictions, as it guarantees a minimum and common level of public services is provided everywhere. Therefore, fiscal equalisation could prevent suboptimal mobility choices otherwise driven by asymmetries in the fiscal residual (Buchanan, 1950; Bird and Vaillancourt, 2007).

3 Risks and Disadvantages of Fiscal Equalisation

Although advantages of fiscal equalisation are so relevant as to explain why this kind of scheme is that widespread across federal and quasi-federal countries, it also entails risks or disadvantages related to budgetary efficiency. In fact, fiscal equalisation, particularly when badly designed, can induce suboptimal fiscal policy behaviour on subnational governments, both from the revenue (tax-back problem) and the expenditure (flypaper effect) sides.

3.1 *The Tax-Back Problem*

Fiscal equalisation can lead to excessively high subnational taxation. This is known as the "tax-back problem" and can emerge through two different channels: tax rates or tax bases (Wilson, 2007; Ferede, 2014). First, the tax-back problem can emerge when subnational governments can manipulate the result of the fiscal equalisation formula to absorb more funding by increasing their own tax rates. This is possible both in the Canadian RTS system (Dahlby, 2014; Ferede, 2014) and in the former German own-resource-based formula (Baretti et al., 2002). In this case, the issue could be tackled by fixing the equalisation formula so it cannot be manipulated anymore. For instance, by replacing tax rates or actual revenue as input variables for a proxy of potential revenue or of tax base.

But it is the second channel of the tax-back problem the most difficult to address. Even when the equalisation formula does not alter the transfer allocation in response to changes in subnational taxation, jurisdictions can avoid enforcing growth-enhancing policies in order to erode their tax base, aware of the fact that equalisation would compensate them, at least to some extent, for the revenue loss (Smart and Bird, 1996).

However, even when there is no voluntary intention by subnational governments to manipulate the result of equalisation transfer allocation, equalisation might lead them to set suboptimally high tax rates. This can happen when central government and subnational governments share taxation power over the same tax bases (tax base co-occupation). Equalisation decreases the perceived efficiency cost of taxation for subnational governments, as they are only aware of the tax base loss up to the share of revenue it corresponds to them, neglecting the loss faced by the central government due to subnational decisions on the shared tax bases (Dahlby and Wilson, 1994).

Literature has suggested several responses to the tax-back problem. They range from an increase in tax autonomy to reduce the need for transfers, to reduce federal taxes and spending below the optimal, to avoid tax base sharing between levels of government, or to use matching grants (Sato, 2000). However, it is still not clear to which extent they could be put into practice to prevent the tax-back problem from emerging while preserving the effectiveness of fiscal equalisation in reaching its goals.

3.2 *The Flypaper Effect*

First proposed by Courant et al. (1978), this hypothesis suggests that subnational governments tend to spend more when the income stream comes from intergovernmental transfers than when it stems from own tax revenue. Literature has presented two causes to explain this phenomenon. On the one hand, an increase in received intergovernmental transfers, not necessarily equalisation transfers, allows to keep subnational spending constant with lower taxes. This generates fiscal illusion in subnational governments since they underperceive the efficiency cost of raising taxes as that cost is passed to the central government. Fiscal illusion results in suboptimally high subnational public expenditure (Dahlby, 2011; López-Laborda and Zabalza, 2015).

On the other hand, apart from the fiscal illusion generated by transfers, they can also lead to overspending when self-interested subnational incumbents are looking for re-election. Again, they have two ways to increase spending and improve the welfare of voters living within its jurisdiction, by raising taxes or by increasing received transfers. While the former option would entail also a cost represented by tax increases, the latter would shift the electoral cost of raising new revenue towards the central government, thus setting an incentive for an excessive increase in subnational public spending (Mieszkowski, 1994; Hines and Thaler, 1995).

4 What Can Be Equalised?

Another element at which fiscal equalisation schemes might differ is on the side of the budget considered. While all federations contemplate to some extent fiscal capacity or revenue as criteria to allocate equalisation transfers, not all take into account expenditure needs or costs. Figure 1.3 shows that although in most federations both are to some extent combined, Canada and Germany only consider revenue equalisation; and Korea, Spain, Japan, and the Netherlands, mostly equalise expenditure needs. For their part, Mexico

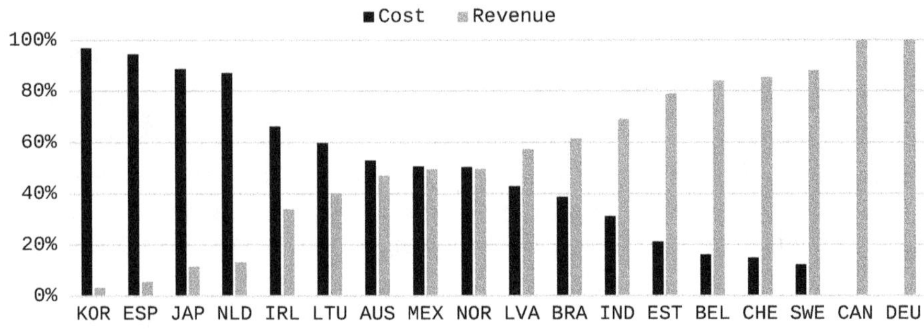

FIGURE 1.3 Share of fiscal equalisation schemes devoted to cost/revenue equalisation across OECD countries (2018 or latest available) (% fiscal equalisation expenditure)
SOURCE: (OECD, 2021, P. 57)

and Norway are examples of perfect equilibrium between revenue and needs equalisation.

4.1 *Fiscal Capacity*

Income-side equalisation focuses on differences in revenue-raising capacities across territories. The aim is to reduce or eliminate differences in budgetary capacity determined by uneven tax base distribution across jurisdictions. While actual revenue differences might be used to allocate transfers, it is often the case, and the recommendation of literature and international organisations, such as the OECD, that potential revenue is considered instead. On the one hand, it makes the formula more difficult to manipulate, limiting the tax-back problem. And, on the other hand, it entails a more efficient incentive scheme, since subnational governments face the consequences of the use of their tax autonomy, closing the door to harmful tax competition.

Fiscal capacity can be measured using all decentralised taxes or just some of them. In addition, target fiscal capacity to be used as a yardstick to measure jurisdictions' fiscal capacity can be based on an average of all or some jurisdictions (e.g. Canadian Representative Tax System) or on a nationally set default threshold (e.g. Spain). In some cases, the fiscal capacity formula includes tax bases that are only centrally taxed, in those cases a territorialisation exercise needs to be run. Proxy variables are then used to measure subnational jurisdictions' tax capacity, such as consumption for VAT or excise duties.

The technical complexity of estimating fiscal capacity in some countries has led to several experts suggest new approaches to simplify it by using macroeconomic variables as a proxy. Proposals range from per capita Gross National Product, or regional GDP, to an adjusted GNP to account for federal benefits (Barro, 2002). Despite this alternative could be useful in some contexts, traditional models based on purely fiscal variables seem to be better proxies as they are directly linked to the actual variable that has to be estimated.

4.2 *Expenditure Needs*

In addition to public income-related information, the transfer allocation formula can distribute funding according to population (on a per capita basis), or alternatively, according to a list of proxies of spending needs. The goal of the latter approach is to try to approximate transfer allocation to how much the population of a specific jurisdiction need the provision of local public services. Proxies might be objective or subjective variables. On the one hand, objective variables are those linked to geography (e.g. population dispersion, land area, insularity …) and other circumstances (e. g. wage level) that make public goods provision costlier. On the other hand, subjective variables translate the population structure of the jurisdiction into the formula by giving more weight to the elderly or underaged population, as they demand more long-term care, healthcare, or education services.

Despite it is not a usual practice, experts, such as Spahn (2007), have proposed introducing fixed costs in the fiscal equalisation formula. The rationale behind it is that disregards it is a small or a large jurisdiction, there are certain public goods that need to be provided. The most straightforward example is institutions. Executive and, in some cases, legislative bodies too, must be established in each jurisdiction to take care of responsibilities attributed to this layer of government. The global cost of running subnational institutions will be very similar. However, the cost per inhabitant may range a lot depending on how populated a jurisdiction is. This is why recognising fixed costs in certain policy areas would approximate transfer allocation to actual spending needs of subnational governments.

In line with the recommendation of using non-manipulable variables in the equalisation formula, the use of regional wage differentials has been questioned. It is true that wages represent the main cost of public service production as they entail an intense demand for a high-skilled labour force (e.g. doctors, nurses, or professors). In some countries, cross-regional development and income level disparities translate into large heterogeneities in price and wage levels. This makes inputs more expensive and, therefore, public services costlier. If the goal of fiscal equalisation is to allow a similar level of local public services provision despite uneven fiscal capacities and needs, then it could be argued that input price differentials should be considered. However, if wages of civil servants are set by subnational governments, then including this variable in the equalisation formula would set an incentive for setting suboptimally high wages, as subnational governments would be aware of its immediate translation as higher grant entitlements (Boadway and Shah, 2009).

In many cases, the negotiation of the grant allocation formula is the result of a political discussion in which central government and subnational governments need to reach an agreement. They have to agree not only on which proxies to use, but also on which weight each of them is attributed in the formula. The discretion of the variables chosen and the weight given to them in the design of the allocation formula might be controversial and might create coalitions of regions around their own interest. In order to tackle this problem, some countries have opted for a technical, and even econometric approach (e.g. Australia, the Netherlands, or Finland), in which the correlation between provision costs and proxies is assessed. This way, political negotiations can then be based on a previous technical assessment carried out by an expert body.

5 Equalisation Degree: Full or Partial?

Differences in fiscal capacity/revenue and expenditure needs/costs can be fully or partially equalised. The choice between full or partial equalisation is to be decided through the democratic decision-making process as it is the reflection of the extent of redistribution citizens aim for or are ready to tolerate. Indeed, full equalisation might be too unpopular and politically costly so as to be feasible. Although it is a key defining element of any equalisation scheme, it is sometimes not explicitly set in the law, but it needs to be interpreted from its design.

Fiscal equalisation can be partial due to many reasons. It can be because the law explicitly states that only a share of differences in fiscal capacity and/or needs are to be compensated. The percentage of differences equalised is named after the "inclusion rate". However, sometimes the partial nature of equalisation is subtler. For example, because some jurisdictions do not take part in the scheme, because not all revenue bases are considered in the calculation of fiscal capacity, or because there are some public services the formula does not account for.

There are examples of full equalisation in the sense that they compensate for all the differences identified as the objective to be covered by the scheme. This is the case in Australia where costs are fully equalised. In contrast, systems such as the German and Spanish only compensate a (high) percentage of those differences. However, if we consider fiscal differences in broader terms, it is virtually impossible full equalisation exists. Indeed, as long as some jurisdictions (e.g. *foral* Basque and Navarrese regions in Spain), revenue bases (e.g.

natural resource revenues in Canada), or public services (e.g. elderly care) are excluded from the formula, fiscal equalisation will always be partial. For instance, the neglection of cross-jurisdictional environmental externalities' effect on subnational fiscal capacities and needs illustrates the partial nature of fiscal equalisation (Lopez-Laborda et al., 2023).

Literature has posed questions on the efficiency of full equalisation. Some authors (Bucovetsky and Smart, 2006; Martínez-Lopez et al., 2018) argue that total equalisation could reduce incentives for regional development and growth-oriented subnational policies, as fiscal consequences of successful economic policy would be virtually neutralised by equalisation. According to this view, partial equalisation would be superior, even if some equity would be sacrificed at the expense of more efficiency. In contrast, authors (Boadway and Flatters, 1982; Martínez-Lopez et al., 2018) defending full equalisation consider that it does not just ensure a better equity outcome (Boadway and Shah, 2009), but that it is more efficient. According to this view, partial arrangements would only be able to achieve limited advantages related to the efficiency arguments listed in Section 2.3. For example, inefficient migration would only be prevented to the extent that differences in fiscal residual are equalised, but not totally.

6 Financing Fiscal Equalisation

Fiscal equalisation can be centrally financed, this is exclusively by using the federal budget; or, alternatively, it can be funded with subnational revenues, whether they are actually collected by subnational tax administrations or not. The former is the case of the Canadian Federation, where it is the federal budget that faces the full cost of equalisation. In contrast, the latter is the case of Australia, where GST (consumption tax) revenue, which is used to fund equalisation, is owned by states.

Vertically financed fiscal equalisation is meant to close fiscal vertical imbalances derived from the constitutional distribution of revenue and expenditure powers. In addition, it can also contribute to close horizontal imbalances if the formula applied considers differences in fiscal capacities and needs across subnational governments. In contrast, horizontally funded systems cannot address vertical fiscal imbalances. However, schemes based in horizontal transfers can exert positive effects, such as more responsible fiscal behaviour of subnational entities, derived from fiscal co-responsibility and tax autonomy exercised (Olson, 1969).

Regardless the vertical or horizontal nature of grants, fiscal equalisation transfers are always unconditional. This is part of the nature and rationale behind fiscal equalisation, which should allow subnational governments, grants recipients, to provide a differentiated menu of expenditure policies according to citizens' preferences and needs. Therefore, central governments do not set any requirement linked to the policy areas in which grants should be spent. This is true even when allocation formulas consider separate variable sets for equalising specific expenditure needs, such as healthcare or education. Even in those cases, transfers remain non-earmarked to preserve subnational spending autonomy.

According to OECD expert-survey data, illustrated in Figure 1.4 (OECD, 2021), most of fiscal equalisation schemes are fully funded by vertical transfers. This is the case in Korea, Japan, the Netherlands, Greece, Australia, Mexico, Brazil, Indonesia, Estonia, and Canada. It is consistent with the recommendation of keeping redistributive function policies centralised (Oates, 1972). In contrast, Lithuania, Spain, and Latvia support equalisation pre-eminently with horizontal transfers. It is Norway, Ireland, and Portugal, the countries that keep the most equilibrated approach between horizontal and vertical transfers.

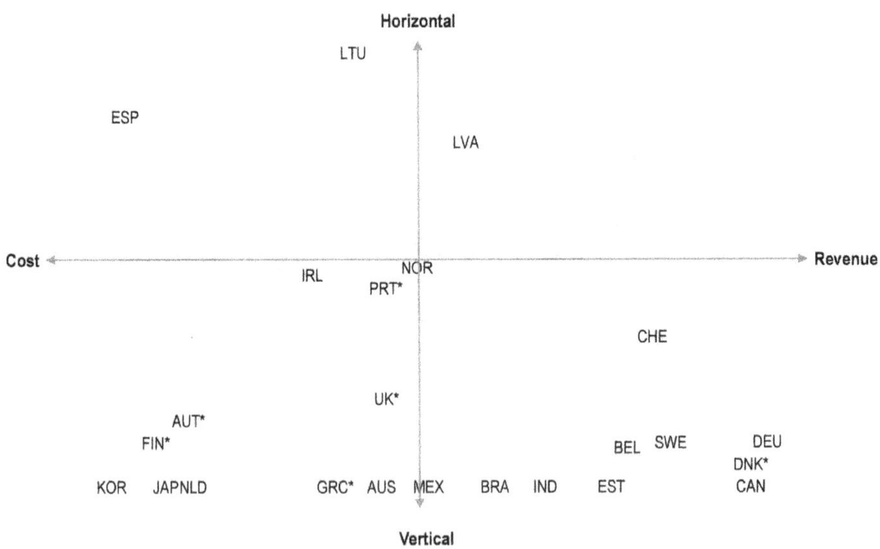

FIGURE 1.4 Comparison of fiscal equalisation systems across the OECD according to their design (2019)
Note: data for countries marked with * corresponds to 2013
SOURCE: (OECD, 2021, P. 48). BASED ON EXPERT'S SURVEY

Interestingly, there is a correlation between the size of equalisation relative to total public expenditure (Figure 1.1) and the vertical character of transfers supporting it (Figure 1.4). Indeed, while large fiscal equalisation schemes are funded by vertical transfers, it is only small schemes that are mainly supported by horizontal transfers. Spain is the only outlier as even if relatively large, its fiscal equalisation system is primarily supported by horizontal grants. Two reasons might be behind this correlation. On the one hand, due to the existence of vertical imbalances, central governments keep a larger financial capacity to fund large transfer schemes. And, on the other hand, vertical transfers should be politically less controversial, as cross-jurisdictional redistribution takes place in a subtler way when carried out through vertical transfers when compared to horizontal transfers. Therefore, large redistribution mechanisms would be more politically feasible when supported by vertical transfers.

All in all, it could be questioned whether vertical transfers actually exist in a philosophical sense. This is because all revenues are paid by residents in a specific jurisdiction within the country, and thus can be territorialised. Consistent with this view, vertical transfers would actually be indirect horizontal transfers, being net contributor territories the financing entities and net recipients the beneficiaries.

7 Future Challenges for Fiscal Equalisation

This chapter has surveyed the economics of fiscal federalism focusing on its objectives, justification, consequences, and possible designs. From this overview, it can be concluded that there exist as many fiscal equalisation arrangements as fiscally decentralised countries, since their configuration largely depends on the institutional context. Looking to the future, it is possible to identify three pending challenges that sooner than later will be necessarily faced.

First, fiscal equalisation should incorporate new flexibility elements to better cope with external shocks. The COVID-19 pandemic evidenced that the lack of automatic mechanisms makes *ad hoc* intervention by the central government indispensable, as it had to step up to protect the decentralised welfare state from the sharp decrease in public revenue (OECD, 2021). This represents a problem because it incorporates uncertainty in the system as different colour cabinets at the central government are unlikely to react consistently. In addition, this could be used as a hidden channel to reduce subnational governments fiscal autonomy without holding a previous public debate or passing an explicit legal or constitutional amendment.

Second, the accelerated progress of climate change is forcing policymakers to use all the tools available to try to cope with this issue. That includes fiscal federalism arrangements which might become very useful to ensure all levels of government are aligned with international and national green agendas. Environmental fiscal transfers (Busch et al., 2021) could serve to set a smarter incentive scheme for subnational governments to pursue more ambitious environmental objectives, and to equip regional and local institutions with the necessary human, technical and financial capabilities to successfully tackle ecological transition (Dougherty and Montes-Nebreda, 2023). Within environmental fiscal transfers, fiscal equalisation could play a central role by incorporating green criteria to improve current fiscal capacities and needs measurement formulas, as proposed by Lopez-Laborda et al. (2023).

Finally, population ageing will continue putting pressure on welfare systems. The WHO forecasts that by 2050 world's population of people aged 60 or more will double compared to 2020. This rapid ageing process will continue increasing the demand for healthcare and elderly-care services, which are most of the time provided by subnational governments. Just as an example, this issue has already led some subnational authorities in the United Kingdom to go bankrupt in 2023. In the long term, if not properly addressed, these imbalances in public finances could translate into macroeconomic systemic risks. Therefore, fiscal equalisation will need to adapt and provide a response (De Biase et al., 2022).

References

Baldwin, R. E., & Krugman, P. (2004). Agglomeration, integration and tax harmonisation. *European economic review*, 48(1), 1–23. https://doi.org/10.1016/S0014-2921(02)00318-5.

Baretti, C., Huber, B., & Lichtblau, K. (2002). A tax on tax revenue: The incentive effects of equalizing transfers: Evidence from Germany. *International Tax and Public Finance*, 9, 631–649. https://doi.org/10.1023/A:1020925812428.

Barro, S. M. (2002). Macroeconomic versus RTS Measures of Fiscal Capacity: Theoretical Foundations and Implications for Canada. *Queen's University. Institute for Intergovernmental Relations*, Kingston, Ontario. https://www.queensu.ca/iigr/sites/iirwww/files/uploaded_files/2002-7StephenBarro.pdf.

Bird, R., & Vaillancourt, F. (2007). Expenditure-Based Equalization Transfers. In J. Martinez-Vazquez, & B. Searle (Eds.), *Fiscal equalization: Challenges in the design of intergovernmental transfers*. Springer Science and Business Media.

Boadway, R. (2004). The theory and practice of equalization. *CESifo Economic Studies*, 50(1), 211–254.

Boadway, R., & Flatters, F. (1982). Efficiency and equalization payments in a federal system of government: A synthesis and extension of recent results. *Canadian Journal of Economics*, 613–633.

Boadway, R. W., & Hobson, P. A. R. (1998). *Equalization: its contribution to Canada's economic and fiscal progress* (Vol. 36). Kingston, Ont.: John Deutsch Institute for the Study of Economic Policy, Queen's University.

Boadway, R., & Keen, M. (1996). Efficiency and the optimal direction of federal-state transfers. *International Tax and Public Finance,* 3, 137–155. https://doi.org/10.1007/BF00399907.

Boadway, R., & Shah, A. (2009). *Fiscal Federalism: Principles and Practice of Multiorder Governance.* Cambridge: Cambridge University Press. https://doi.org/10.1017/CBO9780511626883.

Boadway, R., & Shah, A. (2007). *Intergovernmental Fiscal Transfers: Principles and Practice. Public Sector Governance and Accountability.* Washington, DC: World Bank. https://openknowledge.worldbank.org/handle/10986/7171.

Boadway, R., & Tremblay, J. (2006). A Theory of Fiscal Imbalance. *FinanzArchiv / Public Finance Analysis*, 62(1), 1–27. http://www.jstor.org/stable/40913100.

Boadway, R. W., & Wildasin, D. E. (1984). *Public sector economics.* Little, Brown.

Brennan, G., & Buchanan, J. M. (1980). *The power to tax: Analytic foundations of a fiscal constitution.* Cambridge: Cambridge University Press.

Buchanan, J. M. (1950). Federalism and fiscal equity. *The American Economic Review*, 40(4), 583–599.

Buchanan, J., & Wagner, R. (1970). An efficiency basis for federal fiscal equalisation. In B. Grewal, G. Brennan, & R. Mathews (Eds.), *The Economics of Federalism.* Canberra: Australian National University Press. https://www.nber.org/system/files/chapters/c3353/c3353.pdf.

Bucovetsky, S., & Smart, M. (2006). The efficiency consequences of local revenue equalization: Tax competition and tax distortions. *Journal of Public Economic Theory*, 8(1), 119–144. https://doi.org/10.1111/j.1467-9779.2006.00255.x.

Busch, J., Ring, I., Akullo, M., Amarjargal, O., Borie, M., Cassola, R. S., ... & Zhou, K. (2021). A global review of ecological fiscal transfers. *Nature Sustainability*, 4(9), 756–765. https://doi.org/10.1038/s41893-021-00728-0.

Castells, A. (1988). *Hacienda Autonómica. Una perspectiva de federalismo fiscal.* Barcelona: Ariel Economía.

Courant, P. N., Gramlich, E. M., & Rubinfeld, D. L. (1978). *The stimulative effects of intergovernmental grants: Or why money sticks where it hits.* University of Michigan, Institute of Public Policy Studies.

Dahlby, B. (2011). The marginal cost of public funds and the flypaper effect. *International Tax and Public Finance,* 18, 304–321. https://doi.org/10.1007/s10797-010-9160-x.

Dahlby, B. (2014). Reforming equalization: Balancing efficiency, entitlement and ownership. *SPP Research Paper*, 07.22. https://dx.doi.org/10.2139/ssrn.2510564.

Dahlby, B., & Wilson, L. S. (1994). Fiscal capacity, tax effort, and optimal equalization grants. *Canadian Journal of Economics*, 657–672. https://doi.org/10.2307/135789.

De Biase, P., Dougherty S., & Lorenzoni, L. (2022). Ageing and the long-run fiscal sustainability of health care across levels of government, *OECD Working Papers on Fiscal Federalism*, 38. Paris: OECD Publishing. https://doi.org/10.1787/7c184406-en.

Dougherty, S., & Montes-Nebreda, A. (2023). "The multi-level fiscal governance of ecological transition", *OECD Working Papers on Fiscal Federalism*, 44. Paris: OECD Publishing. https://doi.org/10.1787/2051f0f7-en.

Ferede, E. (2014). The Incentive Effects of Equalization Grants on Fiscal Policy. *SPP Research Paper*, 07.23. https://dx.doi.org/10.2139/ssrn.2510562.

Hines, J., & Thaler, R. (1995). Anomalies. The flypaper effect. *Journal of Economic Perspectives*, 9, 217–226. https://pubs.aeaweb.org/doi/pdf/10.1257/jep.9.4.217.

Kotsogiannis, C. (2010). Federal tax competition and the efficiency consequences for local taxation of revenue equalization. *International Tax and Public Finance*, 17(1), 1–14.

López-Laborda, J. (1991). *Los equilibrios financieros en el estado de las autonomías*. Monografía nº 95. Madrid: Instituto de Estudios Fiscales.

López-Laborda, J., Montes-Nebreda, A., & Onrubia, J. (2023). Going green through local fiscal equalisation. *Fedea Working Papers*, 2023–07.

López-Laborda, J., Montes-Nebreda, A., & Onrubia, J. (2024). Should fiscal equalisation and regional policy goals and tools be disentangled?. *Regional Studies*, 1–15. https://doi.org/10.1080/00343404.2024.2371146.

López-Laborda, J., & Zabalza, A. (2015). Intergovernmental fiscal relations: the efficiency effect of taxes, transfers, and fiscal illusion. *Environment and Planning C: Government and Policy*, 33(1), 136–162. https://doi.org/10.1068/c12284r.

Martínez López, D., Pedraja, F., Monés, M. A., & Colldeforns, M. (2018). Debates sobre la reforma del Sistema de Financiación Autonómica: ii) ¿Nivelación total o parcial?. *Fedea Policy Papers*, 2018–07.

Martinez-Vazquez, J., & Searle, B. (Eds.) (2007). *Fiscal equalization: Challenges in the design of intergovernmental transfers*. Boston: Springer Science and Business Media.

Mieszkowski, P. (1994). Comments on Chapter 5. In J. M. Quigley, & E. Smolensky (Eds.), *Modern public finance* (pp. 157–161). Cambridge: Harvard University Press.

Mieszkowski, P., & Musgrave, R. A. (1999). Federalism, grants, and fiscal equalization. *National Tax Journal*, 239–260.

Musgrave, R.A. (1983). Who should tax, where, and what? In C. E. McLure Jr (Ed.), *Tax Assignment in Federal Countries*. Canberra: Australian National University Press.

Oakland, W. H. (1994). Fiscal equalization: An empty box? *National Tax Journal*, 47(1), 199–209.

Oates, W. E. (1972). *Fiscal federalism*. Northampton: Edward Elgar Publishing.

OECD (2021). *Fiscal Federalism 2022: Making Decentralisation Work*. Paris: OECD Publishing. https://doi.org/10.1787/201c75b6-en.

Olson, M. (1969). The principle of "fiscal equivalence": the division of responsibilities among different levels of government. *The American Economic Review*, 59(2), 479–487.

Onrubia, J., & Ruiz-Huerta Carbonell, J. (2019). Estado y haciendas territoriales: la salida del laberinto. In M. J. Garde, J. Gascón, & T. Merola (Eds.), *Hacienda Pública y gobernanza fiscal en España: desafíos 2020. En reconocimiento a la trayectoria profesional en el sector público de D. Juan Antonio Garde Roca* (2019). Madrid: Instituto de Estudios Fiscales.

Pérez, F., Reig, E., Mollá, S., Pérez, J., & Vicente, I. (2020). Los costes de la no autonomía. *IVIE Lab,* Entregable nº5. http://w3.argos.gva.es/documents/165533218/169881490/Informe+5_Los+costes+de+la+no+autonom%C3%ADa.pdf/9d108e51-62da-4d3d-9064-453c90b2f171.

Sato, M. (2000). Fiscal externalities and efficient transfers in a federation. *International Tax and Public Finance*, 7(2), 119–139. https://doi.org/10.1023/A:1008709203069.

Shah, A. (1994). *The reform of intergovernmental fiscal relations in developing and emerging market economies*. Washington, DC: The World Bank. https://elibrary.worldbank.org/doi/abs/10.1596/0-8213-2836-0.

Sinn, Hans-Werner (2003). *The new systems competition*. Oxford, UK: Blackwell Publishing.

Smart, M. (1998). Taxation and deadweight loss in a system of intergovernmental transfers. *Canadian Journal of Economics*, 31(1), 189–206.

Smart, M., & Bird, R. (1996). Federal Fiscal Arrangements in Canada: An Analysis of Incentives. *Proceedings of the Annual Conference on Taxation Held under the Auspices of the National Tax Association-Tax Institute of America*, 89, 1–10. http://www.jstor.org/stable/42912113.

Spahn, P. B. (2007). Equity and efficiency aspects of interagency transfers in a multigovernment framework. In R. Boadway, & A. Shah (Eds.), *Intergovernmental Fiscal Transfers: Principles and Practice* (pp. 225–258). Washington, DC: The World Bank.

Tiebout, C. M. (1956). A pure theory of local expenditures. *Journal of political economy*, 64(5), 416–424.

Usher, D. (1995). *The uneasy case for equalization payments*. Vancouver: Fraser Institute.

Wilson, L. S. (2007). Macro formulas for equalization. In R. Boadway, & A. Shah (Eds.), *Intergovernmental Fiscal Transfers: Principles and Practice* (pp. 225–258). Washington, DC: The World Bank.

Zodrow, G. R., & Mieszkowski, P. (1986). Pigou, Tiebout, property taxation, and the underprovision of local public goods. *Journal of urban economics*, 19(3), 356–370.

CHAPTER 2

Paradigms of Subnational Government Participation in Equalisation Mechanisms: A Comparative and Constitutional Outlook

Francisco Javier Romero Caro
Senior Researcher at the Eurac Research Institute for Comparative Federalism

Alice Valdesalici
Research Group Leader on Governance and Policies and Senior Researcher at the Eurac Research Institute for Comparative Federalism

1 Introduction

Today many federal systems encounter a loss of solidarity and an upsurge of interregional disparities. These have exacerbated dormant tensions and intergovernmental conflicts. Although central to intergovernmental relations, equalisation is scarcely addressed by comparative constitutional scholars, except for the studies on the solidarity principle, which however rarely delve into comparing the functioning of equalisation mechanisms (Belser et al., 2021; Delaney & Mason, 2022).

To bridge the gap, this chapter explores the different sets of legal tools that can be traced back to the category of 'equalisation mechanisms'. In particular, the analysis is limited to those mechanisms of subnational financing that in serving the purpose of solidarity put in place an inter-territorial redistribution of fiscal resources, with the aim to reduce fiscal inequalities. The components of the category 'equalisation mechanisms' are selected by process of elimination, including all grants whose amount is not linked to the principle of territoriality (Blöchliger & King, 2006, pp. 166–68). Along this line, subnational revenue coming from grants should theoretically be higher for poorer units than for richer ones. In practice, however, the extent to which this occurs differs greatly depending on the determinants of the entire process. By and large, the overall result is strongly affected by the existing legal framework, the institutional and procedural guarantees in place and the legal constraints inherent to it. As such, in the real-world, intergovernmental grants are often used for expanding the political support rather than for reducing horizontal

 | DOI:10.1163/9789004524514_004

imbalances. The impact of political momentum is always present and lies at the core of every equalisation process. Nevertheless, the margin of discretion, the constraints on the political process and the interests that drive decisions can differ greatly from one case to another.

Against this theoretical background, this chapter investigates the rules that design and govern different systems of equalisation having regard to institutional actors and decision-making procedures, exploring the role of subnational governments (SNGs) in making equalisation-related decisions with the purpose to show the coexistence of a plurality of equalisation paradigms and to verify whether and to what extent common trends do emerge in practice.

The precondition of this study is that institutions and procedures governing equalisation mechanisms are determinant of the functioning of a federal system and the federal equilibrium. Put differently, the level of government in charge of defining the scheme of intergovernmental transfers, the existing guarantees and the institutions that govern intergovernmental relations and settle intergovernmental conflicts are central features of a system and its functioning (Bahl, 2000, p. 429). This lies on the assumption that the extent and the way SNGs are involved is not without consequences in terms of transparency, equity, autonomy, but also of democratic accountability. The procedural and institutional dimensions of equalisation schemes end up determining the interests that are channeled through the process and its results. Besides being central in drawing a line between constitutional rules and political processes, these elements contribute to determine the overall federal equilibrium. As a matter of fact, the degree to which SNGs are involved in the decision-making process is telling about the impact on subnational accountability and autonomy, the overall acceptance of the redistributive scheme, and hence the extent to which solidarity is instrumental to the unity of the federal system, and does not end up in challenging the system itself. Background idea is that the design of '*a grant system*' can have '*undesired drawbacks*' (Ambrosanio et al., 2018, p. 123).

Along this line of investigation, the chapter adopts a case-study approach. Different federal systems have been identified with the aim to portray the existing variety of 'architectural' solutions around the globe. Accordingly, the following four cases are investigated: Australia as the prototype of tax-revenue sharing on a 'technical base' (*Commonwealth Grants Commission*); Canada representing the paradigm of federal-provincial diplomacy with little, if any, legal entrenchment; Germany as the prototype of tax-revenue sharing on a 'legislative-assembly base' (*Bundestag* + *Bundesrat*); and Spain with the (quasi-constitutional) institutionalisation of the CPFF as a forum for intergovernmental financial relations.

The cases will be investigated integrating a static dimension – If, where and to what extent is inter-territorial solidarity regulated? – with a dynamic dimension – Who makes the rules? Who can amend them? This is done by looking at fiscal constitutions in their broad understanding, including constitutional documents, the implementing legislation, as well as the existing intergovernmental agreements. Therefore, the following issues shall be addressed:

Is there any constitutional entrenchment? Are equalisation mechanisms/revenue-redistribution tools embedded in a constitutional document, or in other legal acts? To what extent are decisions left to the political bargain? Are there any constitutional or legal constraints? What is the role of IGR-agreements and practice?

How are rules approved and amended? Unilaterally from the centre or with direct (or indirect) participation of SNGs? How does their involvement look like in practice? Is the participation of SNGs in the rule-making process of binding or non-binding nature from a legal or political perspective?

2 Australia: The Prototype of a Tax-Revenue Sharing Scheme on a 'Technical Base'

From a comparative perspective, the Australian system of fiscal equalisation can be considered as the prototype of a tax-revenue sharing scheme on a 'technical base'. The design and the degree of equalisation have been considered as a technical problem credited to the independent Commonwealth Grants Commission (CGC). The result is that the Australian equalisation mechanism is '*the most elaborate system of horizontal fiscal equalization of any federation*' (Madden, 2006, p. 85).

Unlike other federal systems, equalisation is not entrenched in the Australian Constitution. There is only a provision that enables the federal Parliament to '*grant financial assistance to the States on such terms and conditions as the Parliament thinks fit*' (sec. 96 Constit.). Nevertheless, this function is central due to the existence of an ample horizontal imbalance coupled with a wide vertical fiscal imbalance. While States have extensive powers in carrying on expensive services in the field of education, health, or law and order, the power to tax is strongly centralised. Over time the federal government has increased its fiscal strength, because of political negotiations with the States and judicial decisions. At the same time, among the six States and two self-governing Territories large discrepancies exist in fiscal capacity and costs for providing services.[1] SNGs differ widely in terms of community size, population growth and composition, remoteness, indigenous status, and economic strength. Such territorial diversity gives rise to strong horizontal imbalances.

In 1998, the Special Premiers' Conference had reached the Intergovernmental Agreement on the Reform of Commonwealth–State Financial Relations. The Goods and Services Tax (GST) Act of 1999 rests on this agreement. Ten years later, the Intergovernmental Agreement on Federal Financial Relations (IGA-FFR) was developed through the Council of Australian Governments (COAG). It is designed to be a living document, with detailed arrangements which can eventually be updated by another agreement. The Federal Financial Relations Act of 2009, which is meant to provide an overarching framework for financial transfers between the Commonwealth and the States and for related collaboration on policy development and service delivery, is based on this agreement (OECD, 2012). For this purpose, two types of transfers are provided. A first one under the main responsibility of the CGC, is based on the distribution of GST revenues according to the principles of horizontal equalisation, and results in untied transfers to the States. A second group instead consists of a series of special transfers, comprising the national payments for specific purposes in areas administered by States, the National Health Reform Funding, and the National partnership payments, which are key to facilitate reforms or to support specified projects. In 2018–2019, transfers amounted altogether to 45% of all State revenues (CGC, 2019).

Within this framework, the CGC is vested with the task to advise the Commonwealth on the GST redistribution among States and Territories, providing recommendations in accordance with the Treasuries' terms of reference.[2] Pursuant to the CGC Act of 1973, the body is composed of the chairperson and not less than two other members (currently three), which are appointed by the Governor-General of the Commonwealth on advice from the Federal Executive Council, without any requirement of State representation. However, this usually occurs after consultation with the States and it is no coincidence that in many cases these experts have previously worked for States.

In practice the Commission defines the methodology for GST redistribution. The evaluation process is of dynamic nature, as it is based on a quinquennial review of the methodology and annual updates of the calculations, to ensure

1 Despite Territories having a different constitutional position compared to States, when it comes to financial relations they are treated equally. They have been included in the horizontal fiscal equalisation (HFE) respectively in 1988 (Northern Territory) and in 1993 (Australian Capital Territory).

2 On the evolution of the CGC role over time, see: Wilkinson (2002) and Ross (2021).

the distribution reflects changes in State circumstances. Calculations are based on 'relativities', i.e., an index of relative needs designed on a complex formula that starts from the assessment of the difference between expenditure and revenue. Besides, in the assessment of the relative needs only factors beyond the State control are considered (Koutsogeorgopoulou, 2007, p. 16). Accordingly, States with below average revenue-raising capacity or above average spending needs receive a larger share.[3]

Over time the Commission has gained a reputation for independence and impartiality. Despite the lack of any explicit constitutional provision, the legitimacy of the CGC is considered under section 96 of the Constitution. Also, the principle of horizontal equalisation is neither enshrined in the Constitution, nor is mandated by legislation. Instead, the definition of the concept is provided by the CGC itself. Accordingly, 'State governments should receive funding from the Goods and Services Tax revenue such that, if each made the same effort to raise revenue from its own sources and operated at the same level of efficiency, each would have the capacity to provide services at the same standard' (CGC, 2010, p. 30). Basic assumption is that each State shall have the resources to provide services at national average levels of efficiency. Put differently, horizontal fiscal equalisation should ensure that citizens in different States have access to equal standards of government services.

With the Treasury Laws Amendment Act of 2018, the CGC Act of 1973 and the Federal Financial Relations Act of 2009 have been changed with the aim to ensure a gradual transition from full to reasonable equalisation.

Despite the central role the CGC plays in the apportionment of resources in general and in equalisation in particular, its role is complemented in practice by another institutional element based on 'sophisticated institutional arrangements', in which 'the States are complicit and adept at working the system to their advantage' (Galligan, 2012, p. 321).

With one notable exception (sec. 105A Const.), no reference is made by the Constitution to the institutional and procedural dimension. However, the financial rules of subnational financing are mostly the result of intergovernmental agreements. In Australia, financial settings have changed dramatically over time. This never occurred because of constitutional amendment, but rather as a result of intergovernmental agreement. Intergovernmental institutions and agreements have evolved over time to manage the political

3 In the year 2018–19, New South Wales, Victoria and Western Australia have received less revenues from GST than the ones they would have received if the apportionment would have been made on a population basis and a certain criticism on the unfairness of such a system is raising from their side (CGC, 2019).

dimension of fiscal federalism, to the point that federal-state financial relations are considered an emblematic expression of the intergovernmental dimension, as well as a key item of the collaborative nature of Australian federalism (Madden, 2006, p. 86).

Numerous forums exist for easing financial relations between the Commonwealth and the States, involving the respective executive at both levels. At the peak there is the Council of Australian Government (COAG) – now substituted by the National Cabinet –, through which the Commonwealth and the States enter into agreements and make all political decisions related to financial relations.

Under the COAG, the Council on Federal Financial Relations (CFFR) comprises the treasurers of the Commonwealth, the States, and the Territories. The latter oversees federal-state financial relations and is responsible for broad economic and fiscal issues and legislative oversight of GST operations. After the abolition of the COAG, the Council now reports to the National Cabinet and is a member of the National Federation Reform Council (further on this: Saunders, 2020).

This 'whole process of intergovernmentalism, headed by COAG [now National Cabinet] but with plenty of levels down below, is a big contributing factor to (omissis) hyperexecutive federalism' (Saunders, 2015).[4] At the same time, the circumstance that neither the power to enter into intergovernmental agreements nor intergovernmental institutions are entrenched in the Australian Constitution, leaves questions about their validity and legal effect to be governed by general principles of law (Saunders, 2005, p. 298). Intergovernmental agreements were eventually transposed into legal acts approved by the national Parliament, but in the absence of legislation the legal effect of an agreement between the governments is disputed. They are political compacts, and the related provisions cannot bind future legislators. Although they mainly originate and remain 'soft law', it seems too simplistic to recognise its provisions of merely political nature. In many cases, it is the agreement itself that prescribes its force by stipulating that it is binding for all parties involved. However, an act approved by the Parliament could in theory amend the agreement that is 'unenforceable as a matter of constitutional law' (Saunders 2000, 99). Practice however shows that such agreements are stable over time because they are backed by a strong political commitment, and a broad consensus is needed to change the *status quo*. The IGA-FFR of 1999, for

4 For a critical view on the Australian federal system on this perspective, see (Saunders & Crommelin, 2015).

instance, has endured for more than a decade, as only in 2009 a new intergovernmental agreement has been signed. The practice of entering into intergovernmental agreements has taken hold also in respect to tied Specific Purpose Payments to the States, with the objective of ensuring coordinated actions in areas of State competence.

In Australia, intergovernmental relations are adversarial and when it comes to public finance the debate is episodic as it follows the periodical reviews carried on by the CGC, or the discussions on reform that from time to time spice up the debate. Different views on the features and the scope of equalisation on the part of the States emerge during the States' consultations carried on by the CGC and mostly reflect their economic strength. While some States have changed or mitigated their position over time, the discussion mostly focuses on the impact equalisation has on efficiency and incentives to growth. As equalisation in Australia is a zero-sum game and the system is meant to provide full compensation of existing differences, the richest States, such as Western Australia, tend to question the merits and effectiveness of the system (Eccleston & Woolley, 2014, p. 235). In the 2020 CGC review, it emerged that divergent opinions are expressed on the degree of equalisation, although all States support the objective of horizontal fiscal equalisation (HFE) except for New South Wales, which argues that GST revenue should be distributed on a population share or equal per capita basis (CGC, 2009, p. 9).

The intergovernmental institutional framework ends up circumscribing the Commission's margin of discretion. At the same time, it mitigates the Commonwealth dominance in fiscal issues. The federal power is not unlimited and has to come to term with States interests as channeled through institutions and practices of intergovernmental relations. This occurs not only by setting the general trajectories of the system via intergovernmental agreements, but also through the terms of reference delivered to the CGC. The latter is the instrument that links the political to the technical dimension of equalisation, allowing that policy objectives and political decisions are reflected in the technical implementation and functioning of the system (Spasovejic & Nicholas, 2013, p. 318). The CFFR meets in advance to discuss and *de facto* define such terms, although the Australian government theoretically has the final say.

At the same time, the recommendations processed by the Commission after consultations with the States are generally accepted by the Commonwealth. In theory, they are considered by the CFFR, with the federal treasurer having the final say in determining how revenues are shared (Ross, 2005, p. 110). But as a norm, the CFFR does not make use of its power to dissent on the Commission recommendations (Warren, 2008, p. 548). As such, the space left for politics is smaller than in other federal systems. This is probably due to the nature of the Commission's recommendations on the methodology. In fact, these are the result of experts' evaluations adopted after consultation with the States. The (counter-)effect being that equalisation is based on complex formulas that hamper an effective understanding by politicians (Shah, 2017, p. 30), making accountability very difficult to be achieved. Besides that, the CGC solution has the advantage to move a highly divisive issues like equalisation outside the political arena. Although this system is functional to combine the different visions of the subnational funding system, it lacks accountability and transparency, as it is primarily based on 'closed door' negotiations and political bargaining, with the legislative assemblies at all levels being mostly left aside (Warren, 2008, p. 530).

3 Canada: The Paradigm of Federal-Provincial Diplomacy

Although Canada is one of the federal states in which SNGs have greater fiscal autonomy, federal transfers continue to be important. The evolution of Canadian federalism in financial-related matters has resulted in the consolidation of a model that represents the paradigm of federal-provincial diplomacy through which the provinces try to influence the federal government's decision-making in managing the three main sources of federal transfers: the Canada Health Transfer, the Canada Social Transfer and equalisation to mitigate interregional disparities.

The idea of territorial solidarity is as old as the Confederation, since the constitutional design of 1867 (sections 118 and 119), already included federal per capita subsidies to the provinces. Equalisation was introduced as a federal program in 1957 under the Tax Rental Agreements. These agreements were the result of cooperation between the federal government and the provinces as the provincial governments had to pass legislation authorising the rental of their taxes to the federal level (Janigan, 2020, pp. 247–250). Equalisation was designed as a guarantee of the financial stability for the provinces through the allocation of unconditional payments to each province equal to the amounts needed to bring the per capita proceeds of rental payments (or of the allowed abatement) to the level of the average per capita yield of the two provinces with the highest direct tax yield. In a certain way, the system was conceived as a sort of compensation for the centralisation of most tax sources and social programs. Likewise, equalisation was also aimed at fiscally integrating Quebec. Still, the province declined to participate in all tax rental or tax collecting agreements (Béland & Lecours, 2014, pp. 343–344).

Equalisation was given constitutional status only later, in 1982, as part of the patriation process that allowed Canada to achieve full constitutional sovereignty. It was incorporated into section 36.2 of the 1982 Constitution, highlighting the importance of territorial solidarity for modern Canada. The constitutional entrenchment of the program was however limited in scope as section 36.2 only commits both Parliament and the federal government to the principle of making equalisation payments but does not establish any formal obligation to make those transfers. The constitutional provision on equalisation has nevertheless not prevented the general acceptance of the need to articulate inter-territorial solidarity by means of an equalisation program by all political actors, although they frequently disagree on its nature and extent. The inclusion of equalisation in the Constitution did not have a significant impact in the functioning of the program in practice due to the vagueness and reduced scope of section 36.2 as equalisation continued to be governed by an act of Parliament. The main legal instrument that governs equalisation is the Federal-Provincial Fiscal Arrangements Act of 1985, which regulates the technicalities and operational aspects of the program such as the timing (art. 3.94) or the method of calculation (art. 3.2). Thus, the principle of equalisation anchored in section 36.2 of the Constitution does not constitute a substantial constrain for the federal legislator, who enjoys full discretion to establish, modify, and terminate the terms of transfers. Consequently, the decision-making power is vested solely in the federal government (Boadway, 2008, p. 132).

Although provinces are sometimes consulted, there is no legal obligation to do so, and the federal government may unilaterally alter or extend the compact. This was the case in 2018 and 2023 when the federal government decided to extend the current program until 2024 and later to 2029, without changes.

The Federal-Provincial-Territorial Meeting of Ministers of Finance is an intergovernmental body composed by the federal Minister of Finance and its provincial and territorial counterparts that generally meets twice a year to discuss economic and fiscal issues. Within this forum there is a specific committee – the Fiscal Arrangements Committee – that conducts consultations on fiscal transfers, including the equalisation program. This forum serves as a venue where the provinces can express their views and concerns about equalisation and demand changes to the compact from the federal government. However, these meetings are solely consultative. Any agreement that may be reached is a mere recommendation to the federal government.

Provinces have also recurred to horizontal cooperation to assert their positions and try to influence the federal government during the periodic renewal processes of the equalisation compact. The Council of the Federation (COF), an intergovernmental body created in 2003 that groups the provinces and territories, has adopted a proactive role on this regard. After Paul Martin's decision to implement a new funding formula framework in 2004, the COF decided to commission a group of experts to form an independent advisory panel with a mandate to examine the vertical and horizontal fiscal balances and make recommendations as to how any imbalances should be addressed. This advisory panel ran in parallel with an expert panel appointed by the federal government that explicitly focused on equalisation. The government of Stephen Harper adopted most of their recommendations which were for the most part similar to those of the advisory panel commissioned by the provinces in the COF. In addition, the federal government introduced a couple of novelties regarding the treatment of income derived from natural resources in the formula. With this decision, the federal government was attempting to accommodate the demands of resource-rich provinces such as Alberta and Saskatchewan, which had been very critical of the system and were key to the Conservative's accession to power while also maintaining special regimes for Newfoundland and Labrador and Nova Scotia so these provinces could keep their payments determined by the old framework to avoid the new fiscal capacity cap (Feehan, 2014, p. 4).

Since the mid-2000s equalisation has become a major source of intergovernmental conflict in Canada due to politicisation as both federal and provincial politicians have articulated claims and threats around the program with these increasing during periods of economic recession (Béland & Lecours, 2011, pp. 207–208). Consequently, successive federal governments have used equalisation as a tool to court certain provincial electorates, either offering special arrangements or implementing tweaks to the formula to avoid sudden losses in equalisation revenue (Feehan, 2020, p. 9). As an alternative to intergovernmental bargaining and with the aim of reducing the existing politicisation of the system, Béland and Lecours (2016, p. 12–13) have proposed the creation of an independent advisory body following the example of the Australian CGC. However, this possibility was rejected by the majority of the provinces when asked by an expert panel in 2006, as they wished to maintain their capacity to lobby the federal government.

The federal unilateralism that characterises the governance of equalisation in Canada, together with the nature of the compact as a zero-sum game where any change in the revenue redistribution results in winners and losers, has contributed to fuel intergovernmental conflicts between receiving and not receiving provinces, with Quebec often being the scapegoat as it gets the lion share of equalisation. Resource rich provinces such as Alberta or Saskatchewan that are not eligible to receive funds from the program as their fiscal capacities are above the average frequently portrait equalisation as if it were of horizontal nature. These provinces tend to argue that the program is funded by their wealth and subsidise other parts of the country without getting anything in return. This claim has increased recently as most of the have provinces – those that have a fiscal capacity above the average – were running deficits while those that were receiving equalisation, such as Quebec, had sizeable budgetary surpluses (Feehan, 2020, p. 12). As a response, Saskatchewan called for a 50/50 solution, i.e., a reform of the system in which half of the funds would be distributed per capita; a solution that would denaturalise the system, undermining the principle enshrined in article 36.2 of the Constitution. Alberta, for its part, has repeatedly demanded for the system to be reformed complaining about a lack of financing as it considers the system unfair and a privilege towards Quebec as if it were a reward in exchange for staying in the federation (Béland & Lecours, 2014, p. 348).[5]

In view of the controversy that equalisation creates in some parts of the country and in order to avoid further intergovernmental tensions with the provinces, the federal government decided in 2018 to quietly renew the program under its current conditions until 2024. This decision was not explicitly announced, and the lack of transparency was such that opposition MPs and provincial governments apparently were not aware that within the 584 pages long Budget Implementation Act there was that provision. The news was later reported by the press and confirmed by the Finance Minister. The government denied any intention of concealing the decision to the provinces and emphasised that federal officials had been in close contact with their provincial counterparts during the previous months including a brief discussion during the Federal-Provincial-Territorial Meeting of Ministers of Finance. Despite this, the Premiers of Saskatchewan and Alberta complained that although provinces knew that the federal government was in favour of maintaining the *status-quo*, there was no formal notification about the decision. Moreover, they also expressed their frustration due to the lack of will of the federal government to open discussions on their proposals to reform the compact and alter the current distribution of funds among the provinces. Despite these criticisms and several calls for reform, the federal government proceeded in similar fashion in 2023, extending the system until 2029 with a provision buried in an omnibus motion in Parliament that sought to implement budget measures.

5 The importance of equalisation for Quebec has been recognized by the province's Premier François Legault who considers it part of the "original deal" of Confederation – although the term equalisation was not coined until the 1940s – and thus a right for Quebec, highlighting its contribution to maintaining the province within the federation.

The federal government's intention to ease tensions over equalisation does not seem to have had the desired effect. Quite the opposite, as Alberta quickly deemed the federal refusal to change the nature of the system to be 'a slap in face', subsequently demanding equalisation to be abolished from the Constitution. Furthermore, the province decided to move forward with its intention to hold a referendum on the issue. This non-binding consultation was a, rather failed, attempt to increase the pressure on the federal government and other provinces to negotiate changes in the equalisation formula in favour of resource-rich provinces, with 60% of voters supporting the removal of equalisation from the Constitution but at a turnout of just 38%.

The processes that led to the renewal of the equalisation compact in 2018 and 2023 perfectly illustrate the internal traits of Canadian federalism with respect to financial relations: the dominance of federal unilateralism and limited intergovernmental cooperation which is generally held behind closed doors and mostly informally; a model generally described as executive federalism (Watts, 1989, pp. 3–6).[6] In an attempt to modulate federal unilateralism, some opposition MPs tabled a bill in Parliament following Alberta's referendum bid that would have forced the federal government to consult with the provinces prior to any change of the method of calculation of the fiscal equalisation payments. Although the proposal was voted down, it could be a first step to articulate mechanisms that enhance provincial participation in the governance of equalisation, reducing the tensions that have accompanied the Canadian system in recent times.

4 Germany: The Prototype of a Tax-Revenue Sharing Mechanism on a 'Legislative-Assembly Base'

As mentioned in the introduction, the German system of equalisation can be classified as the prototype of a tax-revenue sharing mechanism on a 'legislative-assembly base', in which the *Länder* are indirectly involved through a federal second chamber, namely the *Bundesrat*.

As the German *Länder* have practically no autonomous power to tax, revenue sharing is an essential feature of financial relations. Such a system is based on two constitutionally entrenched tools: a tax-revenue sharing scheme on a territorial base and equalisation mechanisms. As to the latter, starting from

6 The dominance of executive federalism has been challenged by Cameron and Simeon (2002) who argue that Canadian federalism was moving towards a more collaborative approach in intergovernmental relations although this collaboration has not yet reached equalisation.

2020 the system rests on two elements: VAT-adjusted revenue sharing and federal supplementary transfers, including general- and special-purpose ones.[7]

The rules governing these components can be found in the Basic Law (Arts. 106–107), with the integration of two federal laws: the Revenue-Sharing Criteria Act (*Maßstäbegesetz*) and the Financial Equalisation Act (*Finanzausgleichsgesetz*) of 2001, as last amended in 2018.

Under the first pillar revenues are distributed according to the derivation principle, and as such are not equalising, whereas VAT-revenue sharing is designed in a way to correct horizontal imbalances. The 2018 constitutional amendment, in fact, makes explicit the instrumental nature of VAT distribution in ensuring an adequate compensation of horizontal imbalances.[8]

Looking in more detail at the VAT-revenue distribution, this consists of two main steps: a first one that aims at defining the respective share of the federal and the subnational level (vertical sharing), and a second one that provides for the distribution of the revenue thereof among the *Länder* (horizontal sharing).

The choice of the constitutional legislator was to introduce a flexible element into the system, which is reflected in the very open nature of the tax-sharing arrangement between the *Bund* and the *Länder*. Indeed, on this point the constitutional document resorts to vague concepts without providing any definition of them (Fischer-Menshausen, 1978, p. 138). Pursuant to article 106.3 BL, the respective shares of the *Bund* and the *Länder* in the VAT-revenue distribution shall be based on the following principles. First, the *Bund* and the *Länder* shall have an equal claim against current revenues to cover their necessary expenditures. Second, the financial requirements of the *Bund* and of the *Länder* shall be coordinated in such a way as to establish a fair balance, avoid excessive burdens on taxpayers, and ensure uniformity of living standards throughout the federal territory. As a result, this mechanism exerts a '*cushioning function*' (Stern, 1980, p. 1158), capable of guaranteeing – through an amendment to a primary and not a constitutional law – a change in the revenues accruing to the various levels of government, in the event of a funding gap in their respective budgets.

Once VAT revenues are vertically shared, the bulk of resources attributed to the subnational level is then horizontally redistributed. This is done with the purpose of ensuring a reasonable equalisation of the disparate financial

7 The horizontal equalisation among the Länder (so-called *Länderfinanzausgleich*) for which Germany is considered an emblematic case has been abolished with the 2018 constitutional reform, ceasing to exist as of 2020.

8 On the new equalisation mechanism and on the impact of the 2018 reform on the federal system as a whole, see (Seiler, 2017, pp. 52–62; Wieland, 2018, pp. 247–261).

capacities. As of 2020 the distribution continues to be based on population, though corrected with additions or deductions based on financial capacity. In sum, entities with a below-average financial capacity will receive a supplement, whereas resources from VAT will be accordingly reduced for the ones with an above-average capacity. Increases or decreases will be applied by considering only the 63% of the deviation from the average financial capacity of the *Länder*. This lifts the financial capacity of all below-average *Länder* closer to the national average but does not nullify existing differences.

On top of that, the poorer *Länder* whose fiscal capacity remain below average even after VAT redistribution will receive additional vertical transfers in the form of general supplementary federal grants (Art. 107.2 BL). Supplementary grants for well-determined special needs are also foreseen. Both types of federal transfers are prescribed by the constitutional provisions and then regulated in detail in the above-mentioned federal laws with the approval of *Länder* via *Bundesrat*. Together with the highly centralised power to tax, this system yields a strongly egalitarian pattern of fiscal equalisation.

A proper understanding of the role of *Länder* in designing the equalisation mechanism requires to start with an investigation of the *Bundesrat*. The German solution consists in the assignment of a co-legislative function to the *Länder*, via the *Bundesrat*. The latter in fact shall approve all constitutional and ordinary laws in financial matters, if and to the extent they affect the *Länder*.[9] Even if the *Bundesrat* is a federal organ, its composition and functioning guarantees the representation of the *Länder*, or rather their executives. The decision-making power lies at the federal level, but the legal act is the outcome of a legislative process that calls for the double approval of the same text. As such, the consent of the *Bundesrat* ensures the integration of the territorial interests in the federal decision-making process, while preserving the uniformity of the system of public finance throughout the entire federal State.

This law-making scheme ensures an equal role of both the *Länder* via *Bundesrat* and the federal level via *Bundestag*, providing a strong safeguard for the autonomy of the subnational level of government. The federal level alone cannot modify the rules of the game. The consent of the *Bundesrat* however does not uphold the autonomy each single *Land* is vested with. It rather provides a form of representation of territorial interests on a merely collective

9 Pursuant to Art. 105.3 GG *'Federal laws relating to taxes the revenue from which accrues wholly or in part to the Länder (omissis) shall require the consent of the Bundesrat'*. The scope of the provision is rather broad, as it includes all major taxes of the system. It is estimated that 85% of overall tax-revenue comes from *Zustimmungsgesetze*, that is, laws that require the consent of both the *Bundestag* and the *Bundesrat*.

dimension. The subnational level participates as if it were a '*second-level federal pact*' (Palermo & Woelk, 1999, p. 1103) and this results in the integration of the single units in the federal legal order (Woelk, 2014, p. 165). The autonomy of each single entity is narrowed down, due to the *Bundesrat* composition and functioning. First, it works on the majority principle which is based on a mitigated formula of territorial representation. The representation of the units is based on population, though not exactly proportional but tempered to favour less-populated *Länder* (pursuant to Arts. 50–53 BL). Second, it does not exclusively channel territorial interests, but integrates multi-faceted interests of political nature, combining federal with regional claims. This is fostered both by the way the *Bundesrat* functions and the role of political opposition to the *Bundestag*, it has taken up in practice (Dolzer, 1999, pp. 7–15).

Though the process formally requires a majority, in practice, all federal laws on equalisation have been approved by unanimity, being challenged later in the Federal Constitutional Court. Besides that, the content often reflects the compromise reached at the *Länder*-level and sees the payers as opposed to the recipients (Lenk & Glinka, 2017, pp. 507–08), showing that economic diversity has a divisive effect when it comes to equalisation.

The change in the VAT vertical sharing approved in 2018 – and into force from 2020 onwards – contributes to proving the political nature of this decision and the weight of intergovernmental agreements in this respect. As a result of the negotiations, the *Länder* obtained an increase in their share from the current 44.6% to 45.2%. However, this has been obtained against an overall consolidation of federal powers (Fraenkel-Haeberle & Valdesalici, 2018). In this sense, the VAT vertical distribution seems to betray the very function for which it was conceived, i.e., the dynamic correction of the vertical fiscal gap, conversely resulting in a bargaining chip used by the federal government in the negotiation process to gain more powers to the detriment of the *Länder* autonomy (Benz, 2017, p. 66). The issues that are channeled in the determination of their respective shares of revenue have in fact little – if nothing – to do with the constitutional principles; the latter are rather used as an argument for catalysing consensus (Hettlage, 1981, p. 124). In fact, the issues regarding the interpretation of the constitutional rules are reflected in a wide-ranging debate that moves away from the level of technical decisions towards a dimension governed exclusively by the dynamics of compromise among divergent interests.

Furthermore, from a procedural point of view the way in which the 2018 compromise was reached is unprecedented. Initially the proposal was to convene a commission reflecting the composition of the federal legislator, nonetheless such institutional solution never materialised. At a first stage discussions took place behind closed doors among the Prime Ministers and Ministers of Finance of both *Bund* and *Länder*. Later, negotiations alternated between phases in which only the *Länder* were involved through the Conference of Prime Ministers (an informal institution of horizontal self-coordination) and occasions in which the federal level took also part in the negotiations. After some back and forth, the *Länder* came to an agreement in December 2015 and one year later an intergovernmental agreement with the federal level was finally signed in the form of a '*package deal*' (Benz & Sonnickesen, 2017, p. 150). This solution is criticized for its lack of transparency and is known as the '*Barter*' (Seiler, 2017, p. 58).

If this arrangement confirms the structure of joint decision-making the German Federation grounds on, at the same time, it results in the legislative assemblies being substantially deprived of their authority. The decision-making arena has shifted more and more from the parliamentary institutions to the executives of the various levels of government involved, reducing the role of the legislator to merely ratifying their decisions (Häde, 1996, p. 199).

Besides being limited, in 2018 the parliamentary debate has shown an interesting feature of intergovernmental relations in the German federation: financial relations, which should be the responsibility of the *Bund*, in order to guarantee '*uniform living conditions throughout the federal territory*' (Art. 72.1 BL), have been left to the horizontal negotiations of the *Länder*. Conversely, issues related to the allocation of competences, especially administrative ones, have been drawn into the gravitational sphere of the *Bundestag*, even though they touch the core of the *Länder*'s political autonomy (Benz, 2017, p. 67).

This deviation from the constitutional and legal framework raises perplexities in terms of constitutional legitimacy. The Federal Constitutional Court in this respect warns that the legislator would be obliged to act within the limits of the constitutional provisions and underlines that the BL sets forth legal constraints that should guide the political compromise (BVerfGE, 1, 117, [131]; BVerfGE, 101, 158, [220]). Despite that, substantial decisions on the system of equalisation are left to the political process, even though strong constraints do exist. First, the Federal Constitutional Court has mandated the co-existence of three different laws: the Basic law setting the fundamental principles, the *Maßstäbegesetz* defining *a priori* the general criteria of distribution, the *Finanzausgleichsgesetz* providing for the more specific and time-constrained rules of revenue-sharing. Second, if the use of vague concepts in the constitutional documents is meant to leave the legislator (wide) margins of adjustment to the changing of circumstances, these are not soft laws (Siekmann, 2011, parr. 24–33). Finally, the constitutional jurisprudence has worked effectively over time also in determining substantial constraints to the margin of discretion.

If in the earlier judgements (BVerfGE 86, 148 [264]; BVerfGE 72, 330 [386]) a sense of solidarity prevailed (so-called *Solidargemeinschaft* between *Bund* and *Länder*), this approach has been mitigated from 1999 onwards, when the Court has stated that a certain competition among the *Länder* is a physiologic and necessary component of the federal order and the *Länder* financial autonomy.

5 Spain: The Quasi-constitutional Institutionalisation of the Fiscal and Financial Policy Council (CPFF) as a Forum for Intergovernmental Financial Relations

The Constitutional architecture in Spain is characterised by a strict silence regarding intergovernmental relations – in financial or any other matter – due to the particularities of the constituent process and the *Transición* from dictatorship to democracy (Fernández Allés, 2004, p. 51). However, this silence has not been an obstacle for the Spanish model to develop its own framework to manage financial relations leading to the quasi-constitutional institutionalisation of the CPFF as a center-dominated forum for intergovernmental financial relations.

The process of political decentralisation undertaken in Spain after the approval of the 1978 Constitution initially enshrined a model of gradual and asymmetrical autonomy in which some territories – the Basque Country, Catalonia, Galicia and subsequently Andalusia – rapidly gained access to a higher level of competencies than the rest, although the model has evolved towards a gradual homogenisation of competences (Aja, 2014, p. 36–66). The first steps of decentralisation were centered on the assumption of public policy competencies by the Autonomous Communities (ACs), without this process being accompanied by a transfer of fiscal space: the fiscal autonomy of common regime[10] ACs was rather low as most tax bases – VAT, income and corporate tax – remained under full control of the central State after the approval of the LOFCA (Organic Law on Financing of the Autonomous Communities 8/1980) in 1980 (Ruiz-Huerta, 2014, pp. 185–186). The process of fiscal decentralisation gained momentum with the reform of the LOFCA in 1997 which allowed the ACs the power to set tax rates and establish tax credits and allowances over ceded taxes. This meant that the system evolved from a highly centralised tax

10 The common regime is applied uniformly to all the ACs on the Spanish peninsula, except for the Basque Autonomous Community and Navarre, which are ruled under the foral regime. The Canary Islands and the two North African enclaves of Ceuta and Melilla have a special tax regime.

sharing model to one where ACs have some margin of discretion over ceded taxes, although the latter are created and regulated by the national legislator in order to maintain a certain homogeneity throughout the common regime territory (Zornoza, 2014, pp. 109–114).

The gradual gain of fiscal autonomy acquired by the ACs through the different reforms of the LOFCA had the side effect of increasing regional disparities. Thus, equalisation emerged as a necessary counterpart to decentralisation to bridge the gap among ACs and prevent the inhabitants of a territory from having to bear a significantly higher tax burden than their fellow citizens to access similar public services. In fact, this circumstance was foreseen by the drafters of the Constitution who included several references to territorial solidarity throughout the text, with the principle of horizontal solidarity being outlined in article 2 and developed in article 138 (Vega García, 2014, pp. 216–218).

Following this logic, equalisation was created by article 13 of the LOFCA as an unconditional transfer targeting needs compensation called *Participación en los Ingresos del Estado*. This transfer, aimed at providing common regime ACs with enough financial resources to cover their spending needs, was asymmetrical as not all ACs had the same level of competences at the time and not all of them benefited from ceded taxes. This model lasted until 2001 when it was reformed and renamed as *Fondo de Suficiencia* (Sufficiency Fund) in an effort to settle equalisation after most ACs had reformed their Statutes of Autonomy to access the maximum level of competences. This fund, which maintained the philosophy of targeting needs compensation, was the result of an intergovernmental agreement reached unanimously by all common regime ACs – the Basque Country and Navarre excluded due to their foral regime – and the central government.

The Fiscal and Financial Policy Council (CPFF), created by article 3 of the LOFCA, is the organ responsible for coordinating the fiscal relations between the central state and the ACs. This intergovernmental body is composed of the National Minister of Finance and the Finance Minister of each Autonomous Community (plus the Finance Councilors of the two Autonomous Cities of Ceuta and Melilla). The agreements reached within the CPFF are not legally – but politically – binding as they take the form of mere recommendations to the central government according to article 10 of the Council charter. In order to adopt these recommendations, a majority of two thirds is required in a first vote while an absolute majority is sufficient in a second vote. Regarding the voting system, it is important to highlight that the central government enjoys a privileged position. Each AC has one vote while the central government has the same number of votes as all the ACs combined. This diminishes the ACs' decision-making capacity as, in a second vote, the central government can move forward with just the support of a single AC.

The standard practice was to publish the agreements of the CPFF in the official gazette but without enacting them in a legal statute. This started to change in 1996 and consolidated when a new system was approved in 2001 as the agreement of the CPFF was codified in Organic Law 7/2001. This decision opened an indirect path for territorial participation in the design of the new framework of territorial financing. Since the LOFCA is an organic law, any amendment to it requires the absolute majority of both houses of Parliament, allowing parties with a strong territorial character, notably nationalist forces in Catalonia and the Basque Country, to exert some influence during the legislative process.

When the first results of this model were published in 2005 it became evident that the equalisation compact presented several shortcomings and needed to be renewed (Ruiz-Huerta & Herrero Alcalde, 2008, pp. 154–158). Finally, after years of public debate, the national government decided to open a formal process of renewal in 2008, stating that one of the main objectives of the new system should be to ensure that all citizens, regardless of their place of residence, have equal access to basic public services. The first step was to hold a series of bilateral meetings with the different ACs to learn about their demands so the central government could elaborate a proposal that would be presented to the ACs in the CPFF. After the first proposal was elaborated, the central government conducted new bilateral meetings with the ACs in a process characterised by a lack of transparency and the predominance of the interests of some ACs over the others. The process of negotiations was conditioned by Catalonia's intention to limit its contribution to horizontal solidarity as its new Statute of Autonomy – later partially invalidated by the Constitutional Court[11] – restricted Catalonia's contribution to equalisation only to the financing of essential public services (health, education and social services). Consequently, the new system had to be built around this idea, which greatly complicated the negotiation process.

Catalonia exercised a notable leadership role during the negotiations, an aspect that aroused mistrust among the ACs governed by the Popular Party (PP), as they considered that the new model was tailor-made for that community. After two failed attempts to reach an agreement, the central government

11 Article 206.3 SAC conditioned Catalonia's contribution to equalisation to other AC's making a similar fiscal effort, an aspect that was declared unconstitutional by the Constitutional Court as it violated the principle of financial autonomy. See STC 31/2010 FJ 134.

presented a third proposal. Accordingly, the ACs could maintain 25% of their revenue instead of the previous proposal of 20%, therefore reducing the horizontal contribution to territorial solidarity. Finally, an agreement was sealed during summer 2009 in the CPFF after more than a hundred meetings over a yearlong negotiation. Still, some ACs complained about a lack of transparency and cooperation by the central government due to the absence of meetings at the highest level, the dominance of bilateralism – as desired by Catalonia – and the impossibility of adding modifications to the latest proposal of the central government. In contrast to the unanimous agreement of 2001, this time there was a clear division along party lines. The central government and the ten ACs with Socialist governments voted in favour of the new system, while the remaining seven, ruled by the People's Party (PP) abstained. The only exception to partisan politics were the favourable votes of the autonomous city of Ceuta – ruled by the PP – and the Canary Islands, with a coalition between a nationalist party and the PP. The decision to abstain was imposed by the leader of the PP, Mariano Rajoy, in an attempt to reconcile the different visions existing within the party. The PP saw the new equalisation compact as a model that improved the positions of the richest communities and that used very arbitrary distribution variables to achieve horizontal solidarity. This rejection to support the reform was also influenced by the Catalonian lead during the negotiations and the need for any reform of the model to be adapted to its new Statute of Autonomy, which the PP had appealed to the Constitutional Court. This exacerbated the tensions with other ACs ruled by the PP, notably Madrid, whose Finance Minister advocated for rejecting the agreement in the CPFF arguing that it was a privilege towards Catalonia as '*a Catalan was worth two Madrilenians*' (El País, 2009). The PP's refusal to support the reform complicated its parliamentary approval, given that the amendment of the LOFCA requires an absolute majority. Eventually, the national executive and its allies in Congress were able to reach the required threshold by a single vote and the new system was formally enacted in Organic Law 3/2009.

The 2009 reform reorganised the equalisation model around four different funds. The first and most important is the *Fondo de Garantía de Servicios Públicos Fundamentales* (Guarantee Fund for Essential Public services), which can be described as equalisation in the proper sense. It is designed to ensure that if each AC makes the same tax effort, it receives the same amount of resources per capita adjusted to finance the essential services (education, health and social services) (Vilalta, 2016, pp. 94–99). The fund combines a horizontal component as ACs contribute to the fund with 75% of their resources and a vertical one fully funded by the central government. The second fund is the *Fondo de Suficiencia Global* (FSG,Global Sufficiency

Fund) also known as the *statu-quo* clause, which is the result of a compromise achieved by all parties during the negotiation process to ensure that all ACs get more resources than in the previous system regardless of their financial needs (Castells, 2015, p. 212). Further, the system also features two convergence funds which, as the FSG, are entirely financed by the State: the *Fondo de Competitividad* (Competitiveness Fund) and the *Fondo de Cooperación* (Cooperation Fund). These convergence funds, the purpose of which is not to promote territorial solidarity *stricto sensu* but competitiveness, fiscal autonomy and regional development, were introduced as a counterpart to certain ACs in order to get them to approve the new system (Herrero Alcalde et al., 2010, p. 186). The combination of these four funds has largely increased the complexity of the system without fully achieving the goal of horizontal equity enshrined in the LOFCA. This is mainly because of the distorting effect created by the FSG and the convergence funds, which respond more to the different political interests of the ACs than to technical considerations of equity (Zabalza & López-Laborda, 2011, pp. 751–752).

The territorial financing system agreed upon in 2009 was to be renewed after five years as prescribed by Law 22/2009. The national government and the ACs agreed in the 2017 *Conferencia de Presidentes* (Presidents Conference) – Spain's main vertical intergovernmental forum – to create an expert panel in charge of elaborating a proposal. This panel was composed of five experts nominated by the central government and one nominated by each AC or Autonomous City. The panel elaborated a proposal which showed the disparity of positions between the different ACs with the proposal to eliminate the *statu-quo* clause being one of the most divisive issues as some ACs feared that this would result in a reduction of their funds. In stark contrast to the previous reform, Catalonia declined to engage in the process – although informally being represented by the Balearic Islands. Furthermore, Catalonia has since then boycotted the CPFF, arguing that no proper discussions are made as everything is decided beforehand by the central government. Catalonia's refusal to participate, the central government's lack of will to open the Pandora box of reform amid a period of instability and the tensions created by the illegal declaration of independence of Catalonia in 2017 ended in a failed reform attempt. Although the pandemic and the disastrous economic situation resulting from it make reform more necessary than ever, political differences have so far prevented from starting it, albeit the current system should have expired in 2014.

6 Comparative Conclusions

This chapter has illustrated the diversity of 'architectural' solutions that can be found around the world when defining the rules that design and govern the different systems of equalisation. The undertaken analysis has identified from 'the law in the books' perspective four different paradigms among federal systems. The first two heavily rely on institutions, with tax-revenue sharing being carried out either by an arm-length agency on a 'technical base' – exemplified by the CGC in Australia – or by 'legislative-assembly base' with Germany's *Bundestag* + *Bundesrat* as reference model. In the other two intergovernmental relations play a decisive role, although with different degrees of institutionalisation, varying from the quasi-constitutional Spanish CPFF as a forum for intergovernmental financial relations to the almost not existent legal entrenchment of the Canadian model of federal-provincial diplomacy.

From a static point of view, the first lesson is that inter-territorial solidarity is inherent to federal systems. The four models feature equalisation programs in their fiscal constitutions, but with different degrees of legal entrenchment. Although constitutional entrenchment is present in most of the models – with just the exception of Australia – this is not per se determinant. In fact, constitutions usually limit themselves to asserting the principle of solidarity, which can then take various forms and lead to very different types of equalisation mechanisms. This is why, in practice, the implementing legislation is the core element in the understanding of the functioning of equalisation, since it is where the different elements that make up the system and determine its operation and limits are regulated in detail.

It is therefore no coincidence that a broad conception of the notion of fiscal constitution should be privileged, as including not only rules 'formally incorporated in some legally binding and explicitly constitutional document', but also unwritten rules like 'customary, traditional, and widely accepted precepts' (Buchanan & Wagner 1977, p. 24). This approach entails three key consequences for the purposes of this analysis. First, it stresses the importance of '[contemplating] the Constitution as a whole, considering provisions not specifically directed [at] fiscal matters and taking into account the federal structure created by the Constitution' (Dam, 1977, p. 272). Second, it justifies the inclusion of all sources of law, which govern the subject matter but do not have formal constitutional status. In this case, substance prevails over form, as these rules deserve to be thought of as quasi-constitutional in nature. Third, it gives weight to economic rules and most importantly to political facts that impact the interpretation and implementation of the rules and determine the way in which a system functions and evolves.

Such a broader perspective leads to the need to incorporate the dynamic dimension into the analysis, paying attention to the procedures of making and amending the rules that govern equalisation with the aim to explore the role of SNGs in determining the level of redistribution, the interests that are channeled into the process, and the existing guarantees of subnational autonomy. In this regard, important differences between the systems can be observed. The Australian model of equalisation on a 'technical base' finds its own *a priori* basis on an intergovernmental agreement, which paves the way for crediting the Commonwealth Grants Commission with the task of advising the Commonwealth on the GST redistribution among States and Territories. Consequently, the CGC defines the methodology in an independent and impartial manner, with direct territorial involvement being rather low, although both the Commonwealth and the States are consulted along the way. The degree of territorial participation is significantly higher in Germany. Equalisation laws are in fact the result of a joint effort between the *Bund* and the *Länder*, with the latter indirectly participating in the legislative process through the *Bundesrat*. In sharp contrast, the Spanish and Canadian models are characterised by the predominance of the center in the rule-making process, with decisions being subject to strong political bargain either during the negotiations in the CPFF in Spain, or via federal-provincial diplomacy through which the provinces try to influence the federal government's unilateral decision-making in respect of equalisation.

Having a closer look at the decision-making processes, into the folds of how the rules work in practice, it emerges a clear trend which leads the different paradigms to converge towards a common point of reference. In all systems, in fact, the involvement of subnational governments undergoes a twist which shows the clear dominance of the intergovernmental dimension and particularly the executives of the levels of government involved. All systems under scrutiny are conditioned by practice and although SNG's participation is not binding from a legal perspective, it is *de facto* advisable or even necessary from a political viewpoint. This is with no doubt the case of Australia, with the States being consulted during the entire process from the appointment of the CGC members to the CGC recommendations. Also, in Canada the federal government usually advances its plans on equalisation to the provinces before implementing them through the federal budget.

Such a converging trend brings to the fore another important element exhibited by all four cases: the relevance of partisan politics and their influence over (re-)distributive politics in federal systems with the political momentum being sometimes decisive to reach agreements as the cases of Germany and Spain clearly illustrate. This being favoured by the vague nature of the constitutional provisions governing this matter. This choice of constitutional design enables that the political dimension of equalisation conditions the performance of the program in practice; in fact, a balance between the best outcome in redistributive terms and what is politically feasible needs to be worked out. As a result, the 'renewal' processes of the different equalisation programs often bring with them high peaks of intergovernmental tension in which the different actors vie for concessions of a larger slice of the pie. Although the controversy generated by these political processes does not (necessarily) question the need for inter-territorial solidarity programs, it offers clear-cut evidence of divergences that exist among SNGs about the level and scope of equalisation. Interestingly, this can be seen in all federations: not only in Canada and Spain but also in homogeneous federations like Australia or Germany. In the latter, all federal laws providing for equalisation have been approved by unanimity of the parties involved, but later have been challenged in front of the Federal Constitutional Court.

Moreover, such a 'political' drift is favoured by the very function of equalisation mechanisms. By pitting the richer/donor subunits against their poorer/receiving counterparts, it thus opens a window of opportunity for subnational governments to mould the system to their own advantage and for the centre to use these mechanisms for expanding their political support rather than for reducing horizontal imbalances. Further, in centre dominated models, solidarity has also become an instrument to maintain the unity of the federal system or, at least, to try to accommodate certain nationalist demands regarding territorial financing within the constitutional boundaries. The Spanish experience, with Catalonia's intention to limit its contribution to horizontal solidarity being a central issue both during the negotiations leading up to the 2009 model and more recently with the proposal of granting this territory a prviledge financial system, or the political impossibility of reforming certain aspects of the Canadian program that would harm Quebec's interests are two examples of this practice.

As previously said, the extent and the way SNGs are involved is not without consequences in terms of subnational autonomy and democratic accountability, but also with respect to the stability and unity of federal systems. In theory, the bigger the role played by SNGs, the stronger the guarantees in these directions will be. However, this is a difficult task due to equalisation being based on complex formulas that hamper an effective understanding by the political actors and the general public and that, for this very reason, can easily be (ab-)used to the advantage of the parties involved. Complexity results in lack of transparency, challenging the extent to which all levels of government are made accountable for equalisation programs. Accountability is exceedingly difficult and even impossible in practice, paving the way for decisions being taken in 'closed door' negotiations – as all four cases clearly show – with the legislative assemblies at all levels being mostly left aside, or seeing its role reduced to a mere ratification of decisions taken in other fora.

Finally, the comparative analysis reveals that the scope SNGs' participation in the decision-making over equalisation is limited even in models like the German one where a cooperative effort between the *Bund* and the *Länder* is mandated. Even if the law contains mechanisms – whether binding or not – for territorial participation, in practice, the influence of SNGs over the final result is rather limited, not least because the interests of the single SNGs are often opposing whereas the participation mechanisms provide only for an involvement of the subnational level of government as whole, so that the autonomy of the single unit is watered down, at best. This increases the political controversy around horizontal solidarity, an issue that is controversial by its own nature, and thus explains the intergovernmental tensions surrounding these programs in their entirety. In fact, in all the models investigated, it is possible to observe that SNGs have taken forceful measures to try to put pressure in the center and force a renegotiation of the terms and conditions, in order to turn the system to their own advantage. However, all this only serves to reinforce the thesis of the importance of articulating effective participatory channels for SNGs to take part in the making (and reform) of the rules that design and govern equalisation mechanism, in order to avoid the surfacing of dormant tensions and prevent the blast of intergovernmental conflicts (Romero Caro & Valdesalici, 2024, p. 343 ff.).

References

Aja, E. (2014). Estado autonómico y reforma federal. Madrid: Alianza Editorial.

Ambrosanio, M. F. & Balduzzi, P. & Peiti, C. (2018). Accountability and revenue assignment across levels of government: rules, practices, and challenges. In A. Valdesalici & F. Palermo (Eds.), Comparing Fiscal Federalism (pp. 119–148). Leiden: Brill.

Bahl, R. (2000). Intergovernmental Transfers in Developing and Transition Countries: Principles and Practices. Washington, DC: World Bank.

Béland, D. & Lecours, A. (2011). The Ideational Dimension of Federalism: The 'Australian Model' and the Politics of Equalisation in Canada. Australian Journal of Political Science, 46(2), 199–212.

Béland, D. & Lecours, A. (2014). Accommodation and the politics of fiscal equalization in multinational states: The case of Canada. Nations and Nationalism 20(2), 337–354.

Béland, D. & Lecours, A. (2016). Canada's Equalization Policy in Comparative Perspective. IRPP Insight 9, 1–17.

Belser, E. M., Bächler, T., Egli, S. & Zünd, L. (Eds.) (2021). The Principle of Equality in Diverse States. Reconciling Autonomy with Equal Rights and Opportunities. Leiden: Brill.

Benz, A. & Sonniksen, J. (2017). Advancing Backwards: Why Institutional Reform of German Federalism Reinforced Joint Decision-Making. Publius 48(1), 134–159.

Benz, A. (2017). Ein Verteilungskampf, in dem alle gewonnen haben?: Oder ein Tauschgeschäft zum Nachteil von Föderalismus und Demokratie?. Jahrbuch des Föderalismus 2017, 63–75.

Blöchliger, H. & King, D. (2006). Less than you thought: the fiscal autonomy of sub-central governments. OECD Economic Studies 43, 155–88.

Boadway, R. (2008). Fiscal Equalization: the Canadian experience. In N. Bosch & J. M. Durán (Eds.), Fiscal Federalism and Political Decentralization. Lessons from Spain, Germany and Canada (pp. 109–136). Cheltenham: Edward Elgar.

Buchanan, J. M. & Wagner, R. E. (1977). Democracy in Deficit: Political Legacy of Lord Keynes. New York: Academic Press.

Cameron, D. & Simeon, R. (2002). Intergovernmental Relations in Canada: The Emergence of Collaborative Federalism. Publius 32(2), 49–71.

Castells, A. (2015). The Relation Catalonia/Spain: Some Financial and Economic Aspects. In G. Pola (Ed.), Principles and Practices of Fiscal Autonomy: Experiences, Debates and Prospects (pp. 203–225). Farnham: Ashgate.

CGC (2009). The Commonwealth Grant Commission: the last 25 years, Commonwealth of Australia. Accessed May 24, 2021. History – Commonwealth Grants Commission – The Last 25 Years.pdf (cgc.gov.au).

CGC (2010). Report on GST Revenue Sharing Relativities. 2010 Review. Accessed May 26, 2021. Reporting | Commonwealth Grants Commission (cgc.gov.au).

CGC (2019). Commonwealth-States relations, 2018–2019. Accessed May 26, 2021. Fiscal Equalisation | Commonwealth Grants Commission (cgc.gov.au).

Dam, K. W. (1977). The American Fiscal Constitution. The University of Chicago Law Review 2, 271–320.

Delaney, E. F. & Mason, R. (2022). Solidarity Federalism. Notre Dam Law Review, 98(2), 617–670.

Dolzer, R. (1999). Das parlamentarische Regierungssystem und der Bundesrat – Entwicklungsstand und Reformbedarf. VVStRL – Veröffentlichungen der Vereinigung der Deutschen Staatsrechtslehrer 58, 7–38.

Eccleston, R. & Woolley, T. (2014). From Calgary to Canberra: Resource Taxation and Fiscal Federalism in Canada and Australia. Publius 45(2), 216–243.

El País (2009). Beteta asegura que hubieran votado en contra de la financiación si no lo impone Rajoy. 15 July 2009 [Online]. [Accessed 10 May 2021]. Available at https://elpais.com/elpais/2009/07/15/actualidad/1247645823_850215.html.

Feehan, J. (2014). Canada's Equalization Formula: Peering Inside the Black Box ... And Beyond. The School of Public Policy Research Papers, 7(4), 1–30.

Feehan, J. (2020). Canada's Equalization Program: Political Debates and Opportunities for Reform. IRPP Insight, 30, 1–20.

Fernández Allés, J. J. (2004). Bases para una teoría constitucional española sobre relaciones intergubernamentales. Revista Española de Derecho Constitucional 72, 51–86.

Fischer-Menshausen, H. (1978). Unbestimmte Rechtsbegriffe in der bundesstaatlichen Finanzverfassung. In W. Dreissig (Ed.), Probleme des Finanzausgleichs I (pp. 135.164). Berlin: Duncker & Humblot.

Fraenkel-Haeberle, C. & Valdesalici, A. (2018). La terza riforma del federalismo tedesco: il «Finanzausgleich» tra vecchie e nuove previsioni normative. Le Regioni 3, 373–412.

Galligan, B. (2012). Fiscal federalism: then and now. In G. Applby, N. Aroney & T. John (Eds.), Future of Australian Federalism: Comparative and Interdisciplinary Perspectives (pp. 320–338). Cambridge: Cambridge University Press.

Häde, U. (1996). Finanzausgleich. Die Verteilung der Aufgaben, Ausgaben und Einnahmen im Recht der Bundesrepublik Deutschland und der Europäischen Union. Tübingen: Mohr Siebeck.

Herrero Alcalde, A., Ruiz-Huerta Carbonell, J. & Vizán Rodríguez, C. (2010). La reforma de la financiación autonómica de 2009. REAF 11, 169–205.

Hettlage, K. M. (1981). Zur Revisionsklausel in der Finanzverfassung. In P. Lerche, H. Zander & P. Badura (Eds.). Festschrift für Theodor Maunz zum 80. Geburtstag am 1. September 1981 (pp. 119–136). München: C.H. Beck.

Janigan, M. (2020). The Art of Sharing: The Richer versus the Poorer Provinces since Confederation. Montreal & Kingston: McGill-Queen's University Press.

Koutsogeorgopoulou, V. (2007). Fiscal Relations Across Levels of Government in Australia. OECD Economics Department Working Papers 541, 1–36.

Lenk, T. & Glinka, P. (2017). Der neue bundesstaatliche Finanzausgleich – eine Reform und viel Reformaufschub. Wirtschafsdienst 7, 506–512.

Madden, J. R. (2006). Central Fiscal Dominance, Collaborative Federalism and Economic Reform. In J. S. Wallack & T. N. Srinivasan (Eds.), Federalism and Economic Reform: International Perspectives (pp. 85–142). Cambridge: Cambridge University Press.

OECD (2012). Australia: The Intergovernmental Agreement on Federal Financial Relations. In OECD (Ed.), Reforming Fiscal Federalism and Local Government: Beyond the Zero-Sum Game. (pp. 27–37). Paris.

Palermo, F. & Woelk, J. (1999). Il Bundesrat tra continuità e ipotesi di riforma. Le Regioni 6, 1097–122.

Romero Caro, F. J. & Valdesalici, A. (2024). Diversity Accommodation and Fiscal Federalism: Comparative Remarks from a Constitutional Law Perspective. In Romero Caro, F. J. & Valdesalici, A. (Eds.), Fiscal Federalism and Diversity Accommodation in Multilevel States: A Comparative Outlook (pp. 333-349). Cham: Palgrave Macmillan.

Ross, A. W. (2005). Federal-State Financial Relations in Australia: The Role of the Commonwealth Grants Commission. The Australian Economic Review 38(1), 108–118.

Ross, A. W. (2021). History of Federal-State Fiscal Relations in Australia: A review of the Methodologies Used. The Australian Economic Review, 45(2), 145–157.

Ruiz-Huerta, J. & Herrero Alcalde, A. (2008). Fiscal Equalization in Spain. In N. Bosch & J. M. Durán (Eds.), Fiscal Federalism and Political Decentralization. Lessons from Spain, Germany and Canada (pp. 147–165). Cheltenham: Edward Elgar.

Ruiz-Huerta, J. (2014). Spanish Decentralization and Fiscal Federalism. In G. Pola (Ed.), Principles and Practices of Fiscal Autonomy: Experiences, Debates and Prospects (pp. 185–202). Farnham: Ashgate.

Saunders, C. & Crommelin, M. (2015). Reforming Australian Federal Democracy. University of Melbourne Legal Studies Research Paper 711.

Saunders, C. (2000). Federal fiscal reform and the GST. Public Law Review 2, 99–105.

Saunders, C. (2005). Intergovernmental agreements and the executive power. Public Law Review 16. 294–313.

Saunders, C. (2015). Cheryl Saunders: ten principles for reforming federalism. Interview by David Donaldson. The Mandarin. July 15, 2015. Accessed May 28, 2021. Cheryl Saunders: ten principles for reforming federalism | The Mandarin.

Saunders, C. (2020). A New Federalism? The Role and Future of the National Cabinet. Governing during Crisis. Policy brief no. 2, Melbourne School of Government. Accessed May 31, 2021. The Role and Future of the National Cabinet (unimelb.edu.au).

Seiler, C. (2017). Flucht in die Intransparenz. In Jahrbuch des Föderalismus 2017, 52–62.

Shah, A. (2017). Horizontal Fiscal Equalization in Australia: Peering Inside the Black Box. Report commissioned by the NSW Government. Accessed May 25, 2021. Submission DR103 – Anwar Shah – Horizontal Fiscal Equalisation – Public inquiry (pc.gov.au).

Siekmann, H. (2011). Art. 104a. In M. Sachs (Ed.), Grundgesetz Kommentar München: C.H. Beck.

Spasovejic, J. & Nicholas, M. (2013). Fiscal Equalisation in Australia. Australian Journal of Public Administration, 72(3), 316–329.

Stern, K. (1980). Das Staatsrecht der Bundesrepublik Deutschland. München: C.H. Beck.

Vega García, A. (2014). El principio constitucional de solidaridad interterritorial en España y en Alemania: aplicación y límites. REAF 20, 214–277.

Vilalta, M. (2016). Pasado, presente y futuro de la nivelación en el modelo de financiación de las Comunidades Autónomas. Mediterráneo Económico 30, 87–116.

Warren, N. (2008). Reform of the Commonwealth Grant Commission: It's all in the detail. IUSNW Law Journal 31(2), 530–552.

Watts, R. L. (1989). Executive Federalism: A comparative analysis. Kingston: Institute of Intergovernmental Relations.

Wieland, J. (2018). Notwendigkeit einer Föderalismusreform III – Wie kann die Finanzverfassung zukunftsfest gemacht werden?. In T. Schweisfurth & W. Voß (Eds.), Haushalts- und Finanzwirtschaft der Länder in der Bundesrepublik Deutschland (pp. 247–261). Berlin: Berliner Wissenschafts-Verlag.

Wilkinson, J. (2002). Horizontal fiscal equalization. Research note no. 1, Department of the Parliamentary Library. Accessed May 20, 2021. Horizontal Fiscal Equalisation (aph.gov.au).

Woelk, J. (2014). La forma segue la funzione: il Consiglio federale tedesco (Bundesrat). In E. Rossi (Ed.), Studi pisani sul Parlamento (pp. 157–174). Pisa University Press.

Zabalza, A. & López-Laborda, J. (2011). The new Spanish system of intergovernmental transfers. Int Tax Public Finance 18, 750–786.

Zornoza, J. (2014). New Trends in Fiscal Decentralization: a Spanish View. In S. A. Lütgeau, (Ed.), Fiscal Federalism and Fiscal Decentralization in Europe. Comparative Case Studies on Spain, Austria, the United Kingdom and Italy (pp. 105–126). Innsbruck: Studienverlag.

PART 2

Fiscal Federalism and Equalisation in Practice: Case Studies

CHAPTER 3

Redistribution and Equalisation in Fiscal Federalism and the Structure of Territorial Imbalances in Argentina

Miguel Ángel Asensio, Florencia Martino and Pamela Fadul
Institute of Federalism of the National Academy of Law and Social Sciences of Córdoba (IFANDCS) & Faculty of Economic Sciences (UNL – Universidad Nacional del Litoral)

1 Introduction

The establishment of equalisation or "fiscal compensation" systems in countries with a federal or decentralised organization is a characteristic that usually occurs in them, although the doctrine has been in charge of establishing differences in their particular structures[1]. Regional and economic disparities are common in federations, affecting the fiscal capacities and influencing the delivery of public services in each jurisdiction. Francois Perroux (1961) stated many years ago that "it is not possible to achieve the same level of development in all places and economic sectors at the same time". Fiscal equalisation is an important objective although it is not always or has been a priority in certain relevant cases.

Consequently, a difference could be established between systems that aim simply to distribute or redistribute, on the one hand, or to equalise, on the other. In some cases, simply, an effort has been made to establish systems for the distribution of fiscal resources among federal partners adhered to a minimum rationality, where in addition to economic ones, legal, social and political factors have had an important weight.

In the Argentine case, as in others, personal levelling may not be equivalent to regional levelling. As a consequence, this introduces an additional difficulty in the search for the said rationality. As Richard M. Bird has pointed out, transferring resources with a geographically redistributive orientation may imply transferring resources to the rich in poor regions, which would not

1 In this respect, see the words included in (Mangiamelli, 2013).

coincide with personal redistribution criteria, where the opposite would occur (Bird, 1986).

The document proposes to expose the problems to reach a formula where equalisation in a broad sense, understood as "equitable" had an important start half a century ago in Argentina, to then gradually sink towards a system of patches or mends (patchwork system) for which an attempt has been made to change it by a precise constitutional mandate, where equalisation in the aforementioned sense has been explicitly incorporated.

Accordingly, it is possible to assert that the system of intergovernmental fiscal relations in Argentina[2] has evolved from one based on rationality guidelines, to another of "permanent provisionality" where the addition or subtraction of components by legal means, led the experts to baptise it as "tax labyrinth", attentive to the incidence of those "patches" in a picture that originally claimed to be more sophisticated.

Therefore, a brief description of the nature and historical evolution of the system is required, showing the main reforms addressed and their operation before and since the beginning of this century.

In order to achieve a formula that overcomes the aforementioned weaknesses; however, specific information and statistical inputs are required to reach that equalising objective. Fortunately, at present, it is available the data from the National Census 2022 but the last data for provincial and regional GDP is outdated and it is a strong deficit for adequate decisions on the matter of identification for the main territorial country's imbalances, which may be solved. So, statistical data is essential.

After this preliminary Introduction, we mention the territorial inequalities and recover very briefly the regional landscape until the early XXI century, in one hand, and the characters and historical trajectory of the different fiscal interjurisdictional regimes in the last half a century of revenue sharing and intergovernmental transfers linked to it that is mentioned in previous works, in the other. Immediately, we afford the task of elaborating a reestimation of the GDP[3] for getting a renewed overview of the regional and territorial scenario which could be indicative for the building of a more rational system of fiscal federalism with equalising goals, avoiding the patchwork and usual provisionality as demanded for the Reformed National Constitution, which requires such a guideline of equity. In the end we attempt some brief conclusions, not

2 For a broad approach about the intergovernmental relations in Argentina, see (Cetrángolo & Jiménez, 2004).

3 The authors thank the Statistician, Professor Dr. Roberto D. Meyer (Faculty of Economic Sciences, UNL) for his technical assistance in the matter.

omitting considerations for the Argentine case, which as such has not only shown high economic volatility in recent decades, but also fragility in the institutional-fiscal field that surrounds the analysis outlined.

2 Regional Inequalities and Territorial Imbalances in Argentina

Territorial inequalities in Argentina have their roots in the 19th century and were consolidated in the 20th with the economic expansion based on the wet Pampa, which also concentrated the majority of the population (Asensio, 2020). Nearly a quarter of the 21st century has passed, the regional spectrum has experienced significant nuances, although without definitively distorting a predominant regional structure.

The magnitude of territorial, provincial and regional imbalances is visible through various indicators. Unlike advanced federations, the per capita income gap between provinces is very wide (Altavilla y Soares, 2022). A comparative measurement recently placed it at a level five times higher than that of the United States between the richest state and the poorest.

In that direction, provinces such as Corrientes, Formosa, Chaco or Santiago del Estero recorded that their Human Development Index (HDI) was far from the national averages. The same has been observed with respect to Coverage of Basic Needs (CBN) (Cao & Vaca, 2006; Asensio, 2018 & 2021).

Having said that, considering the span of the last half century, it is possible to locate in 1970 an initial peak ratifying the clear pre-eminence of the traditional Pampean region, in terms of its significance within the country as a whole, which without prejudice to certain variations, shows its substantial volume in comparison with the rest.

However, at the beginning of the present century, it was also not possible to omit that at least in one case, a clear alternative growth was viewable. Against a reduction in the weight of the Pampean area, the advance of the Patagonian region was visible, which more than doubled its relative weight within the whole, without ignoring other important but perhaps less striking changes.

In dynamic terms, the aforementioned growth acquires significance since in 1970, Patagonia was the territorial area with the lowest economic participation within the total, and even within the extra-Pampean area. The second advance of importance was until then (2004) that of the Cuyo region, in the west of the country.

Although in the northern area of the national territory the growth of the Northwest (NOA) appeared as positive, the provinces that make up the Northeast (NEA) showed a worrying negative result that relegated them in the

TABLE 3.1 Unequal weight of the Argentine regions (1970 and 2004) (% of GDP and GDP pc)

Regions	1970	2004	Differences (+/-)	GDP pc index
Pampean	81.6	75.07	−6.5	120.64
Patagonia	3.5	8.31	+4.8	182.80
NOA	6.1	6.46	+0.4	56.32
Cuyo	5.5	6.41	+0.9	96.58
NEA	4.5	3.75	−0.7	43.65

SOURCE: ELABORATED BY THE AUTHORS BASED ON ASENSIO (2018) AND PER CAPITA GDP IN 2004 (GDP INDEX IN 2004)

group. In relation to the growth of Patagonia, Cuyo and NOA, the setbacks of the Pampean Region – whose overwhelming weight of origin also maintains it as a determinant – and especially of the NEA were not irrelevant.

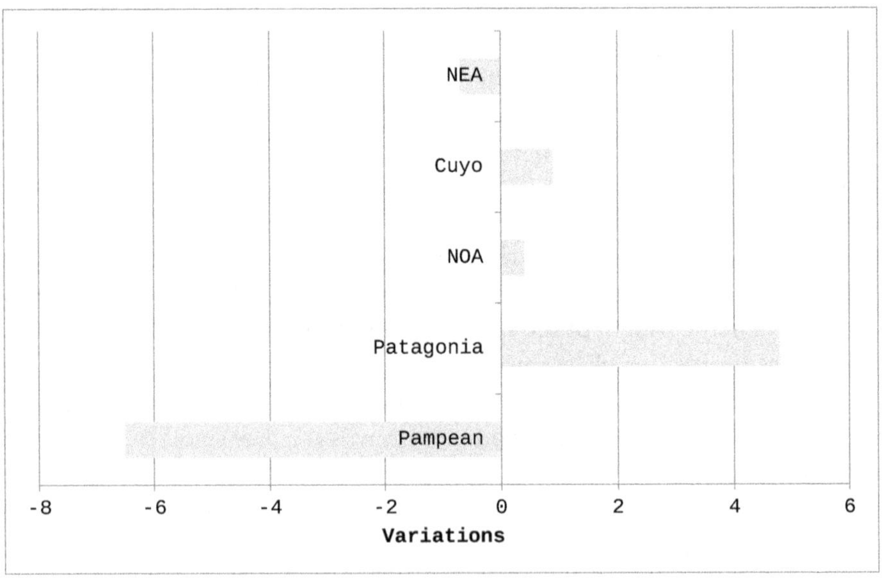

FIGURE 3.1 Percentage variations in the regional weight in GDP in the period 1970–2004 (in %)
SOURCE: ELABORATED BY THE AUTHORS BASED ON ASENSIO (2018) AND OFFICIAL GDP (INDEC)

This already demonstrated the existence of gradual transformations that occurred in the mentioned decades that modified the regional situation. On the other hand, we cannot fail to mention that in recent years up to the present, there have been changes in the primary and secondary sectors that suggest a scenario with some changes, perhaps not very visible at present but surely more evident in the future. We allude to the availability of one of the most important hydrocarbon deposits on an international scale, located in Northern Patagonia, and the growing importance of mining located mainly in the Northwest of the country.

In the latter case, it is worth noting, together with explorations such as gold, copper or other conventional minerals, the appearance of lithium as a resource of transcendent importance in the short, medium and long term, given Argentina's participation in the so-called "lithium triangle" which also covers Bolivia and Chile. This without neglecting to consider renewed conditions for the traditional crops of the Pampean Area, in addition to those that may emerge as a food-producing space by the latter, given the war situation in Ukraine.

It should also be considered that within each region, there are provinces that are especially decisive in the results. Therefore, as well as the territorial aggregates that include them, the importance of the provinces themselves must be taken into account, which on the other hand are the formative subjects of the Federal State and the effective recipients of fiscal transfers within the federal fiscal system.

Hence the crucial importance of having adjusted and close measurements in time of economic capacity and the consequent observable imbalances at a provincial and regional level, all of which is the basis for the necessary effort to obtain updated estimates that denote with greater precision the order and range of the different regions and provinces within the group, as well as their importance in terms of economic level per inhabitant, as is attempted below.

3 Argentine Fiscal Federalism and Equalisation

3.1 *Nature of the System*

As is known, among the different existing intergovernmental financial coordination options (Shoup, 1980; Nuñez Miñana, 1994; Tanzi, 2010; Anderson, 2010), in Argentina, for nine decades, a system of "revenue sharing" has prevailed (Porto, 1990; Asensio, 2015, 2016 & 2023), which under certain criteria translates into intergovernmental fiscal transfers to federative actors. This implies not only the determination of these amounts for the transfers, but also the kind or type designated for them, that determine their financial and equalising impact.

If we remember in this regard the recommendations of a classic like Wheare, such transfers should not be essentially "conditioned", in order to enhance the independence and autonomy of the recipients. Therefore, they should be predominantly "free" or "unconditioned" (Wheare, 1964).

However, these transfers must improve or strengthen the fiscal capacity of the less endowed regions, provinces or territories in relation to those with greater economic and fiscal power given scenarios of "horizontal" fiscal imbalance. Equalisation systems aim to reduce this fiscal and budgetary imbalance or "gap".

Ultimately, in "Musgravian" terms, it is about achieving a greater relationship between fiscal capacity and fiscal need for each of the districts in federated or decentralised contexts, which must enable them to provide better public services to their citizens (Musgrave, 1992).

Consequently, it is worth investigating how the total fiscal capacity of these units is formed, whether rich, intermediate or poor. It is necessary to distinguish between a fiscal capacity of its own, or arising from taxes over which they have powers that are inherent to them, on the one hand, and a fiscal capacity received or transferred, on the other. The sum of both configures its total capacity. And the "equalising" redistribution must reinforce the weak areas by postponing or somewhat moderating the weight of the most gifted.

In the Argentine case, large taxes, essentially the income tax and the value added tax, rest by constitutional means or by legal delegation in the national government. Therefore, with these taxes, plus others such as those on fuel and financial operations, as well as in particular one of great recent importance: export withholdings. Federal government is the one that achieves a clear favourable vertical fiscal imbalance, which allows it to make equalising transfers to the provinces, in addition to expanding its space and institutional power in the federation.

The provinces retain the power over the gross receipts tax (turnover tax), taxes on real estate and vehicle property and the stamp tax, as well as other minor taxes. The tax on the exploitation of subsoil natural resources located in their territories must be added, a right enjoyed since the National Constitution reformed in 1994. Municipalities mainly collect duties called *tasas* on sales and personal property. These tributes make up the main sources of the fiscal capacity of the two subnational levels.

If we remember that we have previously pointed out that to such fiscal capacities we must add the transfers that the national government must make to the provinces based on the aforementioned favourable vertical fiscal imbalance

TABLE 3.2 Matrix of tax resources and fiscal capacity in Argentina

	Government level	Total tax income of each level
1	National	Own + Shared
2	Provincial	Own + National participated
3	Municipal	Own + National and provincial participated

SOURCE: ELABORATED BY THE AUTHORS

that it enjoys, as well as that which the provinces make to their municipalities, we conclude in which the total fiscal capacity of each federative entity (Nation, Provinces, Municipalities) is integrated with its own taxes plus shared taxes, the latter being derived from transfers from another level of government, the federal or that of each province. And we say "shared" taxes, since they are those that derive from the revenue sharing system between the federal and provincial levels, as well as revenue sharing between the provincial and municipal levels. In terms of Argentine legislation, this is equivalent to saying that all budgets at the three levels make up their resource matrix (or total fiscal capacities), adding to the own taxes themselves the co-participating taxes which, as such, are said taxes shared between the three federative levels (Asensio, 2015).

Returning to the problem of equalisation, it will then be the intergovernmental transfers that, adding to the own fiscal capacity, manage to increase the total fiscal capacity of the remaining levels of government and therefore of the territories involved. In some cases, this total fiscal capacity will be almost overwhelmingly composed of transferred or participated resources, given the meagre importance of the tax revenues of the less powerful jurisdictions in an economic sense. Table 3.3 below shows that three provinces depended on more than 90% on national transfers in 2005 and four on more than 80% in 2022.

The proportion of national income allocated to the provinces (and through them to the municipalities) has been established in the so-called "tax sharing laws", which specify predominantly, although not exclusively, the aforementioned increase in the fiscal capacity of the latter and reduce the imbalances between them. This proportion has fluctuated in half a century, along with variations in subnational tax powers and the proration coefficients established in the law for each provincial state.

This has occurred in a context where the national government collects around 85% of total budgetary revenues and spends just over 50%, while

TABLE 3.3 Own fiscal capacity and transfers received by region (2005 and 2022) (% of the total)

Provinces and caba	2005			2022		
	Own fiscal capacity	Transferred fiscal capacity	Total	Own fiscal capacity	Transferred fiscal capacity	Total
Buenos Aires	54.407	45.593	100.000	67.158	32.842	100.000
CABA (Autonomous City of Buenos Aires)	88.557	11.443	100.000	85.261	14.739	100.000
Catamarca	8.896	91.104	100.000	19.739	80.261	100.000
Córdoba	33.411	66.589	100.000	49.807	50.193	100.000
Corrientes	11.038	88.962	100.000	21.504	78.496	100.000
Chaco	10.778	89.222	100.000	22.719	77.281	100.000
Chubut	29.299	70.701	100.000	49.739	50.261	100.000
Entre ríos	23.903	76.097	100.000	37.828	62.172	100.000
Formosa	5.230	94.770	100.000	13.556	86.444	100.000
Jujuy	10.556	89.444	100.000	22.701	77.299	100.000
La pampa	26.112	73.888	100.000	42.784	57.216	100.000
La rioja	8.031	91.969	100.000	16.709	83.291	100.000
Mendoza	34.856	65.144	100.000	50.113	49.887	100.000
Misiones	18.251	81.749	100.000	51.144	48.856	100.000
Neuquen	43.272	56.728	100.000	67.430	32.570	100.000
Río negro	26.146	73.854	100.000	38.315	61.685	100.000
Salta	20.607	79.393	100.000	36.396	63.604	100.000
San juan	14.226	85.774	100.000	23.011	76.989	100.000
San luis	23.743	76.257	100.000	32.123	67.877	100.000
Santa cruz	27.516	72.484	100.000	42.485	57.515	100.000
Santa fe	34.711	65.289	100.000	46.660	53.340	100.000
Sgo. Del estero	10.266	89.734	100.000	17.703	82.297	100.000
Tucumán	24.470	75.530	100.000	39.373	60.627	100.000
Tierra Del Fuego	26.160	73.840	100.000	41.273	58.727	100.000

SOURCE: ELABORATED BY THE AUTHORS BASED ON NATIONAL DIRECTORATE OF PROVINCIAL AFFAIRS, MINISTRY OF FINANCE OF THE NATION (2023)

the aggregate of provinces and municipalities do not exceed 15–20% of tax resources, but their public spending covers the other 50% for their heavy responsibilities in education, health and security.

As we will see immediately, the process recognises two phases, an initial distribution between the national government and all the provinces and a subsequent distribution of the provincial purse between each of them. As has been noted, such prorations represent coefficients established in such legislation, which translate into intergovernmental participations or transfers.

Put in terms of winners and losers, Table 3.4 shows that the last legislation that established equalising coefficients generated a redistribution produced mainly from the province of Buenos Aires to the others, without prejudice to other movements therein.

3.2 *Brief Historical Background: From Explicit Rationality to its Abandonment, Promise of Recovery and Provisionality*

Considering such framework, the construction of a financial coordination system that balances or levels with an equalising objective the positions of the participants in the federal system of Argentina can be viewed schematically through four main historical moments along the last fifty years. The first two identified with two laws, the third, with the validity of Intergovernmental Agreements and the fourth with the practical coexistence of a "mother of laws", the Constitution itself renewed, and the continuity of such Agreements or Pacts.

This is so insofar as the instance where a system based on an explicitly quantitative rationality was generated by Law 20221, close to the beginning of the last quarter of the 20th century, that is, five decades before the beginning of this essay. We say in this way as long as it is possible to speak of fiscally equalising or redistributive formulas, this was an emblematic experience in that sense.

In said federal tax scheme, within a revenue sharing mechanism or "tax participation system", the group of main national taxes would be incorporated, bringing them together under the figure of the "tax union". It would create the so-called co-participating mass or tax or fiscal bag to be shared or distributed.

As it was anticipated, the latter would recognise two large distributions, an initial primary distribution between the national or federal government (48.5%), the provinces (48.5%) and a Fund for Regional Development (3.0%), on the one hand. Such a distribution would then have a tripartite character. On the other hand, there would be a secondary distribution, which would include the allocation of the provincial part between each of the jurisdictions at that level: 48.5% of provinces were distributed according to population (65%), according to the so-called "development gap" (25%) and according to

TABLE 3.4 Changes in interprovincial distribution of equalising transfers (1973 and 1988) (in %)

Provinces and CABA	1973	1988	Winners and losers
CABA	–	1.4	1.4
Buenos Aires	27.99	21.5	−6.49
Catamarca	1.93	2.86	0.93
Córdoba	8.9	9.22	0.32
Corrientes	3.79	3.86	0.07
Chaco	4.13	5.18	1.05
Chubut	1.86	1.52	−0.34
Entre Ríos	4.56	5.07	0.51
Formosa	2.29	3.78	1.49
Jujuy	2.21	2.95	0.74
La Pampa	1.8	1.95	0.15
La Rioja	1.72	2.15	0.43
Mendoza	4.73	4.33	−0.4
Misiones	2.96	3.43	0.47
Neuquen	1.72	1.68	−0.04
Río Negro	2.29	2.62	0.33
Salta	3.74	3.98	0.24
San Juan	2.55	3.51	0.96
San Luis	1.75	2.37	0.62
Santa Cruz	1.44	1.52	0.08
Santa Fe	9.06	9.28	0.22
Sgo. del Estero	4.01	4.29	0.28
Tucumán	4.55	4.94	0.39
Tierra del Fuego	–	0.7	0.7
Total	100	100	–

SOURCE: ELABORATED BY THE AUTHORS BASED ON LAW 20221/73 AND LAW 23548/88

population dispersion (10%). The development gap of each province is the percentage difference between its level of development and that of the area comprised by the Federal Capital and the Province of Buenos Aires. And to determine such provincial level of development, the simple average of three indices was taken: quality of housing, level of education of human resources

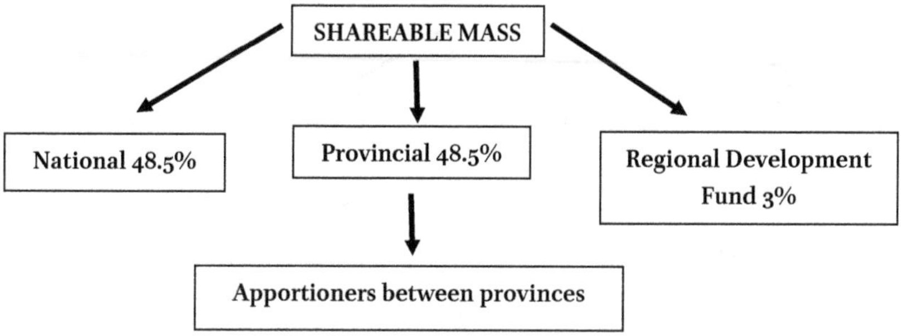

FIGURE 3.2 Distribution under the National Law N° 2022
SOURCE: ELABORATED BY THE AUTHORS BASED ON LAW 20221/73

and automobiles per inhabitant, all emerging from the National Population Census (Articles 3 and 4 Law 20221).

In such a way, the fundamental compensatory, redistributive or equalising mechanism would rest on this second distribution, since objective distribution criteria were foreseen to determine the part of each province. If it is possible to speak of a formula, this part of the mechanism housed it, at least in its essential part.

As of 1–1–1988, when the democratic system was restored, that system was renewed, where the existence of two distributions, primary and secondary, was ratified, but the FDR was replaced by the Contributions Fund of the National Treasury to the Provinces. However, the parts of each province would not arise as in the previous system of a formula where there would be objective criteria for distribution, but rather they emerged from a crude political negotiation concluded at dawn in a close parliamentary discussion.

Both instances disagreed about the validity of formulas in its distribution, but they recognised a substantial common aspect. Despite previous symptoms, they did not explicitly include consideration of the financial crisis that the national social security system was already outlining, financed under a pay-as-you-go scheme, through contributions coming from employees and employers that showed signs of exhaustion. This would affect the early end of its validity.

The third moment in recent history is made up of the beginning of the so-called "era of pacts" or intergovernmental tax agreements, which was mainly identified with two of them, in 1992 and 1993. The first of those mentioned (1992) recognised a pre-primary deduction to the co-participating mass which would be used to finance the retirement system with tax resources, taking into account the aforementioned aspect and not explicitly contemplated in the previous instances. The second (1993) would introduce limitations on the tax autonomy previously exercised by the provinces in relation to their own taxes,

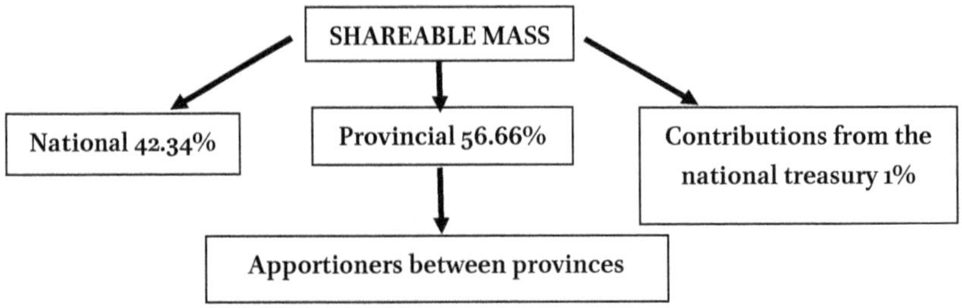

FIGURE 3.3 National Law N° 23548
SOURCE: ELABORATED BY THE AUTHORS BASED ON LAW 23548/88

especially with respect to taxes considered distortive, such as the stamp tax and the tax applied on gross incomes.

The fourth moment includes the approval of the New Reformed Constitution in 1994, which did not eliminate the validity of the previous Fiscal Pacts, although without alluding to them, and raised the obligation to implement a co-participation based on "objective distribution criteria". That is to say, within the same Constitution, the return to a formula or set of principles including equalising goals was established, just as it had happened in 1973, a little more than two decades before: "An agreement law, based on agreements between the Nation and the provinces, will institute co-participation regimes ... guaranteeing automaticity in the remission of funds ... The distribution between

TABLE 3.5 Relevant instances in the transformation of fiscal federalism in Argentina (1973–2023)

Instances	Denomination	Characters
1 (1973–87)	Revenue Sharing on a rational basis	Objective distribution coefficients among provinces
2 (1988–91)	Politically based Revenue Sharing	Equalising coefficients with political agreement
3 (1991–94)	Nation-Provinces Federal Agreements	With Revenue Sharing mass removals
4 (1994–2023)	National Constitution plus Fiscal Pacts and Consensus	Effective Pacts and Latent Constitution

SOURCE: ELABORATED BY THE AUTHORS

the Nation, the provinces and the city of Buenos Aires and between them, will be carried out in direct relation to the powers, services and functions of each of them, contemplating objective distribution criteria, it will be equitable, supportive and will give priority to an equivalent degree of development, quality of life and equal opportunities throughout the national territory" (Garat, 2016; Art. 75, inc. 2, National Constitution).

Such implementation of a return to specific guidelines has not been made effective, continuing a mechanism of periodic agreements. This formed a phase of maintenance of Fiscal Pacts and then Fiscal Consensus without enforcing and not implementing the constitutional mandate. Thus, until now, the validity of a contaminated tax participation or system of "patches" or "repairs" was configured (Asensio, 2018).

But by keeping the distribution coefficients between provinces frozen (Law 23,548) and altering its own fiscal capacities since the beginning of the 1990s in a positive sense (as in the case of granting fiscal power over natural resources) and negative (by promoting the elimination of taxes considered distortive) the equalising impact of the fiscal federalism system as a whole was altered, which is seriously outdated, making its reform a significant challenge.

As a consequence, the promise or claim of the National Constitution reformed in 1994 subsists to establish a rational system based on such "objective criteria of distribution". In such a context, to know with accuracy the magnitude and extent of regional imbalances is essential in order to establish a redistributive and equalising system replacing the present and "quasi eternal" provisionality.

For this purpose, given the availability of provisional figures from a new National Population Census for 2022, we proceed below to carry out a projection of the GDP figures by province, region and per capita from the last comprehensive calculation of 2004 originating from the INDEC (*Instituto Nacional de Estadística y Censos*, 2016).[4] This, with the understanding that in any distribution scheme with redistribution or equalisation the economic capacity of the territories will have to be considered. It is a main goal of this chapter and the essential object of what follows.

4 In spite of being perhaps a something crude or raw reestimation of the Gross Geographical Domestic Product since the one from INDEC (2004), the statistical controls effectuated let us to be confident in the results.

4 In Search of Regional/Provincial Coefficients. Recalculation of Magnitudes

4.1 *General Framing and Methodological Notes*

The above mentioned affects the rationality of any scheme of tax or expenditure assignment as well as equalisation transfers, which compounds the basic structure in a system of fiscal federalism with equalising attributes, that remain on fragile basis meanwhile the alluded indicators are not adjusted.

Due to the lack of updated statistics since 2004,[5] we have resorted to evaluating criteria that would allow us to estimate with a reasonable approximation the evolution of the different economic and demographic contexts of the Argentine provinces in order to obtain evidence referring to their evolution.

Here is presented a brief contribution, mainly quantitative, on the evolution of the Geographic (Provincial/Regional) Gross Product (GDP) and Per Capita (GDPpc) from 2004 to 2022, by provinces and regions (reestimated GDP or RGDP). An important limitation has been the possibility of having data and information in a systematic and continuous way in previous years and intermediate between such extremes.

For this purpose, databases of economic electric power consumption, cement consumption and number of workers in the private sector registered in the mentioned period were used. For the consumption of economic electrical energy in the case of the Autonomous City of Buenos Aires (CABA), the data after 2006 until 2022 were estimated. With the variable number of formal private employees, forecasts were made for the year 2022. For its part, a complete database has been obtained of cement consumption.

The information on electric power comes from the yearbooks of the National Secretariat of Energy, up to the year 2016, and of the Association of Electric Power Distributors of the Argentine Republic, for the remaining years. Those referring to cement consumption were extracted from the database of the Portland Cement Manufacturers Association of the Argentine Nation. The data on registered workers in the private sector were extracted from the Undersecretariat of Policies for Development with Regional Equity of the Ministry of the Interior of the Argentine Nation.[6]

---

5 Although a "statistical cutoff" has also been available for 2005, based on other studies, we prefer here to start from those available for 2004 as they are adjusted to new revisions originating from the National Institute of Statistics and Censuses (INDEC, 2022).

6 https://www.argentina.gob.ar/interior/subsecretaria-de-politicas-para-el-desarrollo-con-equidad-regional/series-estadisticas-historicas.

Regarding the number of members of the population, it was estimated for the period 2007 to 2009 by the method of time series forecasts. In accordance with what was previously indicated, 2004 was considered as the base year, and from this individual index was constructed, to obtain a subsequent Combined Indicator through simple averages.

With this indicator, the evolution of GDP and GDPpc (RGDP) was estimated up to and including the year 2022, taking 2004 GDP as the base year at constant prices. Subsequently, they were regionalised and the empirical evidence obtained was analysed, tending to determine the aforementioned regional-provincial relative weights and levels per inhabitant that emerge from having built the 2004–2022 series of the GDP.

4.2 *Criteria for Selection of Indicators*

As noted, three indicators were selected, available at the National Energy Secretariat and ADEERA (Argentine Distributor's Association of Electric Energy), at the Argentine Chamber of Construction, and at INDEC (2016). They are individually relevant indicators, since they explain particular aspects of the country's economic activity, in addition to complying with the following attributes:

a) Relevance in the determination of relative provincial and regional differences.
b) Absence of correlation with the rest of selected indicators.
c) Non-existence of a high level of uniformity given that it is wished to observe disparities among provinces and along time per provinces.
d) Absence of observations very atypical which must be discarded.
e) Existence of data for these indicators, for the selected period for each one of the jurisdictions.
f) Intertemporal comparability for the data, given that the indicators own to the same period of time.
g) Absence of distortive biases for specific causes inherent to the indicator, like years of pandemic or ways for capturing it.

4.3 *Regionalisation Criteria*

Without ignoring the existence of other territorial units (Velázquez, 2012), the analysis of territorial imbalances in Argentina can be addressed primarily between provinces or between regions. For our purposes, in line with the situations already stated above, the following five regions were considered:

- Pampean Region: CABA, Buenos Aires Province, Santa Fe, Córdoba, Entre Ríos and La Pampa;
- Cuyo: Mendoza, San Juan and San Luis;

– Patagonia: Río Negro, Neuquén, Chubut, Santa Cruz and Tierra del Fuego;
– NOA: Jujuy, Salta, Tucumán, Catamarca, Santiago del Estero and La Rioja;
– NEA: Corrientes, Chaco, Formosa and Misiones.

5 Results

Based on the estimates made or adopted of the Provincial Gross Geographic Product, those of the Regional Gross Geographic Product were prepared. Once this was achieved, based on the available population projections, we proceeded to calculate the GDP per inhabitant by provinces and regions.

Figure 3.4 shows the magnitudes corresponding to the five large regions that make up the national territorial spectrum. It is expressive of the considerable volume of the Pampean area within the complex and the notorious distance with respect to any of the rest, indicating in this sense its persistence as an area of greater relative size within the Nation.

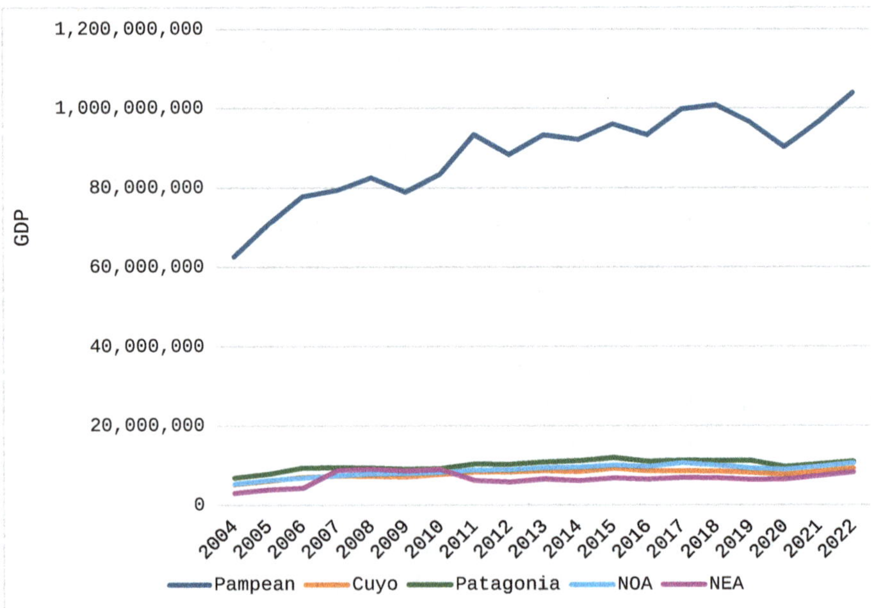

FIGURE 3.4 Modern changes in the Regional Geographic Gross Product (2004–2022) (in constant pesos base year 2004)
SOURCE: ELABORATED BY THE AUTHORS BASED ON ESTIMATION OF GDP SUPPORTED BY THE CONSTRUCTION OF A COMBINED INDICATOR OF ECONOMIC ACTIVITY FOR THE PERIOD 2004–2022

However, considering the existence of previous studies, it is also appreciable that in relative terms such importance has continued to indicate a slight but persistent decline for that region in relation to the country as a whole. Furthermore, it becomes unequivocal in the time period 2004–2022.

In the same way, the support of the position reached by the Patagonian Area also emerges – the second in importance due to the economic weight achieved – that the same studies denoted increased after a progressive process of increase in its importance (Asensio, 2021, p. 235).

In this sense, however, it is observable, together with the maintenance of the Cuyo's Region, an increase in the economic capacity of the NOA and NEA within the group, which can be linked to productive transformations that occurred during the period considered. This, together with other processes, influences the fact that in the same period the weight of the "extra-pampean" Area has increased, which from less than 25% in 2004, now represents 27.3%.

The previous concepts can be exposed by means of two additional synthetic expressions. These are the data that emerge from the Table 3.6 and Figure 3.6 that brings together the large regions, on the one hand, and their dynamics of change for the afore mentioned period of two decades between 2004 and 2022,

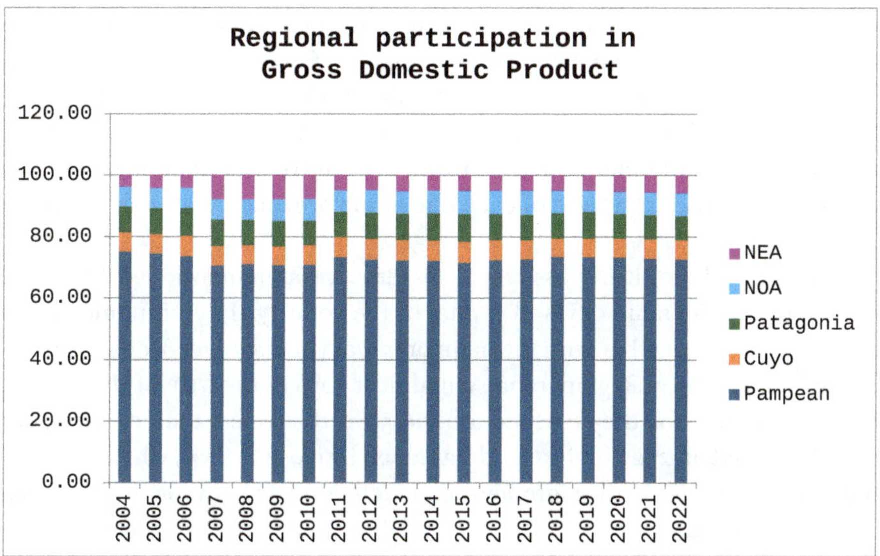

FIGURE 3.5 Relative regional importance (2004–2022) (% GNP of annual participation)
SOURCE: ELABORATED BY THE AUTHORS BASED ON AN ESTIMATION OF GDP SUPPORTED BY THE CONSTRUCTION OF A COMBINED INDICATOR OF ECONOMIC ACTIVITY

TABLE 3.6 Participation of the Argentine regions (2004 and 2022) (GDPR & GDP pc)

Regions	2004	2022	Differences (+/−)	GDPpc index
Pampean	75.07	72.64	−2.43	121.97
Patagonia	8.31	7.7	−0.61	148.37
NOA	6.46	7.44	+0.98	64.56
Cuyo	6.41	6.45	+0.04	96.34
NEA	3.75	5.77	+2.02	68.76

SOURCE: ELABORATED BY THE AUTHORS BASED ON AN ESTIMATION OF REGIONAL GDP SUPPORTED BY THE CONSTRUCTION OF A COMBINED INDICATOR FOR ECONOMIC ACTIVITY IN THE PERIOD 2004–2022 (GDPPC INDEX IN 2022)

which are then exposed under the same criteria as the most used above for the interregnum 1970–2004.

From Table 3.6, the recovery of the northern regions emerges, particularly the NEA, as well as the relative sustainability of the Cuyo Region thanks to slight growth. A new reduction in the weight of the Pampean Region is unequivocal, and after an already indicated phase of expansion, a moderate but visible decline in Patagonia, which does not, however, alter its great long-term expansion. The statement can be seen in Figure 3.6.

It should be stressed that such magnitudes obviously depend on the significance of each of the provinces that are members or components of the large regions selected and mentioned above as main territorial groupings. For this reason, the individual weight of each one of the provinces that make up them cannot be ignored.

And again there, it is possible to discern the aforementioned historical matrix, where the main city and capital of the country, the Autonomous City of Buenos Aires, together with the main province (Buenos Aires), crucial members of the Pampean Region, represent almost 50% of the GDP of the Nation. Despite this, in 2004 they reached around 54%, that is less than two decades ago. Given that, in 2022 their record has fallen by close to 50%, which is surely linked to the change in the aforementioned relationship between the Pampean and Non-Pampean space.

Next, it is appropriate to stop at the magnitudes of the product per inhabitant, as determinants of the situation compared both between regions and between provinces. In the first case, the statistical exercise carried out confirms that this variable place the Patagonian Region in first ubication.

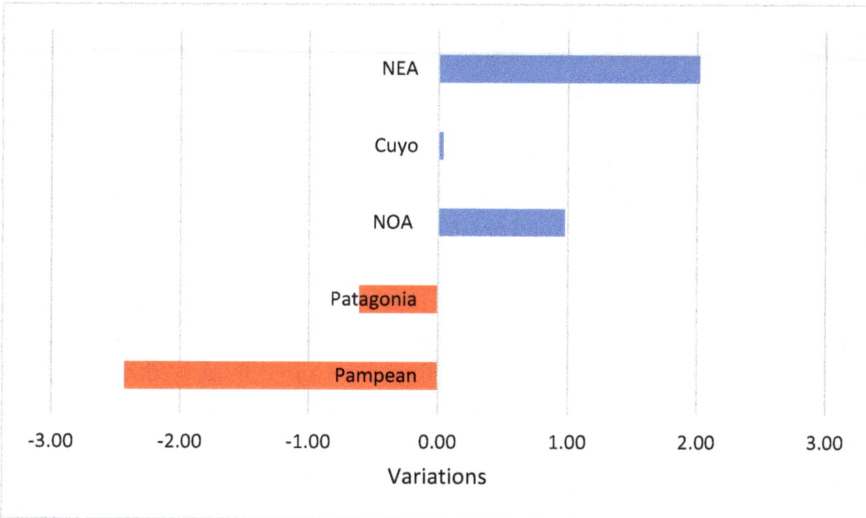

FIGURE 3.6 Percentage variations in the regional GDP by regions (2004–2022) (% GDP)
SOURCE: ELABORATED BY THE AUTHORS. SAME AS IN FIGURES 3.4, 3.5 AND TABLE 3.6

This is significant, as it occurs having relegated the Pampean Region to second position during the first twenty years of the 21st century, a region that was the axis of national historical development since the post-colonial stage in the 19th century. And at the same time, in an inconspicuous way, while confirming a long-term position, it shows the Cuyo Region with an individual income higher than that of NOA and NEA.

In turn, given the provincial composition of the different regions or territorial spaces, it is important to consider the GDP per inhabitant and per province, which implies an approximation to the "well-being" of each individual located in those territorial jurisdictions, whose magnitudes affect, obviously, in the values for the respective regional groupings – or simply regions – of belonging.

Table 3.8 shows the emerging imbalances and asymmetries using the dimension "province". Mindful of its new institutional character since the 1994 Constitution granted it such attribute, the Autonomous City of Buenos Aires is discriminated separately for comparative purposes, although it is clear that this implies dehomogenising the evaluated spaces, considering one of characteristics essentially urban, with others that recognizes the existence of cities and "urbanity" plus territories and "rurality".

In this framework, the Patagonian Tierra del Fuego, Santa Cruz and Neuquén appear as determinants. The first of these provinces, manages to surpass the

TABLE 3.7 Participation of each province in the GDP (2004–2022)

Provinces	2004	2005	2006	2007	2008	2009	2010	2011	2012
CABA	18.57	18.70	17.67	16.57	16.72	16.21	15.53	16.17	14.53
Buenos Aires	35.09	34.68	34.73	34.52	34.84	35.41	35.93	35.83	36.64
Catamarca	0.74	0.77	0.75	0.76	0.77	0.75	0.71	0.69	0.72
Chaco	1.18	1.42	1.32	3.90	4.02	4.28	4.27	1.74	1.73
Chubut	2.13	2.17	2.30	1.81	1.84	1.71	1.72	1.91	1.89
Córdoba	8.32	8.18	8.41	6.38	6.41	6.42	6.53	8.57	8.62
Corrientes	0.96	1.02	1.00	2.12	2.05	1.69	1.54	1.20	1.03
Entre Ríos	2.49	2.45	2.44	2.51	2.53	2.78	2.73	2.85	2.85
Formosa	0.46	0.55	0.56	0.62	0.61	0.61	0.62	0.69	0.70
Jujuy	0.78	0.74	0.73	0.72	0.74	0.79	0.75	0.75	0.80
La Pampa	0.84	0.89	0.87	0.92	0.86	0.86	0.81	0.83	0.83
La Rioja	0.67	0.72	0.67	0.66	0.63	0.65	0.68	0.67	0.68
Mendoza	4.01	3.96	4.00	3.98	3.77	3.79	3.86	3.89	4.04
Misiones	1.16	1.17	1.19	1.19	1.14	1.18	1.26	1.31	1.36
Neuquén	2.70	2.55	2.53	2.64	2.57	2.72	2.41	2.42	2.65
Rio Negro	1.23	1.26	1.47	1.45	1.37	1.33	1.35	1.36	1.32
Salta	1.61	1.59	1.59	1.64	1.63	1.79	1.74	1.74	1.78
San Juan	0.99	0.98	1.05	1.04	1.04	1.05	1.03	1.15	1.27
San Luis	1.41	1.52	1.67	1.54	1.46	1.52	1.77	1.52	1.57
Santa Cruz	1.40	1.40	1.53	1.57	1.35	1.46	1.41	1.41	1.53
Santa Fe	9.78	9.58	9.61	9.61	9.65	8.96	9.22	9.17	9.02
Santiago del Estero	1.01	1.04	1.05	1.10	1.22	1.31	1.39	1.31	1.43
Tucumán	1.66	1.73	1.75	1.77	1.78	1.82	1.76	1.78	1.96
Tierra del Fuego	0.85	0.92	1.10	0.96	1.02	0.89	0.96	1.04	1.05
Total country	100.00	100.00	100.00	100.00	100.00	100.00	100.00	100.00	100.00

SOURCE: ELABORATED BY THE AUTHORS BASED ON ESTIMATION OF PROVINCIAL GDP SUPPORTED BY THE COMBINED INDICATOR OF ECONOMIC ACTIVITY (GDPPC INDEX IN 2022)

2013	2014	2015	2016	2017	2018	2019	2020	2021	2022
14.57	14.62	14.48	14.99	14.82	15.52	15.79	15.37	14.38	14.46
36.58	36.14	35.58	36.04	36.01	35.73	35.80	35.92	36.02	35.44
0.75	0.76	0.74	0.71	0.76	0.61	0.51	0.63	0.64	0.66
1.73	1.78	1.81	1.71	1.78	1.77	1.66	1.80	1.99	2.12
1.84	1.93	1.92	1.80	1.81	1.82	1.94	1.50	1.45	1.41
8.46	8.55	8.76	8.52	8.78	9.01	8.81	8.77	9.06	9.36
1.32	0.96	1.25	1.25	1.25	1.24	1.24	1.40	1.50	1.49
2.87	2.88	2.88	2.86	2.86	2.84	2.91	3.16	3.19	3.16
0.67	0.70	0.70	0.69	0.64	0.62	0.65	0.62	0.65	0.67
0.82	0.85	0.88	0.84	0.81	0.77	0.74	0.79	0.79	0.80
0.85	0.87	0.85	0.86	0.92	0.93	0.90	0.93	0.91	0.92
0.73	0.73	0.73	0.69	0.71	0.63	0.65	0.72	0.67	0.66
3.93	3.83	4.14	3.98	3.77	3.81	3.82	3.87	3.90	3.88
1.47	1.40	1.35	1.38	1.39	1.37	1.35	1.47	1.46	1.49
2.59	2.76	2.89	2.66	2.62	2.63	2.84	2.61	2.63	2.68
1.32	1.32	1.37	1.35	1.26	1.23	1.29	1.30	1.27	1.26
1.76	1.80	1.79	1.87	1.91	1.86	1.83	1.89	1.84	1.78
1.29	1.21	1.13	1.14	1.10	1.10	1.10	1.09	1.11	1.14
1.53	1.57	1.69	1.53	1.43	1.32	1.34	1.33	1.39	1.43
1.52	1.64	1.72	1.56	1.46	1.37	1.40	1.39	1.42	1.32
8.99	9.18	8.91	9.01	9.23	9.29	9.09	9.09	9.30	9.30
1.45	1.54	1.56	1.60	1.67	1.63	1.59	1.64	1.65	1.67
1.82	1.85	1.81	1.81	1.91	1.81	1.73	1.66	1.77	1.87
1.15	1.11	1.05	1.14	1.09	1.08	1.04	1.08	1.04	1.03
100.00	100.00	100.00	100.00	100.00	100.00	100.00	100.00	100.00	100.00

TABLE 3.8 Reestimated GDP by province per capita (2004–2022) (in constant pesos base year 2004)

Provinces	2004	2005	2006	2007	2008	2009	2010	2011	2012
CABA	51421	58935	61644	61498	63956	61273	63376	67804	58318
Buenos Aires	20142	22511	24794	26069	27012	26376	27128	28650	27757
Catamarca	17191	19966	21239	22389	23502	22151	22851	23037	22861
Chaco	9676	13186	13445	41212	43541	44475	47725	20288	19079
Chubut	40301	46325	53888	43442	44324	38332	39955	46375	43182
Córdoba	21498	23911	27024	21868	22628	21747	23294	31962	30455
Corrientes	8213	9902	10680	24299	24121	19020	18348	14863	12034
Entre Ríos	17198	19155	20943	22960	23887	25208	26074	28574	27073
Formosa	7460	10068	11312	13372	13398	12928	13746	15793	15126
Jujuy	10076	10800	11704	12234	12919	13081	13194	13708	13835
La Pampa	22003	26391	28194	32115	30867	29980	29951	31854	30452
La Rioja	17809	21325	21702	22546	21976	21748	24155	24674	23439
Mendoza	20166	22478	24916	26099	25321	24450	26154	27559	27078
Misiones	9514	10795	11992	12560	12408	11964	13545	14789	14502
Neuquén	44033	46514	50277	55293	54752	55399	51677	53028	54547
Río Negro	17578	20423	26181	27319	25649	23472	24906	26232	24162
Salta	11772	13035	14208	15495	15850	16614	16925	17565	16951
San Juan	12581	13936	16318	17236	17864	17321	17807	20761	21731
San Luis	29451	35426	42116	41083	39897	39736	48205	42822	41800
Santa Cruz	55579	62270	74342	76970	61958	61410	60742	63071	63801
Santa Fe	25849	28682	31697	33789	35092	31413	34064	35503	33220
S. del Estero	10086	11751	13121	14447	16437	16879	18795	18760	19470
Tucumán	9867	11602	12852	13839	14334	14031	14363	15013	15650
Tierra del Fuego	63094	75641	97355	90260	96639	79316	88863	97101	91227

SOURCE: ELABORATED BY THE AUTHORS. SAME AS TABLE 3.7 AND FIGURE 3.7 AND NATIONAL POPULATION CENSUS 2022 FROM INDEC

2013	2014	2015	2016	2017	2018	2019	2020	2021	2022
61785	61192	63710	63274	66501	69548	67670	61546	61886	66309
28979	27992	28703	27638	29082	28573	27135	25225	26950	28857
24903	24748	25182	22860	25869	20675	16457	18575	20124	21973
20010	20121	21234	19148	20897	20644	18349	18379	21635	26504
43417	44229	45548	40350	42239	41866	41958	29873	30618	33538
31296	30924	33015	30523	33108	33631	31176	28735	31617	33661
16198	11534	15671	14963	15755	15497	14722	15361	17555	17856
28550	28109	29316	27661	29146	28687	27857	28095	30205	31671
15295	15671	16127	15192	14895	14263	14149	12626	14101	15770
14889	15135	16304	14739	14997	14036	12708	12690	13513	14360
32530	32608	33420	32053	36339	36450	33493	32059	33529	36131
26181	25825	26775	23995	25861	22714	21890	22384	22216	24691
27509	26211	29502	26978	26869	26893	25536	23942	25677	27574
16320	15240	15237	14765	15635	15248	14279	14328	15138	16611
55515	57652	62614	54635	56540	56004	57057	48342	51765	52716
25019	24499	26327	24537	24134	23279	22952	21367	22190	23626
17573	17461	18060	17908	19195	18373	17086	16367	16894	17702
23095	21216	20520	19777	20072	19746	18708	17170	18664	19917
42528	42730	47658	41023	40092	36653	35046	32203	35751	37736
65042	67378	72064	61227	59097	54132	51764	46801	50111	56813
34713	34773	35240	33966	36749	36700	34095	31650	34566	37396
20556	21383	22571	21986	24196	23453	21605	20672	22062	22652
15171	14993	15274	14467	16075	15081	13578	12097	13660	15673
103473	95601	92920	93669	93405	89627	80696	76477	77310	77045

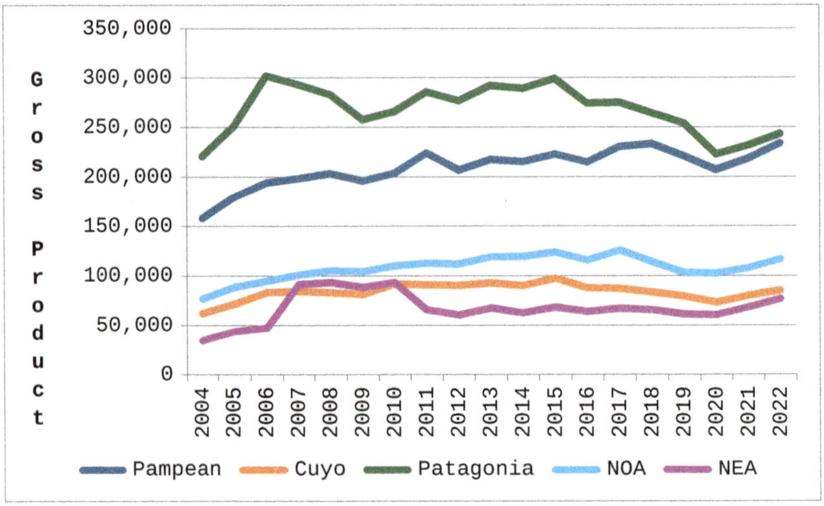

FIGURE 3.7 Evolution of the Regional Gross Product per capita (2004–2022) (in constant pesos base year 2004)
SOURCE: ELABORATED BY THE AUTHORS. SAME AS FIGURES 3.5, 3.6 AND TABLES 3.6 AND 3.7

emblematic level of the main city of the country, the so-called CABA. In doing so, another trio is formed that by their order make up Tierra del Fuego, CABA and Santa Cruz, which indicates the three leading jurisdictions in terms of per capita income.

On the other hand, in the NOA and NEA are low-income jurisdictions. Formosa, Tucumán and Jujuy become the provincial districts with the lowest individual income. A substantive change appears on the scene: the difference between the province with the highest income (Tierra del Fuego) and the one with the lowest income (Jujuy) has narrowed from more than eight times in 2004 to more than five times in 2022.

Going back, it can be observed that in all the regions there has been a growth that has been verified "between extremes", to a greater or lesser extent, despite the fact that towards the interior of the period examined, which covers some eighteen years, oscillations are observable. with not insignificant rises and declines, in accordance with the shaky recent economic history of the country.

The production of the selected regions registers a variety based on geographic, climatic and demographic conditions, as well as specific variations in the internal and international markets that absorb their respective volumes generated in a continental surface that with its almost 2.8 million square kilometres is the eighth in the world.

Such variations are the ones that are strongly linked, attentive to the historical differences with the most important – the Pampean one – to the possibility of establishing a compatible and comprehensive federal fiscal system with the reduction of regional inequalities and the capacity to provide public services to the throughout the country under equitable conditions, avoiding intolerable differences – particularly emphasised aspects for its reconfiguration in the Constitutional Reform of 1994. Precisely, such is the goal of the above mentioned Article 75, paragraph 2 with reference to the system of distribution of fiscal resources, in the reformed Argentine National Constitution.

Despite this, the process of unequal economic growth between regions and provinces has continued and, a quarter of a century after the sanction of the reform of the original Magna Carta, the new system of co-participation demanded by the Constitution has not come into force, except for particular modifications arising from different Intergovernmental Agreements (Asensio, 2021).

Then, a recurring reason for conflict pointed out from the most important areas, in a landscape of winners and losers, is the lack of relationship between their own economic capacity, and therefore their ability to generate fiscal resources, with the scarce recovery of the same through the federal fiscal system. That is, their role as contributors who, as such, redistribute income towards the less favoured group.

Table 3.7 primarily exhibits such a problem, which cannot by itself define, together with demographic or social components, among others, the achievement of constitutional requirements, which necessarily imply finding a formula that contemplates all its complexity in a specific context of federative associates where it is possible to reconcile the role of the most advanced in relation to the least wealthy.[7]

6 Conclusions

The compensatory, redistribution or equalisation systems have to do with marked economic and fiscal imbalances. They are embodied in fiscal federalism schemes through strategies that, in short, consider the importance of interregional solidarity to allow a basic provision of public services in a context of different relative developments, by federative actors.

7 In this regard, works such as those by Castells and Queralt (2002) or Cuadrado and Mancha (2005) denote such importance in the European context.

TABLE 3.9 Federal revenue sharing in comparison with the economic importance of each jurisdiction in the country

Individual provinces and CABA	Secondary distribution percentages in federal sharing	Economic weight (2022)	Positive and negative divergences
CABA	1.4	14.46	−13.06
Buenos Aires	21.5	35.44	−13.94
Catamarca	2.86	0.66	2.2
Chaco	5.18	2.12	3.06
Chubut	1.52	1.41	0.11
Córdoba	9.22	9.36	−0.14
Corrientes	3.86	1.49	2.37
Entre Ríos	5.07	3.16	1.91
Formosa	3.78	0.67	3.11
Jujuy	2.95	0.8	2.15
La Pampa	1.95	0.92	1.03
La Rioja	2.15	0.66	1.49
Mendoza	4.33	3.88	0.45
Misiones	3.43	1.49	1.94
Neuquén	1.68	2.68	−1.00
Rio Negro	2.62	1.26	1.36
Salta	3.98	1.78	2.2
San Juan	3.51	1.14	2.37
San Luis	2.37	1.43	0.94
Santa Cruz	1.52	1.32	0.2
Santa Fe	9.28	9.3	−0.02
Santiago del Estero	4.29	1.67	2.62
Tucumán	4.94	1.87	3.07
Tierra del Fuego	0.7	1.03	−0.33

SOURCE: ELABORATED BY THE AUTHORS BASED ON TABLE 3.7, ABOVE, AND LAW 23548

The so-called "horizontal imbalances" are of great importance in economic and social matters, and also with regard to public finances. The issue of horizontal fiscal imbalance is closely related to the existence of horizontal economic imbalances (Bird, 1986; Bird & Vaillancourt, 1999). In a tax participation system, the consequent fiscal transfers must embody that solidarity under "objective distribution criteria" as required in Argentina by the 1994 Constitution. At a minimum, this implies knowing the economic and fiscal capacity of the participants, which an attempt has been made in this work with a "gross" reestimation of its geographic (provincial and regional) gross product (GDP).

The gaps in territorial income, ultimately, refer not only to the coverage of fiscal needs, but also to the greater autonomy or fiscal dependence of some provinces with respect to others, within the national design of fiscal federalism. For federal countries, it is a great challenge to reduce such imbalances, in the sense that the validation of the territorial orientation generated by economic forces has expanded and can strengthen concentration, and its ignorance could generate non-optimal options (Asensio, 2013).

Among the main questions that led to the estimates that we present, was the verification of regional and intraregional changes in the first two decades of the 21st century, after other previous efforts. The results that emerge from the previous analysis indicate that the predominant importance of the Pampean Area has continued, but the same exercise shows a predominance that does not alter a continued tendency to be less accentuated. This would confirm the long-term trends emerging from such previous studies (Asensio, 2013, 2018 and 2021).

In this line, Cao and Vaca (2006) have highlighted the pre-eminence of the "central area" (that essentially involves the Pampean area) beyond changes in the political, economic and social structure of the country; added to the relative backwardness of the provinces of the peripheral area originated and reproduced for a long time from a set of structural factors.[8]

On the other hand, the per capita product data again highlights the importance of the Patagonian Region,[9] which, as such, clearly differs even from the Pampean one. This is linked to its productive matrix in particular, as well as to a scarce demography, recognising its valuable energy matrix, despite thousands of hectares of desert landscape.

The leaderships in this aspect show facets of interest both in advanced jurisdictions and in the most backward ones, considering a smaller difference between higher and lower levels, as has been pointed out.[10] However, certain

8 In this important study, as the cited authors indicate, Central Area refers to CABA, province of Buenos Aires, Santa Fe and Córdoba. Peripheral area includes San Luis, La Rioja, Catamarca, Santiago del Estero, Jujuy, Corrientes and Formosa.

9 And as stated above, of any of the provinces that make it up in relation to such values of PBGR per inhabitant.

10 The appearance of Tucumán and Jujuy among the least favoured, is a novelty compared to the existing scenario at the beginning of the 21st century.

signs would appear in some of the minor participants, which include the NOA, Cuyo and NEA regions, which could be reflecting the transformations in the national economic structure that we hinted at above.

It should be noted, as we did previously, in relation to the federal finance model to be adopted, that the resources of each jurisdiction are made up of its own resources, on the one hand, and resources shared between the Nation and the Provinces, on the other. The latter are those derived from revenue sharing transfers with its equalising impact.

The aforementioned National Constitution of 1994 granted tax income originating in the natural resources of the subsoil to the Argentine provinces, which for specific purposes include those of the Andean cordon and the Patagonia, as a result of which they can receive royalties that have since modified their relative situation in relation to the traditional agro-industrial area of the country, which is the Pampean.

For the fiscal federalism schemes to be adopted in the future, on the other hand, it should be remembered that up to now and due to its complexity, we have not yet included in the discussion the "off-shore" resources that refer to the very vast Argentine Sea.

From the point of view of fiscal redistribution and equalisation achievable through the federal fiscal system, the existing discrepancy between the flows established by law for some provinces and their own fiscal capacity is appreciable. This keeps the interest open in reaching rational formulas such as those used in the past, to get out of the contemporary "ad hoc" scheme and produce another that responds to the ambitious promise emerging from the Constitution reformed in 1994.

Profound specific changes in the financial coordination mechanism caused by the crises of both 2008 and 2020–2021 (COVID-19) cannot be pointed out in the specific operations of the regime, and it is up to us to refer the interested reader to recent contributions in this regard (Asensio & Martino, 2023).

References

Altavilla, C. y Soares, M. (2022). Federalismo fiscal y desigualdad social en Argentina y Brasil, *Revista de estudios regionales*, N° 125.

Anderson, G. (2010). *Fiscal Federalism: A Comparative Introduction*. Oxford: Oxford University Press.

Asensio, M. A. (2013). Territorial Imbalances and Regional Disparities within a Federal Context: The Case of Argentina. In S. Mangiamelli (Ed.), *Federalism, Regionalism and Territory* (pp. 93–105). Milano: Giuffré.

Asensio, M. A. (2015). Subnational Tax Powers in Argentina, *Occasional Paper Series*, 16 (pp. 1–40). Ottawa: Forum of Federations.

Asensio, M. A., P. M. Garat & L. Di Gresia (Eds.) (2016). *Aportes para el debate fiscal federal.* Buenos Aires: Fundación Civilidad.

Asensio, M. A. (2018). Repasando Medio Siglo de Evolución Regional en Argentina: Matemáticas del Desequilibrio Territorial, *Revista de la Junta Provincial de Estudios Históricos*, LXXIV, 107–125.

Asensio, M. A. (2020). Formación económica, institucional y regional de la Argentina en perspectiva y comparaciones con Canadá. In M. A. Asensio (Ed.), *El federalismo en Argentina y Canadá. Desafíos económicos e institucionales* (pp. 61–68). Santa Fe: UNL.

Asensio, M. A. (2021). Equality, Development Equivalence and Federal Finance in Argentina. In E. M. Belser, T. Bächler, S. Egli & L. Zünd (Eds.), *The Principle of Equality in Diverse States. Reconciling Autonomy with Equal Rights and Opportunities* (pp. 224–252). Leiden: Brill-Nijhoff.

Asensio, M. A. & F. Martino, (2023). Fiscal federalism and subnational finance in Argentina before and after the pandemic storm. *Revista "Cuadernos Manuel Giménez Abad"*, (9), 6–32.

Bird, R. M. (1986). *Federal Finance in Comparative Perspective*, Toronto: Toronto Tax Foundation.

Bird, R. M. & F. Vaillancourt (Eds.) (1999). *Fiscal Decentralization in Developing Countries*. Cambridge: Cambridge University Press.

Cao, H. & J. Vaca (2006). Desarrollo regional en la Argentina: la centenaria vigencia de un patrón de asimetría territorial. *EURE*, 32(95), 95–111.

Castells, A. & Espasa Queralt, M. (2002). Desequilibrios territoriales y políticas de cohesión en la Unión Europea. *Papeles de Economía Española*, 91, 253–278.

Cetrángolo, O. & J. P. Jiménez (2004). Las relaciones entre niveles de gobierno en Argentina. *Revista de la CEPAL*, 84, 117–134.

Cuadrado, J. R. & T. Mancha (2005). Política Regional y de Cohesión. In Jordán Galduf, J. M. *Economía de la Unión Europea*, Madrid: Civitas.

Garat, P. M. (2016). Aportes desde el derecho constitucional al debate sobre la relación fiscal federal. In M. A. Asensio, P. M. Garat. & L. Di Gresia (Eds.). *Aportes para el debate sobre la cuestión fiscal federal*, (pp. 11–140). Buenos Aires: Fundación Civilidad-Fundación Hans Seidel.

INDEC (2016). *Cuentas Nacionales. Metodología de estimación, Metodología INDEC N° 21*, Buenos Aires: Instituto Nacional de Estadística y Censos.

INDEC (2022). *Argentina: Censo Nacional de población, familias y vivienda*, Buenos Aires: Instituto Nacional de Estadística y Censos.

Mangiamelli, S. (2013). *Federalism, Regionalsm and Territory, Consiglio Nazionale delle Ricerche*, Milano: Giuffre Editore,

Musgrave, R. A. & Musgrave, P. (1992). *Haciendo Pública: Teórica y aplicada.* Madrid: McGraw-Hill.

Núnez Miñana, H. (1994). *Finanzas Públicas*, Buenos Aires: Macchi.

Perroux, F. (1961). *Nota sobre la Noción de Polo de Crecimiento.* Buenos Aires: CFI.

Porto, A. (1990). *Federalismo fiscal.* Buenos Aires: Tesis-Norma.

Shoup, C. (1980). *Hacienda Pública*, Madrid: Instituto de Estudios Fiscales.

Tanzi, V. (2010). Revenue Sharing Arrangements: Options and Relative Merits, *The Mabub ul Haq Memorial Lecture*, unpublished paper, Islamabad: PDSE 26th Annual General Meeting and Conference, December 28.

Velázquez, G. A. (2012). *Geografía y calidad de vida en Argentina. Análisis regional y departamental.* Tandil: Universidad Nacional del Centro.

Wheare, K. (1964). *Federal Government*, Oxford: Oxford University Press, Galaxy Books.

CHAPTER 4

From Full to Partial Equalisation: The Case of Horizontal Fiscal Equalisation in Australia

Tracy B. Fenwick
Associate Professor at Australian Centre for Federalism, School of Politics (Australian National University)

Miranda Stewart
Professor at Melbourne Law School (The University of Melbourne) & Honorary Professor at Crawford School of Public Policy (The Australian National University)

1 Introduction

The pursuit of both policy diversity and revenue-maximisation means that federations often end up with an uneven distribution of wealth and unequal access to public services of comparable standards across a country (Riker, 1975; Rodden and Wibbels, 2002). Keith Banting (2006) further contends that the inherent characteristics of federalism may even be at odds with the goals of social citizenship. Efforts to remedy the potential inequities of too much power and too many resources at any one level of government in a federal democracy are dependent on a plethora of constitutional, fiscal, political, administrative, and cultural-societal factors.

Two definitive characteristics about Australian fiscal federalism are well established in the literature. First, Australia, in contrast to other more decentralised federal systems, has a strong vertical fiscal imbalance (VFI). VFI refers simply to when one level of government – in this case the Australian Federal Government – collects more revenue than it spends. In both theory and in practice, this structural factor preconditions the states to be fiscally dependent on the centre. Second, Australia has one of the most egalitarian horizontal fiscal equalisation systems (HFE) in the world. These two characteristics appear to be sequentially connected; it is logical that one both permits and necessitates the other. The existence of an egalitarian HFE, however, does not mean the Australian Federal Government (known in Australia as the 'Commonwealth') never encroaches upon the states. As the late Australian federal theorist Brian

DOI:10.1163/9789004524514_006

Galligan (2012, p. 322) succinctly observed, 'money talks politically and buys policy influence'.

Notwithstanding, due to the extent of VFI in Australia, the Commonwealth Government is in a good position to work out the problems of territorial inequality and uneven economic development to ensure all Australians enjoy equal rights of social citizenship. The norm of 'equality' is deeply entrenched in Australian society, in particular with regards to labour rights and social welfare (Braun, 2006, p. 12). As this chapter will explore, however, Australia's HFE system still generates tensions between the states and territories, in particular between the poorer and the wealthier ones.

2 Fiscal Federalism in Australia

To understand fiscal federalism in Australia and the purpose of its HFE, it is essential to begin with a brief overview of fiscal constitutionalism (for more detail, see Stewart 2023). Australia's federation was created in 1901, and now comprises six sovereign states (originally five) and two territories: New South Wales (NSW), Queensland (Qld), South Australia (SA), Tasmania (Tas), Victoria (Vic), Western Australia (WA), Australian Capital Territory (ACT), Northern Territory (NT). The territories are subject to federal legislative control with delegated tax and administrative powers (for brevity, we will henceforth refer to the constituent units of the Australian federation simply as 'the states'). The Australian constitution is very difficult to amend, requiring a referendum to be supported both by an overall majority of votes and by a majority of states (excluding the territories). It has therefore rarely been amended. From the outset, it was recognised that both the Commonwealth and the states would need revenues to support their expenditure needs. At federation, therefore, the Commonwealth was ceded exclusive control over customs and excise, the main tax source at this time.

2.1 *Federal Revenue Powers*

In term of revenues, the Constitution provides the foundation of the federal power to tax, limits some taxation powers in the states, and sets up a basic framework for federal–state fiscal relations. S51(ii) provides concurrent general tax power to the Commonwealth to make laws with respect to taxation but not so as to discriminate between states or parts of states; moreover, the Commonwealth is prohibited from giving preference to one state or another in taxation (S99) and from taxing the states (S114). The Commonwealth has exclusive power to levy duties of customs and excise (S90); this has been interpreted broadly to preclude the states from levying sales or consumption taxes, as discussed below. Regarding the income tax, until 1942, there was taxation competition between the Commonwealth's income tax first enacted in 1915, and the income taxes levied by the states (previously the colonies) during the first decades of federation.

Leading up to and during the Second World War, in order to bolster government revenues to fund the war effort, the Commonwealth and states concurrently enacted the Uniform Income Tax Act (1936), specified as being for the duration of the war. In 1942, four acts were passed enabling the Commonwealth to take over all income taxation, known as the Uniform Tax Scheme, under which the states could no longer impose their own income tax and the Commonwealth took over state tax offices and personnel. Legal challenges (*South Australia* v. *Commonwealth*, First Uniform Tax Case (1942) 65 CLR 373) failed, signalling the High Court's leading decision on centralising Australian fiscal federalism. This decision was due in part to deference to the nation's defence efforts. Even though the state premiers originally opposed converting this temporary war measure into a permanent policy, that is in fact what occurred. Victoria and New South Wales (NSW) challenged its constitutionality again (*Victoria v Commonwealth*, Second Uniform Tax Case (1957) 99 CLR 575 to no avail).

The key finding of the High Court was that it was constitutional for the Commonwealth to make grants to the states under S96, conditional upon the states not levying state income taxes. This is a critical juncture in Australian fiscal federalism, as it led to a significantly increased VFI. The legal condition that states had to refrain from imposing income taxes in order to receive federal grants under S96 was lifted during the 1970s, but to date no state has enacted a state income tax.

Because of the extensive taxation rights bestowed by the constitution on the Commonwealth, state and local governments in Australia currently collect less than 20% of the country's tax revenue, thus raising only half of the revenues they require to fund their expenditures (Stewart, 2023, p. 9). In 2020–21, the Australian government contributed 46.4% of states' spending; and approximately half of the sums supplied by the Commonwealth was tied to national goals, priorities and programs (Australian Treasury, 2022). The size of discretionary transfers relative to non-discretionary transfers therefore provides the Commonwealth considerable leeway to set the direction of policy priorities and directions, meanwhile claiming credit for co-financed policy successes along the way (Fenwick, 2023).

2.2 *Federal Spending Power*

Turning now to federal spending power, under SS81 and 83 of the Constitution, the federal government must appropriate funds by a law of the Commonwealth Parliament to be spent 'for purposes of the Commonwealth'. This is an important *de jure* constraint on Commonwealth spending power. Both major political parties – the centre-left Australian Labor Party (ALP) and the conservative Liberal–National Party Coalition (LNP) – have used Commonwealth expenditure powers under these sections to prioritise national spending during exceptional emergency crises. The ALP did so during the global financial crisis, via the Tax Bonus Act (2009), and more recently the Coalition did so during the COVID-19 crisis via the Commonwealth's Jobkeeper (2020) and Jobseeker (2020) programs.

As previously outlined, S96 of the constitution provides the Commonwealth with considerable power to control and deliver policy and expenditures across the federation. This so-called 'grants power' affords the centre considerable sway over the states, being able to 'grant financial assistance to any State on such terms and conditions as the Parliament thinks fit'. The original purpose of this section was to protect Tasmania and Western Australia (WA) as weaker regions, and to quell WA's secession movement. It also provided a future blank cheque for the Commonwealth to make 'tied' grants to the states (Galligan, 2012, p. 327), including for a range of purposes inside the states' legal jurisdiction, such as infrastructure, drought relief, national fitness, and state universities. As Galligan states (2012), VFI was not precluded; indeed, it was there at the beginning, and after 1942, the federal government's grants power under S96 became the primary mechanism to both finance and equalise the unintended inequities that often arise in federal systems.

Such extensive federal spending power and centralised taxation power could lead to stark inequality across the states and exacerbate intergovernmental tensions. In the Australian case, however, this propensity was historically mitigated by three main types of financial assistance from the Commonwealth to the states under S96 of the Constitution: general revenue sharing, special grants to claimant states based on Commonwealth Grants Commission (CGC) calculations, and specific purpose payments (for more detail, see Sanders, 2023).

3 Recognition of the Need for Fiscal Redistribution

From the early days of federation, it was clear that the states required different levels of fiscal support; specifically, the states that were smaller in respect of population, although not always in respect of geographical size, needed more support. In 1926 a referendum was held on the proposal to entrench in the constitution the principle of awarding federal grants to the states on a *per capita* basis, but it failed – possibly because the *per capita* formula was already perceived to disadvantage some states (Saunders, 1990). Equally importantly, a High Court judgment under S96 confirmed the ability of the Commonwealth to impose 'such terms and conditions' on grants to the states as it 'thinks fit' (Fenna, 2023). By the outset of the Great Depression, three states were receiving special disadvantage grants from the Commonwealth to cover expenses they could not: Tasmania, WA, and South Australia (SA). By 1929, the growing fiscal needs of the states had brought home to the Commonwealth Government the need for some sort of fiscal uniformity or standardising efforts to equalise the states within the federation, and it established a Royal Commission into the Australian Constitution.

There is no doubt that efforts to seek a national solution to federal–state fiscal relations were further propelled by WA's referendum in April 1933, where nearly two-thirds of voters supported secession, but it nevertheless failed to be implemented. This referendum occurred under a Nationalist Party Premier, within the wider context of an ALP Federal Government. In the small states, talk of secession had been growing out of their fears of industrial and population centralisation in the larger states, particularly NSW and Victoria whose population shares had grown, from federation to 1931, to 39.2% and 27.5% respectively, while Tasmania's fell to 3.5% and SA's to 8.8% (Sanders, 2023). Australia's HFE system and its arms-length agency that recommends how Commonwealth funds are to be redistributed to the states, therefore, emerged out of both fiscal and political factors.

3.1 *Development of the HFE and the History of the CGC*

The Commonwealth Grants Commission (CGC) was established in 1933 with a mandate to make recommendations on special grants to the states, the intention being to enable claimants to achieve financial order equivalent to the other states. It was created as an independent 'expert' agency under Commonwealth legislation and not by Constitutional amendment. The CGC is an example of 'rationalising policymaking': that is, taking an important policy area out of the hands of politicians and avoiding politicised distributional struggles (Braun, 2006, p. 13). The CGC produced its first three reports between 1935 and 1937, when the sitting Prime Minister, Joseph Lyons, was also the former Premier of Tasmania, a fiscally weaker state that had received special grants. Perhaps Lyons understood better than most government executives why rationalisation was needed in this policy area. In these early reports, based on states' submissions, it became clear that Australian HFE would adopt 'a fiscal needs approach', making it possible for a claimant State 'by reasonable effort to function at a standard not appreciably below that of other States' (Productivity Commission, 2018). Prior to the establishment of the CGC, special grants, debt assistance, and payments were made on an *ad hoc* basis.

When the Commonwealth took over income taxation in Australia during the Second World War, the VFI increased, and the capacity of all states – including the largest, NSW and Victoria – to raise their own revenue to cover their expenditure needs fell. In the post-war period, while a portion of payments continued to be made to 'claimant states' based on equalisation calculations made by the CGC, 'specific-purpose payments' became a more important mechanism to financially assist and influence the delivery of services and infrastructures in the states. Specific-purpose payments are conditional and reflect the priorities of the federal government. In addition to tied grants, states were granted a share of united income tax reimbursements and general financial assistance calculated according to a formula based largely on population (with adjustments).

A considerable change occurred in the early 1970s. The CGC was re-established as an independent statutory authority when the Whitlam government (ALP) moved it out of the Prime Minister's portfolio. Financial grants were to be replaced by income-tax-sharing arrangements, and the Premiers decided that revenue under this arrangement was to be distributed on the basis of relativities based on equalisation principles (Productivity Commission, 2018). The purpose of CGC calculations was to 'make it possible for a State, by reasonable effort, to function at a standard not appreciably below the standards of the other states'. Since 1978, under the States' Amendment Act, the same funding source was used to address both vertical and horizontal inequality, and the CGC recommendations would affect all states, not just those in fiscal need, making HFE in Australia *de facto* a zero-sum game. Any efforts to make a state better off would result in another being worse off. In 1981, the wording was further amended to 'same standards', representing a principle of full equalisation that was maintained until 2018.

3.2 *The Institutionalisation of HFE: Method and Principles in Practice*

It was the application of CGC methods to the larger portion of revenues to be redistributed (general revenue sharing) from the 1980s that established the CGC as an institution of fiscal federalism in Australia (Sanders, 2023). The CGC's 'Direct Assessment Method' entailed that various expenditure disability and revenue capacity factors could be measured in standardised state budgets and summed to give a total state factor, or relativity, compared to all other states, thus applying the relativities to all general revenue sharing on a per capita basis and financial assistance grants to claimant states to combine the two categories (Sanders, 2023).While the distribution game between the states remained zero-sum until 2018, the amount of the pie to be divided between them decreased from 1985 onwards, because of federal efforts to reduce budget deficits.

The ability of the states to cover their expenditure needs was further diminished in 1997 when the High Court declared in *Ha* v. *New South Wales* 189 CLR 465 that tobacco franchise fees were 'duties of excise' that are within the exclusive power of the Commonwealth (S96). In *Ha,* the High Court interpreted S90 of the Constitution to mean that a 'duty of excise' is a tax on the production, manufacture, distribution, or sale of goods up to the point of consumption. This case substantially undermined state tax bases and was a critical factor in the introduction of the Goods and Services Tax (GST) (value-added tax) to replace the former Commonwealth wholesale sales tax in 2000 (Twomey, 2008). The extent of the Commonwealth's exclusive power over all taxes related to goods was recently extended even further to the consumption of goods, in the case of *Vanderstock v State of Victoria* [2023] HCA 30. In *Vanderstock*, the High Court found by a 4:3 majority that Victoria's electric vehicle charging regime in the Zero and Low Emission Vehicle Distance-based Charge Act 2021 (Vic) was unconstitutional, as applied to the 'consumption' of the goods being the electric vehicles and could affect the supply and price of, or demand for, such vehicles, and was therefore an excise.

The reform that introduced the GST in 2000 also led to the methods and principles of HFE becoming much clearer and more firmly institutionalised. The GST replaced not only the unconstitutional franchise fees, but also many of the earlier financial assistance grants (Braun, 2006, p. 27). The GST was enacted as a Commonwealth tax but was to be collected and administered by the Commonwealth on behalf of the states (who paid an agreed sum for the administration each year). The entire GST was distributed to the states and territories, in the same way as previous Commonwealth grants to the states, equalised with the help of the CGC. From 2000 until 2018, the Commonwealth Government had little involvement in this process, aside from the Treasurer's implicit support of GST relativities, and regular reviews of HFE methodology (Productivity Commission, 2018). The GST did reduce the states' dependence on annual revenue decisions and improve their fiscal security; it did not, however, increase their fiscal autonomy, given that approximately half of Australian government payments to the states remain tied to specific purposes (Australian Treasury, 2022).

Between 2000 and 2018, the CGC recommended the distribution of the GST according to the following principle (Productivity Commission 2018, p. 21):

> State Governments should receive funding from the pool of goods and services tax revenue such that, after allowing for material factors affecting revenues and expenditures, each would have the fiscal capacity to provide services and the associated infrastructure at the same standard, if each made the same effort to raise revenue from its own sources and operated at the same level of efficiency.

The CGC's aim of achieving 'full equalisation' was guided by four principles: what the states do collectively; policy neutrality that does not disincentivise individual state actions; practicality; and contemporaneity. Conceptually, the CGC formula, which is very complex and comprehensive and covers all state general government activities, does the following: states with relatively low fiscal capacities are raised to the average (pre-GST) fiscal capacity of all states; all states are then raised to the capacity of the fiscally strongest state (historically NSW or Victoria, but WA after 2008–9); any remaining revenue from the GST pool is distributed to all states on an equity per capita basis (Productivity Commission, 2018).

However, the calculations of the distribution, because of their complexity, are well known to entail a time lag. GST equalisation analysis is carried out each year by the CGC, based on a three-year average level of revenue collection and service delivery across states, and calculated over the previous three years. For example, an assessment in 2018–19 would average the result over the *previous* three years (2017–18, 2016–17, 2015–16), and the relativity factor would then be applied for the *next* year (2019–20) – that is, only in the fourth year are the relativities updated. Actual expenditures or policies are not relevant, except in so far as they may affect the average against which all states are judged. The equalisation process pushes states towards the national average expenditure (neither more nor less). Assume that a hypothetical state decided to build specialised hospitals in every area of 20,000 people and these health expenses are calculated by the CGC based on how many sick people there are in the state, the state would have to fund any spending on a health choice that was higher than the *national average*. Applying the average, the GST relativity is calculated for each state or territory, which is then used to modify the per capita allocation.

The inherent tensions within the HFE system pre-2018 were based on the logic that to lift up states with lower-than-average revenue capacity (calculated tax by tax for every state), other states must be made worse off. As Thomson (2023) lucidly explains, this means that, in any given year, some states will have relativities less than one, indicating that they will receive an entitlement smaller than their per capita share of the GST pool, while to balance this, other states will receive more than their per capita share.

The factors that have the biggest impact on differences between states leading to HFE relativities are mining royalties; land and property sales and taxable land values; remoteness of the population; the share of Indigenous people in the population; payrolls of large companies; the existence of big cities; and the existence of Commonwealth Payments for Specific Purposes (grants). The HFE determination applies directly only to the GST, but the effect of specific grants is 'equalised' away over time, because most state taxes and other federal grants are considered in applying the formula. In practice, this is significant because it depoliticises the impact of specific-purpose grants that are made in agreement between the Commonwealth and the states, lowering the propensity of these grants to have a punish and reward effort, or to be used as 'pork-barrel' politics – a common practice more frequently observed in more competitive models of federalism such as the USA.

To illustrate, the pre-reform distribution of GST revenues and relativities for 2017–18 are shown in Table 4.1. NSW received 87.67% of its per capita GST revenue, Victoria 93.24%, while WA received a very low 34.43%. Among the recipient states, SA received 144% of its per capita allocation and the Northern Territory (NT) an enormous 466% (the categories of mining royalties, remoteness, and Indigenous population are significant here).

4 Political Challenges to HFE: The 2018 Reforms

All federal systems undertaking the territorial redistribution of fiscal resources by means of equalisation programs designed to resolve horizontal and vertical fiscal imbalances run the risk of generating intergovernmental tensions. Australia is no exception, even though, compared to other more decentralised federal systems such as Canada and, more recently, Spain, such intergovernmental conflicts remain relatively low (see Lecours and Beland, 2013). The territorial allocation of resources creates 'winners' and 'losers' and finding an equilibrium – both empirically and politically – is no small feat. As explained above, the CGC is a quasi-autonomous arm's-length technocratic agency that recommends to the Commonwealth Treasurer annual GST revenue-sharing relativities. These recommendations are based on the reported principles and methodology of the CGC. It is important to note that the CGC does not engage in the politics of equalisation; its recommendations derive from the terms of reference set forth by the Commonwealth under its *de jure* S96 powers and *de facto* as a product of intergovernmental financial agreements involving both

TABLE 4.1 GST distribution relativities and outcomes (2017–18)

	NSW	VIC	QLD	WA	SA	TAS	ACT	NT
2017–18 GST relativity	0.87672	0.93239	1.18769	0.34434	1.43997	1.80477	1.19496	4.66024
Population[a]	7,915,069	6,385,849	4,965,033	2,584,768	1,728,053	524,677	415,916	246,726
Total GST received $m[b]	17,791	15,268	15,110	2,285	6,374	2,417	1,266	2,928
2018–19 GST relativity	0.85517	0.98670	1.09584	0.47287	1.47727	1.76706	1.18070	4.25816
Population[c]	8,052,909	6,532,744	5,041,416	2,617,739	1,740,939	525,707	420,123	245,946
GST entitlement $m[b]	18,442	17,261	14,794	3,315	6,887	2,488	1,328	2,805
Average relativity since 2000[d]	0.90126	0.89103	1.03502	0.72395	1.28004	1.68175	1.20221	5.09715

[a] As at 31 December 2017. Source: Australian Demographic Statistics, Dec 2017 (ABS Cat. No. 3101.0).
[b] Estimate. Based on GST pool forecasts as presented in the Commonwealth's 2018–19 Budget.
[c] Estimate as of 31 December 2018. Based on state population forecasts as presented in the Commonwealth's 2018–19 Budget.
[d] Average from 2000–1 to 2018–19. Relativities prior to 2009–10 reflect the CGC's calculation of a pool comprising of GST only (relativities previously recommended by the CGC were based on a pool comprising both GST and healthcare grants)

SOURCE: (STEWART, 2023, P. 30)

the Commonwealth and state governments. In 2018, however, the rules of the equalisation game were changed in both practice and procedure.

Following receipt of the Productivity Commission report (2018), the Commonwealth Government amended the Federal Financial Relations Act and Commonwealth Grants Commission Act to adopt a new equalisation formula, commencing in 2021–22 (Parliament of the Commonwealth of Australia, 2018a, p. 7 [1.11]). This reform was mainly in response to political pressure from WA, where the CGC's decisions on GST calculations reviewed every three years were regarded as 'unacceptable to Western Australians' (Premier Colin Barnett, 2010, quoted in Zimmermann, 2012). It is notable that the new approach was not achieved by an amendment to the Intergovernmental Agreement on Federal Financial Relations (which would have required unanimous agreement of all the states and territories); nor does it implement many of the recommendations in the Productivity Commission report. The Explanatory Memorandum for the reform explained that the GST distribution system had worked reasonably well but 'the mining boom revealed that it does not function well when faced with economic shocks'. In essence, questions were being raised in some wealthier states around the 'fairness' of full equalisation. When the new act was passed in the House of Representatives, on 18 October 2018, the Coalition Treasurer, Josh Frydenberg, stated (House of Representatives, 2018, No. 10396):

> The government has consulted extensively with all states on its proposal since the release of its interim response [to the Productivity Commission Inquiry]. But, unlike changes to the rate and the base of the GST, changes to the distribution of GST revenue do not require the approval of the states and territories. It is the Commonwealth's job to govern for all Australians.

4.1 *The Reform Package*

The updated HFE system came into full effect from 2021–22 (Bill 143, 2018), with the new arrangements were originally intended to apply in full for 2026–27. The new updated system transitions from full equalisation to 'reasonable' equalisation via three steps:

1. The Commonwealth will provide short-term transition payments to ensure no State or Territory receives less than 70 cents per person per dollar of GST revenue and the Government will ensure the NT keeps at least its 2017–18 share of GST revenue (pre-reform). This is a guarantee that no state is 'worse off' than under the previous system.
2. Under the new system, the States will be equalised to the standard of the fiscally stronger of NSW or Victoria from 2021–22 to 2026–27. By 2024–25, the floor will be raised to 0.75 per person per dollar of GST revenue. In

addition, the Government will permanently boost the GST revenue pool by increasing monies sourced from other Commonwealth revenues.

3. By 2026–27 the transition should be complete with the 'no worse off' guarantee effectively ceasing.

The GST pool top-up, therefore, is an external payment in perpetuity, set at a fixed amount intended to provide a slight increase to the GST distribution (eventually making all states better off). It was not intended to alter the zero-sum logic of the HFE system, whereby to lift up some state, other states must be made worse off. The transitional 'no worse off' payments, however, which are not to be made in perpetuity (although this is what the states would have collectively preferred), are being funded externally to the GST pool. This clause was extended on the 6th of December 2023 to 2029–30 (Australian Treasury 2023). Therefore, this first extension, has already signalled the HFE is transitioning to a positive sum-game – a game that in other federations is known to generate greater intergovernmental political tensions.

4.2 *Structural Challenges to HFE: Territorial Diversity and Variation in Fiscal Dependence*

Prior to the 2018 reform described above, challenges from the states were based on their structural realities. Since the introduction of the GST in 2000, the GST pool in any given year is fixed – which creates the parameters of a zero-sum game. This game leads to challenges *between* the states, based on accusations of unfairness over who gets what – not challenges towards the Commonwealth over the amount of the pool to be distributed. Most of the reasons behind the CGC calculations that determine why states receive differing GST shares are not controversial – such as variation in demographic and social circumstances. Economic circumstances within a particular state, however, such as mining resources, are controversial. For example, mining royalties provided $14.8 billion in revenue for the state (and territory) governments in 2018–19, which accounts for an average contribution of 18% to own-state revenue (Freebairn and Griffiths, 2023, p. 192). The contribution of royalty revenues to state budgets, however, varies considerably across the states.

Australia has a *dominant state problem*, whereby its mineral base is concentrated in a few states (Qld, SA, WA). Why is this a problem? In 2018, for example, the royalty rates for iron ore, bauxite, and onshore oil and gas were higher than for other minerals such as copper and nickel. This means, under the pre-2018 HFE assessment rules, that states which increase the production of those higher-value minerals (not including offshore oil and gas-LNG) can lose more in GST revenue than they raise in royalty revenue (CGC, 2018). Across the states, the share in the value of production of these major minerals also

TABLE 4.2 Share of value of production (2016–17) (in %)

Group	NSW	Vic	Qld	WA	SA	Tas	ACT	NT	Total
Major Minerals*	15.7	0.4	30.6	51.5	1.0	0.4	0.0	0.4	100
Other Minerals	11.5	3.4	15.2	49.1	10.0	2.7	0.0	8.2	100

SOURCE: (CGC, 2018, P. 6). *MAJOR MINERALS ARE IRON ORE, BAUXITE, AND ONSHORE OIL AND GAS

varies considerably. This means that the HFE revenue assessments can operate as a performance disincentive in these valuable national areas of revenue production (see Table 4.2). Moreover, this effect – which is considered by states such as WA as 'unfair' – contravenes the CGC's principle of 'policy neutrality'.

In 2015, all the Premiers of the States and Territories, except for WA, collectively wrote to the Treasurer (Coalition) arguing against any potential special treatment of WA to offset its growing economic volatility caused by declining iron ore prices (Letter to Hon. J. B. Hockey, 16 April 2015). From its own perspective, however, WA argued that the fact its per capita relativity fell in 2015 to less than 30 cent per dollar of GST was 'unfair' (see Table 4.3).

To offset the potential intergovernmental tensions generated by the 2018 GST deal for WA, the Commonwealth offered, as it had done previously in 2000 with the introduction of the GST, its so-called compensatory 'worse-off'

TABLE 4.3 Per capita relativities across the states and territories (2010–2020)

	NSW	Vic	ACT	Tas	SA	Qld	WA	NT
*R2010	0.95205	0.93995	1.15295	1.62091	1.28497	0.91322	0.68298	5.07383
*U2012	0.95312	0.92106	1.19757	1.58088	1.28472	0.98477	0.55105	5.52818
R2015	0.94737	0.89254	1.10012	1.81906	1.35883	1.12753	0.29999	5.57053
U2018	0.85517	0.98670	1.18070	1.76706	1.47727	1.09584	0.47287	4.25816
R2020	0.91808	0.95992	1.15112	1.89742	1.35765	1.04907	0.44970	4.76893

Notes: *U refers to CGC "updates" whereas *R refers to CGC reviews
SOURCE: (SANDERS, 2023)

payments. This frequently used mechanism in Australian fiscal federalism in practice buys the acquiescence of the states to fiscal reform. It was well understood, however, by executives at all levels of government that agreed to the new HFE rules, that the efficiency of the new system would be dependent on WA's relativity. If, for example, WA's assessed relativity is consistently lower than the guaranteed floor, the new system disadvantages the other states – particularly when the 'no worse-off' guarantee ceases in 2030. Because of the rebound of iron ore prices in 2017, WA's iron ore royalties, relative wage levels and population growth have resulted in precisely this scenario. WA's 'assessed relativity' (which means under the old HFE system) in 2022 was 0.15784 – well below its guaranteed floor of 0.70 (CGC 2022; see Table 4.4 below).

4.3 *Fiscal Challenges to HFE: No-Worse-Off Guarantees*

The Australian Treasury explained (Parliament of the Commonwealth of Australia, 2018a) that, under the new HFE reform bill, short-term transition payments would be made during the first three years, 2019–22, and that by 2022–23, the floor guarantee would be implemented, but that no jurisdiction's 'assessed' relativity was expected to fall below 0.70. It estimated, when the reforms were legislated in 2018, that the additional funding required to support the transition would cost the Commonwealth nearly $9 billion over ten years. However, because WA's assessed relativity did fall well below 0.7 in 2022–23 (see Table 4.4), the additional funding required was well above the 2018 estimates.

In federal budget paper no. 3 (Australian Treasury, 2022), the government estimated the transition payments at $15.7 billion. The GST pool top-up of $4 billion dollars alone could not guarantee that the states were not worse off than they were under the previous HFE system, in 2022–23, when the GST relativity floor of 0.70 operated from within the GST pool. Thus, as WA and the NT would receive an increased share of the GST pool in 2022–23, all the other states would receive less, thereby triggering no-worse-off payments by the Commonwealth. Under the new system, WA is now assessed to have revenue per capita greater than its assessed expenditure per capita, and all the other states are assessed to have slightly less assessed revenue than assessed expenditure (CGC 2022, p. 19) – this is why the new HFE system that redistributes Australia's untied grants is now considered to equate to 'partial equalisation' and not full.[1] This raises key questions as to the efficiency of partial

1 General revenue assistance as discussed herein – as delivered through the distribution of GST revenues – is only part of the fiscal relationship between the Commonwealth and the States (for more detail, see Thomson, 2023).

TABLE 4.4 Assessed relativities (old system) to GST relativities (2022–23)

	Assessed relativities	Standard state relativities	Blended relativities	GST relativities
NSW	1.01373	0.93448	0.98742	0.95065
Vic	0.92170	0.84245	0.89538	0.85861
Qld	1.09684	1.01758	1.07053	1.03377
WA	0.15784	0.84245	0.38608	0.70000
SA	1.34715	1.26790	1.32087	1.28411
Tas	1.91658	1.83733	1.89037	1.85360
ACT	1.15556	1.07631	1.12927	1.09250
NT	4.93255	4.85329	4.90665	4.86988

SOURCE: (CGC, 2022, COMMISSION CALCULATIONS, P. 20)

compared to full equalisation, as well as issues over fiscal sustainability of the new system, given that the no-worse-off payments are covered by external Commonwealth funds.

The standard state relativities reflect what the system was supposed to look like in 2026–27, when the transition was to be completed, and all states were to be raised to the 'standard state', which in this case is Victoria. If the GST pool by 2030 now is 'fixed – that is, no more no-worse-off payments are made, and thus the equalisation game returns to being zero-sum – states fiscally stronger than the standard state are winners, and all other states are losers. Without the no-worse-off payments in 2022–23, Victoria is the biggest loser under the new rules. With the floor now in place, WA will receive $3.7 billion dollars of GST more than it did in the previous year.

As can be seen in Table 4.5, in 2022–23 all the states except for WA will receive a no-worse-off payment external to the GST pool, equivalent to the amount reflected in the difference between the old system offset by the perpetual GST top-ups, and the new HFE system. It should be noted that none of the changes to the distribution of the GST to the states in 2022–23 was related to the COVID-19 pandemic. The Treasurer has the discretion to exclude some Commonwealth payments from the CGC assessments. Therefore, even though the COVID-19 pandemic affected states' revenue raising and expenditures, Commonwealth-funded payments made to the states attached to national

TABLE 4.5 Impact of 2018 legislated arrangements on the distribution of the GST pool (excludes no-worse-off payments) (2022–23)

	NSW	Vic	Qld	WA	SA	Tas	ACT	NT	Total
	$m	$m	$m	$m	$m	$m	$m	$m	$m
Estimated GST pool distribution	23.218	17.167	16.384	5.682	6.865	3.035	1.421	3.644	77.416
Distribution under previous arrangements	24.565	18.285	17.248	1.271	7.145	3.113	1.492	3.662	76.780
Difference	−1.347	−1.117	−863	4.410	−281	−79	−70	−18	636

SOURCE: (CGC, 2022, COMMISSION CALCULATIONS, P. 44)

response initiatives were not included as revenue by the CGC in assessing how much GST a state requires.

4.4 *Future Political Challenges to the No-Worse-Off Payments: Policy Feedbacks*

It is well established that policies create feedback effects over time that affect future policy adjustments, wholesale reforms, and/or termination (Beland, 2010, *inter alia*). As Pierson's (1993) seminal work established, the main mechanism that produces these feedbacks is, quite simply, politics. Policies both create and change politics, and the Treasury Laws Amendment Bill (2018) is no exception. As Australia's HFE system transitions from full to partial equalisation, indeed, it has created new intergovernmental politics over the territorial distribution of resources and new Intergovernmental Relations tensions that amount to more than 'low level state grumblings' (Lecours and Beland 2013). The new partial equalisation system was legislated to include two future dated federal reviews: the 2025 CGC methodology review, and a 2026 inquiry by the Productivity Commission into its efficiency. As we noted in the previous section, however, the dominant-state problem and the unprecedented surge in iron ore prices, followed consequentially by the blowout to the fiscal cost of the no-worse-off payments, are already calling into question the updated system's longer-term fiscal sustainability and 'efficiency'. The new financial split between resource-endowed states versus those not reaping the rewards of the mining boom also calls into question the 'equity' of the HFE – a longstanding norm in Australian fiscal federalism. Only two states are currently clear winners, first WA, and now Queensland.

According to modelling scenarios conducted by the states themselves, most of them had expected to remain worse off under the new HFE system when the guaranteed payments had originally been set to expire in 2026–27 (see Tasmania State Government, 2021; Victoria State Government, 2022). In contrast to full equalisation, a system of 'partial' equalisation is designed to generate a certain degree of horizontal inequity. Whether or not this is accepted is often a societal question unique to each federation – according to Beland and Lecours (2014), for example, both societal factors, such as the degree of support for social citizenship, and institutional factors, such as any threat to national and territorial unity, come into play. For Beland and Lecours (2014), Australia's equalisation programme is associated with an egalitarian creed even bolder than that stated in the 1982 Canadian constitution.

In the post-2018 Australian context, with a revenue floor now locked in and the current Labor government assuring Western Australians that 'it will be preserved' (West Australian, 2023), it remains to be seen if these new changes will undermine the egalitarian ethos of Australia's HFE. If the revenue floor is indeed maintained, the question remaining is what future reform options are feasible to prevent an Australia fiscally divided between resource-rich states and the populous and increasingly highly indebted states such as Victoria and SA. Although state-level public-sector debt in Australia is currently fiscally sustainable, since 2009 it has increased unevenly (Fenwick, 2023). In 2020–21, for example, the NT had the highest ratio of state net debt to GSP of 20.4%, followed by Victoria at 13.5%, and SA at 10.5% (ABS, Customised Report, 2022).

The Premiers clearly asserted to the Senate Standing Committee on Economics in November 2018 that the states would prefer an in-perpetuity guarantee, noting that the current guarantee was to effectively cease in 2026–27 (Parliament of Australia, 2018b), but has since been extended to 2029–30 (Australian Treasury, 2023). All states (except WA, Tasmania, and the NT) had a net deficit operating balance in 2021–22 (Fenwick 2023); in 2023 Queensland achieved a record budget surplus of $12 billion, thanks to increasing coal royalties (Queensland Treasury, 2023). As the Premier of SA succinctly put it, therefore, 'extending the top-up payments would appease his state's concerns' (Peter Malinauskas, quoted in the West Australian, 2023).

With political pressure from the Premiers, extending the no-worse off guarantees was the only feasible solution in 2023. The commitment by the Treasury Laws Amendment (2018) to the Federal Financial Relations Act 2009 to 'guarantee that each State and Territory will get funding equal to the better of the current distribution system or the update distribution during the transition period' and to 'permanently boost the GST pool with additional Commonwealth assistance' implies, at least to the states, opening the door, both *de facto* and *de jure,* to a positive-sum fiscal game. This is because, first, making WA better off, did not, at least until 20, make the other states and territories worse off and, second, the HFE reforms of 2018 changed the rules of the game because the GST pool is no longer finite – that is, financed exclusively from annual GST revenues. While this is certainly a new direction in the politics of equalisation in Australia, other alternatives exist. For example, Stewart (2023) suggests that equalisation could apply to 50% of income tax and 50% of GST which would expand the pool considerably and shift funding from 'tied' to 'untied' grants.

The other feasible option, according to the CGC, is to revert to the old system of 'full' equalisation (Interview, 2023).[2] This would seem unlikely, however, given the cost and efforts undertaken to transform the older system into one of 'reasonable' equalisation, to avoid charges of 'unfairness'. Moreover, in 2023, all the states and territories, bar Tasmania, are politically aligned with the Commonwealth government, enhancing the prospects of negotiation and compromise. Nevertheless, restoring the old system remains, legally at least, a possibility, as the Treasurer has full discretion to set the terms of reference that the CGC must follow.

5 Conclusions

The goal of this chapter is to outline the key defining characteristics of fiscal federalism in Australia, highlight recent reforms, and frame future challenges. Even though Australia has one of the most dramatic vertical fiscal imbalances among federal systems globally, it also has one of the most egalitarian systems of fiscal equalisation. There are many examples throughout the federation's history, of constituent units (states and territories), voluntarily, or through various types of transactional negotiations, delegating their revenue powers to the Commonwealth. Over time this has consequently produced an even more fiscally centralised federation. These federal bargains were often based on promises of more predictable revenue flows during times of fiscal turbulence, such as the world wars, the Great Depression, and more recent recessions.

2 In person interview by Fenwick with Anonymous Senior Consultant, CGC, 4th of April 2023, Canberra.

Following the introduction of the GST in Australia in 2000, the HFE system and the agency that oversees its implementation, the CGC, were both firmly institutionalised with a consistent methodology and policy intention: to achieve 'full equalisation'. Yet although it is agreed that Australia's HFE has never generated high levels of intergovernmental conflict, territorial diversity (*the dominant-state problem*), and the variation in fiscal dependence on Commonwealth transfers, led to structural challenges to the HFE system. The 2018 reform package, transforming its purpose from 'full'to 'partial' equalisation, was an attempt to meet these challenges.

Two main unintended policy-feedback effects that will affect future reforms and policy developments can be observed as a result of the HFE updates: clear fiscal divisions between the resource-rich states of WA and Queensland and the larger indebted south-eastern states of NSW and Victoria; and the signal from the Commonwealth that the rules of the game have transformed from zero-sum to positive-sum. The former leads to the sort of territorial inequality that has not been seen in Australia since the early days of federation – there are clear winners and losers. Regardless of partisanship, therefore, the states aligned to press the Commonwealth to continue their 'no-worse-off guarantees' until 2029–30 – this is a clear indication of a critical juncture in Commonwealth–state fiscal relations.

The second unintended policy effect of the updated HFE system is that it has opened the door to a positive-sum game whereby the Commonwealth must keep using revenues generated externally to the GST to compensate the losing states. This in turn is known as a 'lock-in effect', a key mechanism that explains how policy choices affect politics, and how those politics constrain future policy developments (see Beland 2010). Stated briefly, the Commonwealth's guarantee to every state of a revenue floor of 75 cents to every dollar contributed, regardless of its revenue-raising capacity, offset by temporarily compensating the other states for any revenue loss, greatly increases the cost of either reverting or adopting once-possible alternatives. Only time will tell what will occur in 2029–30 when the no-worse-off guarantees cease, but a return to full equalisation is unlikely.

References

ABS [Australian Bureau of Statistics] (2022). *Customised Report*. Canberra: ABS.

Australian Treasury (2022). *Budget October 2022–2023*. Budget paper no. 3: Federal financial relations. Canberra: Commonwealth of Australia, Department of the Treasury.

Australian Treasury (2023). "Extension of "No Worse Off" deal to help fund essential services" *Media Brief*, 6th of December. Available at https://ministers.treasury.gov.au/ministers/jim-chalmers-2022/media-releases/extension-no-worse-deal-help-fund-essential-services.

Beland, D. (2010). Reconsidering policy feedback: how policies affect politics. *Administration & Society*, 42(5), 568–590.

Beland, D. and A. Lecours (2014). Fiscal federalism and American exceptionalism: why is there no federal equalisation in the United States? *Journal of Public Policy*, 34(2), 303–329.

Banting, K. G. (2006). Social citizenship and federalism: is a federal welfare state a contradiction in terms? In S. Greer (Ed.), *Territory, Democracy, and Justice* (pp. 44–67). New York: Palgrave Macmillan.

Braun, D. (2006). Between market-preserving federalism and intergovernmental coordination: the case of Australia. *Swiss Political Science Review*, 12(2), 1–36.

CGC [Commonwealth Grants Commission] (2018). *Improving the policy neutrality of the mining revenue assessment.* Staff discussion paper CGC 2018–07-S. Canberra: Commonwealth of Australia.

CGC [Commonwealth Grants Commission] (2022). *GST revenue sharing relativities: 2022 update (March)*. Canberra: Commonwealth of Australia.

Fenna, A. (2023). The revival of Australian federalism? Trends and developments in Commonwealth–state relations. In A. Podger, H. S. Chan, T. Su, & J. Wanna (Eds.), *Dilemmas in Public Management in Greater China and Australia: Rising Tensions but Common Challenges* (pp. 117–144). Canberra: ANU Press.

Fenwick, T. B. (2023). Borrowing to compete or survive a pandemic? New directions in Australian federalism. *Cuadernos Manuel Gimenez Abad*, Special Issue 9, 35–53.

Freebairn, J. & W. Griffiths (2023). Volatile mining revenues and state government budget decisions. *Australian Economic Review*, 56(2), 192–203.

Galligan, B. (2012). Fiscal federalism: then and now. In G. Appleby, N. Aroney & T. John (Eds.), *The Future of Australian Federalism* (pp. 320–338). Cambridge: Cambridge University Press.

House of Representatives, Parliament of Australia (2018). *Official Hansard*, no. 14, 18 October. Canberra: Commonwealth of Australia.

Lecours, A. & D. Beland (2013). The institutional politics of territorial redistribution: federalism and equalization policy in Australia and Canada. *Canadian Journal of Political Science*, 46(1), 93–113.

Parliament of the Commonwealth of Australia (2018a). *Treasury Laws Amendment (Making sure every state and territory gets their fair share of the GS) Bill 2018. Explanatory Memorandum.* Canberra: Commonwealth of Australia.

Parliament of the Commonwealth of Australia (2018b). *Treasury Laws Amendment (Making sure every state and territory gets their fair share of the GS) Bill 2018. Bills Digest,* no. 42, 12 November. Canberra: Commonwealth of Australia.

Pierson, P. (1993). When effect becomes cause: policy feedback and political change. *World Politics,* 45, 595–628.

Productivity Commission (2018). *Horizontal fiscal equalization.* Report no. 88, 15 May. Canberra: Commonwealth of Australia.

Queensland Treasury (2023). Budget Overview, 2023–2023. Government of Queensland. Available at https://www.treasury.qld.gov.au/resource/state-budget-2023-24/.

Riker, W. (1975). Federalism. In F. J. Greenstein and N. W. Polsby (Eds.), *Handbook of Political Science,* vol. 5 (pp. 93–173). MASS: Addison Wesley.

Rodden, J. and E. Wibbels (2002). Beyond the fiction of federalism: macroeconomic management in multitiered systems. *World Politics,* 54(4), 494–531.

Sanders, W. (2023). Fiscal equalisation in Australian federalism: managing diversity of size among subnational jurisdictions. In F. Romero Caro (Ed.), *Fiscal Federalism and Diversity Accommodation in Multilevel States.* New York: Palgrave Macmillan.

Saunders, C. (1990). Government borrowing in Australia. *Publius: The Journal of Federalism,* 20(4), 35–52.

Stewart, M. (2023). Australia. In J. F. Tremblay (Ed.), *The Forum of Federations Handbook on Fiscal Federalism* (pp. 1–59). New York: Palgrave Macmillan.

Tasmania State Government (2021). *Occasional paper: New GST distribution arrangements, September.* Hobart: Government of Tasmania, Department of Treasury and Finance.

Thomson, R. (2023). Federal financial relations in Australia. In A. Podger, H. S. Chan, T. Su & J. Wanna (Eds.), *Dilemmas in Public Management in Greater China and Australia: Rising Tensions but Common Challenges* (pp. 145–162). Canberra: ANU Press.

Twomey, A. (2008). Reforming Australia's federal system. *Federal Law Review,* 36(1), 57–81.

Victoria State Government (2022). The fiscal impacts of the new GST system on Victoria. *Victoria's Economic Bulletin,* 3(3), 1–14.

West Australian (2023). The east smells blood on WA's GST deal, 31 May.

Zimmermann, A. (2012). The still reluctant state: Western Australia and the conceptual foundations of Australian federalism. In G. Appelby, N. Aroney & T. John (Eds.), *The Future of Australian Federalism* (pp. 66–74). Cambridge: Cambridge University Press.

CHAPTER 5

The Political Economy of Federal Equalisation Policy in Canada

Olivier Jacques
Department of health policy management and evaluation, School of Public Health (Université de Montréal) & Centre d'Analyse Politique – Constitution et Fédéralisme

Daniel Béland
Department of Political Science and Director of the McGill Institute for the Study of Canada (McGill University)

André Lecours
School of Political Studies (University of Ottawa)

1 Introduction

Equalisation policy is a central and contentious aspect of fiscal federalism in Canada (Lecours et al., 2023). This chapter analyses the political economy of equalisation in Canada and is divided into three main sections. The first section discusses the structure of the equalisation and transfer programs to highlight their main goals, formulas, and results, while considering their current problems. To do so, it presents the historical evolution of the program and of the level of transfers achieved by each of the three major transfer programs over time. We contend that we cannot understand the political, distributive and, economic dimensions of equalisation in Canada without also referring to the Canada Health Transfer (CHT) and the Canada Social Transfer (CST) and therefore, we broaden our analysis to these two major federal intergovernmental transfers.

The second section builds on our previous research on the politics of equalisation and intergovernmental transfers (Borwein et al., 2023; Jacques, 2024; Jacques et al., 2021a; Jacques & Graefe, 2023; Lecours & Béland, 2010) and analyses public opinion about these issues by relying on representative surveys of the Canadian population conducted annually from 2019 to 2023. We demonstrate that support for equalisation is generally well entrenched in public opinion, but we reveal important divisions based on ideology, place-based

DOI:10.1163/9789004524514_007

resentment, and identity within richer provinces. Intergovernmental transfers, in contrast to equalisation, are significantly more consensual among different segments of the public and across provinces. The third section concludes the chapter by discussing the limits of the equalisation and intergovernmental transfer systems as evidenced by the COVID-19 crisis and the future challenges related to an aging population.

2 The Structure of the Program and Historical Landmarks

2.1 *Goals of Equalisation and of Transfers*

The objective of the federal equalisation program is to reduce horizontal fiscal disparities among the 10 provinces "to ensure that provincial governments have sufficient revenues to provide reasonably comparable levels of public services at reasonably comparable levels of taxation." (Subsection 36(2), Constitution Act, 1982) In contrasts to CHT and the CST payments, federal equalisation payments do not have any strings attached, a situation that preserves the autonomy of receiving provinces, who are entitled to equalisation when they fall under a national average of provincial fiscal capacity calculated through a formula based on the Representative Tax System. In contrast to equalisation programs in other federal countries, Canada's equalisation program only calculates transfers based on fiscal capacity, which means that expenditure needs are not taken into consideration (Béland et al., 2017).

The CHT and the CST are block grants that allocate payments to the provinces on a per capita basis to fulfil their responsibilities in specific policy areas. In contrast to equalisation, which only makes payments to provinces whose fiscal capacity falls under a national average, these two transfers target all the provinces but also to the three territories (Northwest Territory, Nunavut, and Yukon). The CHT and CST exist because, while the provinces and territories have major health care and social policy responsibilities within Canada's highly decentralised welfare state, the federal government has more fiscal capacity, which creates the need for a federal fiscal contribution. Although the two transfers are conditional, their infringement on provincial autonomy is quite limited in nature, as the principles the jurisdictions have to follow to receive full funding are very broad and not always strongly enforced by the federal government. This is especially clear regarding the CHT, which is tied to the 1984 Canada Health Act and its five principles: public administration, comprehensiveness, universality, portability, and accessibility. The federal government can withdraw a fraction of the transfer if provinces do not respect one of these principles, but in practice, provinces have been able to allow for some degree of private delivery and funding of health care services without seeing their transfers withdrawn. Although all the provinces and territories receive CHT and CST money from the federal government on a per capita basis, there is some implicit redistribution involved because richer provinces with a stronger tax base contribute more to the federal budget than poorer provinces (Béland et al., 2017).

2.2 *Historical Evolution*

The federal equalisation program was created in 1957. Fiscal federalism in Canada changed during World War II as the federal government 'rented' tax space from the provinces in order to maximise its fiscal capacity to contribute to the war effort. These 'tax rentals' survived the end of the war in most provinces, but Québec refused to renew this agreement, choosing instead to impose its own corporate and personal income tax for financing its activities. Breaking the fiscal isolation of Québec was a key motivation for the creation of the fiscal equalisation program along with the broader objective of achieving consistent financing for provinces with weaker fiscal capacity.

Equalisation underwent several different types of changes since its creation. The first involves the type of tax revenues included in the formula. Originally, there were only three (personal income tax, corporate tax, and succession duties), but this number increased steadily, reaching 33 in the 1980s. This increase was a major contributor to the mounting complexity of the program, and the number of tax bases was eventually streamlined to five: personal income tax, corporate tax, sales tax, property tax, and natural resource revenue. The second features the number of provinces whose fiscal capacity is considered to establish an 'equalisation standard' (roughly corresponding to the average fiscal capacity). This number was originally two but is currently ten (and it has also been five between 1982 and 2007, when the objective was to reduce the overall equalisation cost by excluding Alberta and its high, oil revenue-derived, fiscal capacity from the formula). The third type of change involved natural resources, a controversial question in Canada since provinces that produce oil and gas (most importantly Alberta) want these revenues shielded from the equalisation formula. To make a compromise with oil-producing provinces, only 50% of the revenues from natural resources are included into the calculation of provincial fiscal capacity, although there has been full inclusion of these revenues in the past. Importantly, there is a 'cap' that stops equalisation payment before they bring the fiscal capacity of a receiving province above that of a non-receiving province.

The principle of making equalisation payments (rather than the equalisation program itself) was enshrined in the *Constitution Act, 1982*, which gives it not only protection against dismantlement but also great legitimacy. Reflective of such legitimacy and of the notion of equalisation as the glue that holds the federation together is the fact that that program essentially escaped all of Canada's periods of austerity and cutback. As Figure 5.1 shows, equalisation payments as a proportion of GDP have been relatively constant overtime, despite declining from the mid 1990s to the early 2000s, from about 1% of GDP to about 0.65%.

Figure 5.1 also reveals that equalisation payments have contributed to a significant part of the budget of Manitoba, New Brunswick, Nova Scotia, Prince Edward Island (regrouped together in the small recipient category), and, to a slightly lesser degree, of Québec. These payments were an extremely important contributor to the budget of Newfoundland and Labrador until oil revenues strongly kick in by the early 2010s while they also made a difference for Saskatchewan, albeit more sporadically, for decades until about the same period. Ontario has almost never received equalisation payments (and when it has, they have been very small). Alberta is the outlier, not having been a recipient province since the early 1960. Therefore, on the face of it, there are good reasons for support for the equalisation program to be strong as most provinces benefited from it at some point.

Equalisation became particularly salient politically in the early 2000s, when pressure from recipient provinces to boost the program arose, as equalisation payments were decreasing and the federal government was running large budget surpluses, achieved partly by significantly reducing federal transfers in the mid-1990s. A particularly contentious issue at the time, which is

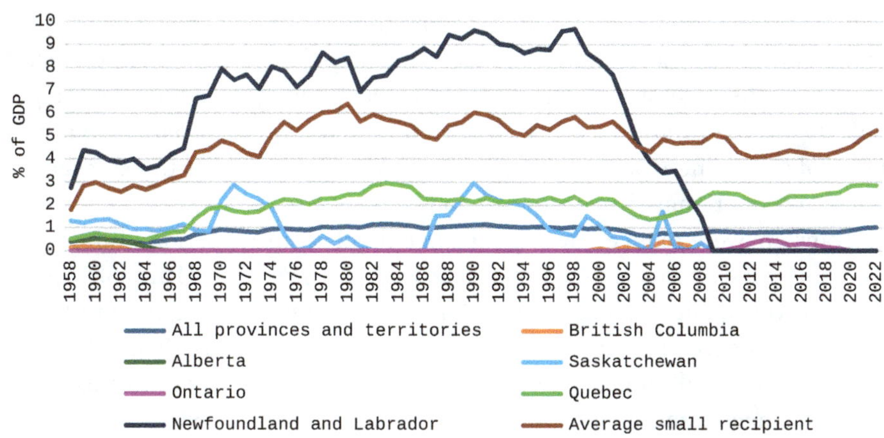

FIGURE 5.1 Evolution of equalisation payments by province (1958–2022) (% of GDP)
SOURCE: FINANCE OF THE NATION, EQUALISATION ENTITLEMENTS

controversial to this day, was the status of non-renewable natural resources in the calculation of provincial fiscal capacity (Lecours & Béland, 2010). The minority Martin government (2004–2006), whose political weakness forced it to agree to some provincial demands to stay in power, enacted a new framework for equalisation but this framework caused even more discontent. In this context, the Liberal Party of Canada (LPC) government led by Paul Martin appointed an Expert Panel on Equalisation and Territorial Formula Financing, which issued its report in May 2006, months after the Conservatives party of Canada (CPC) of Stephen Harper had formed a minority government. Although the panel was launched by a Liberal Prime Minister, his Conservative successor implemented most of the panel's suggestions in his own equalisation reform, which proved very contentious in provinces such as Saskatchewan, Newfoundland and Labrador. Another source of political tension over equalisation occurred in aftermath of the 2008 financial crisis, when Ontario qualified for equalisation payments for the first time in history, a situation that pushed the Harper government to implement new measures to further control the program's spending (Béland et al., 2017).

Regarding the other main intergovernmental transfers excluding equalisation, they grew from 1.6% of GDP in the late 1950s to 3.4% in 1976. This growth corresponds to the creation of a universal health care system, financed by a cost-sharing program between the provinces and the federal government, as well as the introduction of the Canada Assistance Plan and the growth in federal transfer costs for higher education. Transfer costs were reduced when the federal government moved in 1977 from a system of cost-shared programs to a system of essentially unconditional block funding. The federal government felt that cost-sharing programs encouraged the provinces to overspend, since half of the expenses incurred by these programs would be borne by the federal government, and therefore in part by the taxpayers of the other provinces. Moreover, the federal Department of Finance, seeking to reduce the budget deficit, wanted to avoid having its spending determined in part by another order of government, and preferred to be able to determine its transfer spending on a discretionary basis (Simeon, 1982).

Transfers were reduced during the large fiscal austerity period of the 1990s from 2.7% of GDP in 1994 to 1.8% in 2002. Paul Martin's Liberal Party of Canada (LPC) government implemented a significant increase of health care transfers in 2003–2004. This represents an increase in the Canada Health Transfer (CHT) of $41.3 billion over 10 years, on top of the $36.8 billion increase over five years negotiated in 2003, so that the CHT will grow by 6% per year for a decade (Fierlbeck & Palley, 2015). This rare increase in transfers followed the budget surpluses generated by the transfer cut itself. The Conservative Party of Canada came to power in 2006, and as soon as it obtained its only parliamentary majority, the Harper government announced in 2011–12 that the CHT would grow by only 3% per year from 2017 onwards (Fierlbeck & Palley, 2015). The Trudeau government renewed the health transfer imposed by the Harper government in 2017, and increased the CHT modestly in 2023. As such, non-equalisation transfers have been maintained between 2.5% to 3% of GDP since 2004, except from a temporary increase as a response to the COVID-19 pandemic (Jacques, 2024).

2.3 *Results*

Equalisation can be considered as a policy success in the sense that it increases equality in fiscal capacity (and therefore potential ability to fund public services) among the 10 provinces while respecting provincial autonomy, two objectives often portrayed as incompatible with one another. Importantly, some receiving provinces are more dependent on equalisation payments than others. For instance, equalisation payments represent 10% of total public revenues in Quebec, 14% in Manitoba, 16% in Nova Scotia, and around 20% in both Prince Edward Island (PEI) and New Brunswick. Simultaneously, equalisation does not fully equalise fiscal capacity among provinces, which means that, after equalisation, the fiscal capacity of every province is not the same. Indeed, provinces with high fiscal capacity, such as Alberta, retain their superior fiscal capacity rather than being brought down to an average (Béland et al., 2017).

2.4 *Current Issues of the Equalisation and Transfer Systems*

The Canadian equalisation system and the system of transfers work generally well. Still, there is potential for the politicisation of equalisation because it is managed exclusively by the federal government, and such politicisation can then poison intergovernmental relations for a time, provinces find it difficult to forecast equalisation payments, which complicates their budgeting, and the transfers are weakly responsive to program costs.

The Canadian equalisation system, and indeed the whole system of transfer, is ultimately the responsibility of the federal government. The federal government may, and most often does, consult the provinces on all the transfers, but it remains the ultimate decision-maker. On equalisation, this model of executive discretion stands in sharp contrast to an arm's length governance model, such as exists in Australia, where decision-making rests with a group of experts. Executive discretion on equalisation presents the advantage of showing clear lines of democratic accountability but its management by an executive whose members are elected as Members of Parliament means that politics may be seen, in reality or perception, as shaping some aspects of the program.

Because there exists a ceiling on the total equalisation pool, as it is tied with GDP growth, equalisation is a zero-sum game: if a province receives larger payment, others receive smaller ones. Equalisation payments may decline because of a situation (e.g., the fluctuation of oil prices) that is completely out of the control of any government in the federation. All of these dynamics generate significant variation in equalisation payments over time for recipient provinces, which makes it particularly difficult to forecast equalisation payments. This can have a large effect on overall budget forecasts, especially for smaller and poorer provinces whose budgets dependent on a large proportion on equalisation payments (Joanis, 2023).

The main issue with the CHT and the CST is that the total amount of transfers is stagnant as a proportion of GDP while public expenditures in health care, the costliest provincial social program, are growing faster than GDP growth, as shown by Figure 5.2 below. Hence, because the federal government sets the growth of health care transfers at a lower level than the average growth of health care costs, the proportion of health care expenditures funded by the federal government decreases over time. This puts a significant fiscal pressure on provinces that are allocating a growing share of their expenditures to health care, to the detriment of other public programs (Jacques, 2020). As argued elsewhere (Jacques, 2024), the federal government has few political incentives to increase transfer levels. If the federal government increases the two major, virtually unconditional, transfers, provincial governments would be the ones benefiting electorally from presumably better public services. However, to increase transfers to provinces, the federal government must raise taxes, increase deficits, or cut its own programs, which may decrease the government's popularity. Voters are likely to punish the federal government for the visible costs of financing these transfers while they are much less likely to not reward it for a complex and invisible increase in transfers to the provinces. Hence, the Canadian federation is characterised by a low-transfer equilibrium, which puts significant pressure on the funding of social policies. We come back to this issue in the last section of this chapter.

3 The Politics of Equalisation

As we have noted elsewhere, four main factors underlie the occasional politicisation of the equalisation program (Béland et al., 2017; Lecours & Béland, 2010). First, non-renewable natural resources are a provincial jurisdiction and concentrated in certain provinces. Not only are oil and gas an major factor behind Alberta's and Saskatchewan's wealth, but they are also tied to their

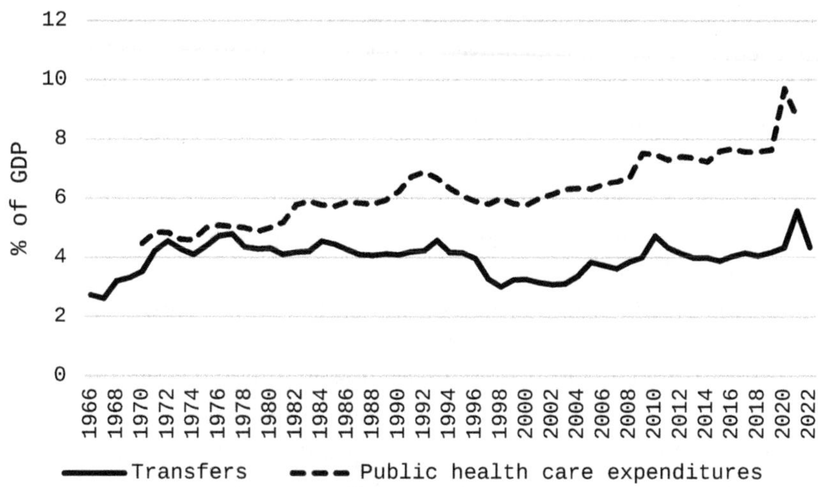

FIGURE 5.2 Evolution of total intergovernmental transfers and of public health care expenditures (1966–2020) (% of GDP)
SOURCE: FINANCE OF THE NATION, AGGREGATE FISCAL TRANSFERS; AND OECD, CURRENT GOVERNMENT EXPENDITURES ON HEALTH CARE

political identity. Hence, in these provinces, equalisation is typically considered as an illegitimate grab on these provinces' oil wealth. The calculation of non-renewable natural resource revenues in provinces' fiscal capacity in the determination of the equalisation formula remains a thorny political issue, which means that the political compromise of 50% inclusion has remained in place for the last 15 years and probably will not be changed any time soon. Moreover, while revenues generated by non-renewable resources depend on the fluctuation of commodity prices on international markets, provinces (such as Quebec) that rely on renewable energy like hydroelectricity, can sell such energy to their population at a low price, which artificially reduces their fiscal capacity and therefore increases their equalisation payments (Lecours & Béland, 2010). This issue of revenues from hydroelectricity and fiscal capacity is, of course, often raised by oil and gas-producing provinces, and it promises to become even more serious as various energy sources other than oil and gas become more widely used.

Second, the governance of equalisation falls exclusively on the federal government. As we explained earlier, there was a period of time in Canadian politics, in the mid-2000s, when the parameters of the equalisation program were in flux and when provinces were jockeying for a reformed program that would favour them.

Third, provincial Premiers benefit from the political strength of the provinces in a federal system characterised by decentralisation and resilient centrifugal forces. As such, Premiers assume that they will be supported by their population if they contest federal changes to the program that are perceived as hurting their province's interests. Moreover, equalisation is often used as a scapegoat to deflect attention from Premiers' own policy decisions.

Fourth, the potential for the politicisation of equalisation is related to Quebec's status in the federation. The mere presence of it symbolises the fiscal benefits for Québec of remaining part of the federation, and the prospect of losing equalisation payments has been one of the main arguments of the "No" side during the 1980 and 1995 referendums on independence (Béland & Lecours, 2014). Politicians and pundits often highlight that Quebec is the main beneficiary of equalisation because it receives the largest amount of equalisation payments, although per capita payments are significantly lower in Quebec (about 8.5 million inhabitants) than in most other, smaller and poorer recipient provinces (less than 2 million in total in the three Maritime provinces, about 1.4 million in Manitoba). Quebec's original (and expensive) social programs (for example, 10$ per day daycare, drug insurance, and the lowest university tuition in the country) raise eyebrows amongst the conservative political leadership of Alberta and Saskatchewan, who tends to spread the false notion that equalisation is a direct transfer from richer provinces to poorer provinces rather than a federal program (Lecours & Béland, 2010).

The 2021 referendum on equalisation in Alberta is a good example of the politicisation of equalisation. The proponents of the "Yes" side wanted to remove the principle of equalisation from the Constitution, arguing that equalisation takes away Alberta's wealth, even when the province is facing a more significant economic downturn than the rest of the country. The referendum was framed as a political weapon against the federal government, but also against Quebec, which benefits from equalisation while opposing pipeline projects deemed crucial to Alberta's economy. The Alberta referendum on equalisation, which the "Yes" side won, cannot lead to the elimination of the program because Alberta cannot unilaterally remove the equalisation principle from the 1982Constitution Act. Still, by focusing on this symbol, then Alberta premier Jason Kenney was seeking to deflect attention from his own policy decisions during the COVID-19 pandemic, which were particularly unpopular, and to blame the federal government and other provinces, particularly Quebec, for Alberta's economic woes (Jacques et al., 2021a).

3.1 *Presentation of the Public Opinion Data*

The next section presents a detailed analysis of public opinion on equalisation and the two major intergovernmental transfers to highlight the drivers of political divisions and agreements about these programs. To do so, we rely on five waves of the Confederation of Tomorrow surveys conducted in Canada in January and February of each year from 2019 to 2023 by the firm Environics. These cross-sectional surveys concern issues related to federalism in general, while asking several specific questions on equalisation and on intergovernmental transfers. We use three different questions as dependent variables. The first asks about general support for the equalisation program and is available in the five surveys. In this question, equalisation is described as a federal program transferring money to poorer provinces in order to ensure that Canadians living in every province have access to similar levels of public services. The answer choices range from a 4 category Likert scale from strongly support to strongly oppose. The second question, available in 2020 and 2022, asks if the respondents want the program to become more generous (coded 1), less generous (–1), or to stay the same (0).

Our third dependent variable measures support for transfer levels, a question that was asked only in the 2022 survey. We told respondents that the federal government transfers money to the provinces to pay for health-care services (hat most important social programs in Canada are delivered by provincial and territorial governments), and that the costs of public health care are expected to rise because of new treatments and medications. We then asked respondents whether the amount of money the federal government transfers to the provinces for health care should increase, decrease, or stay the same. Obviously, support for additional transfers would be very high if respondent were not reminded of the costs of this policy. We presented respondents with three different options to mirror fiscal trade-offs encountered by policymakers, each presented randomly to a third of survey participants. We reminded one third of respondents that higher transfers could lead to tax increases, another the third that higher transfers could lead to a higher federal deficit, while the final third of respondents was asked about their preferences regarding transfers without referring to their costs (for more detail about this survey experimental question see Borwein et al., 2023).

In Figure 5.3, we present the distribution of our three main dependent variables across three groups of provinces: non-recipient provinces of equalisation (Ontario, Saskatchewan, Alberta, and British Columbia), recipient provinces (the four Atlantic provinces and Manitoba) and Quebec. Non-recipient provinces do not receive equalisation payments and maintained a positive fiscal balance in the 2010s. A positive fiscal balance entails that provincial residents pay on average more federal taxes than they receive federal expenditures, including transfers (Tombe, 2018).[1] Recipient provinces receive equalisation payments and maintain a negative fiscal balance during this decade, meaning that they receive more expenditures from the federal government than what they pay.[2] Quebec is a recipient province for equalisation, but its fiscal balance is closer to zero than the other recipient provinces because the it is significantly more dynamic economically than the smaller recipients. Also, because Québec is characterised by the presence of sub-state nationalism and, therefore, it has a significantly higher support for decentralisation and even for political independence (Chassé et al., 2024), the politics of federalism are so different in there that it is pertinent to analyse Québec separately.

Figure 5.3 reveals that the equalisation program remains popular across the country, with 90% of respondents in recipient provinces and in Quebec strongly or somewhat supporting the program.[3] Even in non-recipient provinces, support for equalisation reaches 74% of respondents. However, almost two thirds of respondents in recipient provinces prefer an increase of equalisation payments whereas this option is favoured by only one third of respondents in non-recipient provinces. Higher transfers gather significant support everywhere but remain lower in non-recipient provinces. Only around 6% of respondents prefer lower transfers and the status quo gathers support of about 30% of respondents (not shown).

To analyse the politics of equalisation and transfers, we are focus on three main independent variables: ideology, resentment and identity, which we interact with provincial income. To measure ideology, we rely on federal vote choice and on preferences regarding the size of government. The question on vote choice relies on vote intentions (2019, 2021 and 2023) or vote in the last federal election, if it occurred a few months before the survey (in 2020 and 2022). Respondents who do not know were asked an additional question about which party they lean towards. We use both questions to measure vote choice for the six main political parties: the incumbent centrist Liberal party

1 One could argue that from the point of view of provinces, the fiscal balance should be considered negative if they contribute more than what they receive. However, we prefer to keep the same terms as those proposed by Tombe.

2 Newfoundland has not been receiving equalisation for some years but has one of the largest negative fiscal balances of the federation. Note that during the post-pandemic years, no province had a positive balance because of the significant increase in federal transfers and direct expenditures.

3 Note that the models presented below use the 4-category dependent variable on support for equalisation based on a Likert scale, which has more variation that the dummies presented in the figure.

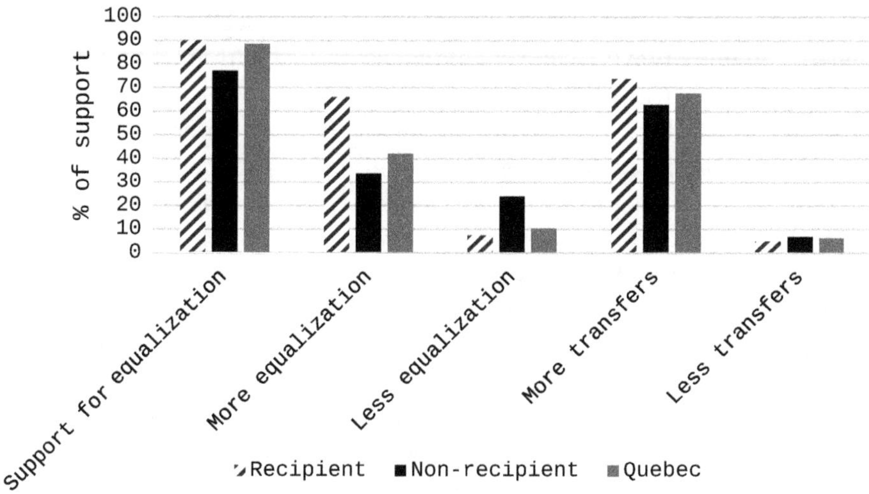

FIGURE 5.3 Distribution of the main dependent variables by the three groups of provinces 2019–2023 (% of support)
SOURCE: CONFEDERATION OF TOMORROW SURVEY

of Canada (35.3% average vote intention), the right-wing Conservative Party of Canada (30.3%), the left-wing New Democratic party (NDP) (18.7%), the regionalist Bloc Québécois (5%), the Greens (7.2%) and the populist radical right People's Party of Canada (PPC) (3.24%). Our other measure of ideology relies on a three-category variable measuring preferences for a larger government offering more services (coded 1) or a smaller government offering fewer services (coded –1) or neither in particular (0), which is available in all surveys except for 2021 (mean = 0.16, SD = 0.74). Left-wing voters should be more likely to support equalisation and higher transfers because both are very redistributive and are tied to the objective of equalising the living conditions of Canadians across the country (Jacques et al., 2021a; Borwein et al., 2023).

We measure territorial identity with the Linz-Moreno question about dual identification to the province and the federal state. Answers are ranging from 1) only a Canadian identification; 2) Canadian first, provincial second; 3) equally Canadian and provincial identification; 4) provincial first and Canadian second; to 5) only a provincial identification (available in all surveys except 2020, mean = 2.73, SD = 1.14). Many studies in Canada and beyond have found that it is a crucial variable to explain preferences for fiscal federalism (Balcells et al., 2015; Borwein et al., 2023; Jacques et al., 2021a). Citizens with a pan-Canadian identity are more likely to support redistribution between provinces even if their own province doesn't benefit directly from it. In contrast, provincial identity constrains the boundaries of the perceived community of solidarity to one's province and should be associated with lower support for inter-provincial redistribution.

We create an index of regional resentment building on the concept of place-based resentment, which has distributional, cultural and representational components. It occurs when people believe that political elites are perceived to cater to the needs of a place-based out-group, while failing to represent the interests of the place-based in-group. The concept has been used to explain the resentment rural communities feel against urban communities and has impacts for political behaviour (Cramer, 2016; Munis, 2022) and similar indices have already been used to study the politics of equalisation (Breton et al., 2022; Jacques et al., 2021a). We build an additive index with responses to three questions asked in all five surveys. The first asks whether respondents believe that their province receives its fair share of federal government spending while the second asks if the province has its fair share of influence on national decisions. Answers to both questions are scored from +1 (less than its fair share) (0 about its fair share) or −1 (more than its fair share). The third asks if the respondents believe that their province is treated with respect, with answers scored +1 (no), 0 (do not know) or −1 (yes).[4] The index ranges from −3 (not resentful) to +3 (very resentful) (mean = 0.84, SD = 1.95).

Tied to resentment, we measure perceptions about Quebec's role in the federation, which, as discussed above, is at the core of the politics of equalisation. We combine two questions asked in different years to maximise our sample size. The first uses a question asking if respondents believe that the federal government treats all regions equally or if it favours one province over the others and, among these respondents, if they believe that Quebec is being favoured (available in 2019 and 2021). The section question asks whether Quebec contributes less than its fair share to the country (available in 2022 and 2023). Both are coded as dummy variables so that respondents are coded 1 if they believe that Quebec is favoured or if it contributes less and 0 if they do not (mean = 0.43, SD = 0.5). Using only one question or the other yields the same results but reduces sample size significantly. We interact this variable with the resentment variable since both combine to generate resentment against the federation and against Quebec, which should be a very powerful predictor of support for equalisation (Jacques et al., 2021a).

4 We put the "do not know" into the neutral category since there are no neutral answer categories for this question, in contrast to the two other questions. Removing them from the analysis doesn't alter the result but significantly reduces sample size.

We also interact the ideology, identity, and both resentment variables with the three provincial categories (Quebec, recipient and non-recipient provinces). We contend that ideology, identity and place-based resentment interact with provincial economic positions to predict support for interregional redistribution. Cavaillé and Trump (2015) distinguish between two facets of redistribution: self-oriented redistribution, which concerns taking from the rich, and other-oriented redistribution, which is about giving to the poor. Self-oriented redistribution is driven by material interests as everyone, but the rich, want to take from the rich (Jacques, 2023). For respondents in poorer provinces, equalisation is self-oriented, as it involves taking from the rich. Concerns related to identity, resentment and perceptions of Quebec should matter less than self-interested considerations in recipient provinces.

In contrast, equalisation is other-oriented in non-recipient provinces because it seemingly involves giving to recipient provinces. Within provinces that do not receive equalisation, other-oriented concerns, which we conceptualise as identity, resentment, and perceptions about Quebec, should matter most (Jacques et al., 2021a). Equalisation is seen as redistribution to Quebec, an out-group characterised by a different language and culture and is particularly likely to be opposed by the anglophone majority if Quebeckers are perceived as not belonging to the majority group (Jacques et al., 2021a). Quebec's quest for increased autonomy is often seen as a form of disengagement with Canada and many perceive that the Government of Canada has gone too far in accommodating Quebec (Chassé et al., 2024; Ferland & Turgeon, 2020; Harell et al., 2022). However, in contrast to equalisation, intergovernmental transfers do not explicitly redistribute from richer to poorer provinces and are more like a universal program that benefit all Canadians, which may dampen the effect of other-oriented concerns, while means-tested ones, like equalisation reinforce them (Muñoz & Pardos-Prado, 2019).

Our models include several control variables such as education, income, perception of economic hardship, gender, immigration status and age. We run ordinary least squares regressions and include provincial and survey years fixed effects, but drop the provincial fixed effects when doing the provincial interactions. We focus on a graphical representation of the results. In the following models, the LPC is used as reference category for vote choice and Alberta is the provincial reference category, while controls as well as survey years fixed effects are included but not shown. Respondents who do not know the answer to a question are excluded from the analysis. Models predicting support for higher transfers also include dummy variables accounting for the experimental condition, that is whether transfers need to be funded by higher taxes and

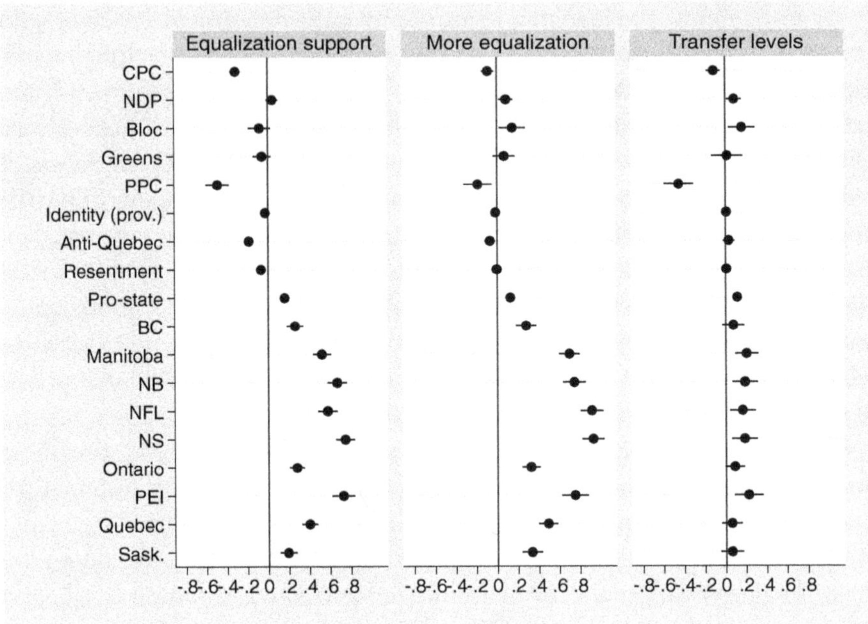

FIGURE 5.4 Result of the main models, higher score means more support (2019–2023)

deficit. Both dummy variable reduce support for transfer, particularly among right-wing respondents (Borwein et al., 2023).

3.2 *Results of the Empirical Analysis*

We present the results of the main models in Figure 5.4. Right-wing voters (CPC, PCC and anti-state) as well as respondents who believe that Quebec is favoured or doesn't pay its fair share are significantly less likely to support equalisation and an increase to equalisation payments. Provincial identifiers and respondents displaying high levels of resentment are less likely to support the program, but the effect of both variable is not significantly related to support for more equalisation. Support for equalisation is higher in all provinces than in Alberta, and significantly higher in recipient provinces outside Quebec. Support for higher transfers is mostly driven by ideology, as we find significantly higher support among the left (pro-state, Bloc and NDP voters). Identity, resentment, and perceptions of Quebec do not influence support for transfer levels. Support for higher transfers is slightly lower in Alberta than in several provinces but remains relatively similar across the country.

Note: First model includes survey from 2019, 2022 and 2023 (N = 6125), second model from 2019 and 2022 (3611), third model is in 2022 (N = 1877). Note: CPC

(Conservative Party of Canada), NDP (New Democratic Party of Canada), PPC (People's Party of Canada), BC (British Columbia), NB (New-Brunswick), NFL (Newfoundland and Labrador), NS (Nova Scotia), PEI (Prince-Edward-Island) and Sask. (Saskatchewan).

Figures 5.5 to 5.7 add interactions to the models presented in Figure 5.4. Figure 5.5 reveals that the effect of resentment is particularly strong among respondents who believe that Quebec is favoured or doesn't contribute its fair share in the federation. In fact, resentment only reduces support for more generous equalisation payment among respondents who believe that Quebec is favoured or doesn't contribute its fair share in the federation but has no effect among respondents who do not hold a grudge against Quebec. Hence, to influence public opinion about the program, resentment must be activated against a significant out-group perceived as benefiting from equalisation.

In Figure 5.6, we reveal that the negative effect of provincial identity and resentment on support for equalisation and for more generous payments is confined to non-recipient provinces, whereas these two variables have no effect in recipient provinces and in Quebec. In fact, resentment increases support for more generous equalisation payments in recipient provinces. The bottom panel of Figure 5.6 also suggests that the negative effect of anti-Quebec sentiments is significantly stronger in non-recipient provinces than in recipient provinces.

Finally, Figure 5.7 reveals some form of left-right consensus in Quebec and the recipient provinces regarding equalisation and support for higher transfers, whereas the effect of ideology is much stronger in non-recipient provinces as conservative voters are likely to oppose equalisation and transfers in these provinces. Additional analyses reveal that none of our main independent variables interact with provinces to predict support for transfers.

These analyses of public opinion reveal a few important considerations for the politics of equalisation and intergovernmental transfers in Canada. They reveal a large consensus in favour of equalisation and of higher intergovernmental transfers. Interestingly, transfers are even less conflictual than equalisation, possibly because redistribution by transfers is implicit and less visible, in contrast to the more explicit redistribution entailed by equalisation. As shown in another study (see Borwein et al., 2023), the main conflict concerning intergovernmental transfers pertain to whether the federal government should impose national standards or if provinces should have the autonomy to decide how to spend the money.

Unsurprisingly, the consensus in favour of equalisation is particularly strong in recipient provinces. In contrast, fiscal federalism is a dividing issue in non-recipient provinces since it represents other-oriented redistribution. There

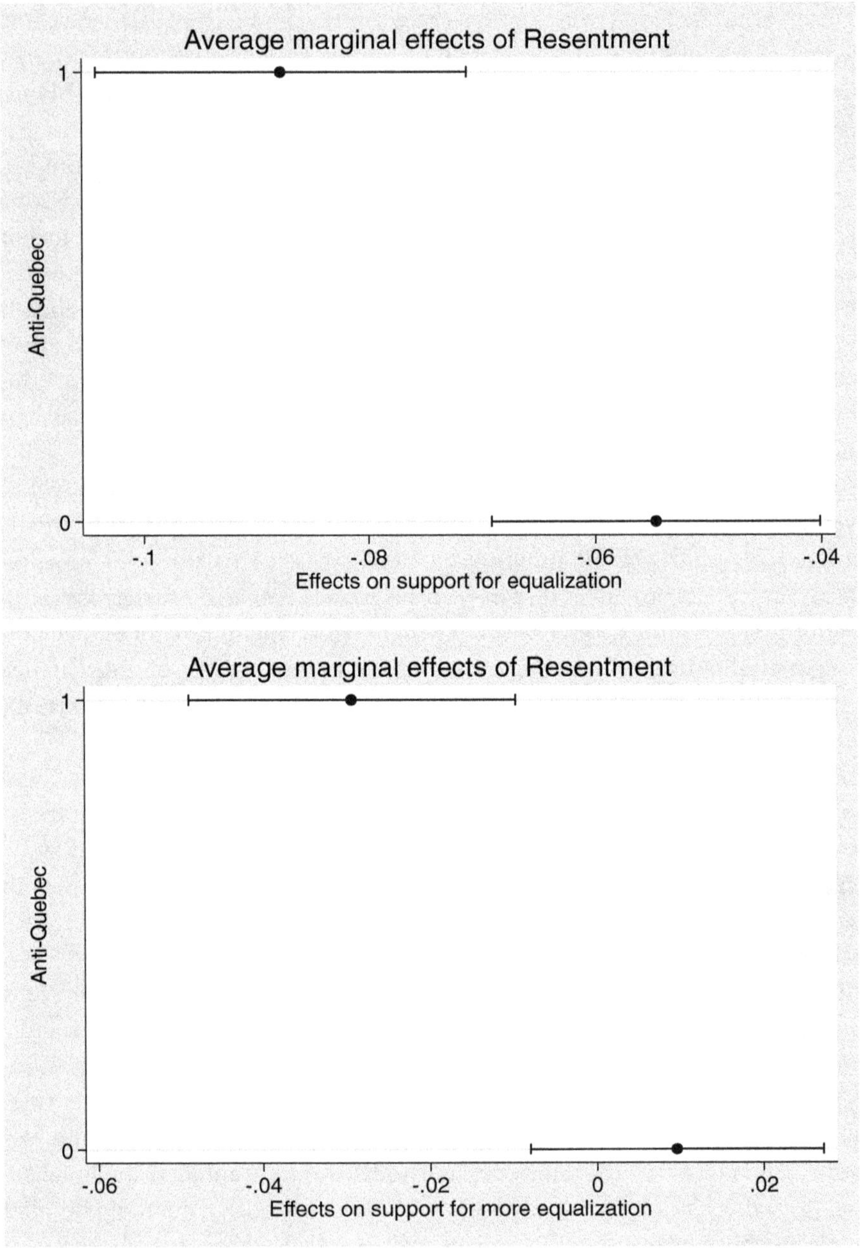

FIGURE 5.5 Interaction of resentment and anti-Quebec sentiments, 2019–2023 (not 2020)

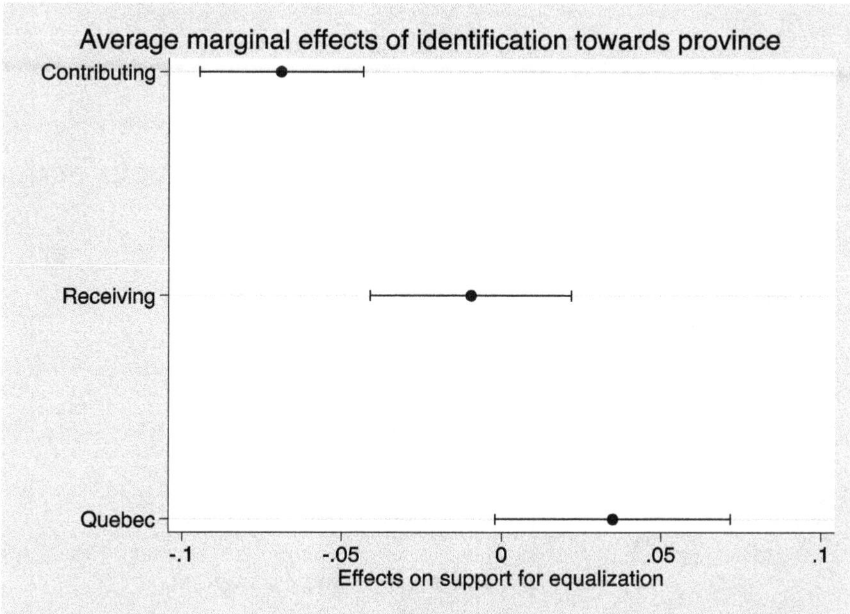
Average marginal effects of identification towards province
Contributing
Receiving
Quebec
-.1
-.05
0
.05
.1
Effects on support for equalization

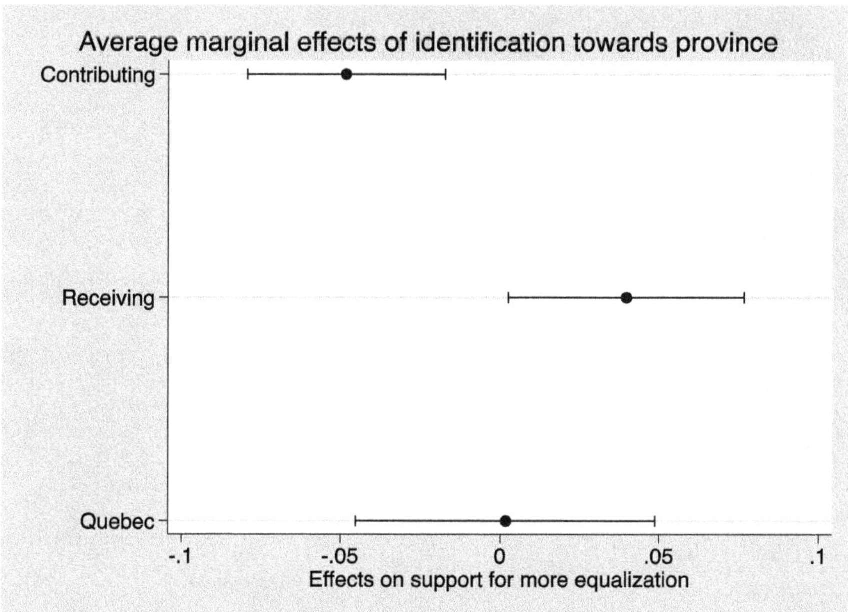
Average marginal effects of identification towards province
Contributing
Receiving
Quebec
-.1
-.05
0
.05
.1
Effects on support for more equalization

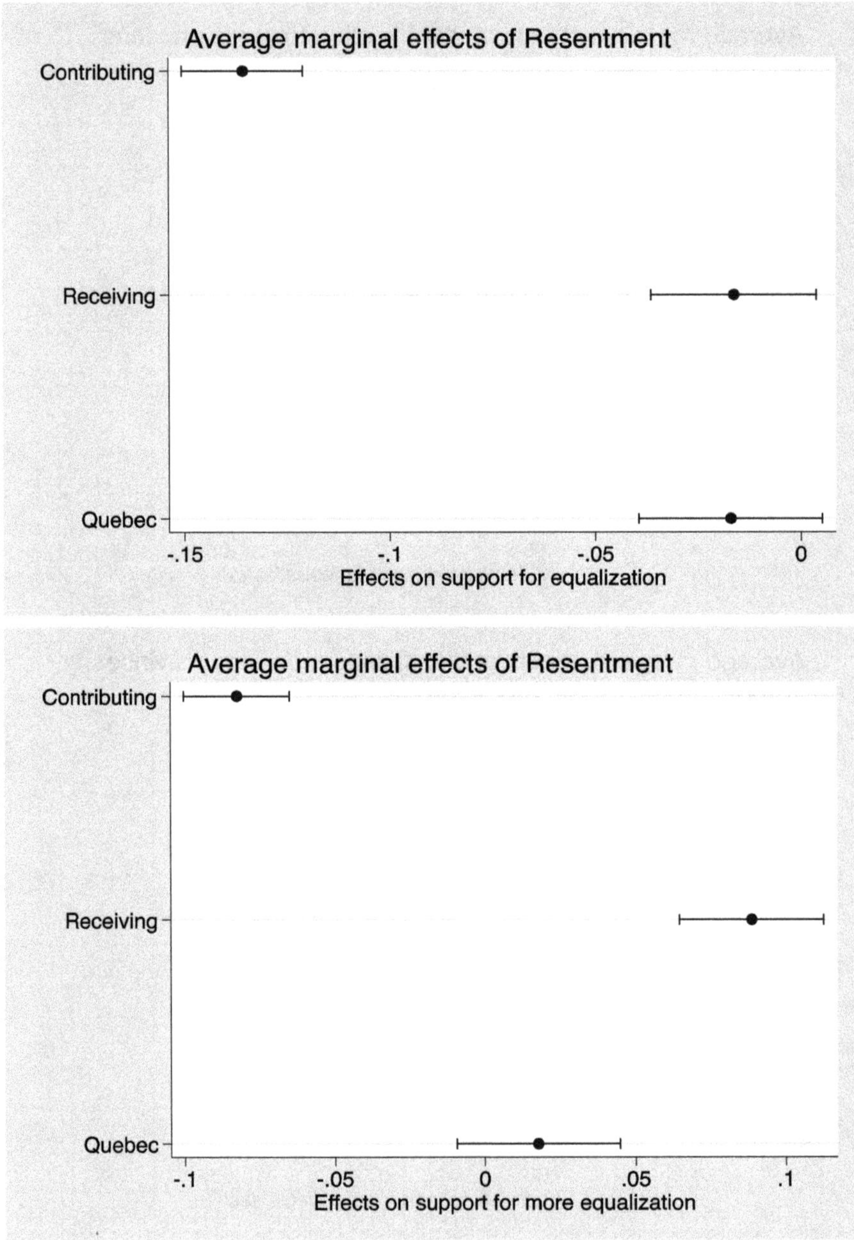
Average marginal effects of Resentment
Contributing
Receiving
Quebec
-.15
-.1
-.05
0
Effects on support for equalization
Average marginal effects of Resentment
Contributing
Receiving
Quebec
-.1
-.05
0
.05
.1
Effects on support for more equalization

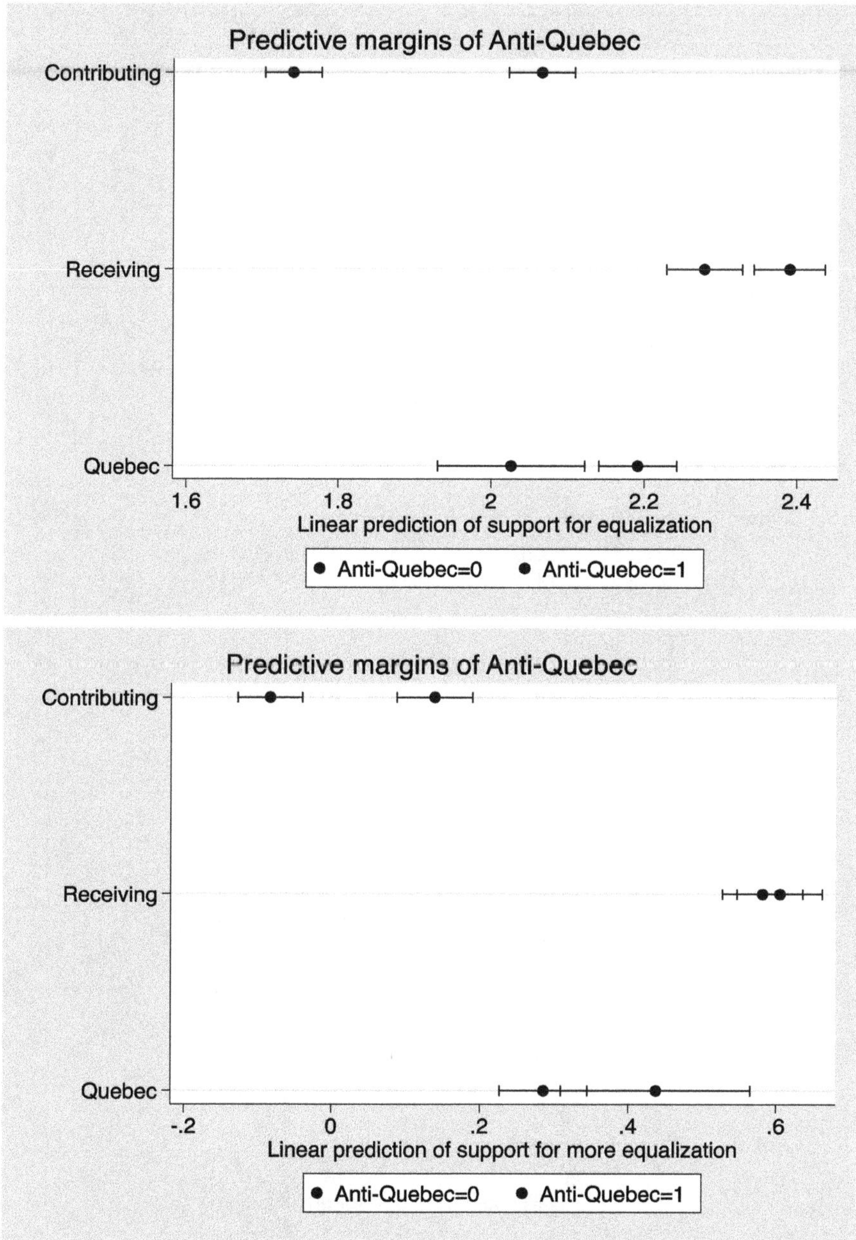

FIGURE 5.6 Interaction of identity, resentment or anti-Quebec sentiments with provincial income (2019–2023, except 2020)

is a significant division between respondents who have a relatively positive conception of the "other" because of their Canadian identity, their lack of

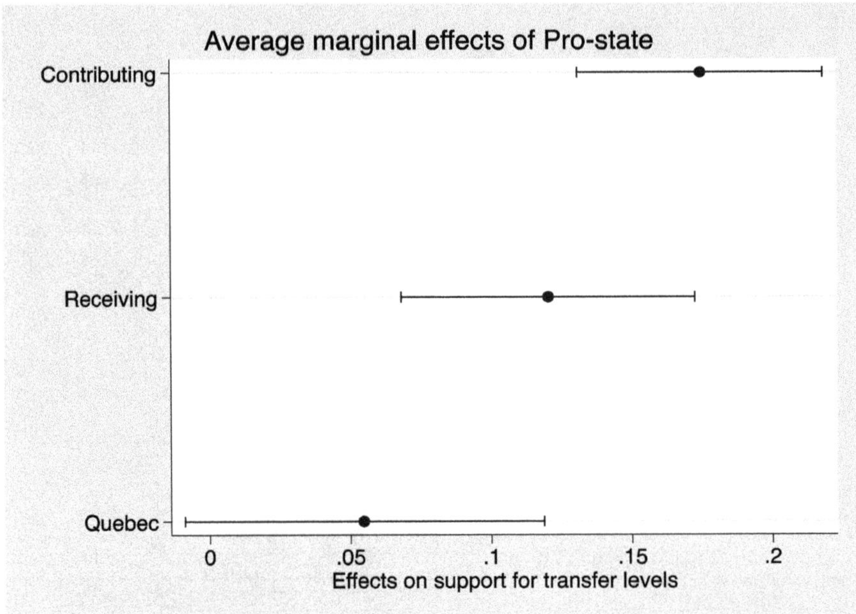
Average marginal effects of Pro-state
Contributing
Receiving
Quebec
0
.05
.1
.15
.2
Effects on support for transfer levels

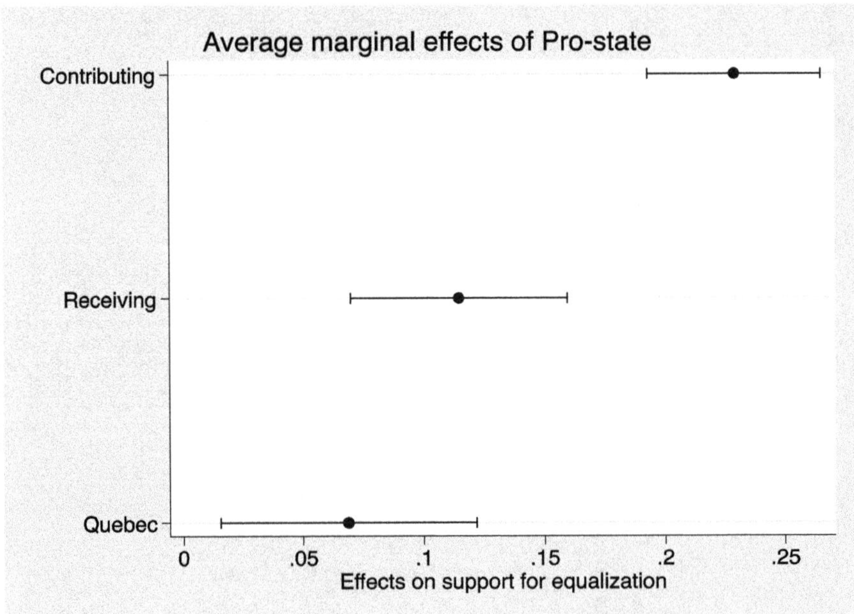
Average marginal effects of Pro-state
Contributing
Receiving
Quebec
0
.05
.1
.15
.2
.25
Effects on support for equalization

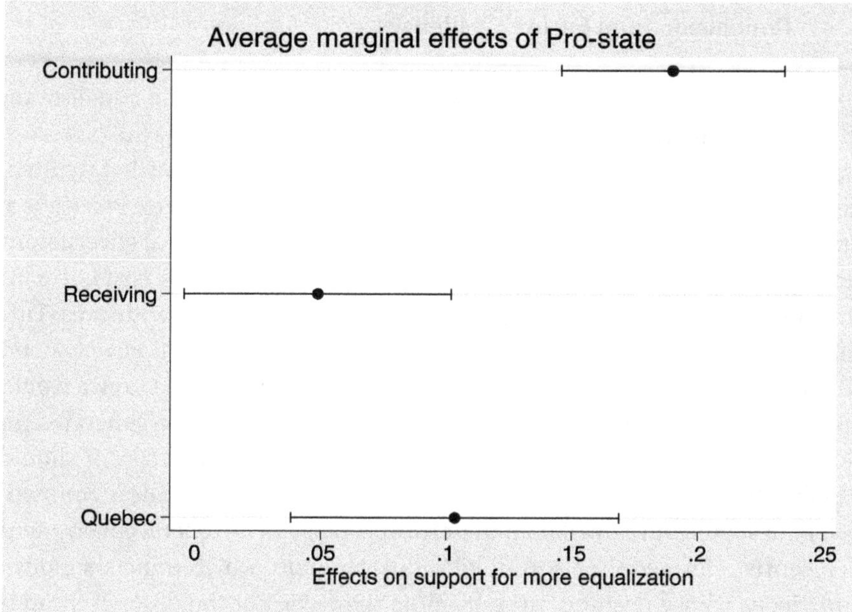

FIGURE 5.7 Interaction of ideology and provinces to predict support for equalisation and for transfers (2019–2023)

resentment and the positive perception of Quebec, on the one hand, and, on the other hand, respondents who resent Quebec and the federation and those that have a provincial identity that limits their perceived community of solidarity to their province. This division is transposed into the political sphere as we observe a clear difference in support for equalisation and intergovernmental transfers between the left and the right in non-recipient provinces.

However, the fact that opposition to equalisation exists only among certain voters in non-recipient provinces make it difficult to marshal a large national-level coalition in favour of cutbacks to (or the dismantlement of) the program. This helps to explain why the Conservatives are not cutting back equalisation despite the strong rhetoric against the program of right-wing parties in Alberta and Saskatchewan. In fact, the federal Conservative party faces a trade-off between their base, which opposes equalisation, and the Canadian median voter, which supports the program.

4 Conclusions and Future Challenges

We conclude by discussing an important future challenge to the equalisation and transfer systems and the limits of the system as evidenced by the COVID-19 crisis. Indeed, the COVID-19 crisis revealed that the current transfer architecture cannot withstand shocks without ad hoc temporary changes. Since 2020, transfers have reached their highest level in history as the federal government made discretionary adjustments to help provinces pay for the costs of pandemic mitigation measures and for additional health care expenditures. This situation leaves significant discretionary powers to the federal government, and it is conceivable that a more conservative party in office in Ottawa would not have increased transfers as significantly, which would have generated an unsustainable fiscal burden for several provinces. Ideally, a program should be built into the system to ensure that provinces can be adequately compensated for a significant downfall in their fiscal capacity. The federal government has recently reformed the fiscal stabilisation program, which transfers money to provinces whose revenues drop by more than 5%, but the program's cap is fixed at approximately 200$ per capita, which is low relatively to current transfer levels (Tombe, 2023). Other reforms will need to be implemented to ensure that Canadian fiscal federalism can withstand major economic shocks.

As discussed in the first section, the growth of intergovernmental transfers is not keeping pace with the growth of provinces' expenditures allocated to their most costly program, health care. This is an issue for all provinces since health care already represents between 40 and 45% of provinces total program expenditures. Recent projections reveal that health care costs will represent at least 3 additional per cent of GDP in the next two to three decades, while more dire predictions suggesting a growth closer to 6% of GDP (Ferguson & Jacques, 2019; PBO, 2022). This is because of inflation in health care costs generated by technological progress, but also due to aging, which increases the average health care expenditure per capita, particularly for the population over 75. Aging also influences the denominator, by decreasing economic growth, therefore increasing health expenditures as a proportion of GDP. Hence, provinces may be spending 75 per cent of their budget on the two core functions of health and education by 2050, leaving few resources for other policy fields and therefore limiting their capacity to provide public spending that responds to citizens demands. As such, public finances are considered as unsustainable over the long-term in a majority of provinces, whereas the public debt of the federal government is under control (PBO, 2022).

This situation may challenge the current division of power in the federation. If cash-strapped provinces cannot respond to public demands, the federal government might use its spending power to implement policies in areas of provincial jurisdiction. Likewise, cash-strapped provinces may be more likely to accept federal conditions imposed on health and social policy intergovernmental transfers. Because the degree of centralisation of the Canadian federation evolves through political dynamics rather than by constitutional means (Lecours, 2019), it is conceivable that these fiscal pressures on provinces may lead towards more centralisation.

The challenges of population aging, growing health-care costs, and inadequate transfers are particularly acute in the Atlantic provinces, which have a more rapidly aging population, combined with a less dynamic economy. The proportion of the population over 65 years old has doubled in Atlantic provinces from 2000 to 2020 and will continue to increase until 2040, while the proportion of the population aged 75+ should represent approximately 17% in 2040 up from 13% in 2030, in contrast to 12.3% in 2040 on average in the other provinces (Saillant, 2023). Facing an aging population and slow economic growth, it is projected that health care expenditures expressed as a proportion of GDP will double from 2013 to 2040 in this region (Saillant, 2016). Hence, the Atlantic provinces' fiscal situation is not sustainable over the medium term unless fiscal federalism changes to accommodate them. Already in 2021, the Bank of Canada had to purchase government bonds of Newfoundland and Labrador since the province was unable to secure financing from financial markets (Saillant, 2023).

One solution to this problem would be to ensure that the CHT is adjusted to the age of the population and therefore higher in older provinces, such as in the Atlantic provinces (Béland & Tombe 2023). However, to make it palatable to other (and more influent) provinces, this age adjustment should be allocated on top of the current per capita transfer, rather than taking money away from younger provinces to give it to older ones. The federal government would therefore have to increase overall levels of transfers to adjust the CHT to age-related health care needs without alienating younger and richer provinces. In any case, Canadian fiscal federalism will need to evolve to address this fundamental demographic and economic inequality between the regions in the country.

References

Balcells, L., Fernández-Albertos, J., & Kuo, A. (2015). Preferences for inter-regional redistribution. *Comparative political studies, 48*(10), 1318–1351.

Béland, D., & Lecours, A. (2014). Accommodation and the politics of fiscal equalization in multinational states: The case of C anada. *Nations and nationalism, 20*(2), 337–354.

Béland, D., Lecours, A., Marchildon, G. P., Mou, H., & Olfert, M. R. (2017). *Fiscal federalism and equalization policy in Canada: Political and economic dimensions.* University of Toronto Press.

Béland, D. & Tombe, T. (2023). Reforming Canada's federal health-cvare funding arrangements. *Canadian Public Administration, 66*(2), 28–44.

Borwein, S., Jacques, O., Béland, D., & Lecours, A. (2023). National standards or territorial autonomy? Public opinion and the politics of fiscal federalism for healthcare in Canada. *Territory, Politics, Governance*, 1–21. https://doi.org/10.1080/21622671.2023.2196303.

Breton, C., Jacques, O., & Parkin, A. (2022). *Resentment in the Canadian Federation* (Bulletin, October, no 3).

Cavaillé, C., & Trump, K.-S. (2015). The two facets of social policy preferences. *The Journal of Politics, 77*(1), 146–160.

Chassé, P., Jacques, O., & Scott, C. (2024). Between decentralization and asymmetry: Explaining preferences about the division of power in Canada. *Publius: The Journal of Federalism*. pjae034, https://doi.org/10.1093/publius/pjae034 .

Cramer, K. J. (2016). *The politics of resentment: Rural consciousness in Wisconsin and the rise of Scott Walker*. University of Chicago Press.

Ferguson, C., & Jacques, O. (2019). Le financement de la santé est absent du débat électoral. *Options politiques*.

Ferland, B., & Turgeon, L. (2020). Understanding majority attitudes toward minority nations in multinational federations: The case of Canada. *Publius: The Journal of Federalism, 50*(2), 188–212.

Fierlbeck, K., & Palley, H. (2015). Canada. In K. Fierlbeck & H. Palley (Eds.), *Comparative Health Care Federalism* (pp. 107–121). Routledge.

Harell, A., Banting, K., Kymlicka, W., & Wallace, R. (2022). Shared membership beyond national identity: Deservingness and solidarity in diverse societies. *Political Studies, 70*(4), 983–1005.

Jacques, O. (2020). Partisan Priorities under Fiscal Constraints in Canadian Provinces. *Canadian Public Policy 46*(4), 458–473.

Jacques, O. (2023a). Explaining Willingness to Pay Taxes: The Role of Income, Education, Ideology. *Journal of European Social Policy*. 33(3), 267-284.

Jacques, O. (2024). Les contraintes politiques et institutionnelles au règlement du déséquilibre fiscal. *Politique et Sociétés*. 43(2).

Jacques, O., Béland, D., & Lecours, A. (2022). Fiscal federalism, social identity and place-based resentment. *Regional Studies*, 56(7), 1210–1223.

Jacques, O., & Graefe, P. (2023). The partisan politics of fiscal federalism in Canada. *Working paper.*

Joanis, M. (2023). Living on Equalization Payments: How Hard Is It for Receiving Provinces to Anticipate Future Equalization Revenues? In A. Lecours, D. Béland, T. Tombe, & É. Champagne (Eds.), *Fiscal Federalism in Canada: Analysis, Evaluation, Prescription* (pp. 132–154). Toronto: University Press.

Lecours, A. (2019). Dynamic de/centralization in Canada, 1867–2010. *Publius: The Journal of Federalism, 49*(1), 57–83.

Lecours, A., Béland, D., Tombe, T. & Champagne, E. (Eds.). (2023). *Fiscal Federalism in Canada. Analysis, Evaluation, Prescription.* Toronto : University of Toronto Press.

Lecours, A., & Béland, D. (2010). Federalism and fiscal policy: The politics of equalization in Canada. *Publius: The Journal of Federalism, 40*(4), 569–596.

Munis, B. K. (2022). Us over here versus them over there … literally: Measuring place resentment in American politics. *Political Behavior, 44*(3), 1057–1078.

Muñoz, J., & Pardos-Prado, S. (2019). Immigration and support for social policy: an experimental comparison of universal and means-tested programs. *Political Science Research and Methods, 7*(4), 717–735.

PBO (2022). *Fiscal Sustainability Report.*

Saillant, R. (2016). *A tale of two countries: How the great demographic imbalance is pulling Canada apart.* Nimbus Publishing.

Saillant, R. (2023). Diversity in Adversity: Fiscal Federalism, the Four Atlantic Provinces, and Canada's Great Demographic Imbalance. In A. Lecours, D. Béland, T. Tombe, & É. Champagne (Eds.), *Fiscal Federalism in Canada: Analysis, Evaluation, Prescription* (pp. 375–394). University of Toronto Press.

Simeon, R. (1982). Fiscal Federalism in Canada: A Review Essay,'. *Canadian Tax Journal, 30*, 41–51.

Tombe, T. (2018). Final and Unalterable-But up for Negotiation: Federal-Provincial Transfers in Canada. *Can. Tax J., 66*, 871.

Tombe, T. (2023). The Challenges and Opportunities Facing Canada's Fiscal Arrangements 19.after COVID- In A. Lecours, D. Béland, T. Tombe, & É. Champagne (Eds.), *Fiscal Federalism in Canada: Analysis, Evaluation, Prescription* (pp. 77–92). University of Toronto Press.

CHAPTER 6

The Political Economy of Federal Grants: Ethiopia's Experience

Bizuneh Yimenu
School of History, Anthropology, Philosophy and Politics (Queen's University Belfast)

1 Introduction

Intergovernmental fiscal transfer, classically known as a federal grant, is among the defining features of federal and non-federal multi-level governments. In theory, subnational governments in federations possess financial independence and separate jurisdictions. However, in practice, vertical fiscal imbalances often arise where the federal government collects more revenue than needed while constituent units lack adequate tax income to finance expenditures (Boadway, 2011; Oates, 1999, p. 1124). Besides, taxes assigned to the constituent units may not yield enough revenues to finance the units' expenses (McLure, 1999). Consequently, federal transfers become vital to bridging fiscal gaps between central and regional governments. Transfers take two primary forms: unconditional (general-purpose) grants that offer spending flexibility and conditional (specific-purpose) grants that limit autonomy by imposing restrictions (Oates, 1999).

The design and practice of intergovernmental fiscal transfers are among the challenging tasks in public finance and fiscal federalism. They require policy and institutional arrangements and should consider social, political, economic, and historical issues. On the other hand, in a system where subnational governments' own-source revenues are minimal, regional autonomy is primarily defined by fiscal transfers. The transfer also limits the magnitude and composition of expenditure at subnational units. Intergovernmental fiscal transfers serve as a defining hallmark within federal systems, offering a critical means to address vertical and horizontal fiscal imbalances. The intricacies of designing and executing these transfer systems encompass complex policy considerations and intricate political dynamics, particularly pronounced in the context of developing countries such as Ethiopia. In such countries, scarce fiscal resources, limited institutional capacity, and the intricate tapestry of diversity all present significant challenges in achieving equitable revenue sharing.

DOI:10.1163/9789004524514_008

This chapter delves into the nuanced political economy that has shaped Ethiopia's intergovernmental transfer system since the inception of its federal Constitution in 1995. It dissects the interplay of political dynamics between the central government and regional entities, as well as among the regions themselves, elucidating how these dynamics have steered the evolution of the transfer mechanism over time. Notably, a central focus lies on the role of the Ethiopian Peoples Revolutionary Democratic Front (EPRDF), Ethiopia's ruling party from 1991 to 2019, in mediating the relationships between the central government and regional administrations while also navigating the power dynamics among the major "developed and big four" regions – Oromia, Amhara, Southern Nations, Nationalities and Peoples (SNNP) and Tigray – and the "developing" and peripheral states of Afar, Benishangul-Gumuz, Gambella and Somali.

Within this framework, the chapter uncovers a significant departure from the constitutional allocation of transfer authority to the House of Federation (HoF), Ethiopia's second chamber. Instead, the federal Ministry of Finance and the EPRDF have exerted considerable influence over determining transfer amounts and devising allocation formulas. In contrast, regional input into the transfer system has been limited, resulting in frequent ad hoc modifications. The resulting volatility is partly attributed to the strategic deployment of transfers as a means of political control and discretion. Looking ahead, the diminishing dominance of the EPRDF and the escalating ethnic stiffness indicate heightened tensions surrounding intergovernmental transfers. Formulating a transparent, rule-based transfer framework that accurately reflects national objectives and regional needs and incorporates diverse voices is imperative for sustaining fiscal federalism in Ethiopia.

The chapter unfolds in the following sequence: It begins with an overview of the Ethiopian Federation, followed by an analysis of the legal framework governing intergovernmental fiscal transfers in the country. Subsequently, it delves into the deermination of transfer pools and scrutinises the determination of subsidy formulas and regional allocations. Moving forward, the chapter critically assesses the interplay between ethno-regional dynamics and fiscal transfers. It then traces the evolution of subsidy allocation methods, followed by an examination of the relationship between grants and regional autonomy in Ethiopia. Finally, the chapter concludes by summarising key insights and implications drawn from the Ethiopian context.

2 Overview of the Ethiopian Federation

Ethiopia's shift from a highly centralised unitary state to a decentralised federal structure began with the ascent of the EPRDF to power in 1991, following its successful insurgency against the Marxist-Leninist Derg regime (Young, 1998). In response to Ethiopia's longstanding issues related to identity, self-rule, and accommodation, the EPRDF adopted a federal system to address these concerns. After a transitional period from 1991 to 1994, Ethiopia officially adopted a federal Constitution in 1995, establishing states commonly known as regions (Lyons, 1996). The Ethiopian federation began with nine states, predominantly named after the dominant ethnic groups in the regions. Subsequently, through referendums, the number of constituent units increased to 12, with the creation of the Sidama region in 2019, the South West Ethiopia Peoples' region in 2021, and two other regions curved from SNNPR in 2023. This expansion reflects the commitment to allow more ethnonationalities to establish a regional government whenever possible as per Article 39 of the federal Constitution, which grants the right to self-determination, including secession.

The regions vary significantly in population size, territorial size, geographical location, ethnic diversity, development levels, economic structures, and urbanisation. Some regions are more developed and politically influential, such as Oromia, Amhara, SNNPR, and Tigray, while others like Afar, Benishangul-Gumuz, Gambella, and Somali lag behind in various development indicators (Gebre-Egziabhere, 2018). The regions also differ in their demographic composition, with some being dominated by a single ethnic group while others host a mix of ethnicities. Geographically, the regions range from central highland areas to peripheral lowland regions. They also differ significantly in size, with some regions consisting of small city-states, such as Harari, with minimal populations and others encompassing large territories, such as Oromia, with significant portions of the country's population. Additionally, some regions are urbanising and economically developed, while others struggle with underdevelopment. The economic structures within these regions vary from promising industrialisation to pastoralism. Notably, lowland regions often face economic challenges, limited development, and meagre own-source revenues (Yimenu, 2023). Despite these asymmetries, all regions hold equal status and powers under the Constitution.

According to the Constitution, both the federal government and the regions are responsible for bearing the financial expenditures necessary to fulfil their respective duties and functions as assigned by law. Hence, revenue sources are constitutionally allocated to both tiers of government. This includes the distribution of taxation powers between the federal and regional governments, encompassing federal, regional, and shared tax sources. While regions possess constitutional powers, the EPRDF, a coalition of four regional parties representing the stronger and more developed regions, effectively controlled all regions through its members and affiliate parties in the less developed regions. This domination persisted until Prime Minister Abiy Ahmed dissolved the EPRDF in 2019, forming Prosperity Party (PP), by merging all regional parties except the Tigray Peoples Liberation Front (TPLF), the Tigray ruling party, which refused to merge PP(Yimenu, 2022). The TPLF was the dominant core in the dominant coalition until Abiy Ahmed came to power following years of protest in Oromia and Amhara regions, forcing the EPRDF to elect Abiy as Prime Minister from Oromia (Kelecha, 2021; Yimenu, 2024).

It is important to note that the identity-based demarcation of Ethiopian regions is further complicated because all regions are governed by ethno-regional parties (Aalen, 2011). Each party in the coalition represented a specific region, creating an ethno-regional alignment that could potentially lead to competition for fiscal allocation. This situation raises concerns that fiscal allocation may be heavily influenced by political considerations and the interests of federal elites in favouring their home regions. Constitutionally, decisions regarding grant allocation are vested in the House of Federation (HoF), Ethiopia's second chamber representing the Nations, Nationalities, and Peoples (NNPs) (See articles 61 and 62). Although the HoF explicitly represents the NNPs, it also functions as a second chamber representing the regions, albeit without legislative power but with adjudicative authority.

3 Legal Framework for Intergovernmental Fiscal Transfers

The landscape of federalism in Ethiopia unveils a distinctive aspect of the division of fiscal authority between the central and regional governments. While the federal Constitution broadly outlines the allocation of responsibilities and functions, it intriguingly lacks a distinct provision for the assignment of expenditure responsibilities. Instead, Article 94 (1) of the Constitution stipulates that both tiers of government are obligated to bear the financial burdens necessary for fulfilling their assigned responsibilities by law. Additionally, the same Article emphasises that unless expressly agreed upon, the delegating party shall bear the financial commitments associated with delegated functions by a State. This provision prevents the imposition of unfunded obligations stemming from delegated functions.

Notably, Article 92 (2) of the Constitution requires the federal government to provide states with emergency, rehabilitation, and development assistance, including loans. These forms of support are extended through federal grants to the regions, aligning with the constitutional objectives. However, Ethiopia's high revenue centralisation and substantial expenditure decentralisation (Yimenu, 2023) create a pronounced vertical fiscal gap across the regions, necessitating federal transfers. Furthermore, the need for financial transfers is amplified by the imperative to address horizontal fiscal disparities originating from variations in revenue generation, developmental levels, and administrative capacities among the "developed" and "developing" regions.

The Constitution confers the power to determine regional subsidies upon the HoF.[1] Intriguingly, a noteworthy turn of events unfolded just two years after the Constitution's adoption. In 1997, the power to determine regional subsidies was bestowed upon the Ministry of Finance and Economic Cooperation (MoFEC) through a regulation enacted by the Council of Ministers (Regulations No.17 /1997.', 1997).[2] This pivotal shift was revised in 2001, as the House of Peoples' Representatives (HPR) enacted Proclamation No. 251/2001, restoring the HoF's authority over subsidies (Proclamation No. 251, 2001).[3] The circumvention of the House's constitutional power via a federal cabinet's law raises several pertinent points. It underscores the executive's substantial influence in unilaterally reshaping constitutional distribution of powers. Additionally, this act of alteration occurs without a constitutional amendment and without any noticeable objections from the House or the regional entities, showing their compliance or lack of independence.

Concomitantly, the legal framework encapsulates pivotal facets germane to the administration of regional subsidies, encompassing the dimensions of notification, reporting, and audit procedures. Article 94(2) of the Constitution states that "the federal government shall have the power to audit and inspect the proportionate development" of the regions. Council of Ministers Regulation No. 17/1997 mandates the federal government's expeditious preparation and notification of subsidies to the regions. A subsequent legislative iteration is manifested in Proclamation No. 648/2009, bestowing authority

1 Article 62 (7) of the Constitution states that the HoF "shall determine the division of revenues derived from joint Federal and State tax sources and the subsidies that the Federal Government may provide to the States".

2 Article 4(4) of Regulation No.17/1997 states that the MoFEC is responsible for the "preparation of estimates of regional subsidies".

3 Article 35 (1) of the proclamation states that "the house shall set a reliable and an ongoing improvement in the formula of subsidies which the federal government may provide to the states, based on the information it secures from relevant executive organs".

upon the central apparatus to scrutinise the utilisation of grants by the regions (Proclamation No. 648, 2009).[4]

This analytical excavation of the legal framework bequeaths elucidation concerning four principal dimensions. Firstly, the paradigm of regional subsidies is forged as a corrective mechanism to mitigate horizontal fiscal disparities. Secondly, legislative edicts governing subsidies, exemplified by Regulation No. 17/1997 and Proclamation No. 648/2009, relegate the regional entities to the status of information providers. Thirdly, the formative epoch of the federal architecture witnesses the conspicuous ascendancy of the Federal Ministry of Finance in determinations, allocations, and administration of subsidies. Fourthly, the jurisdiction of the House of Federation vis-à-vis the determination and allotment of subsidies among regions gains potency after the promulgation of Proclamation No. 251/2001, thus delineating the augmentation of the House's competencies in this realm.

4 The Practice of Determining the Transfer Pool

The utilisation of fiscal transfers is a well-established practice in contemporary states (Boadway, 2011; Sham, 2007). However, the methods employed for designing and allocating intergovernmental fiscal transfers diverge significantly across states. In numerous federal systems, the onus of intergovernmental fiscal transfers rests solely with the federal government. A potential pitfall of this approach is that it can engender excessive central intervention in subnational entities' decision-making, potentially compromising regional autonomy. Efforts to mitigate such challenges have been witnessed in federations like Brazil, which have instituted constitutional safeguards regarding the determination of grants. However, if intergovernmental grants are decided solely by the federal government, they may limit regional autonomy (Sham, 2007, pp. 35–36).

Alternatively, certain federations opt for a distinctive model, where an independent entity or a body composed of representatives from both tiers partakes in designing and enforcing fiscal arrangements. In some federations, a quasi-independent body, like Australia's grant commission, plays a pivotal role. Federations like Germany and Canada adopt an intergovernmental forum for negotiating the conditions and systems governing fiscal transfers (Parker, 2014;

4 Article 68(2) of proclamation No.648/2009 stated that "the federal government shall have the power to audit and inspect the proper utilisation of subsidies it grants to the regional government".

Sham, 2007, pp. 36–37). Each of these approaches entails inherent advantages and disadvantages concerning data requisites, regional autonomy implications, and adherence to the fundamental principles enshrined within the federal framework.

Turning the lens to the Ethiopian context, it becomes evident that the federal government assumes the role of determining the total transfer pool, endowing it with discretionary power over the size of grants. Chanie (2007b, p. 215) provides an insightful depiction of the subsidy allocation process during the early decade of federalism. The sequence unfolds with the Ministry of Finance and Economic Development (MoFED) drafting the distribution pool proposal in consultation with the Economic Affairs Department of the Prime Minister's Office (PMO). Subsequently, a specialised committee within the Council of Ministers (CM), helmed by the Prime Minister, lends its final approval. The proposal then proceeds to receive the rubber-stamp endorsement of the full CM session. Ultimately, the imprimatur of the House of Peoples' Representatives (HPR) is secured during its annual budget ratification session.

Presently, the Ministry of Finance and Economic Cooperation (MoFEC) undertakes the responsibility of formulating the total pool, subjecting it to parliamentary approval at the outset of each fiscal year. Of noteis that the amount of grants is not based on a predetermined formula. Neither premised on ratios nor subject to negotiation, it pivots entirely on the decision of the federal government. An informant notes that:

> After MoFEC prepares the subsidy, the heads of the regional Bureau of Finance and Economic Cooperation and regional Revenues Authority usually attend meetings steered by the Ministry to discuss the subsidies. However, the regional participation is only informative as the regions have no chance of modifying the proposal of the Ministry.[5]

In the realm of subsidy allocation, the involvement of regions is confined primarily to their presence in briefings and discussions. Beyond these participatory meetings, their agency in determining the amount of subsidies is conspicuously absent. The onus of decision-making concerning the transfer pool rests exclusively within the purview of the federal government. Within this construct, the role of the regions is largely relegated to that of information sources, notably limiting their influence in shaping the size of subsidies.

---

5 A Director of Finance and Administration in the Oromia Region Bureau of Finance and Economic Cooperation, April 2019.

Upon the determination of the transfer pool by the Ministry of Finance and Economic Cooperation (MoFEC), the subsequent allocation across regions is subject to a dual-legislative process. The initial stage sees the HoF assigning the subsidies among regions, underpinned by the subsidy distribution formula. Subsequently, the allocation process receives the endorsement of the parliament, signifying both the overall grant amount and the specific allocation apportioned to each region. This comprehensive endorsement transpires concurrently with the ratification of the federal budget. This procedural framework not only underscores the preeminence of federal authority in subsidy allocation but also accentuates the modest latitude afforded to regional entities in shaping this crucial fiscal dimension.

5 Determination of Subsidies Formulas and Regional Shares

The territorial distribution of regional subsidies in Ethiopia is formula-driven. The HoF prepares transfer formulas. The House's Revenue and Budgets Standing Committee plays a leading role in preparing and revising transfer formulas (Yimenu, 2021, p. 143). The House adopted different formulas by using various factors. An official in the Oromia Region stated that "Regions are consulted in the transfer formula approval through representatives of NNPs in the HoF. Besides, as regional presidents are members of the HoF, they can let their concerns heard regarding the subsidy formula, not the transfer pool, during the House's sessions. The sessions sometimes entertain debates as some members raise issues regarding the weights of the variables employed in determining regional subsidies".[6] Such practices indicate that regions have a better opportunity to influence the determination of the subsidy allocation formula than the transfer pool.

There is no fixed time set in Ethiopia to conduct revisions of the transfer formula; however, the practice shows that amendments are made on average every three years. The formula has been revised eight times since the formation of the federation in 1995. The main reasons for the irregularity of the time frame for formula revision are lack of quality data, lack of skilled and experienced workforce, and a viable and independent body to do the task (World Bank, 2010, p. 43).

6 A Director of Finance and Administration in the Oromia Region Bureau of Finance and Economic Cooperation, April 2019.

Two crucial developments in the practices of determination of subsidy formula are noteworthy. First, during the formative stage of the federation, the Federal Ministry of Finance was the main entity responsible for designing and executing the transfer formula (World Bank, 2000, p. 30, 2010, p. 43). Second, though the role of the House has improved over time (World Bank, 2010, p. 43), its mandate was often taken away through the CM Regulation No.17/ 1997, which stretched the Ministry of Finance's authority. Different variables were employed in framing subsidy formulas until 2007. Starting in 2007, differences in potential revenue-raising capacity and expenditure needs became the key determinants of the size of subsidy allocated to regions. The variables and their weights under formula regimes are presented in Table 6.1.

A discerning analysis reveals noteworthy changes in the composition of variables employed in shaping the subsidy formula, ranging from 3 to 6, coupled with substantial shifts in the assigned variable weights. Notably, the significance of the variable 'population size' experienced oscillations, ascending from 30 per cent in 1995 to 65 per cent in 2004. A counterpoint to this trend is the diminishing weights allocated to 'preceding year capital budget' and 'territorial size,' which dwindled from 15 per cent and 10 per cent to 0 per cent, respectively (Table 6.1).

Evidently, population size emerges as a pivotal determinant, commanding paramount importance, shadowed by the considerations of development and revenue-generation endeavours. However, the high reliance of regions on fiscal transfers means fluctuations in variable composition and weightings have

TABLE 6.1 Variables and weights in the subsidies formulas (1995–2007)

Variable	**Weight in per cent**				
	1995	**1997**	**1998**	**2000**	**2004–2007**
Population Size	30	33.33	60	55	65
Level of Development	25	33.33	15	20	25
Revenue Raising Effort	20	33.33	15	15	10
Preceding Year Capital Budget	15	0	0	0	0
Territorial Size	10	0	10	0	0
Poverty Index	0	0	0	10	0

SOURCE: HOF (2017, P. 6)

ramifications on regional planning and budgeting. The implications of these dynamic shifts are profound, warranting scrutiny of the impacts on the magnitude of subsidies allotted to individual regions across periods. The subsequent section delineates the varying proportions of federal grants allocated to each region under distinct formula regimes, shedding light on the interplay between evolving formula dynamics and regional subsidy shares.

Ethiopian regions are classified into: Amhara, Oromia, SNNP, and Tigray as developed regions, in contrast to the remaining regions, termed as developing regions, primarily due to disparities in essential infrastructure, educated human resources, and self-generated revenues (World Bank, 2016a, p. 11, 2016b, p. 20). Within this context, the recalibrations in subsidy formulas have triggered substantial perturbations in the distribution of subsidy shares among regions. Notably, a discernible pattern emerges wherein the share of developed regions, with the exception of Tigray, experienced an ascending trajectory over time. Contrarily, developing regions witnessed a consistent decline in their shares, barring the Somali region, which witnessed a threefold augmentation (Table 6.2).

The examination of standard deviations in grant shares unveils a striking contrast between the variance exhibited by developing and developed regions. Developing regions showcase moderate fluctuations in grant shares over time, indicative of a steady and measured approach in their grant allocation. In contrast, developed regions exhibit considerably higher variability, hinting at a path-dependent model that adjusts to shifting demographics, revenue dynamics, and formulaic factors. This dichotomy underscores an incremental trajectory that characterises grant allocation for developing regions. Stability in fiscal transfers at moderate levels emerges as a priority, rooted in the need to sustain administrative functionality (Chanie, 2007a, p. 377; Moges, 2003, p. 131).

The narrative assumes a divergent course for developed regions, where share fluctuations are considerably broader. For these regions, whose political influence is pronounced, the negotiation of shares extends beyond formula-based considerations to encompass non-formulaic factors. Evidently, institutional inertia casts a substantial influence over grant allocations, intertwining political considerations irrespective of the formula. This observation gains further empirical support through the correlation analysis between population and grant shares, elucidating the intricate nexus between political dynamics and the granular mechanisms governing fiscal allocation.

Analysis reveals a robust positive correlation of 0.99 between population size and grant shares, indicating population is a primary determinant. The most populated regions received the largest transfers, while less populated areas like Afar and Gambella got the smallest. However, Tigray emerged as an

TABLE 6.2 Regional share of federal subsidies (1995–2017) (in %)

Region	Regional share under different formula regimes								Mean	STD	CV	RR	P (%)
	1995	1997	1998	2000	2004	2007	2012	2017					
Tigray	10.5	11.4	9.5	7.6	7.7	6.4	7.2	6.0	8.3	2.0	23.6	36.6	5.8
Afar	4.9	3.3	4.9	6.9	4.7	2.5	3.2	3.0	4.2	1.4	34.5	15.1	2.0
Amhara	20.1	24.6	24.0	21.8	21.6	26.5	23.2	21.6	22.9	2.1	9.0	22.7	23.5
Oromia	32.3	28.1	29.0	27.3	30.1	33.7	32.5	34.5	30.9	2.7	8.6	40.8	38.9
Somali	3.1	2.8	5.0	9.0	7.3	6.7	8.1	10.0	6.5	2.7	40.8	15.7	6.3
B-G	3.4	1.5	3.9	4.8	3.7	1.4	2.1	1.8	2.8	1.3	44.9	17.0	1.2
SNNPR	15.9	20.5	18.6	16.1	18.0	20.7	20.1	20.1	18.7	2.0	10.5	21.0	21.1
Gambella	2.8	2.5	2.5	4.0	2.8	0.9	1.5	1.3	2.3	1.0	43.2	14.4	0.5
Harari	0.8	1.3	1.7	1.8	1.5	0.5	1.0	0.8	1.2	0.5	39.7	23.6	0.3

The correlation between population and grant share = 0.99

Correlation between Ownsource revenues (ROSR) = 0.61

SOURCE: COMPUTED FROM VARIOUS YEARS OF THE HOF FORMULA. NOTE: B-G = BENISHANGUL-GUMUZ; P = POPULATION (2015); AND RR = REGIONAL OWN SOURCE REVENUE

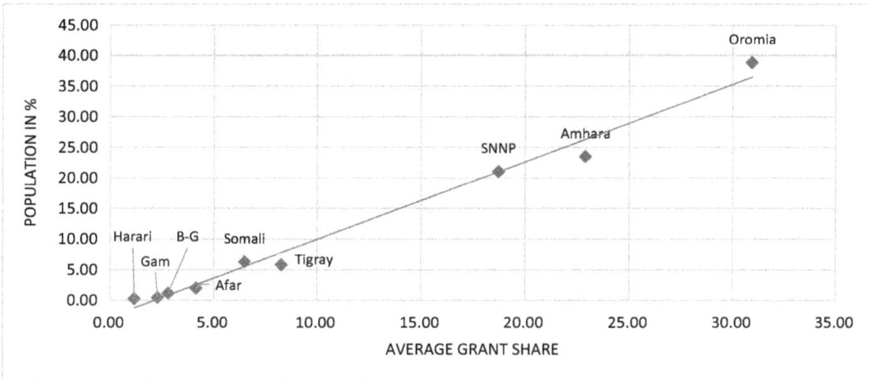

FIGURE 6.1 Population vs. average grant share (2015) (in %)
SOURCE: SEE TABLE 6.2

outlier, receiving a disproportionately high share compared to the more populous Somali region in the 1990s. This deviation from the population-grant proportion suggests significant non-formulaic factors, likely political alignments, shaped Tigray's advantage. Overall, while population strongly predicts grant allocation, Tigray's case demonstrates grants also hinged on ethno-regional politics, especially in the early federal period. This shows objective formula factors alone did not drive intergovernmental transfers.

While population remains a robust predictor of aggregate grant allocation, a granular examination of individual regions unveils noteworthy deviations from this overarching national correlation. Regions such as Amhara, Gambella, and Benishangul-Gumuz defy the expected positive relationship between changes in population and changes in grant shares (Table 6.3). For instance, Amhara's share experienced a 6.4 per cent growth despite a 3 per cent population decline, while Gambella's and Benishangul-Gumuz's shares receded amidst population growth. This discrepancy underscores the potent influence of political dynamics in shaping allocation outcomes, which at times override formulaic calculations.

The augmented share of Amhara epitomises an incremental, negotiation-driven rationale designed to bolster its position relative to other significant regions. This strategic political imperative necessitated circumventing the population-based formula. This empirical insight underscores a dual driving force: the interplay of both national demographic trends and subnational political exigencies in moulding the distribution of grants. Despite a gradual moderation in overt political influences over time, clandestine agreements continued to exert sway, particularly in determining the shares of certain regions.

TABLE 6.3 Regional level correlation between population and grant (1995–2015) (in %)

Year	Tigray		Afar		Amhara		Oromia		Somali		B-G		SNNP		Gambella		Harari	
	P	G	P	G	P	G	P	G	P	G	P	G	P	G	P	G	P	G
1995	6.02	10.5	2.02	4.92	26.48	20.09	35.88	32.25	3.5	3.09	0.88	3.39	19.84	15.85	0.34	2.8	0.25	0.8
2007	5.58	6.38	1.88	2.52	23.35	26.49	36.66	33.72	6.02	6.68	1.06	1.42	20.24	20.72	0.41	0.9	0.24	0.5
2015	5.58	6.03	1.99	3.02	23.53	21.6	38.87	34.46	6.26	9.98	1.16	1.83	21.08	20.11	0.47	1.3	0.27	0.8
Corr	0.75		0.80		−0.72		0.90		0.91		−0.85		0.67		−0.78		0.76	

SOURCE: COMPUTED FROM VARIOUS YEARS' OF HOF'S FORMULA. NOTE: P = POPULATION, G = GRANT; CORR = CORRELATION BETWEEN P AND G

Collectively, this analysis cogently underscores that grant allocation traverses beyond a simple demographic calculus or a technocratic formula. Instead, it embodies a multifaceted and intricate political process where demographic dynamics interact with regional political considerations, resulting in a tapestry of grant allocation that defies simplistic categorisations and underscores the complexity of fiscal distribution mechanisms.

6 Ethno-regional Dynamics and Fiscal Transfers

The disproportionality of Tigray's share in the 1990s is intrinsically tied to the political dominance of the TPLF on a national scale (Chanie, 2007a; Solomon, 2015). Notably, insights from a key informant underscore that TPLF officials justified this skewed distribution by citing the region's tumultuous history of a 17-year conflict against the Derg regime. This included human and infrastructural losses, coupled with their pivotal role in overthrowing the Derg regime.[7] This elucidates how early grant distribution was principally driven by ethno-regional political alignments rather than economic considerations. Transfers were employed as a mechanism to reward TPLF's home region, diverging from needs-based or impartial principles. This politicisation diverted grants from regions like Somali, despite their pressing development requirements. The evidence reveals that fiscal transfers were initially steered along ethno-regional lines, deviating from the constitutional objectives of rectifying regional disparities. It perpetuated the historical marginalisation experienced by lowland areas.

Another conspicuous anomaly emerges in the case of the Somali region, where its grant share is comparatively lower than that of Tigray despite its larger population and elevated expenditure needs. The intricate interplay of factors in sparsely populated lowland areas like Somali highlights their amplified recurrent expenditures due to the challenging geography, translating into pricier service provisions for their sparse settlements (Gebre-Egziabhere, 2018, pp. 16–17; Yimenu, 2023, p. 10). This contextual backdrop anticipates higher grants for these regions compared to their more developed highland counterparts. However, historical grant allocations during the 1990s contravened the constitutional principles of equitable regional development. Rather than aligning with needs-based distribution, Tigray received disproportionate transfers. This divergence underscores the supremacy of ethno-regional

7 A former member of the federal parliament, June 2019, Addis Ababa.

political affiliations over fiscal considerations during the nascent federal era. Partisan objectives superseded the constitutional intent of addressing regional inequalities, thus perpetuating the historical disadvantage of lowland regions.

The evolution of Somali's grant share over time underscores the palpable influence of extra-formulaic political dynamics in shaping allocation. The interplay between centre-periphery negotiations and regional political manoeuvres offers a nuanced explanation for the incremental enhancement of Somali's status (Hagmann, 2005). Interviews corroborate the role of additional political factors. A former HoF member points to Somali's heightened strategic significance in countering insurgent groups like the Ogaden National Liberation Front (ONLF) and militant forces like Al-Shabaab, accentuating the region's bargaining leverage. The shift in power dynamics after the death of Prime Minister Meles Zenawi in 2012 further substantiates this trend as a non-Tigrayan leader's accession to power redistributed influence.[8] Recent political developments underscore the intricate evolution of the centre-region fiscal bargaining dynamics, culminating in a party schism following Oromia-led protests, leading to Abiy Ahmed, an official from Oromia, becoming Prime Minister in 2018. This progression delineates the multifaceted trajectory of power dynamics and its resonance in shaping fiscal allocations.

7 Evolution and Reform of Subsidy Allocation Methodology after 2007

A pivotal shift in federal subsidy allocation was witnessed in 2007 with the adoption of a new formula, which persisted until 2011/12. Acknowledging the limitations of the earlier approach, the House of Federation (HoF) admitted the subjective nature of variables and their assigned weights in estimating expenditure needs (HoF, 2017, p. 7). The method, compared to the prior method critiqued for neglecting potential revenue-generating capacity, was juxtaposed against the Australian Commonwealth Grant Commission system, lauded for its objectivity and minimised lobbying (World Bank, 2010, pp. 23–24). From 2007, emphasis pivoted to disparities in potential revenue generation and expenditure necessities as the bedrock of subsidies.

A subsequent formula spanning 2012–2017 followed same approach. Presently, a 2017 iteration governs subsidy distribution. The revamped methodology sought to integrate changes in population, development, revenue

8 Former member of House of Federation from Somali region, May 2019, Addis Ababa.

capacity, and poverty levels across regions. The new approach hinged on estimating representative revenues and expenditures. Regional revenue estimates were established from primary regional own-source revenues, while expenditure approximations were drawn from main regional expenditures. Taxes constituting 80% of regional revenues and expenditures taking 90% of regional budgets are calculated, and for this calculation, the average revenue of three years was used.

The main tax revenue sources used to estimate revenue generation capacity include agricultural income tax, land use fee, payroll tax, business income tax, turnover tax, and value-added tax. In the previous formula, livestock tax was included in addition to these tax sources to estimate each region's revenue generation capacity. The main expenditure categories included in calculating the expenditure of each region are general services and administration, primary and secondary education, TVET, public health, agriculture and rural development, drinking water development, rural road construction and maintenance, urban development, and micro and small-scale enterprises (HoF, 2017).

The Federal Budget Grant Distribution Formula adopted in 2007 by the HoF combines transfers to manage both vertical and horizontal imbalances. It builds on three main pillars: 1) balancing differences in revenue-raising capacities; 2) balancing differences regarding expenditure needs; 3) reserving one per cent of the distribution pool for Benishangul-Gumuz, Afar, Gambela and Somali Regional States, the four 'developing regions' requiring special attention.

There is no stand-alone fiscal equalisation system in Ethiopia. The 2007 formula introduced a novel approach, channelling 1% of subsidies to developing regions to foster cross-regional development. The four 'developing regions' have significantly lower revenue-raising capacities and higher expenditure needs than the rest of the regions due to different factors, including their historical marginalisation in infrastructure development and investment distribution (Yimenu, 2023). These regions would be unable to catch up with the rest of the region without additional grants. Hence, one per cent of the total grant is reserved for the four emerging regions to address this inequality. The share of these regions, out of that 1 per cent, is 18.6% (Afar), 42.4% (Somali), 28.8% (Benishangul-Gumuz), and 10.3% (Gambella). The share of each region is computed based on weighted indicators relating to the particular situation of these four regional states. The indicators and their weights are area of cultivated land (0.2), population (0.1), Tropical livestock unit (0.15), urban employment (0.1), Spatial price index (0.15), Tax raising effort (0.2) and number of poor people (0.1).

Despite altering the developmental allowance, the proportional stakes of each region from total block grants remained relatively constant. Yet, the paradigm shift bore unforeseen repercussions for specific developing regions. The absolute share of Benishangul-Gumuz and Gambella regions declined compared to the preceding formula. Consequently, deductions were made from regions such as Oromia to offset the developing regions. This recalibration stemmed from political negotiations and regional cooperation, albeit under the ruling party's central committee direction (HoF, 2017, p. 83). Insights from informants, however, hint at adjustments driven by pressure from federal party leaders, propagating down the party hierarchy, emphasising the ruling party's dominance in Ethiopian federalism. Regional officials state that "the adjustment was driven by pressure from federal leaders on members of the HoF through the party structure, following directives from the EPRDF central committee".[9] This is not surprising, considering that intra-party politics takes precedence over federal institutions in Ethiopia (Rohrbach, 2021).

The incongruity between the new formula's intention and its application raises questions about political manipulation's role. Some regions relinquishing their share to bolster others underscores the influence of political dynamics over a purportedly objective framework. Ultimately, the formula's design was undercut by political manoeuvring, failing to reflect the diversity of constituent units and casting doubt on its intended objectivity. The evolution of grant shares unveils a narrative of shifting intra-party and federal-regional negotiations. Heightened assertiveness among regional elites prompted adjustments to the formula, leading to reallocation away from Tigray towards regions like the Somali region. Despite these improvements, persistent shortcomings mar the revised formula. Its intricate calculations pose comprehension challenges for policymakers, and its bias towards regions with larger populations and land sizes contradicts the intended support for developing regions enshrined in the Constitution (Forum of Federations, 2020).

In the Ethiopian context, achieving an apolitical and needs-based distribution proves complex. The intricate interplay of ethno-regional alliances and rivalries complicates the pursuit of equitable allocation. The landscape defies easy technocratic solutions due to the web of interests that connect federal and regional authorities. Grant allocation transcends mere economic considerations, necessitating political equilibrium. The evidence underscores that formula changes unfold through ongoing negotiations and shifts in power

9 An official in the Oromia Region Office of the President, March 2019, Addis Ababa, and A member of HoF from SNNPR, April 2019, Hawassa.

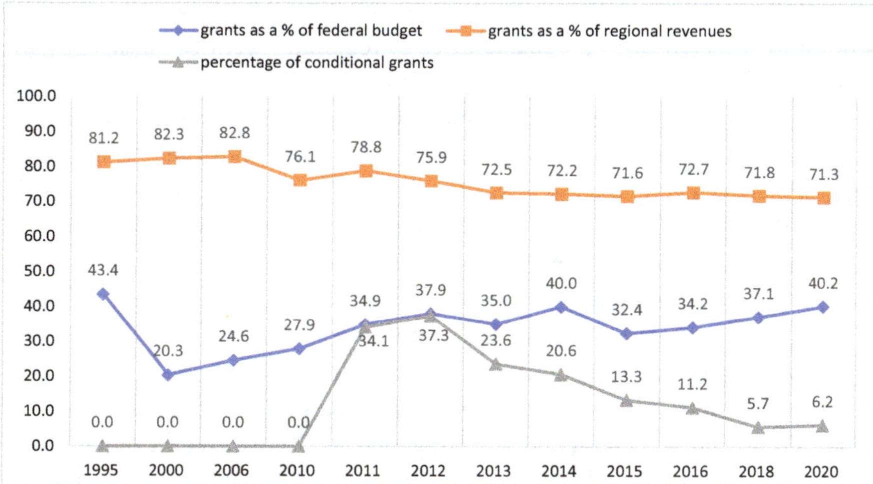

FIGURE 6.2 Subsidies data (1995–2020) (in %)
SOURCE: COMPUTED FROM MOFEC'S VARIOUS YEARS OF DATA

dynamics rather than being products of expert design. This illuminates the limits of technocratic approaches in depoliticising fiscal transfers within a context defined by the intricate interests binding federal and regional actors.

8 Grants and Regional Autonomy in Ethiopia

A thorough examination demonstrates the significance of grants within federal spending, constituting an average of 33% of the budget (Figure 6.2). Despite upward trends, regions argue that transfers remain insufficient due to the imbalance between centralised revenues and decentralised expenditures. This highlights a divergence between subnational aspirations and federal calculations. While an overreliance on transfers threatens regional autonomy, subsidies are indispensable in bridging fiscal shortfalls, with transfers comprising over 75% of regional budgets. The degree of dependence varies, with developing regions heavily relying on grants for approximately 85% of their revenues (Yimenu, 2023, p. 7). This divergence exemplifies the intricate equilibrium that fiscal transfers must navigate between central and regional interests.

Initially granted without restrictions to empower regions, a transition occurred in 2011 when conditional transfers tied to specific sectors aligned with MDGs and SDGs were introduced (UNICEF, 2017). This shift from unrestricted to targeted grants reveals the central government's strategic use of grants to influence regional spending and advance national goals. Regional autonomy is not only affected by grant size relative to regional revenues but also by the proportion of conditional grants within total transfers. Higher shares of conditional grants could undermine regional autonomy (Watts, 2008, p. 106).

Figure 6.2 demonstrates a decline in the share of conditional grants since 2014, reflecting a rebalancing towards regional autonomy. This shift is attributed to the conclusion of MDGs, a priority for both the federal government and donor agencies.[10] The specific conditions attached to grants significantly impact regional autonomy. Evaluating these conditions is crucial as some of the conditions can promote accountability and fiscal effectiveness, yet some conditions may restrict discretion. The level of strictness may also vary. Conditional grants in Ethiopia features earmarking, rigorous monitoring, and demanding reporting, which curtails regional flexibility (World Bank, 2016b, p. 13). As further explored below, these characteristics enable the federal government to steer regional policy priorities.

Earmarked Grants: Conditional grants in Ethiopia confine spending to six sectors: rural roads, drinking water and irrigation, health, education, agriculture, and small and medium enterprise development. While regions maintain control over fund allocation within these sectors, the stipulations intend to emphasise investments in these areas and grant the central government influence over regional priorities. An informant from the Federal Ministry of Finance and Economic Cooperation (MoFEC) highlights that these grants were introduced to counter the prevalence of recurrent expenses in regional budgets, which hindered capital project investments. This strategic shift underscores the central government's attempt to shape regional fiscal direction.[11] Supporting this notion, the World Bank (2016b, p. 27) report affirms that capital expenditure comprised only 25 per cent of total regional spending before 2011, rising to 40 per cent with the introduction of conditional grants. While this shift bolstered investments in key sectors, it overlooked the recurring costs associated with new projects. We may assume that additional money and responsibilities can be attracting. However, it's important to note that conditional grants did not constitute extra funding; rather, they were linked to existing grants, reducing block grants (World Bank, 2016b, pp. 31–33). This reallocation came at the expense of unrestricted funding crucial for day-to-day operations and contributed to increased federal oversight.

10 An Official in the Ministry of Finance and Economic Cooperation, April 2019, Addis Ababa.

11 An Official in the Ministry of Finance and Economic Cooperation, April 2019, Addis Ababa.

Monitoring Project by Project: The federal government's control is upheld through meticulous project-level oversight. Regions must compile project lists within the designated sectors for conditional grant funding and to secure approval from the MoFEC. Once sanctioned, projects within a sector cannot be swapped for those from another sector (World Bank, 2016b, p. 14). Furthermore, the grant obliges regions to plan annual expenditures as though projects were initiated and finalised within a single fiscal year. Consequently, multi-year initiatives grapple with unrealistic annual budgeting regulations, detached from practicalities. Stringent monitoring and limited substitution protocols serve as mechanisms of control, constraining regional financial flexibility. This serves as a testament to how detailed conditions enable federal influence, even within the framework of constitutionally endorsed regional autonomy. These conditions contribute to an enhanced federal role in regional budgetary processes and the setting of priorities, effectively reversing some aspects of decentralisation through regulatory mandates.

Rigorous Reporting: Reporting adheres to the project-by-project monitoring principle, placing a heavy burden on regional administrations in terms of time and effort. The regional financial reporting system is mandated to conform to the stipulations of the federal government (Regulation No. 190, 2010). Moreover, regions are obligated to furnish the central authority with quarterly, semi-annual, and annual financial reports (Art. 51, Regulation No. 190/2010). These reports must include details of revenues, expenditures, and outstanding debts. The World Bank explained the reporting obligations for Ethiopia's conditional grants: Quarterly reports include financial and physical details, not just statistics. These reports trigger MoFEC payments to regions. Funding is performance-based and released post-performance, making it an effective, conditional transfer reliant on timely and satisfactory quarterly reports (World Bank, 2016b, p. 14).

This demonstrates how conditioned grants facilitated regulatory expansion into regional budgetary procedures, centralising some fiscal powers. This process of producing quarterly reports leads to delays for subnational governments. An SNNP informant highlights that "conditional grants, coupled with limited own-source revenues, have become a major challenge." The informant adds that "since policies funded by federal grants are centrally designed with little or no input from the regions, the regions are reduced to executing the federal government's priorities rather than pursuing their own".[12]

12 A Director of Budget Administration in the SNNPR Region Bureau of Finance and Economic Development, May 2019, Hawassa.

Another problematic aspect of conditional grants is their unpredictability. Although the reduction in the proportion of conditional grants (refer to Figure 6.2) increases regional autonomy, the instability in grant amounts led to uncertainty in regional budgeting. A regional official noted, "The region planned several projects based on the first two years' grants and the federal priorities. However, the federal government terminated the MDGs' funding and told the region to finish the ongoing projects from its sources. Thus, we had to shift the budget from other projects to finish the MDGs' projects initiated based on priorities set by the centre".[13] The fluctuation in conditional grant amounts disrupted regional planning due to sudden shifts in federal priorities, resulting in unfinished projects. This further deepened reliance and compromised regional self-governance despite constitutionally granted powers. The trends highlight how discretionary funds intended for regional empowerment can indirectly serve central control if deployed unpredictably.

9 Conclusions

This chapter has offered a comprehensive examination of the political economy dynamics that have shaped Ethiopia's system of intergovernmental fiscal transfers since the inception of its federal Constitution in 1995. The analysis has underscored the critical role of fiscal transfers in addressing vertical and horizontal fiscal imbalances inherent in the country's federal design. However, the chapter has also elucidated the extensive challenges in achieving an equitable, transparent, and effective transfer system within a diverse, developing country like Ethiopia.

A key finding from the analysis is the considerable gap between the constitutional vision for fiscal transfers and the actual practice that has unfolded. Constitutionally, the House of Federation is vested with the authority to determine regional subsidies. However, the federal Ministry of Finance has exerted predominant control over deciding transfer amounts and designing allocation formulas, restricting regional input. This circumvention of the House's intended role underscores the dominance of the executive branch in shaping fiscal federalism, often through non-transparent negotiations within the ruling party apparatus rather than open legislative deliberation.

13 A Director of Budget Administration in the Oromia Region Bureau of Finance and Economic Cooperation, April 2019, Addis Ababa.

The chapter has also demonstrated how political alignments between the federal government and regional administrations, especially the ruling EPRDF coalition dynamics, have strongly influenced fiscal transfers. In the initial federal period, the Tigray region received a disproportionately high allocation, indicative of distribution being driven by ethno-regional affiliations of the TPLF-dominated EPRDF rather than objective economic considerations. Over time, shifts in intra-party bargaining power prompted adjustments, leading to an augmented share for the Oromia and Somali regions. However, the evidence indicates that fiscal transfers have been utilised strategically to reward regional allies, perpetuating historical territorial inequalities that less developed regions face.

Moreover, the analysis has revealed the conditions and monitoring mechanisms attached to federal grants, enabling considerable central oversight over regional budgets and priorities. The introduction of earmarked, conditional grants has briefly reversed aspects of decentralisation, with detailed federal stipulations on project selection, budgets, and reporting curtailing regional autonomy. Unpredictable fluctuations in grant amounts have also disrupted regional planning and self-government.

Evidently, crafting an equitable fiscal transfer system remains an enduring challenge for Ethiopia, requiring transparency and insulation from partisan interests to uphold the principles of fiscal federalism. With the political transition following the EPRDF's dissolution, addressing regional disparities through the transfer system will necessitate balancing diverse regional voices beyond the previous ruling coalition. The diminishing dominance of the federal government also indicates greater bargaining power for states to negotiate their fiscal interests. However, constructively managing these multifaceted dynamics will require strengthening independent institutions like the House of Federation to serve as credible arbiters, upholding constitutional principles over partisan or regional interests. Undeniably, reforming intergovernmental fiscal relations stands among Ethiopia's foremost priorities in this pivotal juncture to sustain national cohesion and equitably uphold regional autonomy. As Ethiopia navigates its transition, concrete reforms to intergovernmental fiscal relations remain imperative to uphold the integrity of its federal system and sustain national harmony.

The insights from Ethiopia's experience offer salient lessons for other federal systems confronting similar challenges of ethnolinguistic diversity, uneven development, and partisan politics. The analysis underscores the need for constitutional safeguards and independent institutions to ensure fiscal transfers adhere to equitable, and objective criteria rather than ethno-regional favoritism. Mechanisms for transparent formula design and negotiation are essential, along with predictable grant allocation resistant to partisan manipulation. Conditions on transfers should balance national priorities and regional autonomy. Overall, insulation from political interests is imperative to uphold the integrity of fiscal federalism.

References

Aalen, L. (2011). The politics of ethnicity in Ethiopia actors, power and mobilisation under ethnic federalism.

Boadway, R. (2011). Mind the Gap: Reflections on Fiscal Balance in Decentralised Federations. In T. J. Courchene, J. R. Allan, C. Leuprecht, & N. Verrelli (Eds.), *The Federal Idea: Essay in Honour of Ronald L. Watts* (pp. 363–377). MacGill-Queen's University Press.

Chanie, P. (2007a). Clientelism and Ethiopia's post-1991 decentralisation. *The Journal of Modern African Studies*, 45(3), 355–384.

Chanie, P. (2007b). *What one hand giveth, the other hand taketh away: Ethiopia's post-1991 decentralisation reform under neo-patrimonialism*. Shaker Publisher.

Forum of Federations (2020). *Terms of Reference: Senior Consultant to Design and Conduct Study to Review the System of Intergovernmental Fiscal Transfers of Ethiopia*. Forum of Federations.

Gebre-Egziabhere, T. (2018). Emerging Regions in Ethiopia: Are they catching up with the rest of Ethiopia? *Eastern Africa Social Science Research Review*, 34(1), 1–36.

Hagmann, T. (2005). Beyond clannishness and colonialism: Understanding political disorder in Ethiopia's Somali Region, 1991–2004. *The Journal of Modern African Studies*, 43(4), 509–536.

HoF (2017). *The Federal General-Purpose Grant Distribution Formula 2017/18–2019/20*. House of Federation.

Kelecha, M. (2021). Oromo Protests, Repression, and Political Change in Ethiopia, 2014–2020. *Northeast African Studies*, 21(2), 183–226.

Lyons, T. (1996). Closing the Transition: The May 1995 Elections in Ethiopia. *The Journal of Modern African Studies*, 34(1), 121–142.

McLure, C. E. (1999). *The tax assignment problem: Conceptual and administrative considerations in achieving subnational fiscal autonomy*. The World Bank.

Moges, A. G. (2003). An Economic Analysis of Fiscal Federalism in Ethiopia. *Northeast African Studies*, 10(2), 111–140.

Oates, W. (1999). An Essay on Fiscal Federalism. *Journal of Economic Literature*, 37(3), 1120–1149.

Parker, J. (2014). *Comparative Federalism and Intergovernmental Agreements: Analysing Australia, Canada, Germany, South Africa, Switzerland and the United States.* Routledge.

Proclamation No. 251 (2001), *Consolidation of the House of the Federation and the Definition of its Powers and Responsibilities.* Federal Negarit Gazeta.

Proclamation No. 648 (2009). *Federal Government of Ethiopia Financial Administration Proclamation*, Federal Negarit Gazeta.

Regulations No.17 (1997). *The Council of Ministers Financial.* Federal Negarit Gazeta.

Regulation No. 190 (2010). *The Council of Ministers Financial Administration Regulation.* Federal Negarit Gazeta.

Rohrbach, L. (2021). Intra-party dynamics and the success of federal arrangements: Ethiopia in comparative perspective. *Regional & Federal Studies*, 31(4), 475–494.

Sham, A. (2007). Introduction: Principles of Fiscal Federalism. In A. Sham (Ed.), *The Practice of Fiscal Federalism: Comparative Perspective* (pp. 3–43). McGill-Queen's University Press.

Solomon, G. (2015). Central Control and Regional States' Autonomy in Ethiopia. In A. C. LeVan, J. O. Fashagba, & E. R. McMahon (Eds.), *African State Governance Subnational Politics and National Power* (pp. 179–197). Palgrave Macmillan.

UNICEF (2017). National Education Sector Budget Brief: 2016/17: Ethiopia. UNICEF ETHIOPIA. https://www.unicef.org/ethiopia/reports/national-and-sector-budget-briefs.

Watts, R. (2008). *Comparing federal systems* (Third Edition). McGill-Queen's University Press.

World Bank (2000). Ethiopia: Regionalisation study (Macroeconomics 2 8898-ET). World Bank Africa Region. https://documents.worldbank.org/curated/pt/781391468749077489/pdf/multi-page.pdf.

World Bank (2010). *ETHIOPIA Public Finance Review 2010* (54952-ET; p. 93). The World Bank.

World Bank (2016a). *Ethiopia Public Expenditure Review 2015* (Report No: ACS14541; p. 166). The World Bank.

World Bank (2016b). *Federal Democratic Republic of Ethiopia Evaluation of MDGs Specific Purpose Grant to Regions* (ACS17500; p. 53). The World Bank.

Yimenu, B. (2021). Implementing federalism in a developing country: The case of Ethiopia, 1995–2020. [University of Kent]. https://doi.org/10.22024/UniKent/01.02.92367.

Yimenu, B. (2022). The Politics of Ethnonational Accommodation Under a Dominant Party Regime: Ethiopias Three Decades Experience. *Journal of Asian and African Studies*, 1–17. https://doi.org/10.1177/00219096221097663.

Yimenu, B. (2023). Measuring and explaining fiscal de/centralisation: Empirical evidence from Ethiopia, 1995–2020. *Public Administration and Development*, 1–15. https://doi.org/10.1002/pad.2020.

Yimenu B. (2024). Continuities and changes in electoral authoritarianism: evidence from Ethiopia. *Regional and Federal Studies*, 1–30 https://doi.org/10.1080/13597566.2024.2315491.

Young, J. (1998). Regionalism and democracy in Ethiopia. *Third World Quarterly*, 19(2), 191–204.

CHAPTER 7

Intergovernmental Fiscal Relations during the COVID 19 Pandemic in Germany: Was the New Fiscal Equalisation Scheme able to Hamper Financial Dislocations?

Gisela Färber
German University of Administrative Sciences Speyer & German Research Institute of Public Administration Speyer

1 Introduction

In Germany, the COVID-19 crisis coincided with the reform of the federal (inter-state) fiscal equalisation scheme in 2020. In the past, particularly during the economic and financial crisis in 2008–09 the equalisation scheme served as an instrument of 'horizontal insurance' against too much divergence among the losses of state and local tax revenues and therefore as stabiliser of subnational expenditures across the country.

This 'insurance function' is to be distinguished from the function of horizontal distribution by 'simply' declining the gaps among the tax revenues of the States. It particularly focusses the very uneven decline of GDP and the therefrom resulting losses of tax revenues in cases of economic crisis which often hit the economically strong Länder more than the poorer ones. That insurance function therefore guarantees the stability of the supply of public services at the level of subnational – state and local – governments in periods of economic crisis and the equivalence of living conditions across Germany. The reform of the inter-state fiscal equalisation scheme in 2020 should – despite the decline of the equalisation rates – be able to perform this function. During the negotiations of the reform, nobody had expected that the challenge for the new scheme would happen the first year after coming into force.

The economic consequences of the COVID crisis indeed hit the states in a divergent manner and had a strong influence on regional economic decline and the following recovery of the growth rates. Growth rates of GDP and of fiscal capacities among the States diverged from the traditional pattern. Most recently, the explosion of energy prices and inflation rates resulting from the

Ukraine war continued the situation of crisis for subnational budgets. As a consequence of ongoing crisis, the new rules of VAT distribution as core of fiscal equalisation and the new Federal Supplementary Grants had to pass a double challenge of distribution and stabilisation of subnational finance.

The paper therefore identifies the 'horizontal' economic and fiscal effects of the COVID and the Ukraine war crisis on regional economic growth and the subnational tax revenues. It analyses if and how the new equalisation scheme was able to stabilise state and local budgets across Germany. As local governments are 'parts' of their Länder, their fiscal capacities play an increasing role for the new – less equalising – equalisation formula and are the base for new supplementary vertical transfer payments. The paper finishes with lessons to be learnt for the intergovernmental financial relations in future crisis situations – the resilience of the system – as well as for the tremendous efforts to be undertaken to manage the changes of the economy and all pubic budgets in the ongoing energy and climate crisis.

2 The Reform of Federal Inter-state Fiscal Equalisation

The fiscal equalisation scheme is the final step of the vertical and horizontal distribution of tax revenues across the three layers of governments. The tax system – almost exclusively under the legislation of the Federation – is dominated by joint tax revenues from the personal and corporate income taxes and the value-added tax. Until 2019, the most famous step was the horizontal equalisation among the States which organised formula-based transfer payments from the rich to the poorer States. Local governments are partly included into the fiscal capacities and financial needs of the States while the Constitution obliges the States to share their revenues from joint taxes and fiscal equalisation with their local communities (for more details see Färber, 2015; Bundesministerium der Finanzen, 2020).

Since the 1980s vertical transfer payments – so-called Federal Supplementary Grants – became more and more important while the willingness to pay of the fiscally strong States declined. Particularly Bavaria and Hesse took several legal actions at the Federal Constitutional Court in order to limit their payments. The largest challenge of the scheme was the inclusion of the extremely poor East German Länder after the German unification in 1995 creating considerable financial strains for the federal and the West German state budgets. That lead to deadlines of the respective equalisation agreements. However, whenever negotiations on the fiscal equalisation scheme started among the Federation and the States the Bund has to compensate losses of the poor states from the lowering of the degree of horizontal equalisation by increasing its federal vertical grants in order to achieve the necessary majority in Bundestag and Bundesrat for the reforms.

In 2020, a long-prepared reform of the federal fiscal equalisation scheme came into force. Background was the expiry of the Federal Supplementary Grants in favour of the East German 'New' Länder by the end of 2019 and the experience that those had not reached an economic and fiscal capacity comparable to those of the West German States. The rich States in the West – particularly Bavaria – were no longer willing to pay considerable horizontal transfers to their poorer neighbours regarding that these revenues from fiscal equalisation enabled them to fund e.g. free kindergarten places which were not the Bavarian political priorities. As the whole system was to expire by the end of 2019, negotiations started in 2013 after the Bavarian and the Hesse governments had – once again – initiated a complaint at the Federal Constitutional Court. The final decisions of the reform were taken in 2017.

The most important changes concern the distribution of the state VAT share which no longer was used for a pre-equalisation for the 'very poor' states and the remaining amount distributed as lump-sum transfer payment according to the size of population. As well were the horizontal payments from the States with above average fiscal capacity to those of an under average fiscal capacity abolished. However, the fundamental structure of the vertical tax sharing regime of income tax and VAT across the Federation, the States and local governments, which covers more than 70% of total public sector tax revenues and includes the obligation of the Länder to share their income tax and VAT revenues with their local communities, remained unchanged. The changes only concerned the rules of horizontal distribution of the state share of VAT revenues and the Federal Supplementary Grants (FSG):

- The VAT-pre-equalisation which formerly used up to 25% of the state share of VAT revenues to raise the tax capacity under 97% of average by 95% and that between 97 and 100% applying a declining compensation rate between 95 and 60% was abolished.
- The horizontal transfer payments were replaced by deductions and add-on of the per capita equally distributed VAT revenues.
- The applied equalisation rate of 63% is lower than before.
- In contrast, the weight of local fiscal capacity which is included into state fiscal capacity has been increased from 64 to 75%.
- The Federation continues to pay FSG to fill up deficient tax capacity remaining after VAT distribution. Fiscal capacity below 99.75% of average is compensated by 80%.

- New FSG have been introduced in order to compensate deficient local tax capacity of less than 80% of average by 53.5% and to counterbalance under average vertical federal transfer payments to research institutes.
- The FSG to compensate above average 'costs of political leadership' of the small and poorer States and for the special burden of high unemployment rates in Eastern Germany remain in principle unchanged, but their amount slightly adjusted.

In Germany, the Länder traditionally vote unanimously on reforms of the state fiscal equalisation scheme. This implies on the one hand that no State will lose as result of reform, and on the other hand that the Federation shift 'fresh money' into the intergovernmental fiscal relations. So was expected that the decline of the horizontal equalisation rate should be compensated by an increase of the FSG closing the gap of under average fiscal capacities after the VAT distribution (see Figure 7.1). The new FSG compensating extremely low local fiscal capacity also aim at increasing low fiscal capacities. Despite the increase of FSG from 2020, they decreased – in relation to the tax revenues of state and local governments – from 5% to 1.9% in 2019 and slightly grew again to 2.2% in 2022.

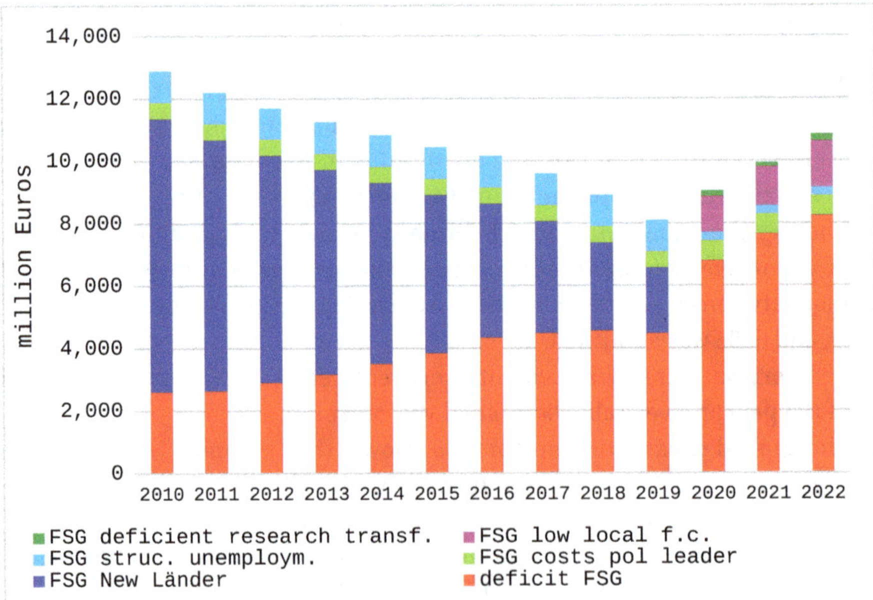

FIGURE 7.1 Federal supplementary grants 2010–2022 (in million euros)
SOURCE: FEDERAL MINISTRY OF FINANCE. ELABORATED BY THE AUTHOR

The new fiscal equalisation scheme is valid for an unlimited period. Its effects however shall be evaluated for the first time in 2030. A denouncement by at least three States is possible at earliest in 2030. The scheme is valid until it will be replaced by a new scheme. These conditions which were agreed unanimously by the Federation and all sixteen Länder however did not prevent Bavaria to start a new complaint at the Federal Constitutional Court recently just before the Bavarian State Parliament election in October 2023.

3 COVID-19 and Ukraine Crisis Effects on the Economic Growth Rates and the Subnational Tax Revenues

The quality of a fiscal equalisation scheme is not only restricted to its 'normal' distributive effects to close the gap between the 'rich' and the 'poor' subnational entities, but also by its capacity to disperse special divergences of tax revenues resulting from economic shocks or crisis among the States as this was the case during the economic and financial crisis 2008–09 (Färber, 2013). The specific question now is whether and how the new fiscal equalisation scheme has been able to support the financial resilience of state and local governments. The first challenge came up with the economic disturbances after the COVID-19 lock-downs particularly in 2020, the second followed quickly by the energy price crisis as a result of the war which Russia has started against Ukraine in 2022.

Although there was an extremely high spread of COVID infections among the Länder (infected from 35,464 in Berlin to 48,057 in Bavaria, death cases from 101 in Schleswig-Holstein to 397 in Saxony, both per 100,000 inhabitants), they had no direct measurable incidence on economic growth and fiscal capacities. The reason probably is that lock-downs and other measures undertaken to prevent the pandemic from even higher infection rates were common decisions of the Federal Chancellor and the Minister-Presidents of the States and were effective all over Germany (Färber, 2021).

The interruption of economic activities in 2020, the supply chain problems mainly resulting from the sharp Chinese shut-Downs, and the explosion of energy prices in 2022 however hit the regional economies unevenly. In 2020, GDP declined in real terms by 2.43% while the consumer prices only increased by 0.47%. The recovery in 2021 brought real growth of 2.65% and an increasing inflation rate of 3.12% before the implications of the Ukraine war caused a real decline of GDP of 0.52% and a growth of consumer Prices of 7.9%. The nominal growth of GDP per inhabitant of the three years, when the population increased by about 1 million, was 10%. The regional growth rates however

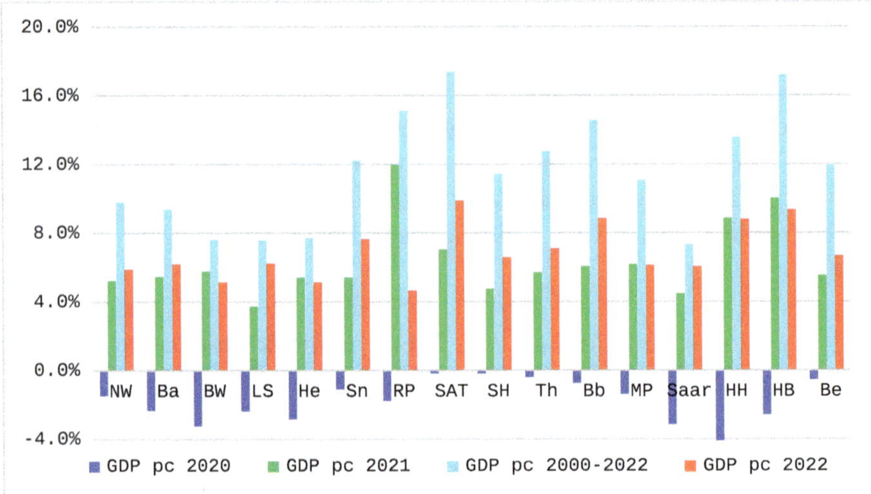

FIGURE 7.2 Growth rates of per capita GDP (2020–2022) (in %)*
*Note: NW – Northrhine-Westfalia, Ba – Bavaria, BW – Baden-Württemberg, LS – Lower Saxony, He – Hesse, Sn – Saxony, RP – Rhineland-Palatinate, SAT – Saxony-Anhalt, SH – Schleswig-Holstein, Th – Thuringia, Bb – Brandenburg, MP – Mecklenburg-Pomerania, Saar – Saarland, HH – Hamburg, HB – Bremen, Be – Berlin.
SOURCE: FEDERAL STATISTICAL OFFICE. ELABORATED BY THE AUTHOR

counted from 7.3% in the Saarland and 17.4% resp. 17–2% in Saxony-Anhalt and Bremen (see Figure 7.2).

The sharpest declines in 2020 took place in the 'rich' industrialised Länder in the West, particularly where the centres of automobile production are located. The biggest losses of 4% appeared in the Hamburg. This city state however leads the recovery in 2021 by 8.8% at the third rank after Bremen (10%, rank 2). Rhineland-Palatinate benefitted from the huge gains of the enterprise Biontech which had developed the first RNMA vaccine against COVID-19. The energy price crisis in 2022 generated under average GDP growth rates in Western Germany, were generated in the three 'rich' Länder Bavaria, Baden-Württemberg and Hesse as well as in the former coal and steel regions Northrhine-Westfalia and Saarland which both still suffer from the economic structural change. While the spread of per capita GDP declined in 2020, it increased in 2020 to a higher value than in the year before the crisis.

Economic capacity and growth rates determine the development of subnational tax revenues and tax capacities. In addition, federal and state governments used tax reductions as an instrument to fight against economic decline during the crisis which lead – according to the rules of intergovernmental tax

TABLE 7.1 GDP per capita growth rates and changes of relation to average (2020–2022) (in %)

	Growth rate GDP pc 2020–2022	GDP pc 2019	GDP pc 2020	GDP pc 2021	GDP pc 2022
NW	9.7%	95.7%	96.3%	95.7%	95.5%
BA	9.4%	117.6%	117.3%	116.9%	116.9%
BW	7.6%	113.3%	112.0%	112.0%	110.8%
LS	7.6%	93.0%	92.7%	90.9%	90.9%
HE	7.7%	112.7%	111.8%	111.4%	110.3%
SN	12.2%	76.6%	77.3%	77.0%	78.1%
RP	15.1%	86.0%	86.2%	91.3%	89.9%
SAT	17.4%	70.3%	71.7%	72.5%	75.0%
SH	11.4%	82.2%	83.7%	82.9%	83.2%
TH	12.7%	71.4%	72.6%	72.6%	73.2%
BB	14.5%	72.3%	73.2%	73.4%	75.3%
MP	11.1%	70.7%	71.2%	71.5%	71.4%
SAAR	7.3%	86.8%	85.8%	84.8%	84.6%
HH	13.5%	162.0%	158.7%	163.3%	167.2%
HB	17.2%	116.2%	115.5%	120.2%	123.7%
BE	11.9%	102.9%	104.5%	104.2%	104.7%
Spatial states	9.7%	98.2%	98.2%	98.1%	97.9%
City states	13.1%	122.0%	121.8%	123.6%	125.4%
Average	10.0%	100.0%	100.0%	100.0%	100.0%
Old Länder	9.4%	104.9%	104.6%	104.6%	104.3%
New Länder + BE	13.1%	79.7%	80.8%	80.9%	82.0%
Variation coefficient	13.5%	23.8%	22.8%	23.7%	24.3%

SOURCE: FEDERAL STATISTICAL OFFICE. ELABORATED BY THE AUTHOR

sharing – to diverging losses of tax revenues. In contrast, inflation creates additional tax revenues for all taxes of a tax elasticity above 1.

In 2020, the tax revenues of the Länder – before VAT distribution – declined by almost 5%. In 2021 tax revenues recovered increasing by 15.3%. The growth of 4.1% in 2022 was lower than the inflation rate. In total, the state tax revenues grew across the three years by 12.8%. Local fiscal capacity exceeded state tax development by a decline of 10.2% in 2020 and a rerise of 15.5% in 2021. In 2022, local governments achieved a growth of their tax capacity by 8.9% higher than the inflation rate.

The decline and recovery of state and local tax revenues however did not correspond with economic development. Usually State and local tax capacities correspond with economic capacity progressively (see Figure 7.3), a result of the vertical tax sharing of taxes with progressive tax rates (personal income tax) or a subnational tax incidence (corporate income tax, local trade tax). Crisis did not change this relation fundamentally, but subnational tax revenues did not change corresponding to economic decline and recovery. There is even no parallel development of state and local growth rates of tax capacities. During crisis the correlation between economic and tax capacity declined as well did the slope indicators. In 2022 however, state tax revenues before VAT were more progressive (1.41) than before crisis (1.174) while the incidence of local tax capacity had declined from 1.04 in 2019 to 0.95 in 2022. The main reason for this development probably is that particularly the tax payments of enterprises show asymmetric pattern in the beginning of an economic decline and in the period of recovery. COVID-19 crisis created besides the 'usual' losers of economic recession new winners as was e.g. the vaccine producer Biontech

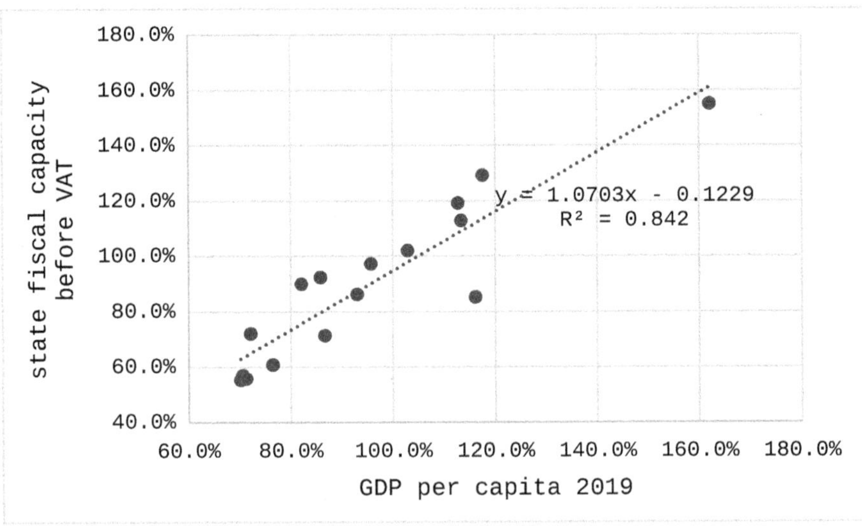

FIGURE 7.3 Relations between per capita GDP and state tax revenues before VAT distribution in 2019 (in %)
SOURCE: FEDERAL STATISTICAL OFFICE, FEDERAL MINISTRY OF FINANCE. ELABORATED BY THE AUTHOR

in Rhineland-Palatinate paying a record amount of taxes to the Land and to its location city Mainz.

Table 7.2 informs on the spread of state and local tax capacities in 2019, the year before crisis, and the accumulated growth rates of subnational tax

TABLE 7.2 State tax revenues (before VAT distribution) and local fiscal capacities per inhabitant 2019 and growth rates (2020–2022)

Euros per capita	State tax revenues before VAT 2019	In % of total	Growth rate 2020–2022	Local fiscal capacity 2019	In % of total	Growth rate 2020–2022
NW	2,202.7	97.2%	7.1%	1,346.8	96.7%	9.7%
BA	2,926.5	129.2%	13.0%	1,715.9	123.3%	12.3%
BW	2,555.9	112.8%	13.3%	1,644.4	118.1%	6.9%
LS	1,952.8	86.2%	13.1%	1,228.0	88.2%	10.8%
HE	2,699.3	119.1%	10.1%	1,620.8	116.4%	16.3%
SN	1,376.5	60.8%	10.3%	865.0	62.1%	19.1%
RP	2,091.2	92.3%	19.3%	1,307.1	93.9%	14.4%
SAT	1,250.7	55.2%	17.9%	879.4	63.2%	5.9%
SH	2,036.8	89.9%	15.1%	1,263.6	90.8%	13.3%
TH	1,261.4	55.7%	13.1%	856.8	61.5%	11.9%
BB	1,631.5	72.0%	10.5%	1,034.8	74.3%	17.1%
MP	1,289.7	56.9%	14.5%	860.8	61.8%	15.4%
SAAR	1,615.0	71.3%	11.8%	1,077.7	77.4%	4.6%
HH	3,509.3	154.9%	26.0%	2,201.4	158.1%	6.1%
HB	1,928.5	85.1%	9.3%	1,423.1	102.2%	16.8%
BE	2,309.8	101.9%	21.5%	1,212.3	87.1%	20.6%
Spatial states	2,236.8	98.7%	11.9%	1,381.0	99.2%	11.4%
City states	2,625.5	115.9%	22.4%	1,530.6	109.9%	14.0%
Average	2,265.7	100.0%	12.8%	1,392.1	100.0%	11.7%
Old Länder	2,430.2	107.3%	12.3%	1,494.2	107.3%	10.8%
New Länder + Be	1,585.8	70.0%	15.7%	970.2	69.7%	16.6%
Variation coefficient	27.8%	27.8%	37.3%	26.1%	26.1%	41.0%

SOURCE: FEDERAL MINISTRY OF FINANCE. ELABORATED BY THE AUTHOR

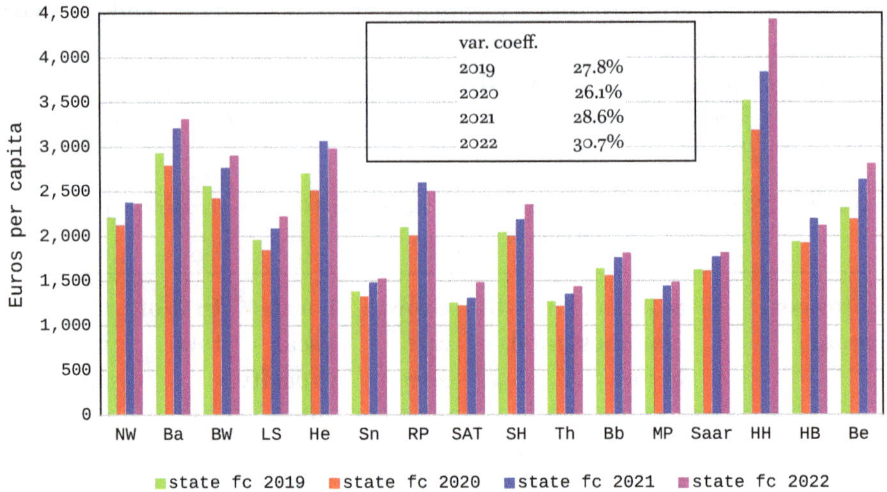

FIGURE 7.4 State fiscal capacity per capita (2019–2022) (in euros)
SOURCE: FEDERAL MINISTRY OF FINANCE. ELABORATED BY THE AUTHOR

revenues across the three years of crisis. The annual decline and growth rates are much more erratic and offer absolutely no systematic relations (correlation coefficients near 0). And the growth rates of state and local tax capacities are often even contrasting as in the case of Hamburg which experienced the highest increase of state tax revenues while the growth of local tax capacity was among the lowest of the Länder. The variation coefficient of the tax capacities is rather high and was higher than in 'normal' periods. That created challenges for the new state fiscal equalisation scheme.

4 Horizontal Changes of State and Local Fiscal Capacities and New Fiscal Equalisation Transfer Payments

The above presented data on state economic and fiscal capacities show the fundamental horizontal problem of the German fiscal equalisation which ever its construction is: The spread particularly of state tax revenues is much higher than that of economic capacities because of the construction of the vertically shared personal and corporate income taxes with a progressive incidence. The uneven growth rates of economic and fiscal capacities during periods of economic crisis increase that equalisation problem particularly in years when tax revenues decline against the pattern of former periods.

In fact, the COVID-crisis brought losses of states tax revenues particularly for the states of higher economic capacity and declined the spread of tax capacity among the Länder while recovery and the most recent Ukraine war and energy price crisis created an explosion of divergence compared with the periods before. Local fiscal capacities, which usually do not show as much divergence as state tax revenues, reacted differently: their spread – measured by the variation coefficients indicated in Figures 7.3 and 7.4 – declined in 2020 and 2021 and was in 2022 even lower than in 2019.

As in the old scheme the distribution of the state share of VAT revenues has to create the main contribution to equalisation among the Länder. While in the past the adds-on for the states of a fiscal capacity below 92% of average closed the biggest gaps before the lump-sum distribution worked for closing down the relative differences and the horizontal transfer payments continued the equalisation process, from 2020 the whole equalisation efforts concerning state revenues burdens on the distribution of the state VAT revenues.

COVID-crisis created here an additional challenge because VAT rates were lowered from 19 to 16% for the second half of 2020 in order to support economic demand during crisis. The state share of VAT therefore slightly declined by 0.02% before in 2021 and 2020 – back to 'normal' tax rates[1] – grew sharply by 10.8% and 12%.

As expected the add-ons and deductions – replacing the former horizontal transfer payments – increased from 2020. The effects of COVID-crisis on state and local tax capacities however attenuated the boost, recovery in 2021 started to show the full results. In 2019, Bavaria, the biggest 'payer' of the former equalisation scheme, had to transfer 6.7 billion Euros to the recipient states, registered in 2020 only a moderate increase of the deduction of 7.8 billion Euros, after all 14.2% of its state revenues including VAT. In 2021 and 2022 as a result of recovery of tax revenues, particularly of the VAT revenues, the deductions grew to 9 billion Euros and 9.9 billion Euros which implies an increasing share of state tax revenues for fiscal equalisation up to 14.7%. The extremely high gains of state tax capacity of Hamburg in 2022 provided an increase of deductions to 814 million Euros or 7.1% of state tax revenues incl. VAT. The Biontech tax payments shifted Rhineland-Palatinate from an 'add-on state' to a 'deduction state' with a rather small and shrinking share of reductions.

Among the 'add-on' states, the East German Länder play a proper role. Despite their success in economic integration indicated by a continuing making up leeway of GDP per inhabitant the German tax system only provides

1 Except a special reduction to 7% for all restaurant services until the end of 2023.

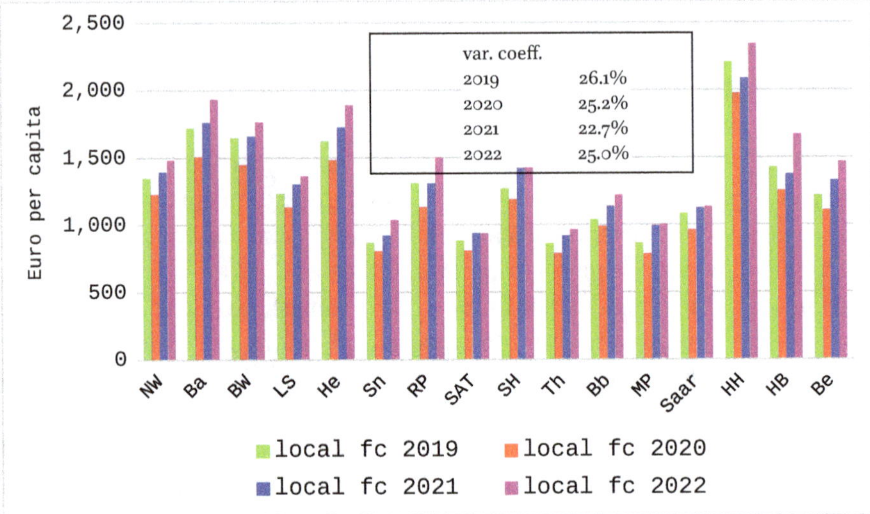

FIGURE 7.5 Local fiscal capacity per capita (2019–2022) (in euros)
SOURCE: FEDERAL MINISTRY OF FINANCE. ELABORATED BY THE AUTHOR

'primes' of a corresponding increase of tax capacity for Berlin. The Eastern spatial states experienced an increase of economic capacity from 73% to 75.3% of average by 2.3 percent points state tax capacity declined from 60.7% of average to 60.6%, and local tax capacity improved slightly from 64.6% to 66.5% of average. Because of that stagnation of fiscal capacities, the East German spatial states Mecklenburg-Pomerania, Brandenburg, Saxony, Saxony-Anhalt and Thuringia remain dependent from 25% to more than 30% of adds-on in order to achieve an aggregated state and local tax capacity of 86–88% on average. Only the city state Bremen profited more from add-ons as a result of the valuation of their citizens by 135% in the fiscal needs indicator combined with its comparatively low fiscal capacity; here the add-ons even increased from 31.6% to 34.2% of state tax revenues.

Further equalisation effects result from the Federal Supplementary Grants. Compared with the proper state and local tax revenues they are rather low. For the supplementation of the equalisation effects of the distribution VAT revenues they are however important because only Länder of an under average fiscal capacity receive FSGs. The highest equalisation effects result from the FSGs compensating further deficient fiscal capacities. The other FSG however are despite their rather low amount of considerable importance particularly for the additional funding of the East German Länder.

TABLE 7.3 Add-ons (+) and deductions (-) of state share VAT lump-sum distribution and their share of total tax revenues (incl. VAT) (2020–2022)

1000 Euros	2020	% of state tax revenues incl. VAT	2021	% of state tax revenues incl. VAT	2022	% of state tax revenues incl. VAT
NW	−624,117	−0.99%	199,668	0.28%	1,240,540	1.69%
BA	−7,770,580	−14.16%	−9,043,527	−14.48%	−9,864,592	−14.74%
BW	−3,674,193	−8.68%	−4,014,681	−8.39%	−4,472,908	−8.64%
LS	1,471,181	5.70%	1,911,447	6.58%	1,789,176	5.62%
HE	−2,530,897	−10.32%	−3,556,309	−12.30%	−3,250,486	−10.89%
SN	2,707,607	24.57%	3,225,129	26.39%	3,303,674	25.07%
RP	333,920	2.40%	−286,955	−1.69%	−107,063	−0.61%
SAT	1,618,773	28.33%	1,978,420	31.96%	1,985,654	28.50%
SH	172,360	1.75%	316,625	2.92%	298,758	2.50%
TH	1,575,693	28.43%	1,856,374	30.37%	1,918,958	28.80%
BB	1,138,668	15.31%	1,370,230	16.41%	1,451,538	16.09%
MP	1,177,050	27.31%	1,325,649	27.62%	1,447,224	27.89%
SAAR	410,533	13.90%	514,388	15.83%	577,260	16.59%
HH	−172,200	−2.04%	−230,479	−2.32%	−814,333	−7.08%
HB	711,763	31.63%	832,253	33.04%	887,912	34.18%
BE	3,454,439	26.38%	3,601,768	23.55%	3,608,688	21.44%
Spatial states	−3,994,002	−1.47%	−4,203,542	−1.37%	−3,682,268	−1.12%
City states	3,994,002	16.79%	4,203,542	15.15%	3,682,268	11.90%
Average	0	0.00%	0	0.00%	0	0.00%
Old Länder	−11,672,229	−4.71%	−13,357,570	−4.74%	−13,715,736	−4.56%
New Länder + BE	11,672,229	24.77%	13,357,570	25.22%	13,715,736	23.71%

SOURCE: FEDERAL MINISTRY OF FINANCE. ELABORATED BY THE AUTHOR

Figure 7.6 visualises the equalisation effects of the steps of the equalisation scheme. The rather huge differences of the mere tax capacities among the states are closed step by step and in the end by the instrument of FSG with additional federal funding. The variation coefficients before and after fiscal

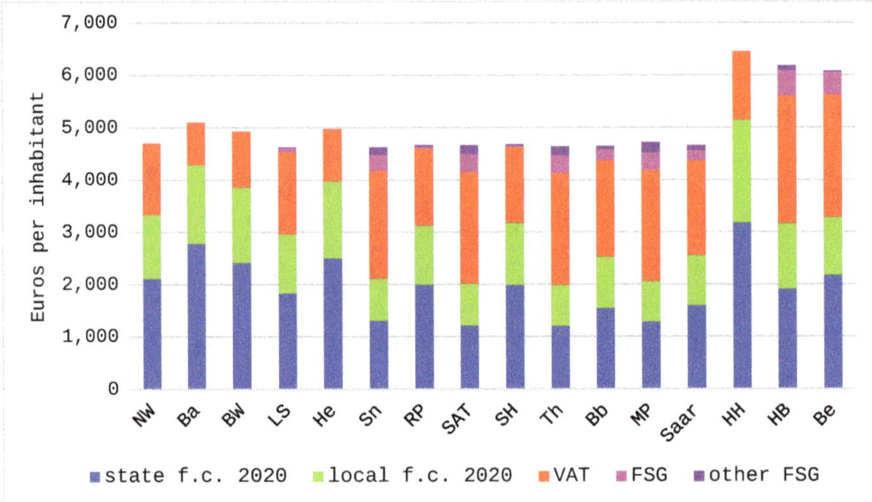

FIGURE 7.6 State and local fiscal capacities after fiscal equalisation and federal supplementary grants in 2020 (in euros)
SOURCE: FEDERAL MINISTRY OF FINANCE. ELABORATED BY THE AUTHOR

equalisation usually fall by more than 50% which measures the intensity of equalisation. The equalisation effect is even larger if the city states and their valuation of citizens by 135% as well as their comparatively high tax capacities are excluded. Among the spatial states the variation coefficients fall by about 85% of the values before fiscal equalisation. Here, the original ranking of the tax capacities is not changed by the equalisation steps.

The data also show that the new equalisation scheme provides a slightly higher equalisation effect than the old one which might be a logic consequence of the de facto necessary unanimous agreement on the new scheme. It does not result from the horizontal effects of tax distribution among the Länder, which are even weaker than before the reform. They come from the additional equalisation effects of the FSGs.

The new equalisation scheme however was not able to cover the losses of tax revenues from COVID-19 recession. Yet is has been able to compensate the unusual spread of fiscal capacities wherever they came from and without regard whether the tax losses were bigger for rich or poor states.

TABLE 7.4 Variation coefficients before and after fiscal equalisation (2019–2022) (in %)

	All Länder		Only spatial states	
	Before fiscal equalisation	**After fiscal equalisation and FSGs**	**Before fiscal equalisation**	**After fiscal equalisation and FSGs**
2019	27.0%	12.8%	23.4%	3.6%
2020	25.6%	12.3%	22.1%	3.1%
2021	26.3%	12.2%	23.6%	3.4%
2022	28.3%	13.0%	23.4%	3.3%

SOURCE: FEDERAL MINISTRY OF FINANCE. ELABORATED BY THE AUTHOR

5 Unsolved Vertical Problems and New Horizontal Conflict?

The analysis of the equalisation effects of the reformed scheme confirmed the expectation that it is still able to stabilise horizontal divergences of state and local tax capacities resulting from economic crisis. The – continuing and even increased – observance of local fiscal capacity within state fiscal capacity and financial needs (based on the size of population) considers that local governments are underequipped with own tax sources and therefore need additional transfer payments as a share of state tax revenues what necessarily creates a special need of horizontal equalisation. However, it should be emphasised that the fiscal equalisation only aims at converging the differences of tax revenues and does not regard disparities of financial needs.[2]

Furthermore, the German *Länderfinanzausgleich* is completely blind against vertical distortions. The instruments used in the fight against economic crisis and for the maintenance of decentralised public services in the pandemic included tax reductions; the resulting losses of tax revenues hit the layers of government according to the vertical assignment of taxes. Economic decline from the crisis mainly occurred for taxes with a base on incomes and profits. Here local governments experienced sharp losses of the revenues of the local trade tax. For 2020, the Federation and the states compensated the losses from

2 Except the higher valuation of citizens of the city states and – for local financial needs – of the population of small thinly populated states.

their budgets considering that local communities are the least capable to compensate high losses of intakes by borrowing.

The continuing crisis combined with the recent climate change policies particularly have generated problems at the expenditure side of the budgets. All levels of government increased their expenditures in a way never observed before. Particularly in 2020, the Federation spent money apparently without limits. The new debt brake was suspended for the Bund and all Länder; most of them were not able to spend the approved crisis budget the same year and started to save the borrowed financial means as reserves for future spending. In many cases even the pure borrowing permit was transferred to future years when the debt brake will probably be back in force (Bundesrechnungshof, 2023).

For the labour market stabilisation social insurances played an important role, particularly the short-time allowances of the Federal Labour Agency. Beside the covering of costs of medical treatments by the Social Health Insurances federal budget funded many special expenditures related to COVID infections or preventions (like the vaccinations) directly. Local governments received special financial assistance e.g. for personnel costs for closed kindergartens, the maintenance of public traffic, and local health care costs.

The best impression of the budgetary effects of the continuing crisis 2020–2022 gives the development of public debt. The excessive borrowing of the Federation increased federal debt by 36.3%, while the Länder and local governments tried to consolidate their budgets and therefore were able to restrict the increase of public debt to 4.8% and 7.1% (see Table 7.6). For many of the special crisis borrowings the period of redemption will take up to 50 years.

6 Further Expectations for the Fight against Energy Crisis and Climate Change Policies

In fact, the Ukraine war and energy crisis and the ongoing fight against climate change creates next challenge for fiscal federalism. An additional burden will be the actual economic crisis; economic institutes and OECD expect a shrinking GDP in 2023 and hope for a recovery in 2024. Here again the effects on the regional GDP might be different. The high energy prices burden the industrial sector extremely. Enterprises threaten to leave Germany and invest abroad if they would not receive more subsidies.

For public budgets arises a special problem from the increasing interest rates. As the European Central Bank has fought against the high inflation rates by increasing its interest rates, the interest payments on public debt have started to grow. In 2020, the federation even earned from borrowing because

TABLE 7.5 Expenditures and revenues of Bund. Länder and local governments (2019–2022) (in euros and %)

	2019	2020		2021		2022	
	Million euros	**Million euros**	**Against 2019**	**Million euros**	**Against 2020**	**Million euros**	**Against 2021**
Expenditures							
Bund	397,003	511,713	28.9%	560,535	9.5%	608,891	8.6%
Länder	417,203	487,220	16.8%	507,171	4.1%	522,250	3.0%
Local governments	276,726	293,177	5.9%	303,374	3.5%	325,780	7.4%
Social insurances	679,929	748,580	10.1%	779,703	4.2%	804,373	3.2%
Total	1,497,437	1,678,622	12.1%	1,762,401	5.0%	1,875,430	6.4%
Tax revenues							
Bund	356,999	315,773	−11.5%	345,386	9.4%	375,491	8.7%
Länder	310,304	295,247	−4.9%	334,484	13.3%	367,570	9.9%
Local governments	104,383	98,418	−5.7%	113,395	15.2%	121,464	7.1%
Social insurances [a]	557,854	566,042	1.5%	592,237	4.6%	622,434	5.1%
Total	1,360,486	1,308,395	−3.8%	1,423,550	8.8%	1,525,275	7.1%

[a] Social insurance contributions

SOURCE: DESTATIS. ELABORATED BY THE AUTHOR

TABLE 7.6 Public debt of levels of government (2019–2022) (in million euros)

	Bund	Länder	Local gov.	Total government
2019	1.027.832	579.136	130.787	1.899.168
2020	1.403.417	635.832	132.496	2.171.798
2021	1.548.469	638.141	116.192	2.319.773
2022	1.620.357	606.883	140.765	2.368.026

SOURCE: DESTATIS. ELABORATED BY THE AUTHOR

of negative interest for its emissions. The extremely high level of federal debt now threatens the budgetary scope of action particularly for necessary military expenditures and subsidies in climate change programs. New federal laws with higher social expenditures will not only burden the budget of the federation, but also local budgets. And at the local level, local communities in some states did not take the chance to reduce their extremely high debt burden and face ugly budgetary problems in the near future.

Before this background, a new political debate on changing the intergovernmental rules of public debt and vertical and horizontal fiscal equalisation will open respectively has already started.

References

Bundesministerium der Finanzen (2020). *The Federal Financial Equalisation System in Germany.* [https://www.bundesfinanzministerium.de/Content/DE/Downloads/Oeffentliche-Finanzen/Foederale-Finanzbeziehungen/Laenderfinanzausgleich/bundesstaatlicher-finanzausgleich-englisch.pdf?__blob=publicationFile&v=5].

Bundesrechnungshof (2023). Bericht nach § 88 Absatz 2 BHO an das Bundesministerium der Finanzen über die Sondervermögen des Bundes und die damit verbundenen Auswirkungen auf die Haushaltstransparenz sowie die Funktionsfähigkeit der Schuldenregel, Bonn. [https://www.bundesrechnungshof.de/SharedDocs/Downloads/DE/Berichte/2023/sondervermoegen-volltext.pdf?__blob=publicationFile&v=6; download 6.10. 2023].

Färber, G. (2013). Auswirkungen der Finanzkrise auf die Handlungsspielräume der deutschen Verwaltung; in: *der moderne staat* 1, 211–230.

Färber, G. (2015). Fiscal Equalization in Germany – Facts, Conflicts and Perspectives. In G. Pola (Ed.), *Principles and Practices of Fiscal Autonomy. Experiences, Debate and Prospects* (pp. 113–134). Ashgate Farnham.

Färber. G. (2021). Germany's fight against COVID-19 – between central regulation and decentralized management. In Steytler, N. (Ed.), *Comparative Federalism and COVID-19 – Combating the Pandemic* (pp. 51–69). Routledge.

CHAPTER 8

Fiscal Federalism and Territorial Inequalities: India's Experience

Govind Bhattacharjee
Centre for Multilevel Federalism

1 Territorial Inequality in India

1.1 *Introduction*

Indian economy was reformed in 1991, liberating it from the hitherto stifling state controls on almost all spheres economic activities. The liberalisation led to inflow of capital and technology from outside while transforming the country's socio-economic landscape. That was the beginning of India's growth story, but the growth came at the cost of inequality. Advent of information and communications technology (ICT) that was transforming life and living in other parts of India could make little inroads within the poorer states, e.g. the states that lay at the remote border areas in the north-east and the north, or in the low-income states like Bihar, Uttar Pradesh, Madhya Pradesh or Rajasthan. As pointed out by Ahluwalia (2000, pp. 1637–48), inter-state disparities in growth rates of GSDP had in fact increased after the reforms of 1991 across the states in India. The process of economic reform has not promoted balanced regional development, but had mostly benefited the already prosperous or well-governed states rather than the laggards. The reform-orientated states had generally performed better than other states since the process was started in 1991 (Bajpai and Sachs, 1999). The poorer states have always been ill-equipped to profit from the reforms because of various impediments like their "less attractive social, economic, and probably, political conditions" (Baddeley, McNay and Cassen, 2006, pp. 999–1022). Kurian (2000, pp. 538–42) noticed widening regional disparities among the states in general and between the forward and the backward states in particular. The forward states, by virtue of their higher income, better physical and social infrastructure, higher per capita transfers and private investments, were much better placed to take advantage of the globalisation and liberalisation process and moved ahead. As a result, richer states became even richer compared to the poorer states. All these indicate that whenever the disparity increases across the states, the poorer category states are the worst sufferers in terms of economic growth and development.

DOI:10.1163/9789004524514_010

Sachs, Bajpai and, Ramiah (2002) also found that there was marked divergence in the growth and income levels among the Indian states during the period 1980–98, as well as during both the pre-reform and post-reform sub-periods, a divergence that was most noticeable within the poorer group of states.

1.2 *Poverty and Inequality in India*

Inequality is rooted in the history and administrative legacy of India; it is multi-layered and has multiple dimensions. As rapid growth has exacerbated the existing inequalities in society, both market and non-market forces have contributed to it. One reason is the agriculture sector which accounts for 19% of the GDP but sustains two-thirds of the population, implying highly suppressed wages for agricultural labourers. The growth of other sectors and the overall economy hinges on the performance of agriculture to a considerable extent through its backward and forward linkages. Agricultural productivity remained in India low historically and the sector grew slowly. The so-called Hindi-heartland states in the Gangetic plain and in the east and north-east of India which heavily depend on agriculture thus suffer from inherent disadvantage compared to the industrialised states in the west and south of India. A disproportionate share of India's population lives in the low-income states:

Economic neglect and lack of development create inequality and disparity; uncontrolled, they ultimately also can lead to violence and militancy which adversely affect development. Predictably, the development-disparity paradigm had stoked the sinister fire of insurgency in many of these low-income states, especially in the north-east of India, leading to decades of political unrest and mindless violence.

In July 2023, an International Monetary Fund (IMF) Working Paper (Arbati-Saxegaard, 2023) studied the impact and drivers of poverty and inequality in India during the pandemic years. While recognising the significant progress made by India in reducing poverty in recent decades, it found, expectedly, that the economic battering by the COVID-19 pandemic has increased poverty and inequality in India but its impact was rather temporary, with both poverty and inequality returning to their pre-pandemic levels by the end of 2021. Demographic and labour market characteristics were identified as the main factors associated with poverty and changes in income and consumption. Their analysis suggested that workers with low skills due to low education and those working in the informal sector lacking in social welfare protection were more negatively impacted during the pandemic. The paper also noted that the government's expansion of food subsidies has "likely played a significant role in mitigating the increase in poverty during the pandemic".

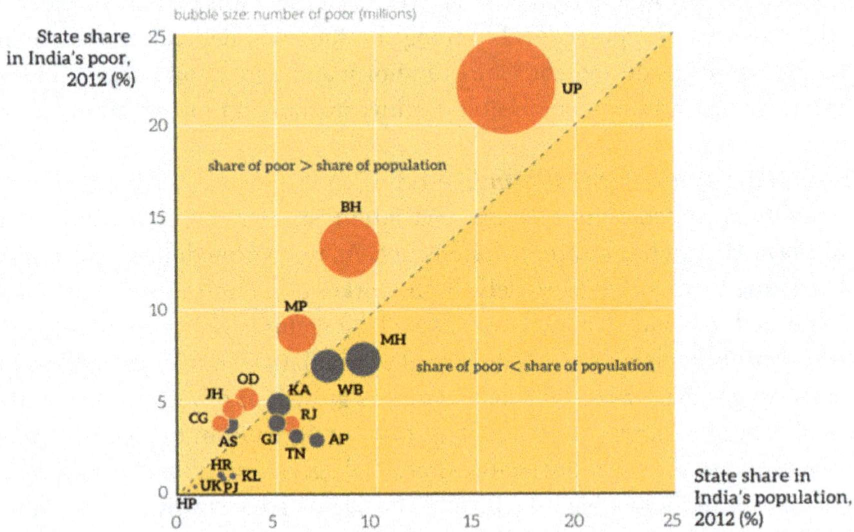

FIGURE 8.1 Sates' share of India's poor (2012) (in %)
Note: The low-income states comprising of Bihar (BH), Chhattisgarh (CG), Jharkhand (JH), Madhya Pradesh (MP), Odisha (OD), Rajasthan (RJ) and Uttar Pradesh (UP) are highlighted in red. The other states (out of the 19 larger states considered here for the analysis) are Andhra Pradesh (AP), Assam (AS), Haryana (HR), Gujarat (GJ), Himachal Pradesh (HP), Karnataka (KA), Kerala (KL), Maharashtra (MH), Punjab (PJ), Tamil Nadu (TN), Uttarakhand (UK) and West Bengal (WB).
SOURCE: INDIA STATES BRIEFS (WORLDBANK.ORG) (HTTPS://WWW.WORLDBANK.ORG/EN/NEWS/FEATURE/2016/05/26/INDIA-STATES-BRIEFS)

India has 28 states besides 8 Union Territories (UTs) of small sizes which are administered directly by the federal government (except two UTs, Delhi and Puducherry, which have elected legislatures with limited autonomy). The IMF paper did not analyse the inequality among them. But in April 2022, the Institute for Competitiveness, at the behest of the Government of India has undertaken another study on inequality and submitted its "The State of Inequality in India Report" which did analyse the inter-state variations. It is a comprehensive study covering the economic variables like income distribution, labour profile and socio-economic variables like health, education and household characteristics that affect inequality. Quoting from the Annual Reports of the Periodic Labour Force Survey (PLFS), it noted that the top 10% of India's labour force earned between 32 and 35% of the total income – more than thrice as much as the bottom 10%, during the fiscal years (FY) 2019, 2019 and 2020. During this period, India's labour force participation increased from

49.8% to 53.5%, but the female labour force participation which was a low 23.8% in FY2018 increased to 30% by FY2020 (male labour participation was above 75% in each year). Unemployment rate which was below 5% in FY2018 increased to almost 6% in FY2020.

Regarding social infrastructure, the report used data from the Rural Health Statistics of the Government of India to point out that while the overall public health infrastructure comprising the primary, secondary and community health centres in the country improved between 2005 and 2020, there were wide differences among the states, with many states registering a decline in their numbers. The shortfalls in primary, secondary and community health centres compared to requirements amounted to more than 50% in each of these categories for some states. The delivery of healthcare services also varied widely among the states. The public infrastructure on school education also showed similar variations across the states, and the differences were acute especially in respect of availability of functional computers and access to internet for students. However, the Gross Enrolment Ratio, especially in primary education was satisfactory (101.25% in primary and 87.74% in upper primary education) and was more or less uniform among the states. Quoting from the government database – Unified District Information System for Education Plus (UDISE +), the report pointed that dropout rates were significant and showed wide variations among states, especially in respect of secondary education (Grades 9–12).

As regards the distribution of wealth among the states, the report used data from the National Family and Health Survey (NFHS-4, 2015–16) to prepare a wealth index based on the quantity and kinds of consumer goods owned by people, like television, vehicle and access to safe drinking water or toilet facilities inside the home. It showed huge gaps in terms of household wealth among the states, and also between rural and urban areas. A 44.4% wealth concentration in the highest quintile in urban areas contrasted with a meagre 7.1% concentration in the highest quintile in rural India where 28.4% households belonged to the lowest quintile, but only 3.1% of households belonged to the lowest quantile in urban areas. 54.9% of the households belonged to the bottom two quintiles of wealth concentration in rural areas where almost two-thirds of India's population live. Among the States and UTs, Chandigarh, Delhi (both UTs), Punjab, and Goa accounted for more than 50% of households in the highest quintile, while Bihar and Jharkhand have recorded the highest concentration in the lowest quintile (51% in Bihar). Both the states have less than 10% of the concentration in the highest quintile as well (3.3% and 8.8% respectively). Between NFHS-4 and NFHS-5 (2019–21), the report found that all states and UTs have significantly improved access to sanitation and improved drinking water due to government's focus on these, supported by Central government's funding for schemes in these areas.

The socio-economic inequities obviously become aggravated due to low earnings. The report noted considerable improvement in solidifying the primary healthcare system especially in the rural areas, but highlighted the challenges of nutritional deprivation affecting the physical and cognitive development of children. It also noted improvement in physical infrastructure in the schools which corrects inequality as accessible and affordable education leads to upward mobility in pulling people above the poverty line, and also by making structural changes in society. Availability of essential commodities and resources in households leads to capability enhancement by raising the standard of living and improved health outcomes.

1.3 *Territorial Distribution of Public Expenditure*

Poor states need higher government investments on sectors like health and education, but per capita investment by government on education and health remains the lowest among poorer states, as seen in Table 8.1 in respect of developmental expenditure (social sector plus economic sector expenditure) and social sector expenditure. However, when we consider the expenditure as percentage of aggregate expenditure by the states/ UTs, no such correlation is seen. The states have different financial capacities, but within their respective capacities, they tend to spend as much as possible on social sectors like education and health. Even the poorer states like Bihar, Uttar Pradesh or Jharkhand spend at the level of, and sometimes higher than, the other states in terms of percentage of total expenditure (TE), though in absolute terms, they are much lower than the advanced states. As a result, the out-of-pocket expenditure (OOPE) on health becomes abnormally high among the poorer states, making their poor populations extremely vulnerable to external shocks like the Covid-19.

The extreme disparity in public healthcare was highlighted in the report of NITI Aayog, Government's thinktank, (Health Index, 2019) which pointed out that while the healthcare scenario in Kerala was comparable to Brazil or Argentina, the situation in Odisha was similar to Sierra Leone. The top five high performing states were Kerala, Andhra Pradesh, Maharashtra, Gujarat, and Punjab, while the bottom five states were Uttarakhand, Madhya Pradesh, Odisha, Bihar, and Uttar Pradesh in that order. Kerala is often cited as a model in public healthcare, as a result of decades of effective public demand, responsive government policies, and the role played by local governance institutions like the Panchayats. A study (Pandey and Gautam, 2020) constructed a composite index of 12 relevant parameters for empowerment of women across the

TABLE 8.1 Per capita expenditure by states, ordered by per capita income (2022) (in indian rupees, INR*)

State/UT	Per capita income (INR)	Per capita developmental expenditure	Per capita social sector expenditure	Expenditure on education as % of TE	Expenditure on health as % of TE
Goa	431,351	62,204	35,673	16.5	5.5
Sikkim	415,045	78,453	47,067	14.5	5.7
Delhi	331,112	18,933	13,796	13.7	5.5
Haryana	229,065	21,172	14,774	10.7	6.3
Telangana	225,663	29,184	16,874	20.7	7.9
Karnataka	221,310	24,348	13,081	14.6	8.8
Tamil Nadu	209,628	23,280	14,104	15.9	7.4
Puducherry	208,453	32,329	18,050	14.4	6.3
Gujarat	207,324	18,115	10,936	14.4	4.6
Kerala	194,432	22,494	16,353	16.8	6.5
Uttarakhand	184,002	23,051	18,009	16.9	6.1
Maharashtra	183,704	17,496	11,537	17.1	6.0
Arunachal Pradesh	181,684	86,862	40,460	15.2	5.7
Himachal Pradesh	177,924	34,622	22,050	13.4	5.4
Mizoram	173,521	52,621	34,244	11.7	3.7
Andhra Pradesh	163,746	22,684	16,716	12.9	5.1
Punjab	150,620	13,435	8,075	15.4	5.7
Nagaland	119,781	32,936	20,381	15.7	5.9
Tripura	118,401	22,146	17,569	8.9	5.1
Rajasthan	115,122	16,932	11,909	15.6	4.3
West Bengal	106,510	12,420	10,650	18.2	5.4
Chhattisgarh	104,788	19,734	12,399	11.4	5.9
Madhya Pradesh	103,654	16,844	11,260	13.6	5.6
Odisha	103,203	18,522	12,771	11.0	7.4
Jammu & Kashmir (UT since 2019)	101,540	27,586	18,464	13.3	6.0
Meghalaya	90,751	27,722	17,856	10.8	5.0
Assam	90,482	15,255	10,194	8.1	3.8
Manipur	75,784	25,977	18,845	13.0	5.2
Jharkhand	69,963	13,185	8,994	20.3	12.2

TABLE 8.1 Per capita expenditure by states, ordered by per capita income (2022) (*cont.*)

State/ UT	Per capita income (INR)	Per capita developmental expenditure	Per capita social sector expenditure	Expenditure on education as % of TE	Expenditure on health as % of TE
Uttar Pradesh	61,434	9,395	6,209	17.6	8.0
Bihar	42,083	9,087	7,063	14.3	8.4

SOURCE: NATIONAL ACCOUNTS STATISTICS, MINISTRY OF STATISTICS AND PROGRAMME IMPLEMENTATION (MOSPI), GOVT. OF INDIA; STATE FINANCES: A STUDY OF BUDGETS, RESERVE BANK OF INDIA, 2023. * 2023 US$1 = 83 INR (APPROXIMATELY)

states, which showed huge inequality across states in terms of value of women empowerment; e.g., women in Bihar were 550% less empowered than women in Sikkim. They also pointed out that regional inequality also hides the social inequality and worst sufferers, both in terms of access and outcome in healthcare, were often those who belong to the marginalised social categories of Scheduled Castes and Scheduled Tribes.

Territorial inequality has different dimensions, one of which is inter-state migration in search of jobs (congestion costs). Only four states (Uttar Pradesh, Bihar, Rajasthan and Madhya Pradesh) account for half of the inter-state migrants in India. As per the 2011 Census, 20.9 million people (37%) migrated from UP and Bihar alone. Their major destinations are Delhi, Maharashtra, Tamil Nadu, Gujarat, Andhra Pradesh and Kerala. The extent of outmigration reflects the limited livelihood options available within their home states, which have experienced higher growth since 2005, but even higher growth could not address the lack of opportunities for employment within the states (Pandey and Gautam, 2020). The growth story of India continues to remain non-inclusive and lopsided.

The inequalities are more prominent among the eight states that lie at the periphery of India in its north-eastern corner (Assam, Meghalaya, Manipur, Mizoram, Nagaland, Tripura, Arunachal Pradesh and Sikkim) and in the three Himalayan states (Jammu & Kashmir – now a UT –, Uttarakhand and Himachal Pradesh), located strategically at the international border of India. They are prima facie disadvantaged due to their difficult mountainous terrains, remoteness of access, sparseness of population, lack of infrastructure and resources, and neglect of centuries, which is why a mechanism of "special category states"

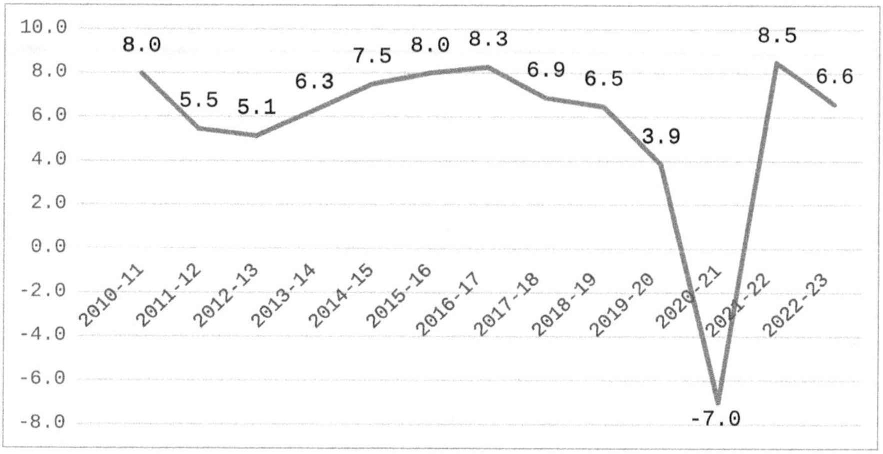

FIGURE 8.2 Growth rate of real GDP in India (2010–2023) (in %)
SOURCE: NATIONAL ACCOUNTS STATISTICS, MINISTRY OF STATISTICS AND PROGRAMME IMPLEMENTATION (MOSPI), GOVT. OF INDIA

was devised to give them access to liberal funding from the Central resources for development. Lack of convergence in income across regions is always connected with rise in conflict and social unrest, and these states have been the victims of such unrest for several decades since the 1970s. Terrorism, insurgency and separatist movements have crippled their development for decades and even though peace has returned now, it will take them decades to catch up with the rest of India. Even the peace has been rather fragile for some, as seen in the ongoing ethnic conflicts in Manipur. The Central Government's focus has been to improve the infrastructure at a rapid pace, especially the road and transportation infrastructure, a task that it has been doing commendably, but it takes time for investments to translate into income and employment which alone can address the problem of inequality.

1.4 *Economic Growth and Inequality*

Between 2010 and 2019, Indian economy has grown spectacularly (see Figure 8.2), but then it started slowing even before the pandemic. Then the pandemic struck. Growth has been the global casualty of the pandemic; only a few countries have somehow been able to absorb the shocks and are now struggling to recover against all odds. Among them, India is the major economy which was growing at the fastest rate before the pandemic and is still growing so after the pandemic. But growth comes at the cost of inequality, and inequality has been growing between the states that constitute the Union of India.

A study (Sinha et al., 2023, pp. 49–58) of growth and inequality among the Indian states in the post reform period (1993–2020) found that the different states have been growing at vastly different rates, from 5.3% for Andhra Pradesh to 14.1% for Sikkim. The distribution of GSDP was also highly skewed in many states, especially the poorer ones. This again confirms our earlier observation that poor states gained very little from the economic reforms, while the richer states surged ahead. The income inequality as measured by the Gini Coefficient also shows wide variations between the states. Andhra Pradesh, Punjab, West Bengal, Nagaland, Jharkhand, and Uttar Pradesh with Gini coefficients between 0.25 and 0.31 showed the lowest income inequality, while Arunachal Pradesh, Mizoram, Karnataka, Uttarakhand, and Sikkim with Gini coefficients between 0.39 and 0.52 showed the highest income inequality. The study found that growth and income inequality were higher in landlocked states than in coastal states, which in another cause of the strong regional inequality. Income was found to be distributed less unequally among the states that had low and medium growth as shown in Table 8.2. The study found evidence to support Gunnar Myrdal's argument that market forces tend to increase rather than decrease the inequalities between competing regions (Sinha et al., 2023). It also proves that the trickle-down theories propagated by the Washington Consensus and market economists make no sense in a country like India.

All the studies cited above clearly indicate that inequality has increased with growth and such high levels of inequality has the potential to impact future growth. As inequality is multi-dimensional, only one of which in income, to address it we need a holistic approach combining many mechanisms and many measures to attain an egalitarian growth, with focus on education, public health infrastructure, employment, and especially on inclusive financial services in which India has achieved remarkable progress in recent years. In the second part of the paper, we investigate whether the existing equalising mechanism are adequate to address the existing range of inequalities.

2 Fiscal Equalisation Program in India

2.1 *Between the Centre and the States*

Under the federal structure in India, in addition to the federal government, also known as the Central or the Union Government, India has 28 states with their own elected legislatures. Their respective legislative powers are delineated in the Constitution, which has separate lists for the Union, States and a Concurrent List of overlapping jurisdictions with residuary powers resting

TABLE 8.2 Inequality vis-à-vis growth in Indian States (1993–2020)

Growth parameter	**Inequality**		
	Low Inequality	Medium Inequality	High Inequality
Low Growth	Andhra Pradesh, Punjab, West Bengal, Nagaland, Jharkhand, Uttar Pradesh	Manipur, Assam, Madhya Pradesh	–
Medium Growth	–	Meghalaya, Maharashtra, Chattisgarh, Odisha, Bihar, Goa, Kerala, Himachal Pradesh, Rajasthan, Tamil Nadu, Gujrat	Mizoram
High Growth		Haryana	Arunachal Pradesh, Karnataka, Sikkim, Uttarakhand

SOURCE: ADAPTED FROM (SINHA ET AL., 2023, P. 53)

with the Centre. States can raise their own tax revenues using their own taxing powers under the constitution, as well as from non-tax revenues from the public services they render. Besides these, they are entitled to a share of the federal taxes and grants via the intermediary of Finance Commission (FC), which is a constitutional mechanism for devolution of resources from the Centre to the states. So far, 15 Finance Commissions have been set up at the federal level beginning with 1952, – one in every five years, and given their recommendations regarding transfer of federal resources to subnational governments. The federal government also gives grants and loans to the states outside this mechanism. At the level of states, there is a similar constitutional mechanism mediated by State Finance Commissions, also constituted once every five years, for transferring resources to the local bodies – the third tier of administration which covers both the urban and rural local bodies. The thrust of the Finance Commission mechanism from the beginning has always been on three guiding principles: equity, equalisation and efficiency, with equalisation being the predominantly guiding factor behind their recommendations. This was natural, given the huge disparity that existed between the states of India from its colonial days before independence in 1947.

After the Indian economy was liberalised, a series of transformational reforms in public finances were undertaken, in areas covering revenue, fiscal discipline and public debt. One important set of reforms was the enactments of fiscal responsibility legislations (Fiscal Responsibility and Budget Management Act, or FRBMA) by the Centre (2003) and by all the states (2006–2010) putting a cap of 3% of GDP or GSDP (Gross State Domestic Product, for the states) on borrowing, which led to significant improvements in public finances. The 12th Finance Commission provided significant incentives to the states for controlling their revenue expenditure by way of writing off part of the huge debts that they owed to the Centre. The states responded and their revenue accounts started generating surpluses, reversing the trends of huge deficits that had hitherto characterised all state finances. The equalising mechanisms applied by the successive FCs and the financial discipline enforced by the FRBMAs saw even the laggard states slowly increasing their growth rates. For some time, it seemed as if they would catch up with the advanced states gradually. But then the pandemic struck, sending the entire country into protracted lockdowns and bringing economic activities to a complete standstill. While both the federal and subnational state governments lost revenue, they had to spend more in providing subsidy to the poor who had lost their sources of income. The result was an increase in debt level across all the states and also at the federal level. Needless to day, the increased debt level exacerbated the existing inequalities as the poor states became more financially stressed. It was not only an Indian phenomenon, all the countries were impacted by it, but the impact was more severe on the emerging economies, and within them, among the poorer regions.

The mechanism of the FC was embedded in the Constitution to address the problem of regional imbalance and to equip and empower the states, where all development takes place. Till 2014, there was a Planning Commission (PC) when India followed the path of centralised planning. At independence, India had adopted a path of centralised planning and set up a PC to guide the socio-economic development of the newly independent nation, impoverished and deindustrialised due to colonial exploitation by the British rulers. PC was not a constitutional body, but was set up by a resolution of the Government of India in 1950 to ensure rapid socio-economic growth of individual states and also to address the disparity that existed between them. Both the FC and the PC – one constitutional and another extra-constitutional body – were thus addressing the same problems – while the FC strove to achieve these objectives by transferring resources from the richer to the poorer states through the constitutional process, the PC tried to address these problems by allocating federal resources through its Five Year Plans to meet the growth needs of individual states by giving higher per capita allocation to the poorer states. During the 1950s and 1960s, about two thirds of the Central resources thus used to be transferred to the states through the agency of the PC. Later, both these Commissions were each responsible for the transfer of approximately half of the total resources transferred from the Centre to the states.

Under this arrangement, public expenditure was classified as plan and non-plan expenditure, plan expenditure, meant for the creation of capital assets, being the prerogative of the PC and non-plan expenditure, meant for maintenance and upkeep of those assets, being the responsibility of the FC. This arrangement was not sanctioned by the Constitution, but the terms of reference of the FCs restricted their scope to recommending devolution of federal resources only in relation to the non-plan expenditure.

While the FC derived their authority from the Constitution, the PC lacked any such sanctity. Its members owed their allegiance to the government of the day, and often made transfers discretionally to suit the interests of the ruling party; this created many distortions and aberrations in our public financial system which severely impacted growth and transparency. It was increasingly being realised that centralised planning was not serving the objectives of growth and development, as the country continued to stagnate in a low-income, low-growth equilibrium for several decades. The PC was finally wound by the newly-elected government in 2014. In the scheme of transfers made to the states at the behest of the PC, discretion of the federal government was objected to by the states, forcing the PC eventually to adopt formula-based transfers, the formula being based on factors like population, area, income inequality, status of infrastructure or backwardness within the states, their special problems, etc. (Appendix 1). Of the total plan transfers which amounted to roughly half the aggregate transfer of resources from the Centre to all states, 30% were earmarked for distribution among the special category states mentioned earlier, and the rest were distributed according to this formula. The 30% share helped the special category states reduce poverty and improve physical and social infrastructure, but was unable to address the problems of income and employment generation or industrialisation within them. It rather created an overwhelming dependence of these states on Central resources, a dependence that continues undiminished even now.

Many a distortion thus characterised the entire planning era (1952–2014), the most damaging of which was the unchecked proliferation of so-called Centrally Sponsored Schemes (CSS), which ate into the formula-based plan transfers and consumed more of the central resources otherwise sharable with the states, which seriously damaged the spirit of federalism, as they were designed by the PC, often without consultation with the states, in areas that mostly belonged to the state's jurisdiction like rural development, education, health, sanitation, etc. Largely financed by the Centre, these schemes were reckoned as huge vote-catchers for the party that ruled at the Centre, and since all parties had a vested interest in continuing with the arrangement, the CSS continued to grow even when governments changed, and they continue till now. The 15th FC (FY 2021–26)[1] itself has pointed out that allocations on these schemes which are transferred to the states "detract from the equalising focus of the transfers extended by the Finance Commissions, and are probably regressive, in the sense that they are positively correlated with per capita incomes of the states ... Thus, there is a strong need to build institutional capacity in the States and shift to well-designed output-based transfers, while rationalising the multiplicity of Union schemes."[2]

A substantial part of the funds for these schemes were even transferred directly to their implementing agencies without routing them through the state budget, which was a requirement of the Constitution, and this kept large amounts of government funds outside the government account. Thankfully, the practice was abolished in 2013 and the PC itself was abolished in 2014. Since then, the FCs have been recommending devolution of all central resources to the states as mandated by the Constitution. They make recommendations for the horizontal and vertical sharing of the net proceeds of Union taxes between the Union and the states and determine the principles for Central grants-in-aid to states, besides also recommending measures to supplement the resources of the Local Bodies.

The FC recommendations are primarily based on the three principles of equity, equalisation and efficiency. Different FCs have used different criteria and weightages thereon for vertical and horizontal devolutions as shown in Table 8.3. The resources to be transferred comprise net proceeds of all taxes

1 The 15th FC was supposed to have given its recommendations covering the period 2020–2025. However due to the intervention of COVID-19, which required it to reassess the requirements of the state and the Union afresh, it gave two reports – one covering the period 2020–21 and the second report, called the report of the COVID-19 Time Commission, covering the period 2021–26.

2 Para 2.36, Second Report of the 15th Finance Commission.

and duties collected by the Centre sans from cesses and surcharges which the Centre can keep for itself, which is a sore point with the states. It can be seen that all FCs have given the maximum weightages to equalisation. From 14th FC onward the environmental criterion was introduced, assessing environmental externalities. The criteria used by the 15th FC for equalisation is the distance of per capita income of a state from the highest per capita income state – the more the distance, the more the share of that state.

As noted earlier, the sluggish pace of growth of agricultural sector contrasted with the rapid growth of the high-skilled service sector, whereas the growth of the manufacturing sector has been rather modest. This unequal growth across sectors has led to growing income inequality between the rich and the poor on the one hand, and between richer and poorer states on the other, and this inequality has widened over time, affecting the fiscal capacity of the states and making them more dependent on the federal financing, which has led to an unwelcome trend towards re-centralisation in federal fiscal relations. As seen from Table 8.4, states' own revenue receipts (RR) meet only a part of their revenue expenditure (RE) needs making them heavily dependent on central transfers for the rest; the RR/RE ratio also varies widely across the states. For some states, the gross financial transfers from centre constitute almost three fourths of their total aggregate expenditure, affecting their autonomy. Table 8.4 also shows the ratios of per capita tax to average state income (GSDP) which is a standard metric of the state's fiscal capacity or tax effort; this also varies widely among the states. For the federal government, on the average it is between 10% and 11% while for all the states combined, it is around 6% so that the total tax to GDP ratio for the country stands at around 17% and this has been rather stagnating at that level for a decade. The high level of dependence of the states upon federal financing does not augur well for healthy federal fiscal relations.

The FC recommendations and transfers have always been non-controversial, being based on objective criteria and formula based. However, the devolution of resources by the 15th FC failed to address the inequality between the states in a fair manner, and their recommendations were even seen as politically coloured. Till the 14th FC, the 1971 population was taken as the reference in order to incentivise the states to control their population, and this was a success because all states save only the six heartland states that speak Hindi, also known as Hindi-Belt states, have reduced their total fertility ratio (TFR) below the replacement level of 2.1. But the Terms of Reference of the 15th FC required it to consider the 2011-population which would have affected the shares of all other states, especially the southern states which have reduced the TFR well below the replacement level. As a result, the six Hindi-belt states – Uttar Pradesh (UP), Madhya Pradesh, Bihar, Jharkhand, Rajasthan and Chattisgarh,

TABLE 8.3 Criteria and respective weightages used by different finance commissions (2005–2026) (in %)

Vertical Devolution				
	FC-12 (2005–10)	FC-13 (2010–2015)	FC-14 (2015–2020)	FC-15 (2020–26)
Percentage of Central resources to be transferred to States (%)	30.5	32	42	41[a]
Horizontal Devolution				
Criteria	*Weights (%)*			
	FC-12	FC-13	FC-14	FC-15
Equity				
Population (1971)	25	25	17.5	
Population (2011)				15
Demographic Change since 1971 (2011 Population)			10	
Area	10	10	15	15
Equalisation				
Income Distance	50		50	45
Fiscal Capacity Distance		47.5		
Efficiency				
Demographic Performance				12.5
Tax Effort	7.5			2.5
Fiscal Discipline	7.5	17.5		
Environment				
Forest and Ecology			7.5	10
Total	*100*	*100*	100	100

a 1 percent is kept for Jammu & Kashmir which has become a UT in 2019. The FC transfers are only for the states. UTs are administered by the Centre

SOURCE: REPORTS OF THE RESPECTIVE FINANCE COMMISSIONS

which together shared 42.75% of India's population as per the 2011 census were given 48.57% of the sharable pool of Union taxes during 2021–26 by the 15th FC. The five southern states – Tamil Nadu, Karnataka, Kerala, Andhra Pradesh and Telangana – with a population share of 21.32% got only 15.8% of

TABLE 8.4 State dependency on federal transfers (2020–21)

State/UT	State's own revenue/ revenue expenditure (%)	Gross transfers from centre/ aggregate expenditure of state (%)	Tax: GSDP ratio (%)
1. Karnataka	59.6	28.0	6.0
2. Goa	59.2	29.4	5.6
3. Telangana	59.0	19.6	7.1
4. Maharashtra	58.0	26.0	6.3
5. Odisha	56.4	44.9	6.4
6. Haryana	54.3	20.8	5.6
7. Gujarat	53.6	29.9	4.3
8. Tamil Nadu	49.3	23.6	5.9
9. Kerala	44.5	33.5	6.2
10. Uttar Pradesh	44.1	45.6	7.3
11. Uttarakhand	43.4	54.4	5.0
12. Chhattisgarh	42.9	42.2	6.6
13. Rajasthan	41.5	31.9	5.9
14. Jharkhand	41.2	46.4	5.6
15. Andhra Pradesh	39.8	32.5	6.0
16. Punjab	39.6	42.0	5.7
17. Madhya Pradesh	39.1	44.5	5.7
18. West Bengal	36.8	42.1	5.2
19. Assam	31.0	58.7	4.8
20. Himachal Pradesh	30.6	599	5.2
21. Bihar	26.2	59.2	5.2
22. Sikkim	25.6	52.5	3.0
23. Meghalaya	22.6	611	6.0
24. Arunachal Pradesh	17.4	81.6	4.6
25. Tripura	16.4	72.3	3.8
26. Mizoram	14.2	67.5	2.7
27. Manipur	11.6	78.3	4.1
28. Nagaland	11.5	78.3	3.3

TABLE 8.4 State dependency on federal transfers (2020–21) (*cont.*)

State/UT	State's own revenue/ revenue expenditure (%)	Gross transfers from centre/ aggregate expenditure of state (%)	Tax: GSDP ratio (%)
Mean	*38.2*	*46.7*	*5.3*
Standard Deviation	*15.4*	*18.3*	*1.6*
Central Government			10.3

SOURCE: STATE FINANCE; A STUDY OF BUDGETS, 2023, RESERVE BANK OF INDIA

the sharable taxes, while the seven western, eastern and northern states with 30.61% of population got 25.31% share of tax proceeds. The eight remote and resource-starved north-eastern states and two Himalayan states (Uttarakhand and Himachal Pradesh) accounting for only 5.32% of population got 10.48% of the tax transfers. Had the 1971 population been considered, the Hindi-belt states which send more legislators to Parliament than other regions, would have got lesser shares, as shown in Table 8.5 (Bhattacharjee, 2021). Besides, the skewed shares of states from this, the recommendations also resulted in some bizarre anomalies.

TABLE 8.5 Share of states vis-à-vis population (1971–2011) (in %)

	Share in population (%)		Share in devolution (%)		
Reference population			**1971**	**1971**	**2011**
	1971	2011	13th FC	14th FC	15th FC
Hindi-Belt States	38.56	42.75	48.83	46.88	48.58
Southern States	25.14	21.32	18.57	17.97	15.80

SOURCE: AUTHOR'S CALCULATIONS BASED ON FC REPORTS

TABLE 8.6 Per capita share of states vis-à-vis tax effort (2021–26)

States	Overall share of states in devolution (%)	Tax effort performance		
		Tax: GSDP ratio (f) per capita (%)	f*2011 population	Per capita share (%)
UP	17.939	7.00	13983008	18.825
Maharashtra	6.317	6.97	7833503	10.546
Bihar	10.058	5.46	5682760	7.651
West Bengal	7.523	5.44	4963550	6.682
MP	7.850	6.72	4881533	6.572
Tamil Nadu	4.079	6.47	4667354	6.284
Rajasthan	6.026	6.12	4192976	5.645
Karnataka	3.647	6.63	4051084	5.454
Gujrat	3.478	5.94	3587565	4.830
Punjab	1.807	6.30	1748247	2.354

SOURCE: REPORT OF THE 15TH FINANCE COMMISSION, VOL 2, ANNEXURE 6.5

The actual *inter-se* shares of the states are influenced by population in more than one way. Thus, the 2011 population enters the calculations in respect of a total weightage of 17.5% (population and tax effort), while the 1971 population enters the calculations in respect of demographic performance with a weightage of 12.5%. Thus tax effort, defined in terms of the ratio of average per capita tax to average state income (GSDP) for three preceding years would have captured the parameter adequately, but multiplying it by the 2011 population to determine the states' shares resulted in Bihar's share in terms of tax effort exceeding that of all other states except UP and Maharashtra, which may not be the true reflection of its relative tax effort (Table 8.6). Similarly, scaling demographic performance, another parameter when defined as the inverse of fertility ratio would have been a correct reflection of a state's performance, by the 1971 population resulted in UP's share from this parameter exceeding that of all other states (Table 8.7); even Bihar's share of 5.513% in terms of demographic performance was better than Gujrat's 5.043%, even though their fertility ratios were vastly different -2.9 and 2.0 respectively (Bhattacharjee & Bhattacharya, 2021, pp. 14–17).

TABLE 8.7 Per capita share of states vis-à-vis demographic performance (2021–26)

States	Population share 2011 (%)	Demographic performance		
		Reciprocal of TFR (f)	f*1971 population	Per capita share (%)
UP	16.959	0.38	32.126	12.318
Maharashtra	9.538	0.52	26.394	10.120
West Bengal	7.747	0.60	26.376	10.113
Tamil Nadu	6.124	0.63	26.075	9.998
Karnataka	5.186	0.55	16.187	6.207
Bihar	8.836	0.34	14.378	5.513
Gujrat	5.130	0.49	13.151	5.043
MP	6.164	0.38	11.413	4.376
Rajasthan	5.818	0.36	9.202	3.528
Punjab	2.355	0.54	7.286	2.793

SOURCE: REPORT OF THE 15TH FINANCE COMMISSION, VOL 2, ANNEXURE 6.1

Thus, the Commission's recommendations hurt the principles of cooperative federalism and created expected discontent among the states. Of course, all Hindi belt states were poorer than the rest, but the recommendations were seen as catering to the interests of the ruling coalition rather than meeting the demands of objectivity and fairness. Even after the tax devolutions, as many as 17 out of 28 states were assessed to be short of adequate revenues to meet their revenue expenditure; they had to be given separate revenue-deficit grants, and this even included rich states like Tamil Nadu. Contrast this to only 11 states that were given such grants by the 14th FC (2015–20) and it becomes clear how the state finances have been devastated by the pandemic, especially in the poorer states.

2.2 *Equalisation Between the States and the Local Bodies*

In the three-tier system of governance in India, the weakest link has always been the last tier of the local bodies. In 1992, the local bodies were given constitutional status through two landmark amendments to the Constitution, 73rd and 74th, for the rural (RLBs) and urban local bodies (ULBs) respectively. The RLBs have a three-tier structure of bodies called Panchayats at the village, block and district levels (called Village Panchayats, Panchayat Samities and Zilla

Parishads respectively), while the ULBs also have a three-tier structure (Nagar Panchayats, Municipal Councils and Municipal Corporations depending on population). There are about 250,000 RLBs and 5000 ULBs in India. They are the institutions of political participation and governance in which one third of seats are reserved for women and are responsible for development at the grassroot level. The constitutional amendments mandated transfer of several functions along with the necessary funds and functionaries from the state to the local bodies. Functions were duly transferred, but many functionaries were missing, and as regards funds, practically their only source of revenue is the tax on property which is grossly inadequate. To address this, the amendments also mandated the constitution of State Finance Commission (SFC) by every state to recommend devolution of state resources to the local bodies. Since states themselves face financial constraints, the Constitution also mandated that the Central Finance Commission would recommend measures to augment their resources. Besides scarcity of funds, the local bodies also suffer from severe constraints upon their capacity, expertise, etc. The 15th FC has recommended a total transfer of INR 4.36 trillion to the local bodies from the Central resource to be distributed among the states on the basis of their population and area (90% and 10% weightages respectively), subject to certain conditions like publishing provisional and audited accounts in the public domain, fixation of minimum floor rates for property taxes by states and improvement in their collection, and also upon the constitution of SFCs by March 2024.

Most states have constituted their SFCs while some states have implemented the recommendations of six SFCs by now. However, many states have not constituted the current SFCs; e.g. in Manipur, the last SFC report covered the period from 2013–18, and the next SFC is yet to be constituted. Just as inequalities exist between states, so also inequalities exist between districts and in most states, due to the availability of infrastructure and institutional capacities in the capital and adjoining districts, they absorb most of the government expenditure for social sector development, while the peripheral districts are starved of funds. There is a huge development-disparity paradigm that develops as a result. An earlier study by the author on intra-state disparities in government expenditure in six states – Bihar, Uttar Pradesh, Jharkhand, Chhattisgarh, Madhya Pradesh and West Bengal – based on the actual treasury data on government expenditure made in the social sectors of education, health and supply of drinking water, revealed shocking disparities within most of these states (Bhattacharya, 2009, pp. 231–37). The situation remains much the same even now, especially among the poorer states. In conflict-ridden Manipur, for example, the average per capita government expenditure in the valley areas inhabited by the majority ethnic group of Meiteis is about two to four times that in the surrounding and underdeveloped hill areas inhabited by the ethnic groups of Kukis who are now fighting the former. Goven that government expenditure constitutes 80% of the GSDP in Manipur without much other economic activity, such skewness creates huge disparity between the core and the periphery. The primary task of the SFCs should be to addressed such disparity through appropriate equalisation measures.

A 2018-study (Chakravarty et al., 2018) of the working of SFCs across the Indian states does not give the impression that they have achieved this objective. While the advanced states in the south have constituted five or six SFCs till now with devolutions covering the current fiscal, some states have not constituted beyond just two SFCs. Their reports often get delayed inordinately, and while some states act promptly upon their recommendations, some show no urgency to act. Their treatment of divisible pool remains non-uniform, with different SFCs defining the divisible pool according to their own judgments, though most SFCs have considered only the state's own revenues (without its share of central taxes). The transfers recommended to the local bodies ranged from 2.5% of the net proceeds of state's own tax receipts for West Bengal to 41% for Karnataka, making comparisons extremely difficult across the SFCs. The study did not find any evidence of relationship between the per-capita income of a state and recommended financial devolution. The per capita transfers showed wide variations across states ranging from INR 146.75 for Odisha to INR 6101.04 for Karnataka, as did the transfers as share of own revenues of the states (1.69% to 41.36% for these two states). The study noted the non-existence and non-availability of data, in the absence of which population and area were mostly considered as criteria for horizontal distribution, without there being any equalising factor like the income distance as in case of Central FCs, though some states have included criteria like remoteness, backwardness, or other vulnerabilities that could be measured. The study noted that for SFCs "to function as an institution to promote decentralisation, the focus needs to be multi-dimensional focusing on improving the process, the data collection and sharing as well as improving the quality of SFC reports."

The situation remains much the same even now, as the author's analysis of a sample of SFC reports covering 8 states selected from different regions and different income strata clearly shows (Appendix 2).

3 Conclusions

Inequality has been the price of growth in India. There are huge inequalities across the Indian states which have increased over the years and pose serious problems for future growth of India. The shock of the pandemic tested the resilience of the equalising federal institutions in India. The constitutional mechanism for devolution of resources mediated by the FCs also faltered, with its emphasis more on the fiscal rather than on the federal, thereby compromising objectivity in the process. FCs have repeatedly emphasised the creation of an independent Fiscal Council to ensure objectivity and fairness in the public financial management system and to check the perpetual tendency of governments to indulge in populism at the cost if state's resources which can be utilised much more productively otherwise, but such recommendations have so far found no acceptance with successive governments. Centralisation of federal fiscal relationship has always been a problem in India, with the Centre encroaching upon states' jurisdictions through the centrally sponsored schemes. To meet the shock of another great pandemic or economic crisis, the public financial management system needs to be more accommodative to the needs and concern of the states. Similarly, the states also must strengthen their own equalising mechanisms which are now delivering sub-optimally, and utilise their resources by increasing efficiency and abstaining from populism. The challenges are serious, and if not manged properly, may impede the growth of the country as a whole.

(The criteria and their explanation is contained a background note appended to Demi-Official: letter No.4/9/96-FR/DCH/3670 dated February 24, 1997 forwarded by Mr. Madhu Dandavate, the then Deputy Chairman, Planning Commission to Mr. Prakash Singh Badal, the then Chief Minister of Punjab.)

APPENDIX 1 Formula used by the planning commission for transfer of plan funds to states (in %)

	Original gadgil formula (1969)	**Modified gadgil formula (1980)**	**NDC revised formula (1990)**	**NDC revisedformula (1991)**
A. Special Category States	*30% share of 3 States*	*30% share of 8 States*	*30% share of 10 States*	*30% share of 11 States*
B. Non-Special Category States				
(i) Population (1971)	60.0	60.0	55.0	60.00
(ii) Per Capita Income of which	10.0	20.0	25.0	25.0

APPENDIX 1 Formula used by the planning commission for transfer of plan funds to states (in %) (*cont.*)

	Original gadgil formula (1969)	Modified gadgil formula (1980)	NDC revised formula (1990)	NDC revisedformula (1991)
(a) According to the deviation method (for States with per capita income less than the national average)	10.0	20.0	20.0	20.0
(b) According to the distance method covering all the States.	0.0	0.0	5.0	5.0
(iii) Performance of which	10.0	10.0	5.0	7.5
(a) Tax effort	10.0	10.0	0.0	2.5
(b) Fiscal Management	0.0	0.0	5.0	2.0
(c) National Objectives	0.0	0.0	0.0	3.0
1. Population Control	0.0	0.0	0.0	1.0
2. Elimination of Female illiteracy	0.0	0.0	0.0	1.0
3. On-time completion of externally aided projects	0.0	0.0	0.0	0.5
4. Success in Land Reforms.	0.0	0.0	0.0	0.5
(iv) Special Problems	10.0	10.0	15.0	7.5
TOTAL	100.0	100.0	100.0	100.0

Notes: NDC = National Development Council, a body of all states (now defunct). The number of special cattery states increased from 3 in 1969 to 11 in 1990, as smaller states were carved out of larger states and given the special category status.

APPENDIX 2 Basis of SFC recommendations in some states, as available now

State	Year of report	Criteria for vertical vevolution	Horizontal devolution formula for RLBs	Horizontal devolution formula for ULBs	Shares of devolution by RLBs and ULBs
Assam	2016–2020	14% of SOTR (Net proceeds of State's Own Tax Revenue)	Population 50% Area 25% Index of Infrastructure [a] 12.5% Per capita Tax Collection 12.5%		60%, 40% Including 6th Schedule Areas
Manipur	2013–2018	10% of SOTR + Share of Central Divisible Pool of Taxes	Population 75% Area 10% Illiterate population: 5% Population without piped water supply 5% Population without electricity 5%		35.28%, 22.49% and 42.23% between PRIs, ULBs and ADCs depending on respective populations
Bihar	2020–2025	10% of SOTR	Different formula for Development, Maintenance and General Funds (30%, 20% and 50% of total devolution respectively both for RLBs and ULBs) Inter-se distribution under each fund based on Population 90%, area 10%.		65%, 35%
Tamil Nadu	2022–2027	10% of SOTR	Population 55% Area 25% SC/ST population 20%	Population 55% Area 25% Slum population 20%	49%, 51%
Maharashtra	2020–2025	11.41% of SOTR	Population 90% Area 10% [b]	Population 90% Area 10%	–

APPENDIX 2 Basis of SFC recommendations in some states, as available now (*cont.*)

State	Year of report	Criteria for vertical vevolution	Horizontal devolution formula for RLBs	Horizontal devolution formula for ULBs	Shares of devolution by RLBs and ULBs
Kerala	2021–2026	28.45% of SOTR	Different formula for different funds, e.g. for the General Purpose Fund: Non-SC/ST population: 40% (50% for BPs and ZPs) Atea 10% Environmental vulnerability [c] 10% Deprivation index [d] 10% Incentive for revenue mobilisation 15%		70%, 30% to 92%, 8% for different funds (General Purpose Fund, Maintenance Find, Development Fund)
Punjab	2021–2026	3.5% of SOTR	Population 80%, Area 10%, SC Population 10%	Population 90%, Area 10%	55%, 45%
West Bengal	2020–2025	1.5% of SOTR with 5% increase in every subsequent year	Population 50% Area 10% Share of Illiterate females 10% Share of Agricultural labourers 10% Share of urban population 10%	Population 33.3% Area 33.3% Share of Illiterate females and Share of marginal workers labourers 33.3%	68%, 32%

a 1. Length of surface roads 2. Length of pucca drains 3. Number of street lights
b For GPs, 100% share based on population
c Floodplain area, coastal length, hazard zone
d Households without LPG connection, electricity or water, below poverty households, distance from highest per capita own revenue weighted with population

SOURCE: REPORTS OF THE RESPECTIVE FINANCE COMMISSIONS

References

Ahluwalia, M. S. (2000). Economic Performance of States in Post Reforms Period. *Economic & Political Weekly*, 35(19).

Arbatli-Saxegaard, E., Coppo, M., Khalil, N., Kotera, S. & Unsal, F. (2023). Inequality and Poverty in India: Impact of COVID-19 Pandemic and Policy Response. *IMF Working Paper* 23/147.

Baddeley, M., McNay, K., & Cassen, R. (2006). Divergence in India: Income Differentials at the State Level, 1970–97. *Journal of Development Studies*, 42(6).

Bajpai, Nirupam and Jeffrey D. (1999). Progress of Policy Reform and Variations in Performance at the Sub-National Level in India. Harvard Institute for International Development (Harvard University), *Development Discussion Paper* No. 730.

Bhattacharjee, G. & Bhattacharya, R. (2021). Fifteenth Finance Commission Recommendations: An Appraisal. *Economic & Political Weekly*, 56(41).

Bhattacharjee, G. (2021). Fifteenth Finance Commission Recommendations: Economics mixed with Politics?. *Mainstream Weekly*, 59(43). http://mainstreamweekly.net /article11623.html.

Bhattacharya, G. (2009). Intra-State Disparity in Government Expenditure: An Analysis. *Economic & Political Weekly*, 44(26–27).

Chakraborty, P.i, Gupta M. & Singh, R. K. (2018). *Overview of State Finance Commission Reports*. National Institute of Public Finance and Policy: New Delhi. Overview of SFC reports.pdf (fincomindia.nic.in).

Health Index India (2019). *Healthy States Progressive India: Report on Rank of States and Union Territories*. Ministry of Health & Family Welfare, Niti Aayog.

Kurian, N.J. (2000). Widening Regional Disparities in India – Some Indicators. *Economic & Political Weekly*, 35 (7).

Pandey, A. & Gautam R. (2020). Regional Inequality in India: A State Level Analysis. *MPRA Paper* No. 101980.

Sachs, J. D., Nirupam B. & Ananthi, R. (2002). Understanding Regional Economic Growth in India. Center for International Development (Harvard University), Working Paper No. 88.

Sinha, M., Ramadas, S. & Ramasundaram, P. (2023). Are Spectacular Growth and High Inequality Two Sides of the Same Coin?, *Economic & Political Weekly*, 58 (19).

CHAPTER 9

Confronting Territorial Inequality among South African Municipalities: Challenges to the Fiscal Equalisation System

Jaap de Visser, Tinashe Chigwata and Nico Steytler
Dullah Omar Institute (University of the Western Cape)

1 Introduction

South Africa is the most unequal country in the world when measured against the common Gini-coefficient. Race is the biggest contributing factor to that inequality (World Bank, 2022) but there is also spatial inequality; poverty is unevenly spread across the country. Under apartheid, the *bantustans* (the then black self-governing territories) were underdeveloped rural areas to serve as labour reserves for mining and urban industries. They were sites of poverty, and public services were far inferior to those in the white areas. The inequality between rural and urban has persisted since 1994 (Visagie & Turok, 2021). This is also reflected at provincial level: residents of the Gauteng and Western Cape provinces are better off when compared to other provinces, with the Eastern Cape, KwaZulu-Natal, and Limpopo housing the poorest (Statistics South Africa, 2020). As the rural-urban divide is also manifest among municipalities across the country, so does inequality among municipal areas (David et al., 2018).

The democratisation of South Africa in 1994 was not only to ensure majority rule, but also to redress the immense inequality and poverty produced by apartheid. The 1993 interim Constitution established a non-racial liberal democracy with a bill of rights. A significant element of the new constitutional dispensation was the establishment of a decentralised system of government: nine provinces and local governments were established, each with a modicum of autonomy (Steytler, 2005). Seven of the nine provinces incorporated the ten bantustans, and inherited their poverty. One of the aims of decentralisation was to ensure the redistribution of resources also between territories. In the 1996 Constitution of the Republic of South Africa, the positions of the provinces were maintained, but the autonomy of local government, as a sphere alongside the national and provincial governments, asserted (De Visser, 2005).

Local government institutions, covering the entire landmass of South Africa, were established in three categories of municipalities: single tier metropolitan municipalities (metros) and district municipalities (which are composed of a number of local municipalities, where the former perform mostly a coordination function and the supply of bulk services to municipalities). District municipalities are again subdivided: nearly half is authorised to provide water services directly to communities, while the other half is not. Through a process of amalgamation, coming into effect in 2000, urban areas were linked to rural areas where possible, and by 2022 there were eight metros, 44 district municipalities, and 205 local municipalities. The metropolitan and local municipalities are further classified by the National Treasury as metros, secondary cities, large towns, small towns, and rural areas (National Treasury, 2012). The financial position of municipalities is highly disparate; urban municipalities have access to their own revenue (property taxes and service fees) but most rural municipalities do not.

The objectives of local government include 'the provision of services to communities in a sustainable manner' (section 152(1)(b) Constitution 1996). These services include water and sanitation services, electricity distribution, and municipal health services (schedule 4B Constitution 1996). Through judicial interpretation, municipalities are obliged to fulfil the socio-economic rights of access to 'sufficient food and water' (section 27 Constitution 1996) and electricity (Steytler & De Visser, 2022, ch. 17).

After the December 2000 municipal elections, which ushered in the new local government dispensation, the national government announced a 'free basic services' policy. This entailed that a basic level of municipal services is provided to all households across the country (DPLG 2001, p 1). Local governments are charged with the service delivery and implementation role, and the national government is responsible for providing the necessary financial resources to municipalities (Steytler & de Visser, 2022, ch. 9–14(9)). Potable water and electricity supply were the first two services to be included (DPLG, 2001, para 3). The national government prescribed that a minimum of six kilolitres of water per household per month had to be provided freely as from 1 July 2001, and from 1 July 2003, free basic electricity of 5kWh/50kWp per household per month. Free sanitation was the next service to be proclaimed in 2008. The provision of the commodities – water, electricity and sanitation – to a household presupposes the necessary infrastructure is in place: a water collection, purification and distribution network, as well as a waterborne sewerage system. Likewise, an electricity distribution system has to provide the connections to each household. The provision of free basic services – water, electricity and sanitation – to indigent households, is then a social wage, initiated and funded by the national government and implemented by local government.

Because poverty is unevenly spread across municipalities, the national funding of free basic services sought to implement an equalisation system of transfers, based largely on the number of indigent households per municipality. The funding was channelled through a municipality's equitable share of revenue raised nationally for the commodities, and conditional grants for the infrastructure.

This chapter addresses three questions in this regard: First, is the intergovernmental fiscal system appropriately designed to ensure that the worst form of inequality – abject poverty – is adequately addressed through a social wage, and if not so, why? Secondly, if so, has the system been properly implemented in addressing this inequality, and if not so, why? Thirdly, if the answers to the two previous questions show weaknesses in design and/or implementation, what could be done?

It is argued, first, that the national law and policies, in the main, genuinely seek to reduce inequality amongst municipalities through a finely tuned redistribution formula for transfers. The municipalities with the highest levels of poverty receive the highest levels of funding per poor household. It applies to both the block grant of the local government equitable share (LGES) of revenue raised nationally, and to conditional grants. However, there are areas where the formula of the LGES and the design of the conditional grants show weaknesses. Secondly, there is a major gap between the intent of the transfers and their implementation; many municipalities do not (and often cannot) give effect to their redistributive aim.

Before commencing with the analysis, an outline of the broad intergovernmental fiscal system is sketched, providing the context in which transfers to local government are situated.

2 South Africa's Intergovernmental Fiscal System

The essential features of South Africa's intergovernmental fiscal system are set out in Chapter 13 of the Constitution 1996. The system is based on provinces and municipalities collecting their own revenue, complemented by fiscal transfers to correct fiscal imbalances. The integrated or centralised nature of South Africa's multi-level government system (Anderson, 2010, p. 12) manifests in, amongst other things, the fact that there is an elaborate system of supervision (i.e. intergovernmental monitoring of financial performance).

2.1 *Provincial Own Revenue*

Unlike federations that assign significant taxing powers to states or provinces, South Africa's Constitution reserves almost all taxing powers for the national government (Khumalo et al., 2015, pp. 207–211). Most provincial functions, such as public health, education and housing, are held concurrently with the national government. This supports the notion that the national government would raise the revenue for these functions. For the vast majority of provincial functions, there is no cost-recovery. Governments do not recover the costs of public health care services, public education and public housing from the recipients of that service. This has informed the minimal tax assignment to provinces. In practice, provincial governments raise very little revenue. It usually does not make up more than 4 or 6 percent of the provincial budget (Khumalo et al., 2015, p. 208). Provinces generally focus on managing expenditure, rather than raising revenue.

2.2 *Municipal Own Revenue*

It is different for municipalities. Section 229 of the Constitution provides that municipalities have powers to impose property taxes and charge fees for the services they provide. This aligns with their constitutional powers. The local government functions in Schedules 4B and 5B of the Constitution are exclusive to municipalities and subject only to national and provincial regulation (Chigwata et al., 2021, pp. 201–203). Furthermore, many municipal functions are trading services where cost recovery is possible (Khumalo et al., 2015, 209). Municipalities may charge individual users for electricity, water, sanitation, and refuse removal. The municipal powers to collect property rates and charge fees for services are constitutionally guaranteed, albeit subject to national regulation. As indicated earlier, the extent to which municipalities raise their own revenue varies greatly from one municipality to the next.

When comparing the constitutional responsibilities of provinces and municipalities with their own revenue, it becomes clear that the fiscal imbalance for provinces is very significant: provinces raise very little of their own revenue (Khumalo et al., 2015, p. 208; Brand, 2006, p. 191). Furthermore, the fiscal imbalance for municipalities varies from one municipality to the next, but is often also significant (Steyler & Ayele, 2018, p. 303).

2.3 *Intergovernmental Fiscal Relations*

The vast majority of intergovernmental transfers are disbursed by the national government. They are decided annually in the Division of Revenue Act (DORA) which is part of the annual national budget.

Aside from setting out the rules on how intergovernmental grants are going to be distributed and managed, DORA determines the vertical division of revenue between the national, provincial and municipal spheres of government. Section 214(1)(a) of the Constitution requires an equitable division of revenue raised nationally between the three spheres of government annually. Nationally raised revenue must be shared fairly between the three spheres, considering their respective expenditure responsibilities. This vertical division of nationally raised revenue takes place following a consultative process (outlined below), and after consideration of a number of factors such as national interests, provision for national debt, subnational fiscal capacity and efficiency of provinces and municipalities (section 214(2) Constitution).

DORA furthermore determines the horizontal division of revenue, i.e. the unconditional and conditional grants to provinces and municipalities. The Act contains appropriations of the vertical and horizontal division of revenue for the upcoming budget year, but also projections for the two 'outer years', to allow subnational governments to plan ahead. Importantly, intergovernmental fiscal transfers complement a provincial government's or a municipality's own revenue, but do not compensate for failures to collect revenue (Khumalo et al., 2015, p. 212).

The Intergovernmental Fiscal Relations Act of 1997 determines a process of intergovernmental consultation on the Division of Revenue Bill, which is repeated annually (Brand, 2006, p. 189). The process towards the annual DORA starts at least ten months before the beginning of the financial year with a report by the Finance and Fiscal Commission (FFC). The FFC is an independent constitutional body, tasked with advising the national government in intergovernmental fiscal relations. Its members are appointed by the President, through a procedure that involves all three spheres of government (Khumalo, et al., 2015, p. 212). In this report, the FFC makes recommendations on the vertical division of revenue and the allocations to provinces and municipalities. The National Treasury then prepares the Division of Revenue Bill. It consults with the FFC, provinces, and organised local government in various intergovernmental forums designed for that purpose (Brand, 2006, p. 189). The National Treasury is obliged to respond to the recommendations by the FFC.

2.4 *Transfers to Provinces*

Section 227 of the Constitution provides that each province is entitled to an equitable share of the revenue raised by the national government. The purpose of the equitable share is to enable provinces to provide basic services, and to perform the functions allocated to them. The equitable share is decided in accordance with a formula comprising six factors. Each factor is weighted, and indicators are used to measure each specific factor. The formula has remained relatively stable since the dawn of democracy in 1994, with only minor adjustments to the factors and the weighting. The elements of the formula are set out below.

The formula is designed to enable provinces to deliver their social services, particularly in education and health. The equitable share is an unconditional grant. However, much of a province's expenditure is indirectly determined by the national government. First, the remuneration schemes, to be paid by provincial governments to their staff, are negotiated by the central government (Khumalo et al., 2015, p. 222). The provincial government thus has limited control over its salary bill. Many of the provincial functions are labour-intensive: the provincial government must employ teachers, nurses, doctors etc. (Steytler & Ayele 2018, p. 304). Secondly, provincial functions are generally carried out in terms of national legislation. The general trend with respect to the concurrent provincial/national functions is that the national government determines the legal and policy framework and the provincial government implements. This is particularly true for functions such as basic education, health care and human settlements. These national laws and policies inevitably influence the scope provincial governments have to determine budget priorities. For example, the minimum standards for education infrastructure are determined nationally (Brand, 2006, p. 186).

Conditional grants to provinces are used by the national government for two reasons. The first is to address historical legacies of underdevelopment in

TABLE 9.1 Summary of equitable share for provinces

Weighting (%)	Factor	Indicator
48	Education	Public school enrolment (Gr R – 12)
27	Health	Risk profile and health system case load
16	Basic	Share of population
5	Institutional	Equal division
3	Poverty	Share of country's poor population, using income data
1	Economic output	Regional gross domestic product

SOURCE: (NATIONAL TREASURY 2022, P. 16)

parts of the country (Khumalo et al., 2015, p. 215). The second is as a mechanism to implement national policy priorities. If the national government wants to drive, for example, school nutrition or extra attention for learners with disabilities, it often designs a conditional grant to get provincial governments to pay attention to these areas. There has been a growth in the number of conditional grants to provinces. At times, the national government consolidates a variety of conditional grants into one comprehensive grant.

2.5 *Transfers to Municipalities*

Every municipality is entitled, in terms of the Constitution, to an equitable share of nationally raised revenue. The main objective of the equitable share for municipalities is to enable municipalities to deliver basic services. The equitable share allocation is unconditional. Like the equitable share for provinces, the equitable share for municipalities is determined according to a formula, using independently sourced data, with the focus primarily on redistribution and poverty alleviation. The details of this transfer are discussed in the next section.

There are two broad categories of conditional grants to municipalities. The first category comprises capacity building grants, aimed at assisting municipalities in building capacity in key areas of municipal governance. Most municipalities do not raise sufficient revenue to fund capital expenditure. This is why the second category of conditional grants comprises infrastructure grants, aimed at assisting municipalities, particularly with pro-poor capital and infrastructure investment (National Treasury, 2022, p. 44; Khumalo et al., 2015, p. 215). The most important of those, the Municipal Infrastructure Grant (MIG) is further discussed in the next section.

All in all, the intergovernmental fiscal system reflects the integrated and centralised system of multilevel government. The national government has a virtual monopoly on all taxation, but expenditure responsibilities are spread across the three spheres of government. This then necessitates an intricate system of intergovernmental fiscal transfers that seeks to follow that division of responsibilities. The system for deciding on intergovernmental fiscal transfers is predictable, formula-based and backed by independently obtained data. It is also transparent and includes input by provinces and organised local government.

3 Evolution of National Transfers to Municipalities

The system of national transfers to municipalities for equalisation purposes in the provision of basic municipal services has evolved over the past three decades, affecting both the local government equitable share and conditional grants. The evolution shows a continued pre-occupation with improving the redistributive effect of intergovernmental grants.

3.1 *Local Government Equitable Share – Vertical Equalisation*

From the onset of the post-apartheid local government system, it has been the government's intention that the LGES must provide a "standardised subsidy mechanism for all poor households" (White Paper on Local Government, 1998, p. 21). The LGES was dispersed for the first time to municipalities on 1 July 1998 with the coming into effect of the 1996 Constitution. Two questions are significant for local government's redistribution role: (1) what is the size of local government's share of revenue raised nationally? and (2) how is the LGES shared horizontally among municipalities?

As indicated earlier, the size of the LGES is determined in terms of the annual national budget process, where also the shares of the national and provincial spheres of government are determined.

The LGES has grown rapidly since its inception in 1998. It increased from 6 billion (3%) South African Rand (R) in 2000/01 to around R100 billion (9%) in 2015/16 of the national budget (Ncube & Monnakgotla, 2016, p. 225). By 2019/20 the LGES had declined to R65.6 billion (8.3%) and was estimated to rise to R83.7 billion (8.7%) in 2022/23 financial year (National Treasury, 2023a, p. 72). Thus, LGES has consistently been less than 10% of nationally raised revenues available for sharing among the three spheres of government. This raises questions about its adequacy given local government's demanding service delivery and development mandate. It is often argued that many municipalities, particularly secondary cities and rural ones, are struggling to provide services and develop the necessary infrastructure needed for service delivery due to insufficient funding from the LGES and conditional grant funding (Public Affairs Research Institute, 2019, p. 4; Ncube & Monnakgotla, 2016, p. 225).

3.2 *Local Government Equitable Share – Horizontal Equalisation*

Once the LGES has been determined through the vertical division of revenue, the next step is the sharing of the LGES among municipalities. Ever since the introduction of the equitable share in 1998, this horizontal division of revenue has been based on a formula. The formula uses objective data to ensure transparency, objectiveness and predictability in the sharing of revenue among municipalities. This makes the manipulation of the formula to benefit certain municipalities difficult, since there is no discretion in the allocation of funds.

The first formula was introduced in 1998, at a time when funding for the operationalisation of the new system of government was a priority. But equity was already the overriding objective of the intergovernmental fiscal system. The 1998 White Paper on Local Government identified five key objectives for horizontal equalisation: equity, efficiency, ensuring a basic level of administrative capacity in the most resource-poor municipalities, predictability, and incentives for proper financial management at the local level (White Paper on Local Government, 1998, p. 120). To achieve these objectives, the initially proposed formula comprised of four subgrants, namely –

1. The basic services grant.
2. The municipal institution grant.
3. The tax base equalisation grant.
4. The matching grant.

The basic services grant (S) subsidised the provision of basic services to poor households while the municipal institution (I) grant funded municipal institutional and political structures. The tax base equalisation grant and the matching grant were not implemented and subsequently removed from the formula. The S and I subgrants determined the LGES allocations to municipalities between 1998/9 and 2004/5 (National Treasury, 2012, p. 3). Equity, in particular the provision of basic services to the poor by all municipalities, was the underlying objective of the formula during this period. The existence of infrastructure backlogs, particularly in rural areas and townships, with some communities receiving no services at all, was identified as a major challenge. Therefore, the LGES was meant to fund the costs of basic service delivery to the urban and rural poor, phased in over a number of years (White Paper on Local Government, 1998). The White Paper emphasised the need for the LGES to go to municipalities with actual service delivery and governance expenditure. Hence, the LGES was initially shared between metropolitan and local municipalities, and only when a local municipality lacked capacity was the LGES dispersed through the relevant district municipality.

After 2000, there were a number of changes to the LGES. From the 2000/01 financial year, a subgrant was introduced to fund municipalities in the former *bantustans* (the so-called former R293 towns) to carry out tasks previously undertaken by provinces. A year later, the abovementioned indicative three-year LGES allocations were introduced to provide predictability for budgeting purposes. In 2001, the national government adopted the Free Basic Services Policy, mentioned in paragraph 1, under which municipalities were required to provide a portion of water, electricity, sanitation and refuse to poor households free of charge. The costs for the delivery of these free basic services was covered through an additional allocation in the LGES from the 2003/04 financial year. Following the 2001 census, the population data was updated in 2004, with some changes to poverty measurement. Prior to this update, a household which earned less than R800 per month was classified as poor, this bracket was enlarged to households earning less than R1100 per month. With increased urbanisation, metros received increased LGES allocations. By 2004/5, the LGES was comprised of the S-grant (67%), I-grant (7%), free basic services (water, sanitation and refuse removal) (12%), free basic electricity (7%), R293 allocations (4%) and nodal allocations (3%) (National Treasury, 2004, p. 272). Each of these subgrants were determined by a separate formula. For instance, the nodal allocations were administered largely outside of the LGSE formula under a separate funding window. This put the equity principle at risk. Lastly, each municipality was guaranteed 70 per cent of its previous year's allocation and a minimum allocation of R1 million (National Treasury, 2012, p. 7).

In the period between 1998 and 2004 the LGES came under attack (National Treasury, 2012, p. 7). Some stakeholders attacked the formula for its lack of transparency, while others criticised the existence of different funding windows which undermined objective and equitable allocations. Against this background, a review of the formula commenced in 2004, culminating in the adoption of a new formula in 2005. The 2005 formula comprised the Basic Services Component (BS), Institutional Component (I), Development Component (D), Revenue Raising Capacity Correction Component (RRC), Correction and Stabilisation Factor (C). The LGES was calculated as $BS + I + D - RRC \pm C$. The Basic Services Component for the subsidised delivery of electricity, water, sanitation and refuse removal remained the largest in the formula, allocated to municipalities that were authorised to undertake the relevant functions, whether it was a metropolitan, district, or local municipality. Poor households that were connected to municipal services received a full subsidy while un-serviced poor households – houses not connected to service delivery infrastructure – received a partial subsidy set at 45% of the value of the serviced households (National Treasury, 2012, p. 13). This was meant to ensure that municipalities do not receive subsidies for services they were not providing. Inadvertently, metros benefited more from the BS even though they only had a combined 1.6 million poor households relative to the 1.9 million poor households in rural municipalities, in terms of the 2001 census data. This was partially because metros had more poor households connected to service delivery infrastructure than rural municipalities and, therefore, received the full subsidy. The D Component was not implemented as there was a lack of consensus regarding its objectives and calculation.

Between 2007 and 2011, several changes were made to the 2005 formula. However, four changes stand out. First, funding for environmental health services was introduced for the 2007/08 financial year as part of the BS component. Second, the measurement of the differentiated tax system in the RRC component was changed from the 2009/10 financial year. This was in recognition of the greater fiscal capacity of metros to cross-subsidise service delivery to poor households in their areas from their own revenue. The change resulted in a slight increment in the LGES share for rural municipalities (National Treasury, 2012, p. 27). Following the increases in bulk electricity prices by Eskom – the national electricity supplier – the subsidy levels in the BS component were adjusted from the 2010/11 financial year to factor in the increment. Lastly, the population escalation factor was replaced with a poverty factor and the BS subsidies for both serviced and un-serviced households were reweighted from the 2011/12 financial year (National Treasury, 2012, p. 8).

The overall effect of these changes is that the growth in allocations to metros was reduced with more funding allocated to rural municipalities. However, for the 2012/13 year, metros still received 34% of the BS relative to 13% allocated to rural municipalities (National Treasury, 2012, p. 17). Nonetheless, district municipalities, many of whom preside over rural areas, received 34%. The formula thus remained largely redistributive in nature. The BS also remained the biggest component in the formula accounting for 92.4 percent of the LGES allocations for the same financial year, demonstrating that it is the main tool for horizontal equalisation (National Treasury, 2012, p. 13). Overall, as shown in Figure 9.2 below, between 2002 and 2012, metros received the largest share of the LGES in every financial year except for the 2002/03 to 2003/04 period, when rural municipalities received the largest share of any category.

In 2012, another review of the formula was undertaken resulting in the formula that was in place at the time of writing. As with the previous reviews, the review only targeted the sharing of revenue among municipalities and did not focus on vertical equalisation. With updated data available, following the 2011 census, the review was necessary to ensure that the formula remained as objective as possible. However, there were also other concerns with the LGES formula. These include the formula's primary focus on only the major basic services, the absence of an accurate way of costing the delivery of services in different municipal environments, the non-implementation of the development component, the population bias of the formula, and the fact that service delivery gains between census were not factored in the formula (National Treasury, 2012, p. 30). Once again, the review culminated in a new or revised formula which was implemented gradually from the 2013/14 financial year

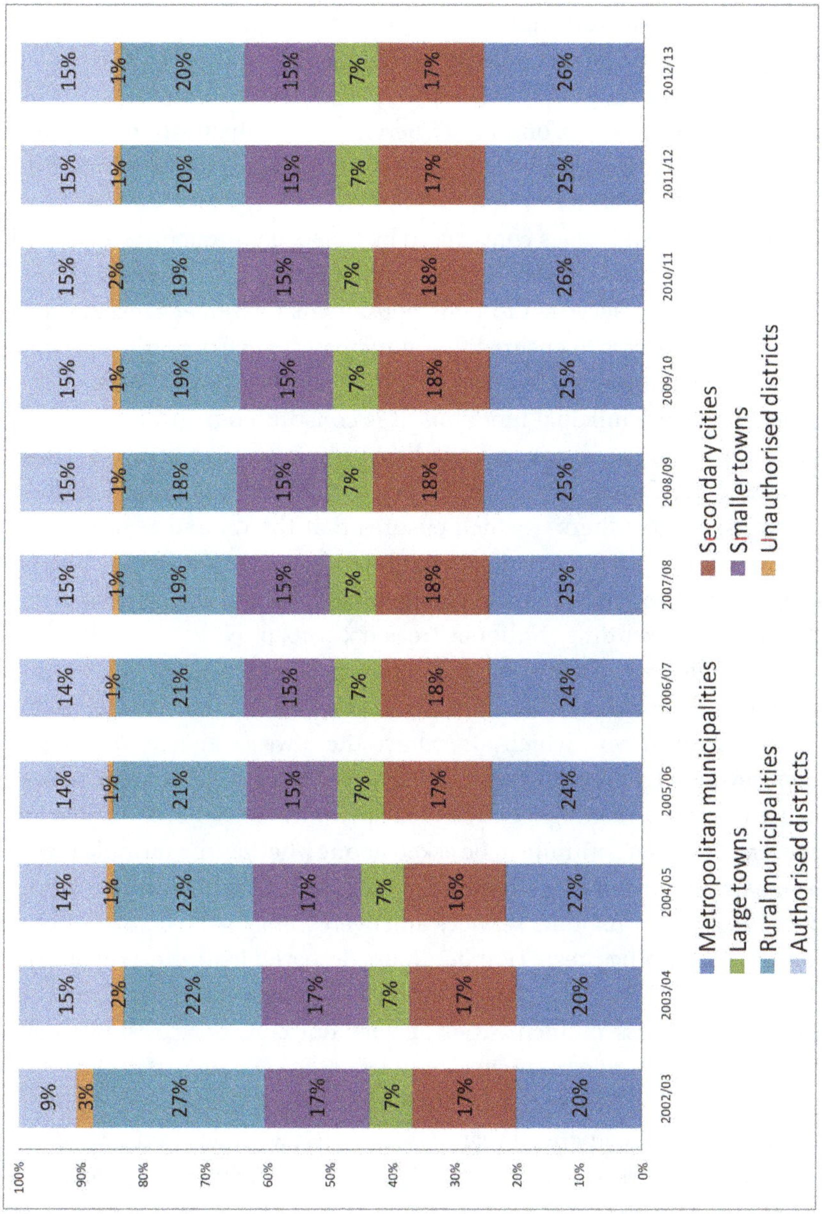

FIGURE 9.1 Distribution of the LGES (2002–2012) (in %)
SOURCE: (NATIONAL TREASURY, 2012, P. 26). AUTHORISED DISTRICTS REFER TO THOSE DISTRICT MUNICIPALITIES THAT ARE WATER AUTHORITIES AND SERVICE PROVIDERS OF WATER (SEE PARA 1 OF THE INTRODUCTION)

over a period of five years (Ncube & Monnakgotla, 2016, p. 225; Public Affairs Research Institute, 2019, p. 28).

Like previous formulas, the new formula relies on demographic and other data to calculate each municipality's share of the LGES (National Treasury, 2016, p. 33). It has three parts, made up of five components:

> Basic Services (BS) + Community Service (CS) + Institutional Funding (I) × Revenue Adjustment (RA) +/– Correction and Stabilization (C).

The first part of the formula is constituted by the BS component, which funds the delivery of free basic services (water, electricity, sanitation, refuse removal and municipal health services) to poor households (National Treasury, 2016, p. 33). The second part is to ensure that municipalities, particularly poor ones, have the required administrative and governance capacity and are in a position to perform key municipal functions. It is constituted by (a) the I component, which provides a subsidy to cover basic administrative costs; (b) the CS component, which funds other core municipal services excluded from the BS such as parks; and (c) the RA, which ensures that the CS and I components benefit poor municipalities the most (National Treasury, 2016, p. 33). The last part, the C component, ensures that changes in allocations to each municipality are evened out over time (National Treasury, 2016, p. 33).

As shown in Figure 9.3 below, in comparison to the old formula (the adjusted 2005 formula), the 2012 formula shifts allocations more towards rural municipalities and small towns, which often have the lowest capacity to generate their own revenue (Ncube & Monnakgotla, 2016, p. 225). These poor municipalities are now receiving higher allocations per poor household.

However, questions continue to be asked about whether the formula is sufficiently redistributive. It has been argued, for instance, that the formula "underestimates the cost of providing services and overestimates the contribution of own revenue to funding these" (Public Affairs Research Institute, 2019, p. 2). It is further contended that, given that the LGES funding model applies uniform cost parameters across municipalities, it does not consider cost-influencing factors that vary from one municipality to the other (Public Affairs Research Institute, 2019, p. 59). Hence, for example, there was an estimated R2 billion shortfall for the 2018/19 financial year between what was allocated through the LGES to municipalities and the actual cost of service delivery to poor households (Public Affairs Research Institute, 2019, p. 34). Further, the formula does not factor in certain services (firefighting services, roads, stormwater etc) that are not provided on a cost-recovery basis. Hence, it is widely acknowledged by many stakeholders that another review of the formula may be necessary.

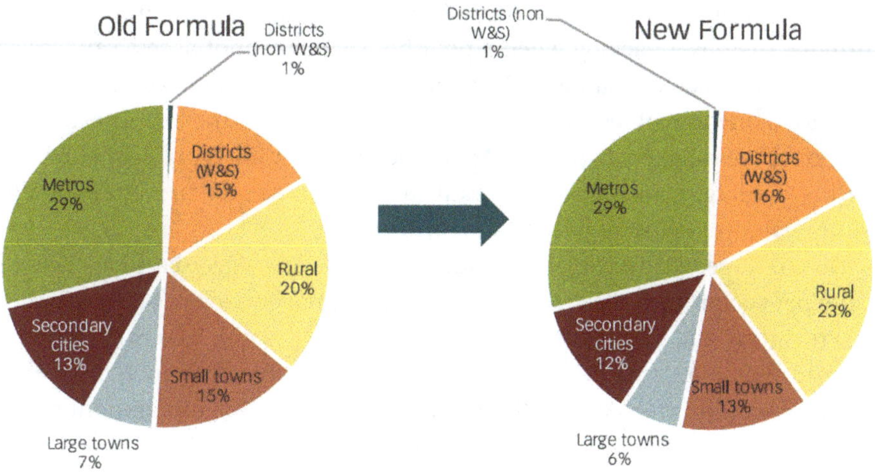

FIGURE 9.2 Redistributive impact of LGES between the revised 2005 (left) and 2012 (right) formulas
SOURCE: (NCUBE & MONNAKGOTLA, 2016, P. 229)

3.3 *Municipal Infrastructure Grant*

Besides the LGES, the national government provides, from its segment of the national budget, a number of conditional grants to municipalities to realise national objectives at the local level. One of those is the equalisation of basic services. Like the LGES, the conditional grants are captured in the DORA. They are administered by various national departments, which also oversee the relevant projects at municipal level. Some of the grants can be accessed only on the basis of a prior application which is approved by various national government agencies. One conditional grant, the Municipal Infrastructure Grant (MIG), comes into focus because of its emphasis on redistribution and its complementarity to the LGES.

The MIG was introduced in 2004 following the consolidation of a number of infrastructure grants. Its original aim was to eliminate, by 2013, municipal services backlogs through the provision of capital finance to municipalities (Government of South Africa, 2004, p. 1). It is a conditional grant so municipalities must comply with certain conditions, and spend the funds in line with their integrated development plans and approved budgets. MIG funds may not be used to cover operational expenditure related to public infrastructure.

The MIG is divided at vertical and horizontal levels. The horizontal division allocates resources between sectors (such as water, sanitation, roads, electricity etc.) and thus gives expression to the national prioritisation of sectors. The horizontal division considers water, sanitation, roads and other backlogs as well as the number of poor households in municipalities. For purposes of the formula, there is a backlog when a poor household cannot access services as determined by sector standards. Furthermore, a household is classified as poor if it has an income of less than R2 300 per month, as per the 2011 Census data (National Treasury, 2022, p. 100). As can be observed in Figure 9.4 below, the MIG is the largest infrastructure grant to local governments. It grew significantly from its inception until the 2009/10 year.

Due to its redistributive effect, municipalities with bigger backlogs benefit more per sector from the MIG than those with smaller backlogs (Department of Provincial and Local Government, (unknown), p. 14). The MIG formula ensures that municipalities with weak fiscal capacity, often rural, and with the largest proportions of poor households, receive the highest amount of the grant and per household (Shai et al., 2021, p. 111).

4 The Implementation of Pro-poor Equalisation Transfers

Both the LGES and the local government conditional grants are geared towards assisting municipalities that face the greatest demand for free basic services. However, in practice this result is often not achieved, both because of the design of the transfers, and the way municipalities make use of them.

4.1 *Local Government Equitable Share*

As indicated earlier, the LGES has two main objectives, namely to enable municipalities to (1) provide basic services to poor households, and (2) to afford basic administrative and governance capacity and perform core municipal functions.

The first objective of the LGES represents a key pillar of the national government's efforts to reduce inequality amongst municipalities. It seeks to guarantee a basic standard of water, electricity, sanitation and refuse removal for everyone. In that sense, the LGES aims to implement the Bill of Rights, and in particular the socio-economic rights to water, sanitation and basic municipal services (Fuo, 2014, p. 194).

The National Treasury pursues this redistributive objective by identifying poor households and allocating subsidies to the municipalities where they live. The National Treasury estimates the number of poor households that reside in each municipality. It uses census and household survey data, collected by Statistics South Africa (StatsSA), which is South Africa's independent national statistics agency. The poverty threshold, used by the National Treasury is two old age state pensions per month which, in 2023 terms, is equivalent to

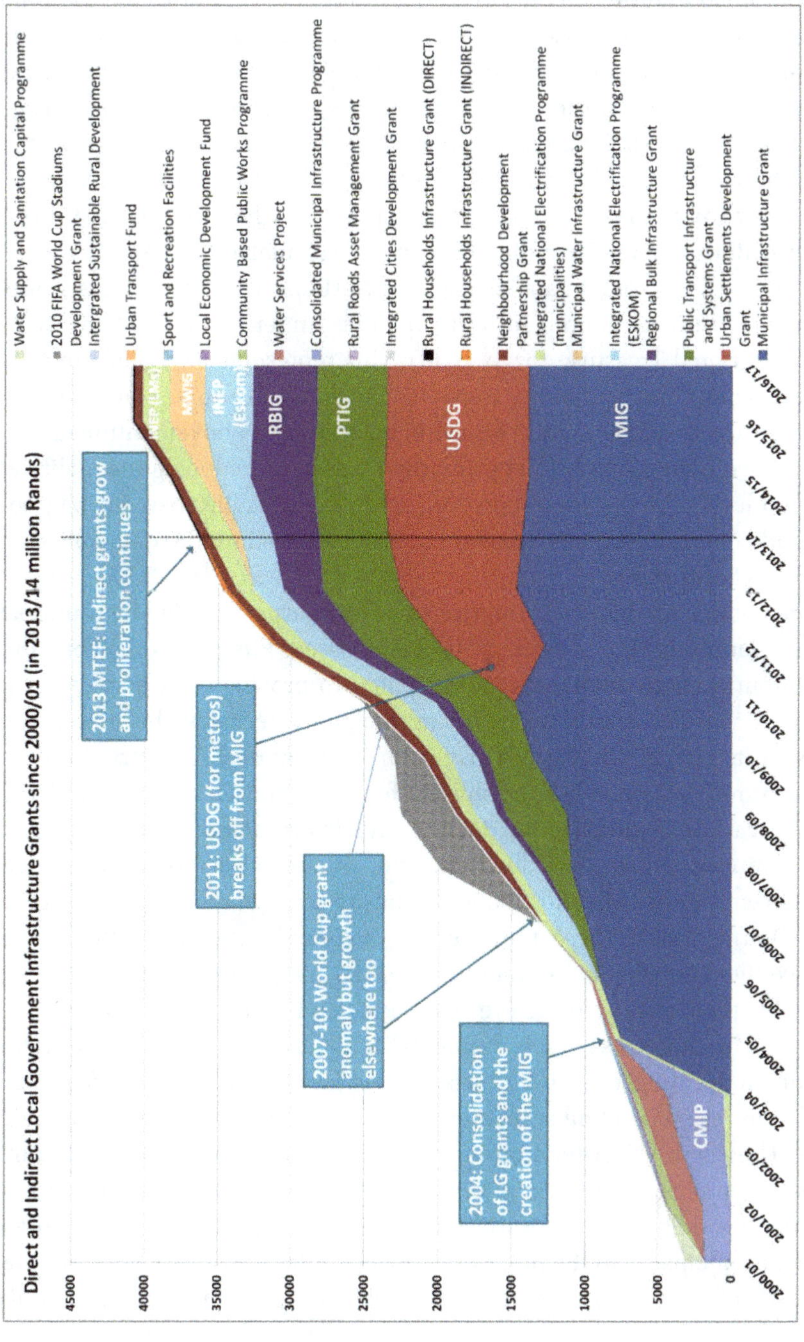

FIGURE 9.3 Infrastructure grants to local government (2000/01–2013/14) (in million Rands)

SOURCE: (NATIONAL TREASURY, 2014, P. 1)

approximately R 4200 (USD 233) per month (National Treasury, 2022, p. 37). If the combined monthly income of a household is less than two old age state pensions, the National Treasury includes a subsidy for that household in the LGES for the municipality in which that household is located. In the 2023/24 financial year, the subsidy was R530 (USD 29) per month for a package of free basic water (six kilolitres per poor household per month), energy (50 kilowatt-hours per month) and basic sanitation and refuse removal (National Treasury, 2022, p. 37). The National Treasury publishes detailed information on how these allocations to each municipality are calculated (National Treasury, 2023a). In the 2023/2024 financial year, the National Treasury will distribute R78.2 billion (USD 4.1 billion) to municipalities under this part of the LGES formula (National Treasury, 2023b, p. 16). This represents 82.5% of the total LGES allocation. The remaining 17.5% is calculated to support institutional costs, community services and councillor salaries (the abovementioned second objective). The LGES is thus primarily focused on reducing inequality at household level. The question, however, is: do the subsidies benefit the poor households that the National Treasury identifies, based on the data collected by Statistics South Africa?

Before answering this question, two important aspects of the institutional design surrounding the LGES must be emphasised. First, while its constitutional intention is to enable the municipality to provide basic services, it is transferred without conditions. The municipality receives the grant, and decides in its budget what it will use it for. The National Treasury does not instruct municipalities to use the subsidy for those households that Statistics South Africa has identified, nor does it have instruments at its disposal to sanction municipalities that don't. Second, municipalities determine their own tariff and debt collection policies and by-laws (Steytler & Ayele, 2018, p. 302). On the basis of these, they identify the poor households in their areas and place them on what is commonly called the 'indigent register'. These poor households then qualify to receive free basic services from the municipality (subsidised by the LGES). Each municipality determines its own criteria for inclusion on the indigent register. Usually, residents must apply to be placed on the indigent register and must regularly renew their indigent status to remain eligible. The eligibility criteria often include means testing, which is administratively complex, controversial (Groundup, 2023), and brings unintended consequences, such as stigmatisation (Fuo, 2014, p. 203). The criteria also differ from one municipality to the next, sometimes fundamentally so. For example, in his study of indigent policies, Fuo concludes that some municipalities only include citizens, others include permanent residents and refugees as well (Fuo, 2020, pp. 291–300). In general, municipal indigent policies are implemented

TABLE 9.2 Free basic services subsidy (2019/20) (in million households)

Service	Million households identified for subsidy	Million households that received subsidy	Difference (millions)
Electricity	10.1	1.9	8.2
Water	10.1	2.1	8
Sanitation	10.1	1.5	8.6
Refuse	10.1	2	8.1

SOURCE: (LEDGER, 2021)

through dense and inaccessible bureaucracies, aimed at reducing the number as much as possible.

The result is that the national government's effort to implement a social wage by subsidising municipalities to provide free basic services is not fulfilling its objective. A recent study by Ledger of the implementation of the LGES basic services subsidy in 2019/20 reveals a staggering gap between the number of households targeted in the formula by the National Treasury, and the number of households identified and assisted by municipalities. In 2019/20, the National Treasury included a free basic service subsidy in the LGES for a total 10.1 million households. However, Table 9.2, based on Ledger's findings, indicates that less than a quarter of those households received the subsidy from their municipality.

In monetary value, the difference between the number of households identified for a subsidy, and the number of households that received a subsidy, amounts to more than R 40 Billion (USD 2.2 billion) (Ledger, 2021, p. 13). In other words, R 40 billion in carefully calculated national poverty alleviation funds is a hit and miss, because local governments exclude many poor households from it.

The context for this disjuncture is complicated, and there are many reasons why local governments are diverting the equitable share away from poverty alleviation (Ledger, 2021, p. 14). However, it is safe to say that part of the reason is the unwillingness or inability of municipalities to spend the LGES in accordance with its constitutional objective.

4.2 *Municipal Infrastructure Grant*

The MIG is another critical tool for redistribution and complements the LGES. However, its redistributive impact has been undermined by both design and implementation flaws. For instance, the MIG capital finance is primarily oriented towards new infrastructure and does not prioritise infrastructure renewal and maintenance. Coupled with municipalities' under-budgeting for repairs and maintenance, this means that the developed infrastructure progressively deteriorates. Also, the formula includes a component which guarantees every deserving municipality a certain minimum allocation, irrespective of their fiscal capacity and infrastructure needs. This diverts funds towards stronger municipalities and therefore, undermines the MIG's redistribution potential (Shai et al., 2021, p. 110).

When it comes to implementation, there are a number of problems. First, many municipalities, particularly rural ones, lack the necessary capacity to administer and spend the grant. Second, given the strict conditions attached to the MIG, municipalities are preoccupied with spending the MIG at the expense of other capital projects, for example those funded from their own source revenue (Shai et al., 2021, pp. 111–113). This means that other capital projects that can make a difference in service delivery often lie idle. Also, MIG funds are sometimes not used for their intended purpose but to fund salaries and creditors, for example (Business Day, 2017). For instance, the Thaba Chweu Municipality in Mpumalanga, which is facing financial problems, is reported to have dug into the MIG to pay salaries for municipal councillors and staff in February of 2014 (Citizen, 2014).

These and many other reasons explain why the grant failed to eliminate the infrastructure backlogs as set out in the MIG policy in 2004. The target to eliminate infrastructure backlogs by 2013 was not only missed, the backlogs are still existing in 2023, a decade later.

5 Towards Greater Equalisation and Poverty Reduction

There is a clear constitutional mandate for all three spheres of government to reduce poverty. National government has the necessary policies in place, funding mechanisms are provided for, and local governments are structured and mandated for the task. Yet, the equalisation mission is not fully executed. What can be done to ensure that the LGES and conditional grants perform their functions more effectively?

The solution for the diversion of LGES funding may be sought along three avenues. First, an argument could be made for more local democracy. Organs that exercise external oversight over local government, such as provincial treasuries, the National Treasury, and the Auditor-General may take municipalities to task on the diversion of LGES away from poverty alleviation. However, as alluded to above, their hands are tied because the LGES is an unconditional grant. For example, all that the National Treasury does when it comes across a municipality diverting LGES funding away from free basic services for the poor, is ask for an explanation. In the words of the National Treasury (2022, p. 37):

> if municipalities choose to provide fewer households with free basic services than they are funded for through the local government equitable share, then their budget documentation should clearly set out why they have made this choice and how they have consulted with their community during the budget process.

There is little evidence of local pressure through the channels of local democracy and internal oversight on this matter. Residents, including those left out of the application of the LGES, are represented in municipal councils that pass budgets, adopt tariff policies and subsequently oversee their implementation. Each municipal council has a Municipal Public Accounts Committee, equipped with a mandate and powers to examine the municipality's finances and probe the mayor and the administration on the use of the LGES. It can be argued that these systems ought to do better in highlighting this problem, and extracting accountability from municipal executives and administrations that control the local purse.

Secondly, an argument could be to argue for more conditionality and thus less decentralisation. If the absence of conditionality has led to a diversion of funds meant for poverty alleviation, does this mean that more conditionality is needed to protect the poor? For example, should the basic services component of the LGES be removed from the LGES, and converted into a conditional grant? This would be an unattractive option. First, many of the reasons for the diversion are not located in mischief on the part of local governments, and second, it would undermine South Africa's firm commitment to devolution.

Thirdly, a fundamental relook at the intergovernmental fiscal system should be done. One of the main reasons why municipalities are not devoting the LGES as intended, is that they simply do not have the necessary funds to meet all their expenditure needs. How can this issue be addressed? The first step would be to review the basis for own source revenue. Both the collection of current income sources can be sharpened, as well as the increase of fiscal instruments. However, this will not help rural municipalities much; located in poor areas, there is little space to collect more revenue or impose new taxes. The second step would be to review the vertical division of revenue raised nationally. The less than 10 per cent local government receives is not enough for all the constitutionally imposed tasks and mandates. Although the economy is in decline and the government's financial position consequently in dire straits, with no immediate prospects of improvement in sight, this is a necessity given the rise in inequality and poverty, which, in turn, will endanger social stability. And local government is best geared to ameliorate poverty through free basic services.

With respect to the need to maximise the redistributive effect of conditional grants to local government, in particular the MIG, the answer must include a review of the design of conditional grants. The proliferation of conditional grants must be controlled, because of the risk of compromising the coherence of municipal infrastructure planning. The design of the MIG requires continuous review, to ensure that it targets infrastructure backlogs and poor households. National government, and in particular sector departments, must improve their monitoring of conditional grants to ensure that spending aligns with the conditions. Finally, the national government should increase funding to assist municipalities with addressing backlogs in infrastructure to deliver basic services. This is difficult, given the precarious nature of the government's financial position mentioned above. However, the funding of infrastructure to deliver those services needed for a dignified human existence is surely a priority.

Lastly, no restructuring of formulas or increase in allocations will benefit the poor for as long as recipient local governments are plagued by corruption, maladministration and a general lack of capability and good governance. A concerted effort must be made, across all three spheres of government, to ensure that all municipalities adhere to their constitutional mandate of prioritising the delivery of basic services to the poor.

References

Anderson, G. (2010). *Fiscal Federalism: A Comparative Introduction.* Oxford: Oxford University Press.

Brand, D. (2006). *Financial Constitutional Law – A Comparison between Germany and South Africa.* Johannesburg: Konrad Adenauer Stiftung.

Business Day (2017), 'Broke councils use infrastructure grant funds to meet salary bill' https://www.businesslive.co.za/bd/national/2017-11-27-broke-councils-use-infrastructure-grant-funds-to-meet-salary-bill/ (accessed 3 October 2023).

Chigwata, T., De Visser, J., & Ayele, Z. (2021). Real or Imagined Local Autonomy – Experiences from Local Government in Ethiopia, South Africa and Zimbabwe. In T. Fenwick & A. Banfield (Eds.), *Beyond Autonomy – Practical and Theoretical Challenges to 21st Century Federalism* (pp. 191–216) Boston-Leiden: Brill.

Citizen (2014). 'TCM allegedly misusing fund' https://www.citizen.co.za/lowvelder/news-headlines/2014/02/05/mig-grant-for-salaries/ (accessed 3 October 2023).

David, A., Guilbert, N., Hamaguchi, N., Higashi, Y., Hino, H., Leibbrandt, M., Shifa, M., (2018). *Spatial Poverty and Inequality in South Africa: A Municipality Level Analysis*. Cape Town: SALDRU, UCT (SALDR Working Paper Number 221).

De Visser, J. (2005). *Developmental Local Government: A Case Study of South Africa*. Antwerp & Oxford: Intersentia.

Department of Provincial Affairs and Constitutional Development (1998). *White Paper on Local Government*. Pretoria: Department of Provincial Affairs and Constitutional Development.

Department of Provincial and Local Government (2001). 'Issues to be taken into account when Implementing Free Basic Services'. Departmental Circular: Annexure B.

Department of Provincial and Local Government (2004). *The Municipal Infrastructure Grant (MIG), 2004–2007, From programme to projects to sustainable services*. Pretoria: Department of Provincial and Local Government.

Fuo, O. (2014). Local government indigent policies in the pursuit of social justice in South Africa through the lenses of Fraser. *Stellenbosch Law Review* 25(1), 187–208.

Fuo, O. (2020). Nativism in South African municipal indigent policies through a human rights lens *Law Democracy and Development* 24, 271–31.

Government of South Africa (2004). *Policy Framework for the Introduction of the Municipal Infrastructure Grant, Amended by the Municipal Infrastructure Task Team 5*. Pretoria: Government of South Africa.

Groundup (2023). Swellendam community centre burnt down as residents rampage over electricity hike and indigent policy. *Daily Maverick*, 20 September 2023.

Khumalo, B., Dawood, G., Mahabir, J., (2015). South Africa's Intergovernmental Fiscal Relations System. In N. Steytler & Y. Ghai (Eds.), *Kenya-South Africa Dialogue on Devolution* (pp. 201–226). Cape Town: Juta.

Ledger, T. (2021). *Access to Basic Services – Enabling Progressive Transformation or Entrenching Poverty and Inequality?* Johannesburg: Public Affairs Research Institute.

National Treasury (2022). *2023 Budget Review Explanatory Memorandum to the Division of Revenue*. Pretoria: National Treasury.

National Treasury (2023a). *Local Government Equitable Share Municipal Demonstration Spread Sheet*. available at http://mfma.treasury.gov.za/Media_Releases/LGESDiscussions/Pages/default.aspx (accessed 14 September 2023).

National Treasury (2023b). *Local Government Funding Model*. Pretoria: National Treasury.

National Treasury (2023c). *Budget Review 2023*. Pretoria: National Treasury.

National Treasury (2012). *Local Government Equitable Share Formula Review, Discussion Paper 2: Analysis of the Current Local Government Equitable Share Formula*. Pretoria: National Treasury.

National Treasury (2022). *Budget review*. Pretoria: National Treasury.

National Treasury (2004). *Annexure E to the 2004 Division of Revenue Bill.* Pretoria: National Treasury.

National Treasury (2022). *Division of Revenue Bill for 2022.* Pretoria: National Treasury.

National Treasury (2016). *W1-Explanatory Memorandum to the 2016 Division of Revenue Bill.* Pretoria: National Treasury.

Ncube, M., Monnakgotla, J., (2016). *The Adequacy of Local Equitable Share and Conditional Grants for Rural Development.* Pretoria: Financial and Fiscal Commission.

Public Affairs Research Institute (2019). *A Critical Evaluation of the Local Government Equitable Share (LGES)*. Public Affairs Research Institute: Johannesburg.

Shai, L., Molefinyana, C., & Msomi, A. (2021). The Effect of the Municipal Infrastructure Grant on Capital Funding and Service Delivery Disparities in Recipient Municipalities. In T. Chigwata, J. de Visser & L. Kaywood (Eds.), *Municipal Perspectives on Development, Governance and Service Delivery* (pp. 87–114) Cape Town: Juta.

Statistics South Africa (2020). *How unequal is South Africa?* Pretoria: Statistics South Africa. https://www.statssa.gov.za/?p=12930#:~:text=Eastern%20Cape%20was%20the%20most%20unequal%20province%20in%202015&text=Gauteng%20and%20Western%20Cape%20were,for%20all%20four%20data%20points (accessed 3 October 2023).

Steytler, N. & Ayele, Z. (2018). Local Governments in African Federal and Devolved Systems. In A. Valdesalici & F. Palermo (Eds.), *Comparing Fiscal Federalism* (pp. 299–327). Leiden-Boston: Brill.

Steytler, N. & De Visser, J. (2022). *Local Government Law of South Africa* 14th Issue Durban: LexisNexis.

Steytler, N. (2005). Republic of South Africa. In J. Kincaid & A. Tarr (Eds.), *Constitutional Origins, Structure, and Change in Federal Countries* (pp 311–346). Montreal: McGill-Queen's University Press.

Visagie, J. & Turok, I., (2021). Rural–urban inequalities amplified by COVID-19: evidence from South Africa. *Area Development and Policy* 6:1, 50–62.

World Bank (2022). *South Africa Report.* https://www.worldbank.org/en/country/southafrica/overview#:~:text=South%20Africa%20remains%20a%20dual,coefficient%20of%200.67%20in%202018. (accessed 3 October 2023).

CHAPTER 10

Inter-regional Inequalities and Fiscal Equalisation in Spain

Mario Kölling
Lecturer of Political Science (UNED – Universidad Nacional de Educación a Distancia)

Ana Herrero-Alcalde
Lecturer of Public Economics (UNED – Universidad Nacional de Educación a Distancia)

1 Introduction

In the political economy literature, federalism and decentralisation have been associated with uneven redistribution. For example, Rodden et al. (2003) states that federalism is a negative factor for the growth of redistribution and the welfare state. Oates (1972) claims that if fiscal systems are strongly decentralised, they enable the existence of various communities that support different levels of redistribution in a country, which would result in varying redistribution levels and patterns. This fragmentation attributed to federalism derives from varying decision-making points and through decentralised fiscal structures, which can decide on their own taxation and redistributive policies (İrepoğlu Carreras, 2016). Equalisation systems are important instruments to offset these financial differences between constituent units in federal countries and in this regard important instruments of interregional redistribution. In Spain, although the decentralisation process has been quite successful, questions related to the regional financing system have occupied a large part of the debates on the territorial organisation of power. Moreover, for years now, there have been calls for a revision of the Constitution in order to adapt the text to the current reality of the territorial model and to establish a framework granting unity and diversity, on the one side, and a stronger equilibrium between shared rule and self-rule, on the other. One of the most contentious issues on these debates has been that linked to territorial inequalities, especially the relationship between territorial inequalities and decentralisation; that is, whether the decentralised nature of the system, because its roots on diversity, either fosters them or slows down any fight against them.

DOI:10.1163/9789004524514_012

Although inequalities among autonomous communities (ACs) related to the GDP per capita or unemployment rate decreased significantly from the 1980s until 2007, the recession starting in 2008 hit the Spanish economy with virulence, leading to significant increases of inequalities among ACs. Until 2019, the economy recovered with rates of economic growth among the highest in OECD countries. However, in 2020 Spain was one of the countries hardest hit by COVID-19 worldwide, both in terms of infections and deaths. The decline in public revenue resulting from the crisis affected the spending capacity of the ACs in an asymmetrical way and increased territorial inequalities among public administrations.

This chapter will analyse the challenges posed by territorial inequalities to Spain's internal cohesion and welfare state as well as assess the effectiveness of the fiscal equalisation system to address these territorial inequalities.

According to this, we will firstly give a brief overview of inter-regional inequalities in Spain and the impact of the two crises on the territorial distribution of economic power. Secondly, we will analyse the equalisation system. Thirdly, we will concentrate on the evolution of expenditure of ACs in welfare policies with special focus on the impact of the economic crises of 2008 and the COVID 19 crisis. And fourthly, we will identify the main challenges of the current equalisation system and analyse the ongoing debate on the reform option of the model.

Our results show that there are 1) long-standing socio-economic inequalities among ACs, 2) an important effort of inter-regional solidarity within the equalisation system, 3) asymmetric impacts of both crises on welfare policies among the ACs, and 4) a shortfall in the design of the equalisation system to address (post-crises) inter-regional inequalities.

A preliminary remark is important though; the system of financing the ACs in Spain has an asymmetrical character and is regulated by two differentiated models: the common and the *foral* regime. The former is applied uniformly in all the ACs on the Spanish peninsula,[1] except for the Basque Autonomous Community and Navarre, and in the Balearic Islands. In contrast to the ACs of the common regime, which have a more limited fiscal and financial autonomy, the Basque Country and Navarre enjoy a broad fiscal and financial self-government power that enables them to set and regulate their own tax systems. Moreover, the Basque Country and Navarre do not contribute to the equalisation system, although both ACs contribute to the Compensation Fund (*Fondo*

1 Canary Islands, Ceuta and Melilla have a special tax regime.

de Compensación Interterritorial), which aims to reduce regional disparities in income and wealth in Spain.

2 Structural and Cyclical Economic and Social Inequalities Among ACs

The geographical pattern and persistence of socio-economic inequalities has been historically a burden for the Spanish economic development. The historical roots of inequalities date back to the 19th century. The industrialisation process concentrated mainly in some urban areas of Catalonia, the Basque Country and, later, Madrid. The economic boom of the 1960s and up to 1975 clearly intensified the concentration of the economic development in some parts of the territory and brought about a large flux of internal migrations: many people migrated from rural and economically depressed areas (especially Andalusia, Extremadura and Galicia) to Bilbao, Barcelona and Madrid. These urban areas attracted also most foreign financial investments. 50 years later, the different weights that economic sectors have across the country keeps very much anchored in that historical pattern. While the agriculture sector accounts for about 3% of the Spanish GDP, in some ACs, such as Castile-La Mancha, Extremadura and Andalusia, it represents 9% of their economic activities. In the same line, while 20% of Spanish GDP is generated in industrial activities including mining, manufacturing and energy, the highest specialisation is found in the North-East ACs (Navarre, the Basque Country and La Rioja), with a share close to 30% of the regional GDP. The service sector in Spain accounts for more than half of GDP, with larger shares in Madrid, and the Balearic and the Canary Islands (around 70% of the regional GDP).

Over the initial 30 years of the decentralisation process, Spain enjoyed high rates of economic growth and prosperity, but regional business cycles present a certain degree of heterogeneity. Some synchronisation is found among groups of ACs that share some common features, such as the weight of the industrial sector, or the levels of per capita income, human capital or unemployment (Banco de España, 2018). Taking GDP per capita as a measure of well-being, four broad groups of ACs can be distinguished. The first group encloses the ACs with the highest GDP per capita, actually 20–30% above the national average (Madrid, the Basque Country, Navarre, Catalonia and the Balearic Islands); the second group includes ACs with a GDP per capita between the national average and 10% over (Castile and Leon, La Rioja and Aragon). The third group includes ACs with a GDP per capita just below the national average, including Northern-west ACs (Galicia, Cantabria, Asturias), as well as the Valencian Community, Murcia and the Canary Islands. The fourth group includes those ACs the GPD per capita of which has values 20% below Spain's average (Andalusia, Extremadura and Castile-La Mancha) (Colino et al., 2020).

According to the GDP per capita indicator, inequalities among ACs decreased significantly from the 1980s until 2007. Nevertheless, these groups remained relatively stable. After the outbreak of the economic and financial crisis in 2008, inequalities increased again.

After the crisis, in ACs with a GDP per capita above the Spanish average, the GDP growth was higher than in the ACs with lower GDP per capita, so

TABLE 10.1 GDP per capita and ranking of ACs (1967–2020) (Spain = 100)

	1967	1983	2002	2007	2017	2020
Extremadura	55	62.1	70.7	67.4	70.0	78.5
Andalusia	70.0	73.0	73.9	77.3	74.0	79.8
Murcia	79.6	82.4	79.2	83.4	82.3	82.8
Canary Islands	80.4	95.0	87.0	88.6	82.1	83.2
C.-La Mancha	67.8	76.8	80.9	80.9	79.1	84.2
Valencia	103.4	103.5	101.2	90.4	87.9	89.6
Galicia	72.1	81.5	85.1	85.7	89.4	94.3
Cantabria	112.6	101.2	91.3	93.9	90.6	100
Spain (average)	*100*	*100*	*100*	*100*	*100*	*100*
C.-León	82.3	86.6	94.6	92.4	93.5	100.2
Asturias	103	95.3	85.6	91.1	88.7	102.5
La Rioja	112.7	112.2	113.7	106.7	104.5	103.6
Balearic Islands	136	147.9	125.3	106.7	104.9	104.2
Aragon	100.2	106.4	106.6	109.4	110.3	106.7
Catalonia	141	125.4	122.4	117.7	119.9	113.1
Navarra	117.4	111.8	123.4	123.3	123.1	115.7
Madrid	142.3	128.2	126.9	132.3	135.0	124.9
Basque Country	149.5	112.1	118.6	126.6	131.5	129.1

SOURCE: INSTITUTO NACIONAL DE ESTADÍSTICA (INE). ELABORATED BY THE AUTHORS

that since 2007 the differences between the more prosperous ACs and the less developed ACs have increased slightly. While Spain's GDP per capita in 2017 was 24,999 euros, the highest GDP per capita was that of Madrid with 33,824 euros, 35% higher than the national average, followed by the Basque Country (32%) and Navarre (23%). Extremadura's GDP per capita, 17,262 euros, was the lowest, 30% below the average.

The impact of the pandemic has also been uneven. The central government's crisis management decisions have disproportionately affected industrialised regions (e.g., the Basque Country) and touristic regions (e.g. Canary Islands) but national and EU economic and social measures cushioned the impact of the crisis (e.g. on the labour market). In this regard, there is no evidence of an important increase in the differences in GDP per capita between the ACs triggered by the pandemic. On the contrary, we can see that differences in GDP per capita between the ACs have narrowed. In 2020, the highest GDP per capita was that of the Basque Country (30% above the national average), followed by Madrid and Navarre, with 25% and 15% above the national average respectively. Extremadura's GDP per capita was still the lowest, 22% below the average. Nevertheless, Extremadura was the Autonomous Community that recorded the smallest decline in GDP in volume terms in 2020 (−7%). It was followed by Castile-La Mancha (−8%) and Murcia (−8%). ACs with the most negative GDP variation rates in 2020 were the Balearic Islands (−22%), the Canary Islands (−18%) and Catalonia (−12%).

Regarding the incidence of unemployment, figures show that it tends to be lower in the northern ACs than in the South, and this difference also persists during the different phases of the economic cycle. In the context of the strong economic growth that took place in Spain from the late 1990s until 2007, unemployment rates decreased markedly, so that in 2007 a convergence of unemployment rates between some ACs could be stated.

Since the onset of the economic and financial crisis, differences between ACs have widened, because the recovery process was uneven. It is noteworthy that in 2007 there was a difference of just over 10.5 percentage points between the unemployment rate in Navarre and Extremadura, and in 2017 this difference was almost 15 percentage points. ACs in the North/West registered an unemployment rate above 10% in 2017, while in the South it was around 25%.

In 2022, ACs in the North/West registered an unemployment rate slightly above 10%, while in the South the unemployment rate was around 20%. In this regard, differences between the data among ACs were not as pronounced as in the economic and financial crisis. However, the 2007 values were not reached either. In 2022, the difference between the unemployment rate of the Basque Country and that of the Canary Islands was just over 11.5 percentage points;

TABLE 10.2 Unemployment rate by autonomous community (1987–2022) (in %)

	1987	1997	2007	2017	2022
Ceuta	–	26.4	20.2	26	29.2
Melilla	–	–	17.4	24.6	22.1
Canary Islands	25.5	20.9	10.9	22	20.3
Andalusia	31.1	32	14	24.4	19.4
Extremadura	25.9	29.5	14.8	25.1	19.0
Balearic Islands	13.4	12.2	9.4	12.6	18.0
C. La Mancha	15.1	19.1	8.1	19.7	14.3
Valencia	20.8	21.1	8.6	16.6	13.7
Spain (average)	20.8	21.1	8.6	16.6	13.6
Murcia	21.4	18.3	8.3	17.2	13.4
Asturias	19.7	21.2	8	14.6	12.0
Madrid	16.3	18.4	6.4	13.8	11.9
Galicia	13.4	19.2	7.5	14.7	11.4
La Rioja	13.2	11.8	5.9	11.5	11.2
C.-León	17.6	19.9	6.9	13.7	11.1
Cantabria	18.8	21.1	4.7	13.4	10.5
Navarra	15.1	10	4.3	9.6	10.4
Catalonia	21.8	17.4	6.5	12.6	10.2
Aragon	12.7	14.4	5.1	11.4	10.1
Basque Country	23.2	18.8	5.9	10.6	8.7

SOURCE: INE. ELABORATED BY THE AUTHORS

in 2017 this difference was very similar. The reduced impact of the pandemic on the unemployment rate was mainly due to the Temporary Lay-off Plans (ERTES). ACS with a greater impact of the pandemic on the labour market recorded a higher percentage of workers affected by ERTES.

3 Welfare Spending in the ACS and the Impact of the 2008 Financial and Economic and the COVID 19 Pandemic Crises

ACS enjoy a high degree of autonomy in managing education and health services, since they are entitled to approve their own annual budgets and decide on the distribution of their resources. The evolution of regional spending in health and education since 2002 is an example of 1) the efforts to ensure equivalent access to welfare across the country, 2) the persistent differences between the health/education systems of Spain's 17 CCAA, and 3) the asymmetric impact of both crises on both public policies. However, differences in per capita expenditure can also be explained by 1) differences in preferences/ ideology of the different regional governments; 2) differences in the funding guaranteed to each territory, and (above all); 3) the different conditions under which services are provided in each territory (mainly due to population dispersion/congestion), which might not be sufficiently reflected in the expenditure needs indicator.

As for the health system, shortly after the remaining regions took over public policy responsibilities in 2001, spending became increasingly divergent over the years presumably as a result of different health policy priorities. After the financial crisis of 2008 and the prolonged recession that ensued, public spending decreased for several years before beginning to increase again more recently. The general trend between 2002 and 2021 was towards an increase in per capita spending in all ACs, with the exception of 2012–2014, when expenditure was reduced in almost all ACs. However, differences between the ACs increased significantly since 2009, being quite large in 2020. In the lower spending range, there is a group of ACs with an expenditure of around €1,400-€1,500 per inhabitant (Andalusia and Madrid), while in the upper expenditure range a group of ACs spends around €1,900 (the Basque Country, Navarre, Asturias, Castile and Leon). In general terms, a north-south patter can be observed, with greater expenditure in the more northerly ACs. The data also suggest that per capita spending is lower precisely in those regions with larger populations, while spending has increased in ACs with an ageing population and which are affected by strong negative migration trends, such as Castille and Leon, Aragon and Asturias. Moreover, the political variable must also be underscored. In exercising their health competencies, the governments of the ACs have implanted different policies and directions in the structure of their health services. While some ACs have given priority to strengthening the public health network, in others, outsourcing services and privatisation of the health service have been promoted. Nevertheless, the impact of the COVID 19 crisis seems not to be important in spending among ACs. All of them increased spending in their public health system. Comparing data from 2019 and 2021 the increases have been particularly important in Catalonia, Castile-La Mancha and Murcia, with about 300 euros per capita of larger spending.

Another central area of welfare policy at the ACs level is education. All ACs manage education, at least since 2001, but the size of their regional education systems is very diverse: Andalusia has more than 400.000 students and La

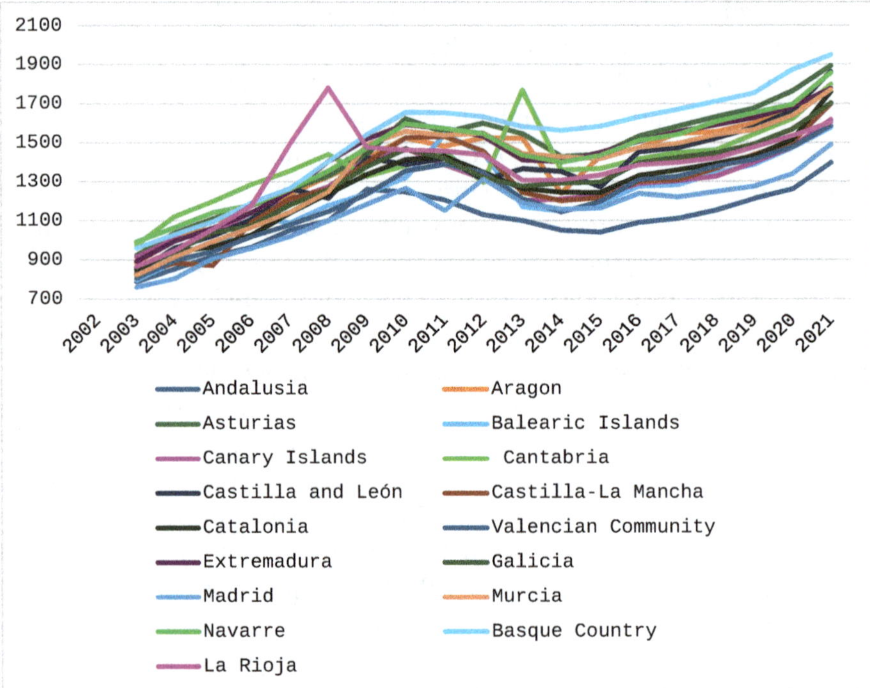

FIGURE 10.1 Public health expenditure per inhabitant (2002–2021) (in euros)
SOURCE: INE. ELABORATED BY THE AUTHORS

Rioja barely reaches 18.000 (2022). In contrast to health spending, decreases in public education spending per student (non-university education) started before 2006 and persisted until 2014. Nevertheless, there were ACs with an increase in spending, such as Extremadura, Castile-La Mancha and Murcia. In this regard, important spending cuts in education due to the impact of the economic crisis can be stated.

The data for 2020 show a significant increase compared to 2014 and in all ACs (with the exception of Madrid) spending exceeds the data prior to the economic crisis. In general terms, it could be said that differences between ACs in terms of per capita education spending are smaller than those observed for health spending.

In the range between 5,000 and 6,000 euros of public education expenditure per student in non-university education, there is a group of ACs with a high density of population. However, it should be mentioned that there are two atypical cases. The Basque Country, with a per-student expenditure of more than 10,000 euros, and Madrid, with a per-student expenditure close to 5,600 euros in 2020. The relatively low level of educational expenditure per

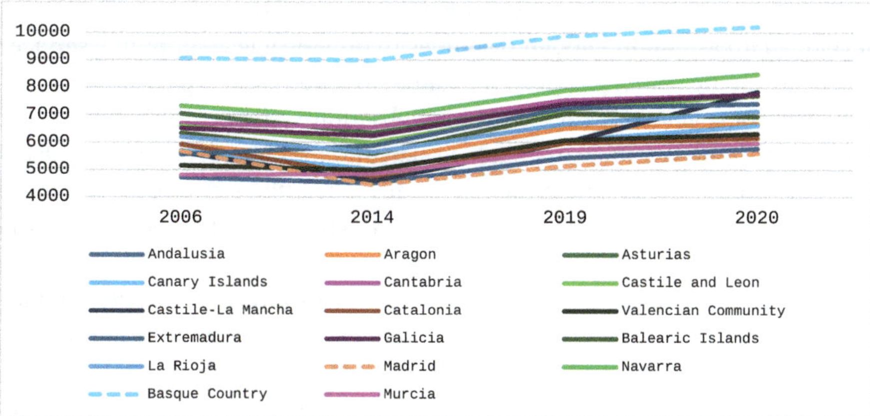

FIGURE 10.2 Public educational expenditure per student (non-university public education) (2006–2020) (in euros)
SOURCE: INE. ELABORATED BY THE AUTHORS

capita in Madrid can be explained not only by the ideology of the governments that have run this ACs in the last three decades, but also by the importance of private educational centres in this community.

Nevertheless, the impact of the economic crises seemed to be the same in all ACs. As already mentioned, there is a decrease in expenditure until 2014, while thereafter expenditure increases. The impact of the COVID 19 crisis is not yet visible considering the 2020 data. Differences in education expenditure between ACSs have not changed significantly over time, although some ACs, such as Extremadura, have increased expenditure more than others.

4 The Equalisation System

4.1 *General Considerations*

The theory of fiscal federalism defines an equalisation system as one that allows all constituent units to provide similar levels of public services if they have a similar level of fiscal effort. This implies that equalisation transfers should allocate more resources into those constituent units with the lowest fiscal capacity, and/or in those units with the highest costs of providing public services. According to Boadway (2004), equalisation transfers are considered to enable a federal country to reach equity without giving up the advantages of decentralisation. The political autonomy of constituent units can be guaranteed by a well-designed system of unconditional transfers, that allows the provision of different levels of public services – responding to differences in preferences –, while keeping horizontal equity among citizens, guaranteeing that the least developed areas obtain enough resources to provide a level of public services similar to the richest ones (Herrero, 2014). However fiscal equalisation is also very country specific. In this regard, equalisation systems are shaped by the wider institutional framework such as size, number and geographical distribution of sub-national governments, the responsibilities and fiscal resources allocated to each jurisdiction, or the mechanics of power sharing between the central and the constituent units (Blöchliger et al., 2007).

Within this framework, the stability of equalisation systems heavily depends on how they reflect the level of inter-regional solidarity desired by the country as a whole. If the redistribution generated by these transfers is too intense, rich constituent units can argue that disincentives for economic growth can emerge for both recipients (more growth leads to bigger tax bases and larger fiscal capacity, and thus to smaller equalisation transfers) and contributors (the more their economies grow, the bigger the transfers they have to pay); on the other hand, if interregional redistribution through the equalisation system is too slight, the internal cohesion of the country can be damaged, as well as its political stability (Herrero, 2014).

An important issue to be solved in this context is whether all levels of government should participate in the decision about the intensity of the inter-regional redistribution desired by the country as a whole. It seems obvious that the central government has something to say about the design and objectives of the equalisation system, especially in the cases where it is implemented through vertical grants. But it is difficult to justify a decision process that completely ignores the ACs' vision about it, if stability of the system is desired (Herrero, 2014). Moreover, the system should be transparent to allow accountability, and it should be based on indicators which could be adapted to changing circumstances.

4.2 *The Spanish Equalisation System*

Overcoming inter-regional inequalities in Spain was one of the great challenges of the decentralisation process and the regional financing system was to be a key instrument for this. The Spanish Constitution (SC) guarantees solidarity between the ACs and the principle of equality of all Spaniards.

Article 158 of the Spanish Constitution defines the instruments to be used to correct inequalities between ACs. These consist of two sets of vertical transfers or flows: one that with an equalisation purpose (Art.158.1) and other with a regional development rationale (Art.158.2). The Constitutional Court underlined in different ruling that the State of the Autonomies has been built on the basis of a "duty of reciprocal aid" or "reciprocal support and mutual loyalty"

(Ruling 18/1982, of 4 May, Ruling 96/1986, of 10 July and Ruling 247/2007, of 12 December).

The equalisation system is adapted by the Fiscal and Financial Policy Council (*Consejo de Política Fiscal y Financiera*), which is a multilateral (asymmetric) institution, where both the central government and the ACs are represented but where all recommendations adapted depend on the final agreement of the central government.

The decentralisation of a substantial part of public expenditure over the past decades made it necessary to update and strengthen the system. In this way, in 2001 and 2009 new Laws of regional financing were passed to strengthen regional revenues and tax autonomy of the ACs as well as to adapt the equalisation system. Even so, the process of decentralisation of revenues was more modest than expenditure and has not resulted in the ACs developing a solid and decisive decision-making power and fiscal autonomy (Lago-Peñas, 2019).

The current *equalisation system* is based on four instruments: the Guarantee Fund for Essential Public Services (Guarantee Fund), the Global Sufficiency Fund, the Competitiveness Fund and the Cooperation Fund. The Guarantee Fund is the main equalisation grant and it tries to guarantee "that if an autonomous community requires its citizens to make the same tax effort on its ceded taxes as the other Communities, it will also be able to provide, if it so wishes, the same level of educational, health and social services" (López Laborda et al., 2023, p. 366). Since 2009, the calculation of the Guarantee Fund occurs in three stages:

(i) The first stage consists of calculating the expenditure needs for public services, which are divided into "essential" and "non-essential" public services. The former represent around 70 percent of AC governments' expenditure and cover areas such as education, health and social services. Relative expenditure needs for fundamental public services are calculated through a set of indicators that reflect cost factors related to the provision of these services: population protected by the public health system according to age groups (38%); total population (30%); population in school age (0–16) (20.5%); population over 65 (8.5%); surface area (1.8%); population density (0.6%); and insularity (0.6%).

(ii) The second stage consists of calculating the fiscal capacity of each AC, which is the normative or potential tax collections of ACs.

(iii) In the third stage the transfer is obtained by subtracting expenditure needs of each AC from 75% of regional tax collections (De la Fuente, 2021). Positive transfers for poorer regions are financed both by negative transfers payed by the richest regions and a vertical transfer from the central government.

"Non-essential public services" – are financed with the remaining vertical transfers and with the remaining 25% of regional tax collections. Expenditure needs for non-essential services are calculated for each AC simply as the difference between the total expenditure guaranteed to that Community by the previous financing model in the base year established by the intergovernmental body CPFF (with some corrections due to the contribution of additional revenues by the central government) and its expenditure needs for essential public services (López Laborda et al., 2023).

Together with the Guarantee and the Global Sufficiency funds, and with the aim of correcting inter-regional subsisting financial disparities among ACs, Law 22/2009 created two unconditional grants: the Competitiveness Fund, which seeks to diminish the differences in the total "per adjusted inhabitant" financing between ACs, and the Cooperation Fund, which aims to stimulate regional convergence. All four transfers are unconditional, so the ACs can freely decide how to use these revenues.

ACs receive in advance equalisation grants from the regional financing system in application of the forecast existing at the time the draft bill for the Spanish general state budget is drawn up. These instalment payments are settled two years later on the basis of the definitive budgetary settlement. If the settlement proves to be negative, ACs must return the excess quantity they had received in advance.

The economic crisis in 2008 and the COVID-19 pandemic increased the need for ad hoc responses by the central government to absorb the impact of the collapse in tax revenues and the sharp increases in expenditure. In this regard, since 2009 the model combines purely fiscal equalisation transfers devoted to finance healthcare, education and social assistance, with regional policy funds and European Union's Structural and Investment funds. Especially in order to address the COVID-19 pandemic in 2020–21, the Royal Decree-Law 22/2020 provided a nonrepayable fund (COVID-Fund) for the ACs of €16 billion to finance costs stemming from the pandemic (Erkoreka et al., 2021) Although decisions about the size and the distribution of the financial resources have been adopted by the central government, the ACs could use the funds according to their needs.

5 Results and Shortcomings of the Equalisation System

Similar to other federal countries, the Spanish equalisation system does not aim to reduce interregional differences in GDP per capita, but it aims to contribute to equity among the ACs, ensuring that all Spanish citizens have access to comparable public services. According to De la Fuente et al. (2016), the horizontal equalisation system generates sizable horizontal flows from rich to poor ACs and greatly reduces regional disparities in terms of financing per adjusted head. However, the effect of vertical transfers is very different. These transfers increase the dispersion of financing per adjusted capita and alter the ordering of the ACs, leaving a final distribution of resources that has very little to do with the original distribution of tax revenues (De la Fuente et al., 2016).

According to Figure 10.3, after operating the various transfers, there is still certain dispersion in the per adjusted inhabitant financing of the ACs. These differences are not related to the tax capacity of the autonomous communities, since the ranking of the ACs according to their tax capacity is sometimes reversed after the transfers. These re-rankings have been quite controversial for years and have diminished the stability of the institutional framework, since some high-fiscal-capacity territories, such as Catalonia, claim to end up with lower final resources than some low-fiscal-capacity regions, such as Extremadura and Castile-La Mancha, after equalising transfers are implemented. This intense redistribution is not generalised, though: a low-fiscal-capacity territory such as Murcia remains on the lower tail of the distribution after equalisation, while Cantabria and Aragon – generally above the national average in terms of fiscal capacity – remain in the upper tail of the distribution when equalisation is finalised.

Two potential explanations of this lack of distributive pattern can be highlighted. First, at the starting point of the devolution process, each AC negotiated with the central government the amount of resources needed to provide public services at the pre-devolution level. These have been political negotiations in which each AC has had a different leverage to get access to different levels of resources. Second, it appears that there is still a strong inertia of the regional distribution of public services existing before the decentralisation of public policies, due to the "no harm" clause that has been applied during each reform of the regional financing system: no AC can end up being in a worse financial situation in terms of per-capita resources after a reform is implemented.

Other important drawbacks of the design of the equalisation system can be highlighted regarding both the fiscal capacity and expenditure needs indexes. The former has traditionally underestimated regional collections on some devolved taxes such as those on the property and transmission of wealth. Specifically, potential or normative tax collections have been usually estimated with the pre-devolution level of collections, updated with the central government's collections growth rate. Due to the different dynamics of central and regional tax bases, the latter behaving more expansively during the last several decades, the result has been a systematic underestimation of regional fiscal capacity.

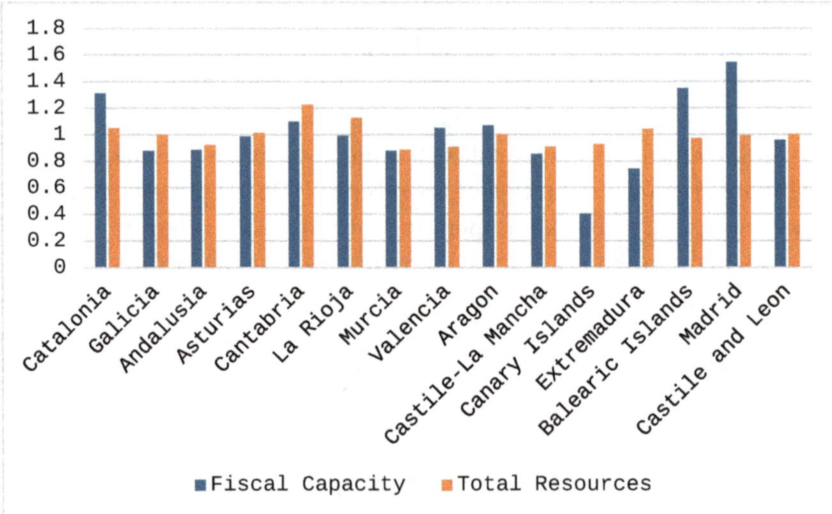

FIGURE 10.3 Fiscal capacity and total financing of the autonomous communities per adjusted inhabitant in 2021 (Average = 100)
SOURCE: SPANISH MINISTRY OF FINANCE (2022). ELABORATED BY THE AUTHORS

Regarding the measurement of expenditure needs, the Spanish equalisation system distributes resources according to each region's share in a set of social and geographic indicators, as previously highlighted. However, the inclusion of those indicators and their respective weights within the expenditure needs formula also is more a result of a political negotiation than the result of previous empirical evidence about the incidence of those variables in the cost of providing public services. Therefore, the distribution of transfers does not guarantee that equalisation is achieved, since some relevant variables – specifically those reflecting the existing of potential economies of scale in the most populated areas – might be absent in the formula or they could be under or over-weighted.

Despite all the previously mentioned drawbacks of the equalisation system, the most controversial part of the regional financing system is the measurement of the vertical gap (the difference between regional potential tax collections and regional expenditure needs considering regional governments as a whole). For many years, ACs have been claiming to deserve a larger share of public resources, since they are in charge of some services which have shown very high elasticities to income. Specifically, both health care and education spending tend to grow faster than the economy on average, absorbing larger shares of public expenditure.

This phenomenon became extremely relevant during the 2008 Great Recession, that triggered a sharp decrease in regional resources, while social expenditure kept its ascending trend. Although many ACs used their fiscal powers to increase their tax collections, the adverse economic situation and the large pressure on the social budget made it difficult to sustain regional finances (CERFA, 2017).

During the COVID 19 pandemic, growth in health and education spending was also very strong, and only ad hoc central government and EU instruments helped to sustain regional finances.

6 Conclusions: Current State of the Regional Financing System, Inter-regional Inequalities in Spain and Future Challenges

There are several reasons why inter-regional differences in Spain have not been reduced and are persistent in time; among the most relevant we could mention: long standing historical differences in development, divergent political priorities, asymmetrical decision making among the levels of government and the socioeconomic characteristics of the ACs. But also the crisis of 2008 and the recovery period afterwards and the COVID 19 pandemic had a pronounced asymmetrical impact on regional revenues and expenditures. The Great Recession brought with it a period of stagnation, fiscal austerity, increasing poverty and income and wealth inequality, which have been accompanied by greater class divisions and a greater demand for economic redistribution, and have consequently led to territorial conflicts and increased political polarisation. The pandemic brought with it enormous social suffering but also an increase in public spending. While differences in economic development and services between ACs increased during the Great Recession, public policies focused on the labour market and the asymmetric impact of the pandemic on economic sectors have led to a more limited increase in the differences between ACs during the health emergency. However, differences in welfare spending are still noticeable even after the two crises.

Questions of regional financing and inter-regional inequalities have become an issue of political confrontation, stirring up a partisan fight between ACs and political parties. In fact, the financing system approved in 2009, which should have been updated in 2014, has still not been revised, mainly due to the lack of consensus amongst political parties and ACs, and the general climate of political tension and economic instability. There is currently an urgent need to review the regional financing system to correct the imbalances of the system, to reduce inequalities between ACs and to improve transparency.

The current Spanish equalisation system does not fulfil all the characteristics and results predicted by theory, but similar to other equalisation systems, its basic structure aims to guarantee the provision of similar levels of public services in all territories. This was successfully reached over time, but the limitations also became visible. Nevertheless, the equalisation system is only one part of the new model. In this regard, a new financing model must provide solutions that take into account not only the problems of autonomy and equalisation among ACs, but also include solutions on how to maintain welfare state policies. In other words, the new system should be anchored in a broader agreement about how to finance the public sector as a whole.

Firstly, the current distribution of responsibilities between the central government and the ACs must be taken into account, as well as the weight of each administration's expenditure on essential public services related to the welfare state. In this context, it should be noted that the role of ACs has increased over the past decade, while the role of the central government decreased in relative terms.

Secondly, the new financing system should be based on the desired size of the public sector in the medium term and the basic dimensions of the spending functions underpinning the welfare state and the priority given to them. Once these priorities are defined, measures on how to protect the financing of these preferential services in case of crisis situations can be designed.

Thirdly, the resources need to be distributed by instruments which are adjusted to the constitutional tasks and socioeconomic characteristics of the different administrations, so that they have the capacity to adjust their level of resources to their expenditure needs. Or to decide how to finance other policies they wish to develop in the exercise of their autonomy.

Fourthly, the decision on what level of resources is considered sufficient and which welfare state policies are priority, is a clearly political decision which must be adopted by all levels of government. It is difficult to justify a decision process that completely ignores the constituent units′ vision about it, if stability of the system is desired.

And finally, the system should be transparent to allow accountability, and it should be based on indicators which could be adapted to changing circumstances.

References

Banco de España (2018). Monitoring the Spanish Economy from a Regional Perspective: Main Elements of Analysis. *Documentos Ocasionales*, no. 1809.

Blöchliger, H., Merk, O., Charbit, C. & Mizell, L. (2007). Fiscal Equalisation in OECD Countries. *OECD Working Papers on Fiscal Federalism*, no. 4.

Boadway, R. (2004). The Theory and Practice of Equalization, *CESifo Economic Studies*, no. 1, 211–254.

Colino, C.; Jaime-Castillo; A. & Kölling, M. (2020). Desigualdades territoriales en España, *Friedrich Ebert Stiftung, Research Paper* https://www.fundacionmgimenezabad.es/es/actividades/jornada-desigualdades-territoriales-las-cuatro-espanas (Accessed: 28 September 2023).

Comisión de Expertos para la revisión del modelo de financiación autonómica (CERFA) (2017). *Informe Final*. Madrid: Ministerio de Hacienda y Función Pública. https://www.hacienda.gob.es/CDI/sist%20financiacion%20y%20deuda/informaci%C3%B3nccaa/informe_final_comisi%C3%B3n_reforma_sfa.pdf (Accessed: 28 September 2023).

de la Fuente, Á. (2021). La evolución de la financiación de las comunidades autónomas de régimen común 2002–2019. *Fedea Policy Papers*, no. 27.

de la Fuente, Á., Thöne, M. & Kastrop, C. (2016). Regional Financing in Germany and Spain: Comparative Reform. *Fedea Policy Papers*, no. 5.

Erkoreka, M., Grau, M. & Kölling, M. (2021). Decentralisation and COVID-19: stress-testing the Spanish territorial system. In N. Steytler (Ed.), *Comparative Federalism and Covid-19. Combating the Pandemic*, (pp. 33–50). London: Routledge.

Herrero, A. (2014). The Spanish Way of fiscal federalism. In S. Lütgenau (Ed.), *Fiscal Federalism and Fiscal Decentralisation in Europe*, (pp. 15–40). Wien: Studienverlag.

İrepoğlu Carreras, Y. (2016). Fiscal decentralization and inequality: the case of Spain. *Regional Studies, Regional Science*, 3(1), 295–302. DOI: 10.1080/21681376.2016.1183513.

Lago-Peñas, S. (2019). Tax decentralisation in Spain: significant progress and remaining challenges. *Spanish Economic and Financial Outlook*, 8(5), 51–58.

López Laborda, J.; Martinez-Vazquez, J.; & Monasterio, C. (2023). Spain. In J.F.s Tremblay (Ed.). *Fiscal Federalism: Comparative Experiences and Challenges*, Forum of Federations, Palgrave Macmillan.

Oates, W. (1972). *Fiscal Federalism*. New York: Harcourt Brace Jovanovich.

Rodden, J; G. Eskeland; & Litvack, J. (2003). Introduction and Overview. In J. Rodden, G. Eskeland, & J. Litvack (Eds.), *Fiscal Decentralization and the Challege of Hard Budget Constraints*, (pp. 3–32). Cambridge: The MIT Press.

Spanish Ministry of Finance (2022). *Informe sobre la financiación definitive de las comunidades autónomas a través del sistema de financiación*. https://www.hacienda.gob.es/es-ES/CDI/Paginas/SistemasFinanciacionDeuda/InformacionCCAAs/Informes%20financiacion%20comunidades%20autonomas2.aspx (Accessed: 28 September 2023).

CHAPTER 11

The Swiss System of Fiscal Equalisation – Balancing Cantonal Tax Autonomy and Federal Solidarity

Eva Maria Belser
Chair for Constitutional and Administrative Law, Institute of Federalism (University of Fribourg)

Mikel Erkoreka
Ituna Center for Basque Economic Agreement and Fiscal Federalism Studies (UPV/EHU – University of the Basque Country)

1 Introduction[1]

Switzerland, originally a Confederation, has a deep-rooted culture of federalism. Ever since the making of the federation in 1848, the cantonal and local governments enjoyed extensive residual powers and exercised broad fiscal autonomy while also assuming the financial costs derived from their own public policy choices. When the Federation came into being, the Cantons thus continued to enjoy (limited) sovereignty but at the prize of being on one's own. The principle of fiscal equivalence – whoever decides, pays, and whoever pays, decides – inseparably links the division of tasks and the distribution of costs.

Given the manyfold demographic, geographic, and economic differences between Swiss Cantons, it comes as no surprise that inequalities increased, and tax burden and service delivery widened over the decades. Ever since the making of the Federation, the arrangement and scope of fiscal equalisation was a highly controversial and much-debated issue. After many years of preparation and deliberation, the Federal Assembly, in 2004, finally adopted a federalism reform which rebalanced cantonal autonomy and federal solidarity. The reform constituted the most far-reaching one in the recent history of Swiss federalism (Cappelletti et al., 2014; Vatter, 2018, p. 168), and of Swiss constitutional

1 This research is part of the research activity of the *Cliobasque* research group (IT1523-22) (University of the Basque Country) and PID2022-136603NB-100 research project (financed by the Ministry of Science, Innovation and Universities of Spain). The authors are grateful to MLaw Lara Torbay and BLaw Annina Wirz for their valuable support in drafting this contribution.

DOI:10.1163/9789004524514_013

law more generally. It was much more profound than the total revision of the Federal Constitution which had occurred in 1999 (and which had been limited to rewording and restructuring the existing constitutional rules).

The mandatory referendum on the "Federal decree on the reorganisation of financial equalisation and the division of tasks between the Confederation and the Cantons (NFA)", held in 2004, was accepted by 20 and a half out of 23 cantonal votes and by 64% of the people. The bundle of measures constituting the federalism reform affected almost half of the provisions of the Federal Constitution and several laws; its implementation hence was complex and took four years. In 2008, the New Financial Equalisation scheme finally entered into force. It deeply revised the framework for the distribution of powers between the Swiss Federation and the Cantons and profoundly reformed the system of fiscal equalisation.

During the reform debates, it was undisputed that the equalisation system, besides its fiscal and financial aspects, comprised important political components and either contributed to or impeded internal cohesion (Béland & Lecours, 2014; Brenton, 2020). Both the Federation and most Cantons agreed that the increasing fiscal inequality of the Cantons needed to be addressed and favoured a reform to revitalise federalism and to strengthen federal solidarity (Kirchgässner, 2012; Linder & Mueller, 2021, pp. 87–91). In the informative dossier jointly published by the Federation and the Cantons prior to the referendum to ratify the reform in 2004, the federal representatives argued that "the new system of fiscal equalisation responds to the principle of solidarity, guarantees healthy competition among Cantons and favours the spirit of innovation, as well as a plural framework of solutions". Along the same line, the cantonal representatives supported this position, arguing that "only a transparent system of fiscal equalisation and a clear distribution of the framework of powers and tasks can guarantee the harmonious coexistence of our four cultures" (Département fédéral des finances & Conférence des gouvernements cantonaux, 2004, pp. 2–3).

The revised model of fiscal equalisation is, on the one hand, still founded on the principles of cantonal self-determination, subsidiarity, and fiscal equivalence. It continues to aim at guaranteeing cantonal diversity, at strengthening democratic and financial accountability ("whoever decides, pays"), and at encouraging tax competition at both the cantonal and municipal levels. On the other hand, it introduces a new regime of federal cohesion in financial matters. It combines horizontal and vertical forms of solidarity with the objective of partially (but not fully) equalise financial resources and burdens.

Before recalling the old financial equalisation regime (section 3) and presenting the current one, its implementation and controversies (section 4), we will briefly present the distribution of the power to levy taxes (section 2). We will conclude by mentioning some important political aspects of and debates about the present and future of the current fiscal equalisation system as it stands (section 5).

2 The Distribution of Tax Powers in Swiss Federalism

The Swiss tax system is a prime example of fiscal federalism and forms the financial backbone of the Cantons and the municipalities' autonomy. Except for some states in the U.S., the Canadian provinces, and a few other autonomous entities, the Cantons of Switzerland enjoy the greatest autonomy in taxing and spending powers (Brühl-Moser, 2012, p. 658; Erkoreka, 2019). Each of Switzerland's 26 Cantons has its own tax law and imposes significantly different burdens on income, wealth, inheritance, and other tax objects. Within the cantonal tax law frameworks, municipalities also levy their taxes and determine their tax rates. The power to levy taxes is thus a parallel power, which belongs to all three levels of government (Meier-Mazzucato, 2022, p. 37).

2.1 *Tax Powers of the Federation*

As the residual power lies with the Cantons, which enjoy original (not delegated) tax sovereignty, the Federal Constitution enumerates all taxing powers delegated to the federation (Article 3 Federal Constitution, Biaggini, 2015, No. 15; BGE 130 I 156, c. 2.5). Some of the powers, which the Constitution attributes to the federation, are *exclusive* and displace the cantonal competencies in the area: the value added tax (VAT), some special consumption taxes, the stamp duty, the withholding tax, and customs duties (art. 130–133 Federal Constitution). There is no federal obligation to levy these exclusive taxes. However, if the federation chooses not to, the competence remains exclusively with the national tier and Cantons remain banned from introducing such taxes (Behnisch, 2014, No. 14). The prevalence of federal taxation provides that "anything that is declared by federal legislation to be subject to, or exempt from value added tax, special consumption taxes, stamp duty or withholding tax may not be made liable to similar taxes by the Cantons or communes" (art.134 Federal Constitution).

The Constitution frames and constrains the exclusive taxing powers of the Federation as their use affects the room for cantonal taxing maneuvers. The Constitution thus sets a maximum rate the federation is allowed to levy for the VAT on the supply and on imports of goods and services (a standard rate of a maximum of 6.5% and at a reduced rate of at least 2.0%). In 2014, the constitution-maker, the Swiss people and the Cantons, decided to increase the maximum rates by 0.1% to finance railway infrastructure. The Constitution also provides that the rate may be increased, should the financing of the Old-Age, Survivors' and Invalidity Insurance no longer be guaranteed due to demographic changes. The supreme law also obliges the Federation to use 4.5% of the non-earmarked VAT income to reduce the health insurance premiums of persons on low incomes (article 130 Federal Constitution).

In contrast to the exclusively federal taxing powers, the Federation's competence to levy direct taxes on the income of private individuals and the net profit of legal entities is *parallel*: the federal power does not limit the power of the Cantons to levy direct taxes on private income and corporate profit as well (Vallender & Cavelti, 2014, No. 3). Several compromises have been made to prevent federal taxation to overuse the tax base and undermine the Cantons' ability to levy taxes. Notably, the federal tax is assessed and collected by the Cantons, not the federation. More importantly, the tax rate the Federation may impose is levelled by the Federal Constitution: the constitutional maximum rate is 11.5% for the income of private individuals and 8.5% for the net profit of legal entities (Article 128 para. 1 Federal Constitution) (Vallender & Cavelti, 2014, No. 2). These limits are set relatively low and guarantee the Cantons a considerable tax base (Hänni, 2021, p. 256). As they are anchored in the Constitution, any increase of the federation's limit on tax rates requires the dual approval of the people and the Cantons in a mandatory referendum. The explicit anchoring of maximum percentage rates in the Constitution consequently provides effective protection of the Cantons' fiscal leeway (Hänni, 2015, No. 1). In addition, when fixing the rate (which must necessarily be below these thresholds), the Federation must take account of the burden of direct taxation imposed by the Cantons and Communes (Article 128 para. 2 Federal Constitution) (Aubert, 2003, No. 26; Vallender & Cavelti, 2014, No. 26). It should be noted, however, that this provision is rather an appeal to the Federation and no legal consequences can be derived from it (Aubert, 2003, No. 12; Valllender & Cavelti, No. 18). However, the Federal Constitution contains a further measure to protect the financial interests of the Cantons: A minimum of 17% of the federal tax income must mandatorily be allocated to the Cantons (Article 128 para. 4 Federal Constitution). The federal competences to levy (and to spend) direct taxes are hence constrained by constitutional law, most plainly by providing a maximum federal tax rate. The Cantons, in contrast, remain autonomous to impose the tax rate they consider adequate to provide adequate services and, simultaneously, be attractive to taxpayers.

2.2 *Tax Powers of the Cantons and Communes*

Since Cantons have residual competences, their taxation powers can be described as the sum of the competences not attributed to and claimed by the Confederation (Reich, 2020, No. 8). Compared to other federal states, the Cantons have a high degree of fiscal and financial autonomy: they have the (parallel) competence to autonomously tax the income and assets of natural persons as well as the profit and capital of legal entities. Most Cantons (and Communes) have also used their autonomy to introduce and apply inheritance and gift taxes (or to lower or abandon these taxes to be more attractive to potential testators and donors), real estate gains and motor vehicle taxes.

The Federal Constitution does not impose the existence of Communes and their financing. The Cantons thus may or may not transfer their tax autonomy to the municipalities which are subordinate to them (Behnisch, 2014, No. 6; Reich, 2020, No. 11). The communes consequently do not have original taxation powers and depend on the Cantons to delegate taxation powers to them (Behnisch, 2014, No. 6; Reich, 2020, No. 11). Such delegation of powers has occurred in all 26 Cantons, either through the cantonal Constitution or through cantonal tax laws (Hänni, 2021, p. 258). The municipalities thus have various sources of revenue to cover their expenditure, but municipal taxes are their main source of revenue. The local derivative tax sovereignty constitutes a major feature of Swiss fiscal federalism. Taxpayers pay direct taxes to three different entities, all applying different tax rates. According to OECD data, almost 40% of all tax revenues in Switzerland were raised at regional and local level in 2021 (OECD Revenue Statistics 2022). Nowadays, the Communes account for about 17% of government spending.

2.3 *Tax Harmonisation*

Due to the great autonomy Cantons enjoy, taxing conflicts may occur between different Cantons keen to tax the same income, assets, or profits. Such double taxation, negatively affecting taxpayers and their rights as well as the internal market, are prohibited by the Federal Constitution. The regulation of the prohibition of inter-cantonal double taxation prevents two or more Cantons to burden, as a consequence of their autonomy, the same person with similar taxes for the same tax substrate for the same period of time (Vallender & Wiederkehr, 2014, No. 57). The Constitution mandates the Federation to take the measures necessary to prevent double taxation (art. 127 para. 3 Federal Constitution). Until today, the Federal Assembly has not made use of this competence; the concretisation of the constitutional ban on double taxation thus lies in the hands of the Federal Supreme Court and inter-cantonal taxation law is regulated by judge's law.

More importantly, the Federation has a constitutional mandate to harmonise Swiss taxation law (art. 129 Federal Constitution). Even though Switzerland mostly constitutes a dual federal system, dividing and sharing power between the federal and cantonal tier, the harmonisation mandate requires the Federation to set out principles harmonising the direct taxes imposed by the Confederation, the Cantons, and the Communes. As the Cantons, also have made and still make their own harmonisation efforts, the Federation is obliged to take account of these efforts (Cavelti, 2008, p. 368).

The harmonisation mandate extends to tax liability, the object of the tax and the tax period, procedural law and the law relating to tax offences. Notably, however, tax scales, tax rates and tax allowances are explicitly excluded from the harmonisation mandate by the Constitution. The Confederation is only allowed to issue regulations preventing unjustified tax benefits (art. 129 para. 2 and 3 Federal Constitution). The "Federal law on the harmonisation of direct taxes of the Cantons and communes" entered into force in 1993 and has frequently been amended since.

There have been several popular initiatives aiming at constraining intercantonal tax competition beyond the harmonisation act. Famously, a popular initiative, called "For fair taxes. Stop the abuse of tax competition", requesting the introduction of minimum tax rates, was rejected at the urns in 2010. In 2015, the inheritance tax reform initiative suffered the same fate. When it comes to tax rates, cantonal autonomy seems to be a principle that the Swiss people and the Cantons uphold. It was hence international pressure mostly that recently motivated the Swiss to introduce minimum taxation for multinational enterprises. After various disputes with the OECD and accusations that Switzerland functions as a tax haven, the Swiss people and the Cantons, on June 18, 2023, approved in a mandatory referendum a constitutional amendment introducing a mandate for the Federation to implement the OECD/G20 Pillar I (market jurisdiction taxation) and Pillar II (global minimum taxation) projects. The implementation of the minimum taxation – a new feature in the Swiss fiscal federalism landscape – is scheduled for 2024. The change will only affect internationally active corporate groups and will not limit the cantonal and local autonomy to tax all other companies at lower rates. The new mandate allows for such inequality of treatment, delegates the transitional implementation to the Federal Council and obliged the executive to present a law to be approved by parliament within a maximum of six years.

It is worth noting that efforts to harmonise taxes between Cantons are not all based on the (limited) constitutional mandate to harmonise taxation and the old and upcoming tax harmonisation law based on it. The Swiss Federal Court also plays an important role in limiting tax competition and obliging Cantons to respect principles of the Federal Constitution when issuing tax policies. This is best exemplified by the *Obwald case* (Supreme Court case 133 II 206). In 2005, the Cantonal Council of Obwald adopted a new taxation law, which contained regressive taxes: once a person had reached the threshold of 300,000 Swiss francs for the taxation on revenue and 5,000,000 Swiss francs for the taxation on capital, tax rates would no longer progress but decrease instead (Case 133 II 206, A). In short, the new cantonal law foresaw that the richer one was, the lower the tax rate was. At the time of the making of the Obwald law, the lowering of the cantonal tax rate for very rich individuals had no negative effects on tax income in the Canton (as very few people in the rural Canton reached the threshold). The new rule was rather adopted in the hope to attract wealthy taxpayers from neighboring Cantons (and countries). Such way of proceeding was deemed unacceptable by the Swiss Supreme Court. Although Cantons enjoy far-reaching taxation power (Case 133 II 206, cons. 5), their autonomy is limited by constitutional principles and fundamental rights. The evolution of tax brackets must thus respect the principle of and right to equality and satisfy the principle of taxation according to one's financial capacity (Case 133 II 206, cons. 7). The constitutional obligation to tax anyone according to the person's financial capacity was (explicitly) only provided for the Federation but was, according to the court, also applicable to the Cantons as it concretised the fundamental right to equality binding on all state actors at all the levels of government. According to the Supreme Court, everyone should hence, in the field of taxation, bear a similar sacrifice, proportionate to one's income and capital. It was judged that regressive taxation does not comply to such fundamental principles of the Swiss Constitution and tax law, and the Obwald law was thus annulled (Case 133 II 206, cons. 13). This is one of the rare cases where the Supreme Court interfered in the fiscal and financial autonomy of Cantons. It made clear that the power that Cantons (and Communes) enjoy in the field of taxation is not boundless, and that their legislations can be scrutinised and even annulled if they contravene the constitutional principles and rights.

In summary, the Swiss fiscal equalisation system has been designed and adapted to a context of tax competition and broad fiscal and financial cantonal autonomy.

3 The Old Fiscal Equalisation System and its Shortcomings

3.1 *Origins and Characteristics*

The first financial program with equalising components was introduced in Switzerland in 1938, in the context of the economic and social crisis of the interwar period. Following the Second World War, in 1958, the Federal Constitution was amended providing the federal government with the power to equalise inter-cantonal disparities. The following year, in 1959, the first federal law of fiscal equalisation in Switzerland was approved (Dafflon, 1995). Although the system introduced in 1959 was partially modified and revised, it was not fully renewed until the reform that came into effect in 2008.

The old system of equalisation was intended to compensate Cantons with fewer resources and those that due to their circumstances suffered from excessive costs in providing public goods. Compensation for excessive costs mainly considered the geographical situation (especially important to the more mountainous Cantons) and population density and obliged the Federation (and the taxpayers of more urbanised Cantons) to financially support the more rural regions of the country.

The classification methodology in effect prior to the reform process classified the Cantons according to a financial capacity index. The formula for calculating the financial strength of each Canton included four elements: per capita income, tax burden, tax revenues and costs of public provision in general (Dafflon & Perritaz, 2002). Once the index had been established, the Cantons were classified in three groups according to their financial capacity: high financial capacity (Cantons with a resource index of 120 or above); intermediate financial capacity (Cantons with a resource index between 61 and 119); low financial capacity (Cantons with a resource index of 60 or less). The distribution of equalisation funds was then established based on this classification.

The federal program, with a vertical, bidirectional character, used three instruments for putting equalisation policies into practice (Dafflon, 2004):

- *Federal grants-in-aid to the Cantons*. The Federation used part of the federal grants policy to strengthen federal solidarity and applied equalising criteria when attributing grants-in-aid. It is worth underscoring that only a part (about one-third) of the Federation's grants had equalising components. In addition, Cantons had to co-finance part of the projects in order to receive conditional federal grants.
- *Revenue sharing in the Federation's incomes*. The equalising criterion was applied in the distribution of transfers according to the Cantons' sharing in certain federal tax revenues and the net benefit of the National Bank.
- *Contribution of the Cantons to certain federal Social Security expenditures*. The methodology to calculate the contribution of the Cantons to the Social Security system included some equalising components.

The system, frequently amended over time, was, on the one hand, blamed for lacking transparency, and, on the other hand, criticised for being insufficiently effective. Most observers agreed that the categorisation system provided limited incentives to low and intermediate capacity Cantons for increasing their tax bases and strengthening their financial self-sustenance, and that the sharing of costs via conditioned grants blurred responsibilities and accountabilities and encouraged overspending.

3.2 *Shortcomings*

In the early 1990s, increasing evidence of the fiscal equalisation system's inefficiency and the growing number of voices criticising its functioning prompted a process of evaluation and revision of the system. In 1994, a commission of experts was formed to study the outputs and possible reforms of the fiscal equalisation system (Frey et al., 1994). Amongst the main shortcomings identified by the commission of experts and other analogous studies and reports, the following points are worth underscoring (Bessard, 2013; Bullinger, 2002, pp. 9–10; Dafflon et al., 1996; Dafflon & Perritaz, 2002):

- The system failed in reducing financial disparities between Cantons. Instead, disparities were increasing.
- The equalising tool via the Social Security system was inefficient.
- The policy of federal grants-in-aid favoured the wealthier Cantons since the Cantons with fewer resources had greater difficulties to come up with their share of the co-financing arrangement. Furthermore, the system of conditional grants created perverse incentives in the provision of public goods and services, as it encouraged non-priority investments due to the mere fact of federal subsidies being available.
- The methodology for calculating the financial capacity index enabled the Cantons to manipulate their fiscal policy to maximise their benefits in the share-out of equalisation funds.
- The system did not establish clear and quantifiable objectives.
- The system was confusing, opaque and had acquired a centralising character. The lack of transparency together with the abovementioned lack of identification of objectives and the diffuse framework of distribution of powers and tasks between the Federation and the Cantons hindered evaluation and accountability. Similarly, it facilitated political discretion in decision-making on the distribution of funds.
- The results of the system were conditioned by variations in the economic cycle. Oscillations in federal resources, whether due to endogenous or exogenous reasons, directly affected the scope and performance of the equalisation policy.

The conclusions of the expert group made it clear and widely undisputed that the Swiss financial equalisation system needed profound reforms. Experts and observers also agreed that the improvement of financial equalisation regime and the strengthening of federal solidarity and the guaranteeing of fair and effective tax competition, required a considerable redesign of the entire federal system. More transparency, accountability, solidarity and efficiency could only come at the expense of reorganising the vertical distribution of tasks and competences and of disentangling intertwined and blurred responsibilities.

4 The Reform Process

The long reform process ended in 2004. Due to the magnitude of the changes, the implementation processes lasted for four additional years. The federalism reform, reorganising the distribution of competences and powers between the Federal and the Cantons, and establishing a new fiscal equalisation system, finally came into effect in 2008. It was based on two interlinked pillars: the redefinition of the framework of distribution of powers and tasks with a view of clarifying responsibilities, and the introduction of a new system of fiscal equalisation aiming at increasing federal solidarity and internal cohesion while incentivising wise spending and providing space for (fair) tax competition.

4.1 *Disentanglement of Powers and Competences*

The first pillar of the reform encompasses the review and redefinition of competences and tasks between the Federation and the Cantons. The countless constitutional reforms (more than a hundred since the making of the Federation), frequent legislative changes, and complex financial grant systems, over time, had produced a almost impenetrable system of mostly shared competences and blurred responsibilities.

The renegotiations of the vertical power sharing arrangement were long and complicated. The adequate balance of diversity and unity (and the financing of both) had always been a highly sensitive and controversial issue and involved constant rivalry since the formation of the Swiss federal state in the 19th century (Vatter, 2018, pp. 167–186). Reorganising a system which had evolved over decades constituted a tremendous task. However, it was clear that a reorganisation of the fiscal equalisation scheme required a disentanglement of the competences and could not remain as deeply intertwined and highly confusing as they were. As long as there was ambiguity about who was in charge of what, and who was obliged to burden what costs, strengthening federal solidarity seemed impossible to achieve.

Consensus was finally reached by agreeing on broad constitutional principles, such as subsidiarity and fiscal equivalence, and using them to update and redefine the framework of distribution of powers. With the objective of (later) clarifying financial responsibilities, priority was given to the allocation of exclusive powers. Seven functions were therefore exclusively assigned to the Federation, and 13 to the Cantons, another 17 remained shared between the two tiers of government. The reform also strengthened the role of cooperation and provided a constitutional framework for both vertical (Federation-Cantons) and horizontal (inter-cantonal) cooperation (Federal Finance Administration, 2012). The aim of this far-reaching updating was to strengthen cantonal autonomy, promote transparency, avoid duplications, facilitate taxation and accountability, and incentivise greater efficiency in the provision of public goods (Département fédéral des finances & Conférence des gouvernements cantonaux, 2004, pp. 16–24). The redefinition of the framework of powers not only helped the implantation of the new system of fiscal equalisation but was widely seen as its precondition.

With the aim of guaranteeing cantonal autonomy and preventing further centralisation – or the re-centralisation of competences (re)allocated to the Cantons – the reform also aimed at strengthening inter-cantonal cooperation. The constitutional framework for cooperation was thus reshaped to strengthen the principle of fiscal equivalence and to prevent and compensate for spillover effects (Frey & Wettstein, 2008). It first emphasised the right of Cantons to enter into agreements with each other to establish inter-cantonal organisation and institutions. The constitutional provisions also clarifies that Cantons can authorise inter-cantonal bodies to issue inter-cantonal legislation implementing inter-cantonal treaties (art. 48 Federal Constitution). Such inter-cantonal agreements have existed before, but have, over the last decades, become more and more important (Belser, 2020). Currently, more than 800 inter-cantonal treaties exist, many of them harmonising cantonal policies, and many of them dealing with the financing of cantonal infrastructure used by outsiders (such as universities, specialised schools, hospitals, prisons, etc.). The Federal Constitution obliges the Cantons to comply with such inter-cantonal law.

The reform, however, went an important step further and provided a constitutional basis for allowing the Federation to impose participation in an inter-cantonal treaty and even to declare such treaty generally applicable to all Cantons (art. 48a Federal Constitution). The idea behind the imposed cooperation was to bring in the Federation in the role of an arbiter with the power to intervene in the framework of inter-cantonal cooperation to prevent individual Cantons from free-riding and from not contributing to (de facto) inter-cantonal services, on the one hand, and to not allow individual Cantons to veto inter-cantonal harmonisation (and thereby provoking demands for centralisation). The policy fields in which such federal intervention may occur is limited to nine specific policy areas (such as cantonal institutions of higher education, cultural institutions of supra-regional importance, waste management and waste water treatment, urban transport, and advanced medical science and specialist clinics). The measure was mainly proposed in response to demands by the central Cantons, to compensate them for goods and services that they provide to neighbouring Cantons (Cappelletti et al., 2014). The practical use of the provision has, however, remained very limited. While the federal interference powers may function as an incentive for inter-cantonal cooperation, inter-cantonal agreement has never been imposed on a Canton which resisted cooperation.

4.2 *Rebalancing Autonomy and Solidarity*

The second pillar of the reform was the implantation of a new system of fiscal equalisation (art. 135 Federal Constitution). The constitutional provision mandates the Federation to issue regulations on the equitable equalisation of financial resources and burdens between the Federation and the Cantons (vertical equalisation) as well as among the Cantons (horizontal equalisation), clarifies the objectives of equalisation and mandates federal solidarity while also limiting it. It grants that the funds for the equalisation of burdens are provided by the Federation, and the funds required for the equalisation of resources both by the Federation and those Cantons with a higher level of resources. This horizontal solidarity is further framed by the Constitution: the payments made by the Cantons with a higher level of resources must amount to a minimum of two thirds of the payments made by the Confederation and may not exceed 80% of the federal payments.

The Federal Law on Fiscal Equalisation and Cost Compensation (*Loi fédérale sur la péréquation financière et la compensation des charges* – PFCC) develops the constitutional mandated and codifies the following goals:
- Strengthen the financial autonomy of the Cantons.
- Reduce disparities among Cantons in matters of financial capacity and tax burdens.
- Maintain the tax competitiveness of the Cantons at the national and international levels.
- Guarantee a minimum provision of financial resources to all Cantons.
- Compensate for excessive costs of the Cantons due to geographical/topographic and socio-demographic factors.
- Guarantee equitable compensation of burdens between Cantons.

The Law on Fiscal Equalisation establishes a mechanism of four-year revision and control. Every four years, the federal government must present a report to the federal parliament evaluating the degree to which the objectives of the equalisation system have been fulfilled and present possible measures and proposals for improvement for the next four-year period. Based on the results of the efficiency report and the adjustments introduced in the system, the federal parliament defines the amount to be contributed by the Federation and the Cantons during the first year of the next four-year period. Subsequently, the Federal Council takes responsibility for adjusting the quantity established for the base year in the following three years of the four-year period.

The law hence provides for a system which is regulated by law but leaves some political leeway to parliament. This political margin of discretion and decision has become very controversial during the last period. The controversy stems from the fact that only six Cantons qualify as contributors while all the others are receivers. Whatever political space the bicameral Assembly enjoys can thus be used to overrule the donors. When the dispute between frustrated contributing Cantons and demanding recipient Cantons became virulent, the Conference of Cantonal Governments decided to set up a joint commission. The federal-cantonal parity commission came up with proposals which eased the political climate. For example, in light of the results of the latest published efficiency report (2016–2019) and recommendations by the commission, a package of measures and adjustments in the equalisation system was approved and came into effect in 2020, with respect to the 2020–2023 four-year period. Its main aim was to uphold federal solidarity while protecting the Cantons feeding into the system by limiting political discretion of parliament.

5 The Revised Fiscal Equalisation System

The system of fiscal equalisation is made up of two mechanisms that function and are financed independently: equalisation of resources and compensation for excessive costs. The system is completed with the cohesion fund and other temporary instruments established to smoothen transition (and find acceptance in Cantons obliged to reorganise their financial system). In order to simplify the new system and make it more transparent, it is organised and taxed with total independence from the rest of the financial transfers and flows of the Swiss financial system.

5.1 *Resource Equalisation*

The resource equalisation is the central mechanism of the equalisation system, concentrating more than 75% of the scheme for equalising flows and transfers. Cantons are no longer classified on the basis of a financial capacity index but in relation to their resource potential instead. The resource potential of a Canton corresponds to the value of its taxable resources, calculated on the basis of the taxable income and assets of natural persons and the taxable profits of legal entities (Dafflon, 2004). The classification of a Canton thus no longer depends on its effective tax income but on the fictive tax income it would provide off if it would apply the federal tax rates. This crucial rule is meant to make federal solidarity more acceptable to contributing Cantons as they must no longer compensate Cantons with lacking appetite to appropriately tax their residents and companies. A Canton following a low tax strategy (thereby putting pressure on other Cantons) has to accept that the categorisation is based on a tax income the Canton does not have – and must explain budget constraints to its population.

By means of the weighted sum of various financial elements, the resource potential per capita of each Canton is calculated. Using the resource potential index, Cantons are classified into two groups: Cantons with an index above the average, that is, above 100, are considered to be financially strong; Cantons situated below that threshold are classified as financially weak (Federal Finance Administration, 2012). The new classification methodology makes it difficult for Cantons to manipulate their taxation systems and tax burden to maximise their benefit in the share-out of the equalisation funds (Bessard, 2013; Kirchgässner, 2012, p. 15).

While the old system of equalisation funds had a vertical character, the new system also includes a horizontal component. Although the Federation continues to be the main financer, the financially strong Cantons are obliged to contribute through horizontal transfers (see Table 11.1). Although the new fiscal equalisation system introduced the horizontal dimension as a novelty in the equalisation system, the number of contributing Cantons is low: between 2008 and 2023, the total number of contributing Cantons oscillated between six and nine. This fact conditions the system's potential, but at the same time, it broadened the range of support needed for its approval (Mueller et al., 2017).

The Cantons below 100 on the index are the beneficiaries of the equalising transfers, both vertical and horizontal. The Federal Council is responsible for annually updating the quantity established for the base year, taking into account the evolution of the resource potential index and fiscal revenue. The Cantons' contributions to the Social Security system are no longer taken into account, nor is the flow of transfers due to the Cantons' sharing in certain federal tax revenues for purposes of equalisation.

The system establishes a partial equalisation goal: initially, it was decided that all Cantons had to reach a minimum of 85 points on the index of resource potential after equalisation (see Table 11.2). Following the adjustments applied to the system in 2020, a more precise formula was introduced to avoid "excessive" financing above the minimum established following equalisation (Conseil fédéral, 2018, pp. 199–200; Vatter, 2018): Cantons with a resource potential below 70 receive equalisation funds until reaching exactly 86.5 points on the index (Federal Finance Administration, 2020). The equalisation system thus strengthens vertical and horizontal solidarity but, as importantly, limits it. The Constitution does not guarantee equal or comparable resources to all Cantons but provides all Cantons with strong incentives to develop economic development strategies and increase tax income.

With autonomy and tax competition in mind, the methodology for sharing-out includes one condition: the order of Cantons on the resource potential index must not be altered after the resource equalisation. Consequently, the distribution of resources amongst Cantons with a lower financial capacity has a progressive character: the financially weak Cantons furthest from the average receive more funds. Conversely, the contributing Cantons give to the equalisation funds proportionately depending on their financial capacity.

Finally, the equalisation funds no longer have a conditional character. Therefore, the Cantons are free to decide where the funds are to be destined. Besides minimising perverse incentives in the provision of goods and services, this spending discretion has the direct effect of increasing cantonal autonomy (Bessard, 2013, pp. 48–49). The decision to not earmark transfers is not trivial but constitutes an essential element of the balance between solidarity and autonomy. Although in the overall calculation of the cantonal funding system, the equalisation funds account for merely about 6% of cantonal budgets, this can exceed 20% amongst financially weaker Cantons (Dafflon, 2014; Soguel, 2019, pp. 299–301). Conditional transfers would thus severely hamper the autonomy of resource-weak Cantons.

5.2 *Cost Compensations*

Compensation for excessive costs is directed at the Alpine Cantons and centrally situated Cantons that for structural reasons face excessive costs in the provision of public goods and services (Federal Finance Administration, 2012). Compensation only covers excessive costs that are assumed by some Cantons in financing certain public policies with respect to the Swiss average. While the need to compensate Alpine Cantons for extra burdens was largely undisputed, the compensation scheme for metropolitan areas came in as a compromise to make the deal acceptable to most Cantons (and prevent it from being vetoed in a referendum). The compensation funds for excessive costs are thus classified on the basis of two factors: compensation for excessive costs of a geographical/topographic (altitude, steep terrain and low population density) and a socio-demographic type (poverty, aging population, immigration and core cities).

TABLE 11.1 Vertical and horizontal distribution of the transfers of the fiscal equalisation system in the 2023 fiscal year (in thousand CHF and percentages)

	Resource equalisation		Cost compensation		Cohesion fund and temporary instruments			Total	
	Contribution	Percentage	Contribution	Percentage	Contribution	Percentage	Temp. Inst.	Contribution	Percentage
Horizontal equalisation (Cantons)	1,737,877	40%	–	–	69,899	33.33%	–	1,807,776	32%
Vertical equalisation (Federation)	2,606,815	60%	880,895	100%	139,798	66.66%	160,000	3,787,509	68%
Total	4,344,692	100%	880,895	100%	209,697	100%	160,000	5,595,285	100%

SOURCE: (ADMINISTRATION FÉDÉRALE DES FINANCES, 2022, P. 40). ELABORATED BY THE AUTHORS

TABLE 11.2 Distribution of the fiscal equalisation system in the 2023 fiscal year (in thousand CHF)

Cantons	Resource index before equalisation	Resource equalisation					Resource ndex after equalisation
		Horizontal		Vertical	Total		
		Contribute	Receive	Receive	Contribute	Receive	
Zurich	123.06	−610,776	0	0	−610,776	0	119
Berne	77.71	0	397,384	596,076	0	993,459	88
Lucerne	92.50	0	26,410	39,616	0	66,026	94
Uri	70.94	0	21,687	32,531	0	54,219	87
Schwyz	173.22	−202,317	0	0	−202,317	0	160
Obwald	107.11	−4,694	0	0	−4,694	0	106
Nidwald	158.13	−43,685	0	0	−43,685	0	147
Glaris	72.91	0	21,409	32,114	0	53,524	87
Zoug	265.93	−368,273	0	0	−368,273	0	235
Fribourg	70.24	0	195,441	293,161	0	488,602	87
Soleure	70.82	0	163,140	244,710	0	407,851	87
Bâle-Ville	153.12	−182,180	0	0	−182,180	0	143
Bâle-Campagne	97.46	0	3,167	4,750	0	7,917	98
Schaffhouse	98.90	0	230	345	0	575	99
Appenzell Rh.-Ext.	85.23	0	10,782	16,173	0	26,955	90
Appenzell Rh.-Int.	101.17	−329	0	0	−329	0	101
St-Gall	83.64	0	117,331	175,997	0	293,328	90
Grisons	83.19	0	49,532	74,298	0	123,831	90
Argovie	81.07	0	198,789	298,183	0	496,972	89
Thurgovie	80.12	0	87,792	131,688	0	219,480	89
Tessin	93.43	0	18,423	27,635	0	46,058	95
Vaud	98.96	0	2,056	3,084	0	5,140	99
Valais	63.78	0	299,978	449,967	0	749,945	87
Neuchâtel	77.46	0	69,539	104,308	0	173,847	88
Genève	137.44	−325,622	0	0	−325,622	0	131
Jura	66.74	0	54,785	82,178	0	136,963	87
Total	**100.00**	**−1,737,877**	**1,737,877**	**2,606,815**	**−1,737,877**	**4,344,692**	

SOURCE: (ADMINISTRATION FÉDÉRALE DES FINANCES, 2022, P. 40). ELABORATED BY THE AUTHORS

Cost compensation			Cohesion fund and temporary instruments				Total
Geographical/ topographic factors	Socio-demographic factors	Total	Cohesion fund			Temp. Inst.	
		Receive	Contribute	Receive	Total	Receive	
0	125,443	125,443	−11,831	0	−11,831	0	−497,164
29,011	0	29,011	−9,231	31,281	22,050	32,113	1,076,633
5,740	0	5,740	−3,347	14,215	10,868	12,701	95,336
11,742	0	11,742	−336	0	−336	1,136	66,761
6,881	0	6,881	−1,239	0	−1,239	0	−196,674
6,198	0	6,198	−312	0	−312	0	1,192
1,414	0	1,414	−358	0	−358	0	−42,629
5,445	0	5,445	−371	4,901	4,530	1,258	64,757
0	3,280	3,280	−951	0	−951	0	−365,944
9,476	1,045	10,521	−2,298	82,368	80,070	9,847	589,040
0	9,250	9,250	−2,351	0	−2,351	8,485	423,235
0	66,325	66,325	−1,865	0	−1,865	0	−117,721
0	0	0	−2,491	0	−2,491	8,934	14,360
0	0	0	−710	0	−710	2,546	2,411
20,741	0	20,741	−517	0	−517	1,710	48,889
9,150	0	9,150	−142	0	−142	0	8,679
1,867	0	1,867	−4,345	0	−4,345	15,739	306,589
140,572	0	140,572	−1,827	0	−1,827	6,352	268,927
0	0	0	−5,239	0	−5,239	20,994	512,728
3,296	0	3,296	−2,204	0	−2,204	8,558	229,130
15,041	384	15,425	−2,975	0	−2,975	11,003	69,511
142	1,24,440	124,582	−6,088	0	−6,088	0	123,635
76,105	9,672	85,777	−2,646	0	−2,646	10,829	843,904
22,994	13,515	36,510	−1,615	65,300	63,685	5,520	279,562
0	1,57,094	157,094	−3,956	0	−3,956	0	−172,484
4,633	0	4,633	−654	11,633	10,978	2,274	154,848
370,448	**510,448**	**880,895**	**−69,899**	**209,697**	**139,798**	**160,000**	**3,787,509**

Financing the excessive cost funds is the exclusive responsibility of the Federation and is independent of the resource equalisation mechanism (it does not take into account the resource potential index). In fact, the compensation for socio-demographic reasons mainly reaches the Cantons situated above the average on the resource index. The fund accounts for about 15% of the fiscal equalisation system (Federal Finance Administration, 2020).

In each four-year revision of the system the amount of the fund is established for the next four years. The Federal Council makes an annual adjustment of the base year's amount due to inflation. To facilitate agreement during the negotiations of the reform, a parity share-out of the fund between both types of excessive costs was agreed on (Cappelletti et al., 2014, pp. 9–11). But subsequently, in the framework of the adjustments introduced in the fiscal equalisation system in 2020 and complying with the demands of the more populous Cantons, it was decided to increase the contribution destined for the Cantons suffering from excessive costs due to socio-demographic reasons (Vatter, 2018, p. 198).

5.3 *Cohesion Fund and Other Temporary Instruments*

The cohesion fund and the temporary instruments function as closure mechanisms of the equalisation system. The reform of 2008 included a compensation mechanism to facilitate the transition of financially weak Cantons that were disadvantaged by the implantation of the new fiscal equalisation system and, without the transitional instruments would have been likely to oppose the change.

The fund was provided with a pre-established and undeflated annual quantity of CHF 366 million (Federal Finance Administration, 2012). It was established that from 2016 the fund would be reduced at an annual rhythm of 5% of the original amount, to definitively disappear by the year 2036, 28 years after the reform had come into effect. The Federation financed two thirds and the Cantons, based on demographic criteria, the remaining third.

When a Canton in some fiscal year exceeded the average in the resource index, it automatically lost the right to receive the fund and could not again access to it even if it later again fell below the average. Similarly, if a financially strong Canton fell below the average, it could not become a beneficiary. Thus, the fund was designed to gradually disappear. It currently still reaches six Cantons but only accounts for 5% of the total transfer scheme of the fiscal equalisation system (Federal Finance Administration, 2020).

Besides the cohesion fund, in order to reduce the impact derived from adjustments in the fiscal equalisation system that came into effect in 2020, a second temporary instrument was approved for the 2021–2025 period, funded exclusively by the Federation. In 2024 a third temporary instrument will be introduced, funded by the Federation for six years, in order to cushion the effects provoked in the fiscal equalisation system by the federal reform in fiscal matters and the financing of the Social Security system (*Le projet RFFA*).

6 Current Situation and Future Challenges

To date three reports have been prepared evaluating the efficiency of the 2008–2011, 2012–2015 and 2016–2019 periods. In 2023, the fourth four-year period of the new fiscal equalisation system will be evaluated. In spite of 16 years not being sufficient time to be able to conclusively evaluate the results of the new fiscal equalisation system, in general terms, at both the politico-institutional and the academic levels, there is consensus on the advantages and benefits of the present system compared to the earlier one. Although some aspects and results of the new system have given rise to debates amongst administrations and specialists, a summary of the main results of the new fiscal equalisation system, based on the efficiency reports published to date (Conseil fédéral, 2010, 2014, 2018), is as follows:

- The system is more transparent and facilitates accountability and evaluation of results. Furthermore, the system is more predictable, and its distribution is resolved prior to the period of cantonal budgetary elaboration.
- The new classification methodology based on resource potential reduces perverse incentives and makes it difficult for Cantons to manipulate their taxation systems to maximise their benefit in the share-out of the equalisation funds. In addition, it has not reduced the capacity of inter-cantonal fiscal competitiveness, and the financially strong Cantons have been able to keep the levels of their tax burden stable. For example, following the introduction of the new fiscal equalisation system, the Canton of Obwalden applied a policy of low taxes to attract contributors to the Canton, without distorting the functioning of the fiscal equalisation system (Kirchgässner, 2012, p. 141; Ladner & Desfontaine, 2019). The Federal Supreme Court had eliminated the tax degression, violating the principle of equality, but did not question the cantonal strategy as such. As a result of the increase of taxable bases, Obwalden climbed the resource potential index, and rose from being a beneficiary Canton in 2008 (even receiving funds from the cohesion mechanism) to become a contributing Canton from 2018 onwards.
- With exception of the 2010 and 2011 fiscal years, in the 2008–2023 period the system has managed to guarantee the minimum level of resources set at 85 points for all Cantons (since 2020: 86.5), also fulfilling the principle

of ordinality. It has withstood the variations in the economic cycle, passing two demanding stress tests for public finances, namely, the financial crisis of 2008 and the COVID-19 crisis in 2020.
- Following the application of the equalisation mechanisms, the system has managed to considerably reduce disparities in resource availability among Cantons. The efficiency report for the 2016–2019 four-year period concluded that "the fiscal equalisation system reduces the disparities among Cantons in terms of financial capacity by approximately one-third" (Conseil fédéral, 2018, p. 12). Nonetheless, if one analyses the evolution of imbalances prior to the application of the equalisation mechanisms, although the inter-cantonal disparities in resource potential have not increased to date, the gap between financially strong and weak Cantons has not been reduced either. As can be seen in Table 11.3, while the resources prior to the equalisation of the group of financially stronger Cantons have increased by over 15% between 2008 and 2023, the resources of the group of financially weaker Cantons have barely increased by 1.8%.
- The grant-in-aid transfers have been reduced and the framework of cantonal powers has been reinforced, strengthening their autonomy. Nonetheless, some studies relativise the reform's impact on its goal of reinforcing the Cantons' effective fiscal autonomy (Arnold, 2020, pp. 196–197; Vatter, 2018).
- The compensation mechanism for excessive costs is insufficient, especially with respect to compensation for socio-demographic factors (Kirchgässner, 2012, p. 17). Thus, starting with adjustments introduced in 2020, the parity in the distribution of the compensation fund for excessive costs was broken, and the quantity destined for compensation due to socio-demographic factors increased.
- The inter-cantonal cooperation related to horizontal compensation for excessive costs derived from externalities has been increased (Vatter, 2018, pp. 191–192).

By way of final reflection, one thing remains clear: the distribution of power and resources has always been the most reformed, questioned and criticised area of Swiss Constitutional law. Debates have raged on ever since the creation of the Swiss modern state and will surely remain present. There are good reasons to argue that the Swiss federal system is in a need of a second federalism reform. Since 2004, the distribution of competences has become complex and confuse again. Most of the competences which have been made exclusive, have become concurrent again. Some of the shortcomings of the old system thus are reappearing. This is also true for the independence of the equalisation scheme from other financial mechanisms. While formally operating separate from each other, countless political deals have let to blurs and overlaps.

TABLE 11.3 The resource potential index before and after equalisation in the five financially strongest and weakest cantons in the 2008 and 2023 fiscal years

	2008			2023		
	Cantons	**Before equalisation**	**After equalisation**	**Cantons**	**Before equalisation**	**After equalisation**
Five financially strongest Cantons	Zoug	214.9	192.0	Zoug	265.9	235.3
	Genève	151.2	140.9	Schwyz	173.2	159.7
	Bâle-Ville	139.8	131.8	Nidwald	158.1	147.4
	Zurich	126.5	121.2	Bâle-Ville	153.1	143.3
	Nidwald	125.4	120.3	Genève	137.4	130.5
	Average	**151.6**	**141.2**	**Average**	**177.6**	**163.2**
Five financially weakest Cantons	Glarus	69.6	86.9	Uri	70.9	86.6
	Valais	69.0	86.9	Soleure	70.8	86.6
	Jura	68.6	86.9	Fribourg	70.2	86.5
	Obwald	67.2	86.7	Jura	66.7	86.5
	Uri	61.8	86.5	Valais	63.8	86.5
	Average	**67.2**	**86.8**	**Average**	**68.5**	**86.5**

SOURCE: (ADMINISTRATION FÉDÉRALE DES FINANCES, 2022, P. 40). ELABORATED BY THE AUTHORS

Walter Turnherr, Chancellor of the Confederation, in a speech in March 2023, emphasised that the Swiss federal system owed a lot – and more than generally perceived – to numerous, mostly vertical money flows. He highlighted that not only formal equalisation measures but considerable other financial flows from the federal government to Cantons, exited and were decisive in the maintenance of political cohesion. Billions are transferred across the country by various means, making sure that any discontent with federal measures impacting cantonal finances does not grow into durable resentment. As Walter Turnherr puts it, the federal government "evened out, weakened or even prevented the emergence of cantonal disparities and, in the longer term, regional animosities". One must then emphasise that a lot of the relative success story of Swiss federalism does not only pertain to constitutional arrangements and legislative measures, but also strongly relies upon the country's considerable wealth, which allows the federal government to soothe potential cantonal frustration with financial transfers.

References

Administration fédérale des finances (2022). *Péréquation financière 2023 entre la Confédération et les Cantons. Rapport pour la prise de position des Cantons.* Confédération suisse.

Arnold, T. (2020). Reforming autonomy? The fiscal impact of the Swiss federal reform 2008. *Regional & Federal Studies*, 30(5), 651–674.

Aubert, J.-F. (2003). Commentary on Art. 128 FedCst. In J.-F. Aubert & P. Mahon (Eds.). *Petit Commentaire de la Constitution fédérale de la Confédération Suisse*, Zurich: Schulthess.

Behnisch, U. (2014). Commentary on Art. 130 FedCst. In B. Ehrenzeller et al. (Eds.), *Die schweizerische Bundesverfassung, St. Galler Kommentar*. Zurich: Schulthess.

Béland, D., & Lecours, A. (2014). Accommodation and the politics of fiscal equalization in multinational states: the case of Canada. *Nations and Nationalism*, 20(2), 337–354.

Belser, E. M. (2020). Heading Together: Intergovernmental Relations and Horizontal Law-Making by Swiss Cantons. In A.-G. Gagnon & J. Pirier (Eds.), *Canadian Federalism and Its Future. Actors and Institutions* (pp. 251–290). eBook: McGill-Queen's University Press.

Bessard, P. (2013). Switzerland's reformed fiscal equalization system. Still substantial room for improvement. In J. Clemens & N. Veldhuis (Eds.), *Federalism and Fiscal Transfers: Essays on Australia, Germany, Switzerland and the United States*. Fraser Institute.

Biaggini, G. (2015). Commentary on Art. 3 FedCst. In B. Waldmann B., E. M. Belser, & A. Epiney (Eds.), *Basler Kommentar*. Basel: Helbing Lichtenhahn.

Brenton, S. (2020). The price of federation: comparing fiscal equalization in Australia, Canada, Germany and Switzerland. *Regional & Federal Studies*, 30(1), 93–111.

Brühl-Moser D. (2012). Der Föderalismus Kanadas: interstaatlich, exekutiv und asymmetrisch. In I. Härtel (Ed.), *Handbuch Föderalismus, Band IV: Föderalismus in Europa und der Welt*. Springer.

Bullinger, A.-B. (2002). Equalization reform in Switzerland: ideal solutions, unpredictable outcomes. *SIPP Public Policy Paper*, 9.

Cappelletti, F., Fischer, M., & Sciarini, P. (2014). "Let's Talk Cash": Cantons' Interests and the Reform of Swiss Federalism. *Regional & Federal Studies*, 24(1), 1–20.

Cavelti, U. (2008). Schranken des Steuerföderalismus. In Rechtswissenschaftliche Abteilung der Universität St. Gallen (Ed.), *Rechtliche Rahmenbedingungen des Wirtschaftsstandortes Schweiz – Festschrift 25 Jahre juristische Abschlüsse an der Universität St. Gallen*, Zurich/St. Gallen: Dike, 367–379.

Conseil fédéral (2010). *Rapport sur l'évaluation de l'efficacité 2008–2011 de la péréquation financière entre la Confédération et les Cantons*. Confédération suisse.

Conseil fédéral (2014). *Rapport sur l'évaluation de l'efficacité 2012–2015 de la péréquation financière entre la Confédération et les Cantons*. Confédération suisse.

Conseil fédéral (2018). *Rapport sur l'évaluation de l'efficacité 2016–2019 de la péréquation financière entre la Confédération et les Cantons*. Confédération suisse.

Dafflon, B. (1995). *Fédéralisme et solidarité: étude de la péréquation en Suisse*. Fribourg: Institut du fédéralisme de Fribourg.

Dafflon, B. (2004). Federal-cantonal equalisation in Switzerland: an overview of the present system and reform in progress. *Chaire de finances publiques et de gestion des finances publiques*, Working Paper 356.

Dafflon, B. (2014). Fiscal equalization: the Swiss way, federal, cantonal, local. *Fiscal Equalization Transfers – International Perspectives: lessons for Poland*, Poland.

Dafflon, B., Frey, R. L., Jeanrenaud, C., Meier, A., & Spillmann, A. (1996). La péréquation financière entre la Confédération et les Cantons en Suisse. *Annuaire des Collectivités locales*, 16, 61–99.

Dafflon, B., & Perritaz, S. (2002). *Federal-Cantonal Equalisation in Switzerland: An Overview of the Present System and Reform in Progress*. Fribourg: University of Fribourg.

Département fédéral des finances, & Conférence des gouvernements cantonaux (2004). *Réforme de la péréquation financiére et de la répartition des tâches entre la Confédération et les Cantons – RPT*. Berne: Département fédéral des finances.

Erkoreka, M. (2019). The Basque and Swiss fiscal systems building processes as a source of lessons for the European integration process. In G. Martínez & X. Irujo (Eds.), *International Perspectives on Fiscal federalism: The Basque Tax System*. Reno: Center for Basque Studies – University of Nevada.

Federal Finance Administration (2012). *National Fiscal Equalization. Strengthening Federalism*. Bern: Federal Finance Administration.

Federal Finance Administration (2020). *National Fiscal Equalization*. Bern: Federal Finance Administration.

Frey, R. L., Dafflon, B., Jeanrenaud, C., & Meier, A. (1994). *La péréquation financière entre la Confédération et les Cantons. Expertise mandatée par l'Administration fédérale des finances et la Conférence des Directeurs cantonaux des Finances*. Berne: Administration fédérale des finances.

Frey, R. L., & Wettstein, G. (2008). Reform of the Swiss fiscal equalisation system. *CESifo DICE Report*, 1/2008, 21–26.

Hänni, P. (2015). Commentary on Art. 135 FedCst. In B. Waldmann, E.M. Belser & A. Epiney (Eds.), *Basler Kommentar*, Basel: Helbing Lichtenhahn.

Hänni, P. (2021). The Swiss Tax System – Between Equality and Diversity. In E. M. Belser, T. Bächler, S. Egli, & L. Zünd (Eds.), *The Principle of Equality in Diverse States – Reconciling Autonomy with Equal Rights and Opportunities*. Leiden-Boston: Brill.

Kirchgässner, G. (2012). The effectiveness of the 2008 reform of fiscal federalism in Switzerland: record of the first period, 2008–2011, and expectations for the second period, 2012–2015. *Cuadernos Manuel Giménez Abad*, 2012(3), 8–25.

Ladner, A., & Desfontaine, L. (2019). *Le fédéralisme suisse. L'organisation territoriale et l'accomplissement des prestations étatiques en Suisse.* Lausanne: Presses polytechniques et universitaires romandes.

Linder, W., & Mueller, S. (2021). *Swiss Democracy. Possible Solutions to Conflict in Multicultural Societies.* Palgrave Macmillan.

Meier-Mazzucato G. (2022). *Steuern Schweiz, Grundriss zu den eidgenössischen und kantonalen Steuern mit Beispielen und Darstellungen*, Bern: Stämpfli.

Mueller, S., Vatter, A., & Schmid, C. (2017). Self-interest or solidarity? The referendum on fiscal equalisation in Switzerland. *Statistics, Politics and Policy*, 7(1–2), 3–28.

Reich, M. (2020). *Steuerrecht*, Zurich: Schulthess.

Soguel, N. (2019). Intergovernmental fiscal transfers and equalization. In A. Ladner, N. Soguel, E. Yves, S. Weerts, & S. Nahrath (Eds.), *Swiss Public Administration. Making the State Work Successfully.* IIAS – Palgrave Macmillan.

Vallender, K.A. & Cavelti, U. (2014). Commentary on Art. 128 FedCst. In B. Ehrenzeller et al. (Eds.), *Die schweizerische Bundesverfassung St. Galler Kommentar.* Zurich: Schulthess.

Vallender, K.A. & Wiederkehr, R. (2014). Commentary on Art. 127 FedCst. In: B. Ehrenzeller et al. (Eds.), *Die schweizerische Bundesverfassung, St. Galler Kommentar.* Zurich: Schulthess.

Vatter, A. (2018). *Swiss Federalism. The Transformation of a Federal Model.* New York: Routledge.

Subject Index